HISTORY

OF THE

WAR IN THE PENINSULA

AND IN THE

SOUTH OF FRANCE

FROM THE YEAR 1807 TO THE YEAR 1814

VOLUME II

HISTORY

WAR IN THE PENINSULA

AND IN THE

SOUTH OF FRANCE,

FROM THE YEAR 1807 TO THE YEAR 1814.

BY

W. F. P. NAPIER, C.B.

COLONEL H. P. FORTY-THIRD REGIMENT, MEMBER OF THE ROYAL SWEDISH ACADEMY OF MILITARY SCIENCES.

VOL. II.

THE SECOND EDITION.

This edition first published in Great Britain 1992
by Constable and Company Limited
3 The Lanchesters, 162 Fulham Palace Road
London W6 9ER

Reprinted 1993, 1995

Originally published in London in 1832
by Thomas and William Boone

ISBN 0 09 471690 0

Printed in Great Britain by
St Edmundsbury Press Limited
Bury St Edmunds, Suffolk

TABLE OF CONTENTS.

BOOK V.

CHAPTER I.

CHAPTER II.

CHAPTER III.

APPENDIX.

LIST OF PLATES.

NOTICE.

GENERAL SEMELÉ'S journal, referred to in this volume, is only an unattested copy; the rest of the manuscript authorities quoted or consulted are original papers belonging to, and communications received from, the duke of Wellington, marshal Soult, marshal Jourdan, Mr. Stuart,* sir J. Cradock,† sir John Moore, and other persons employed either in the British or French armies during the Peninsular War.

The returns of the French army are taken from the emperor Napoleon's original Muster Rolls.

The letter S. marks those papers received from marshal Soult.

* Now lord Stuart de Rothesay.   † Now lord Howden.

HISTORY

OF THE

PENINSULAR WAR.

BOOK V.

CHAPTER I.

THE effect produced in England, by the unfortunate issue of sir John Moore's campaign, was not
in proportion with the importance of the subject.
The people trained to party politics, and possessed
of no real power to rebuke the folly of the cabinet,
regarded both disasters and triumphs with factious
rather than with national feelings, and it was alike
easy to draw their attention from affairs of weight
or to fix it upon matters of little moment. Thus,
the duke of York's conduct being at this time made
the object of parliamentary inquiry, to drag his
private frailties before the world was thought essential to the welfare of the nation, while the incapacity
which had caused England and Spain, to mourn in
tears of blood, was left unprobed. An insular people, who are by their situation protected from the
worst evils of war, may suffer themselves to be thus
deluded ; but if an unfortunate campaign were to
bring a devastating enemy into the heart of the
country, the honour of a general, and the military

policy of the cabinet, would no longer be considered as mere subjects for a vile sophist's talents in
misrepresentation.

It is true that the misfortunes of the campaign
were by many orators, in both houses of parliament
treated with great warmth, but the discussions were
chiefly remarkable, as examples of astute eloquence
without any knowledge of facts. The opposition
speakers, eager to criminate the government, exaggerated the disasters of the retreat, and comprehending neither the motives nor the movements of
sir John Moore, urged several untenable charges
against the ministers, who, disunited by personal
feelings, did not all adopt the same grounds of defence. Thus, lord Castlereagh and lord Liverpool,
passing over those errors of the cabinet, which left
the general only a choice of difficulties at his outset, asserted, and truly, that the advantages derived
from the advance to Sahagun, more than compensated the loss in the subsequent retreat; and both
those statesmen paid an honourable tribute to the
merits of the commander; but Mr. Canning, unscru-
pulously resolute to screen Mr. Frere, assented to all
the erroneous statements of the opposition, and then
with malignant dexterity endeavoured to convert
them into charges against the fallen general. Sir
John Moore was, he said, wholly answerable for the
campaign. Whether glorious or distressing, whether to be admired or deplored, it was his own, he
had kept the government quite ignorant of his proceedings! Being closely pressed on this point by
Mr. C. Hutchinson and Mr. Whitbread, Mr. Canning deliberately repeated the assertion, yet not
long afterwards, sir John Moore's letters to the ministers, written almost daily, and furnishing exact

and copious information of all that was passing in
the Peninsula, were laid before the house!

While the dearest interests of the nation were
thus treated in parliament, the ardour of the English
people was somewhat abated; yet the Spanish
cause, so rightful in itself, was still popular, and a
treaty was concluded with the supreme junta by
which the contracting powers bound themselves to
make common cause against France, and to agree to
no peace except by common consent. But the ministers although professing unbounded confidence in
the result of the struggle, already looked upon the
Peninsula as a secondary object; for the warlike preparations of Austria, and the reputation of the arch-
duke Charles, whose talents were foolishly said to
exceed Napoleon's, had awakened the dormant spirit
of coalitions; and it was more agreeable to the aris-
tocratic feelings of the English cabinet, that the
French should be defeated by a monarch in Germany, than by a plebeian insurrection in Spain.
The obscure intrigues of the princess of Tour and
Taxis, and the secret societies on the continent
emanating as they did from patrician sources, excited the sympathy of the ministers, engaged their
attention, and nourished those distempered feelings
which made them see only weakness and disaffec-
tion in France, when throughout that mighty empire, few desired and none dared to oppose the emperor's wishes; when even secret discontent was
confined to some royalist chiefs and splenetic republicans whose influence was never felt, until after
Napoleon had suffered the direst reverses.

Unable to conceive the extent of that monarch's
views, or to measure the grandeur of his genius,
the ministers attributed the results of his profound

calculations to a blind chance, his victories to treason, to corruption, to any thing, but that admirable
skill, with which he wielded the most powerful
military force that ever obeyed the orders of a single
chief. Thus self-deluded, and misjudging the difficulties to be encountered, they adopted every idle
project, and squandered their resources without any
great or decided effort. While negotiating with the
Spanish junta for the occupation of Cadiz, they
were planning an expedition against Italy, and
while loudly asserting their resolution to defend
Portugal, reserved their principal force for a secret
blow in Holland; their preparations being however
marked by a pomp and publicity totally unsuited to
war. With what a mortal calamity that pageant
closed, shall be noticed hereafter; at present it is
fitting, to trace the operations in Spain, which were
coincident with the retreat of sir John Moore.

It has been already stated that when Madrid surrendered, Napoleon refused to permit Joseph to return there unless the public bodies and the heads of
families would unite to demand his restoration, and
swear, without any mental reservation, to be true
Nellerto. to him. Registers had consequently been opened
in the different quarters of the city, and twenty-
eight thousand six hundred heads of families in-
scribed their names, and voluntarily swore in presence of the host, that they were sincere in their
Azanza
and
O'Farril. desire to receive Joseph. After this, deputations
from all the councils, from the junta of commerce
and money, the hall of the Alcades, and from the
corporation, waited on the emperor at Valladolid,
and being there joined by the municipality of that
town, and by deputies from Astorga, Leon, and
other places, presented the oath, and prayed that

Joseph might be king. Napoleon thus entreated, consented that his brother should reassume his kingly functions.

It would be idle to argue from this apparently voluntary submission to the French emperor, that a change favourable to the usurpation had been produced in the feelings of the Spanish people; but it is evident that Napoleon's victories and policy had been so far effectual, that in the capital, and many other great towns, the multitude as well as the notables were, either from fear or conviction, submissive to his will; and it is but reasonable to suppose, that if his conquests had not been interrupted by extraneous circumstances, this example would have been generally followed, in preference to the more glorious, but ineffectual, resistance made by the inhabitants of those cities, whose fortitude and whose calamities have forced from mankind a sorrowful admiration. The cause of Spain, at this moment, was in truth lost, if any cause, depending upon war, which is but a succession of violent changes, can be called so; for the armies were dispersed, the government bewildered, the people dismayed, the cry of resistance hushed, and the stern voice of Napoleon, answered by the tread of three hundred thousand French veterans, was heard throughout the land. But the hostility of Austria arrested the conqueror's career, and the Spanish energy revived at the abrupt cessation of his terrific warfare.

Joseph, escorted by his French guards, in number between five and six thousand, entered Madrid the 23d of January. He was, however, a king without revenues, and he would have been without even the semblance of authority, if he had not

BOOK
V.

1809.
Jan.
been likewise nominated the emperor's lieutenant in Spain, by virtue of which title he was empowered to move the French army at his will. This power was one extremely unacceptable to the marshals, and he would have found it difficult to enforce it, even though he had restrained the exercise to the limits prescribed by his brother; but disdaining to separate the general from the monarch, King's correspondence captured at Vittoria, MSS. he conveyed his orders to the French army, through his Spanish ministers, and the army in its turn disdained and resisted the assumed authority of men, who, despised for their want of military knowledge, were also suspected as favouring interests essentially differing from those of the troops.

The iron grasp, that had compressed the pride and the ambitious jealousy of the marshals, being thus relaxed, the passions which had ruined the patriots began to work among their enemies, producing indeed less fatal effects, because their scope was more circumscribed, but sufficiently pernicious to stop the course of conquest. The French army, no longer a compact body, terrible alike from its massive strength, and its flexible activity, became a collection of independent bands, each formidable in itself, but, from the disunion of the generals, slow to combine for any great object; and plainly discovering, by irregularities and insubordination, that they knew, when a warrior, and when a voluptuous monarch was at their head. These evils were however only felt at a later period, and the distribution of the troops, when Napoleon quitted Valladolid, still bore the impress of his genius.

The first corps was quartered in La Mancha.

The second corps was destined to invade Portugal.

The third and fifth corps carried on the siege of
Zaragoza.

The fourth corps remained in the valley of the
Tagus.

The sixth corps, wanting its third division, was appointed to hold Gallicia.

The seventh corps continued always in Catalonia.

The imperial guards, directed on Vittoria, contributed to the security of the great communication with France until Zaragoza should fall, and were yet ready to march when wanted for the Austrian war.

General Dessolles, with the third division of the sixth corps, returned to Madrid. General Bonnet, with the fifth division of the second corps, remained in the Montagna St. Andero.

General Lapisse, with the second division of the first corps, was sent to Salamanca, where he was joined by Maupetit's brigade of cavalry, which had crossed the Sierra de Bejar.

The reserve of heavy cavalry being broken up, was distributed, by divisions, in the following order :—

Latour Maubourg's joined the first corps. Lorge's and Lahoussaye's were attached to the second corps. Lassalle's was sent to the fourth corps. The sixth corps was reinforced with two brigades. Milhaud's division remained at Madrid, and Kellerman's guarded the lines of communication between Tudela, Burgos, and Palencia.

Thus, Madrid being still the centre of operations, the French were so distributed, that by a concentric movement on that capital, they could crush every insurrection within the circle of their positions; and the great masses, being kept upon

the principal roads diverging from Madrid to the
extremities of the Peninsula, intercepted all communication between the Provinces: while the second
corps, thrust out, as it were, beyond the circum-
ference, and destined, as the fourth corps had been,
to sweep round from point to point, was sure of
finding a supporting army, and a good line of
retreat, at every great route leading from Madrid
to the yet unsubdued provinces of the Peninsula.
The communication with France was, at the same
time, secured by the fortresses of Burgos, Pampeluna, and St. Sebastian, and by the divisions
posted at St. Ander, Burgos, Bilbao, and Vittoria;
it was also supported by a reserve at Bayonne.

The northern provinces were parcelled out into
military governments, the chiefs of which corresponded with each other, and, by the means of
moveable columns, repressed every petty insurrection. The third and fifth corps, having their
base at Pampeluna, and their line of operations
directed against Zaragoza, served as an additional
covering force to the communication with France,
and were themselves exposed to no flank attacks,
except from the side of Cuença, where the duke of
Infantado commanded; but that general was himself watched by the first corps.

All the lines of correspondence, not only from
France but between the different corps, were maintained by fortified posts, having greater or lesser
garrisons, according to their importance. Between
Bayonne and Burgos there were eleven military
stations. Between Burgos and Madrid, by the road
of Aranda and Somosierra, there were eight; and
eleven others protected the more circuitous route
to the capital, by Valladolid, Segovia, and the

Muster-
rolls of the
French ar-
my, MSS.

Guadarama. Between Valladolid and Zaragoza
the line was secured by fifteen intermediate points.
The communication between Valladolid and St.
Ander contained eight posts ; and nine others connected the former town with Villa Franca del
Bierzo, by the route of Benevente and Astorga;
finally, two were established between Benevente
and Leon.

At this period, the force of the army, exclusive
of Joseph's French guards, was three hundred
and twenty-four thousand four hundred and eleven Appendix, No. 1, sec-
men, about thirty-nine thousand being cavalry. tion 1.

Fifty-eight thousand men were in hospital.

The depôts, governments, garrisons, posts of correspondence, prisoners, and " *battalions of march*,"
composed of stragglers, absorbed about twenty-
five thousand men.

The remainder were under arms, with their
regiments, and consequently, more than two
hundred and forty thousand men were in the field ;
while the great line of communication with France
(the military reader will do well to mark this,
the key-stone of Napoleon's system) was protected
by above fifty thousand men, whose positions were
strengthened by three fortresses and sixty-four posts
of correspondence, each more or less fortified.

Having thus shewn the military state of the
French, I shall now proceed with the narrative of
their operations, following, as in the first volume,
a local rather than a chronological arrangement
of events.

OPERATIONS IN ESTREMADURA AND LA MANCHA.

The defeat of Galluzzo has been incidentally
touched upon before. The duke of Dantzic having

observed, that the Spanish general pretended, with six thousand raw levies, to defend a river line of forty miles, made a feint of crossing the Tagus at Arzobispo, and then suddenly descending to Almaraz, forced a passage over that bridge, on the 24th of December, killing and wounding many Spaniards, and capturing four guns; and so complete was the dispersion, that for a long time after, not a man was to be found in arms throughout Estremadura.

The French cavalry followed the fugitives, but intelligence of sir John Moore's advance to Sahagun, being received, the pursuit ceased at

Merida, and the fourth corps, which had left eight hundred men in garrison at Segovia, then occupied Talavera and Placentia; the duke of Dantzic was recalled to France, and Sebastiani succeeded to his command. At this period also, the first corps, (of which Lapisse's division only had followed the emperor to Astorga,) entered Toledo without opposition, and the French outposts were pushed towards Cuenca, and towards the Sierra Morena.

Meanwhile, the central junta, changing its first design, retired to Seville, instead of Badajos, and being continually urged, both by Mr. Stuart and Mr. Frere, to make some effort to lighten the pressure on the English army, ordered Palafox and the duke of Infantado to advance; the one from Zaragoza towards Tudela, the other from Cuença towards Madrid. The marquis of Palacios, who had been removed from Catalonia, and was now at the head of five or six thousand levies in the Sierra Morena, was also directed to advance into La Mancha; and Galluzzo, deprived of his command, was constituted a prisoner, along with

Cuesta, Castaños, and a number of other culpable or unfortunate officers, who, vainly demanding a judgement on their cases, were dragged from place to place by the government.

Cuesta was, however, so popular in Estremadura, that the central junta, although fearing and detesting him, were forced to place him at the head of Galluzzo's fugitives, part of whom had, when the pursuit ceased, rallied behind the Guadiana, and were now, with the aid of fresh levies, again taking the form, rather than the consistence, of an army. This appointment was an act of deplorable incapacity; the moral effect was to degrade the government by exposing its fears and weakness, and, in a military view, it was destructive, because Cuesta was physically and mentally incapable of command. Obstinate, jealous, and stricken in years, he was heedless of time, circumstances, dispositions or fitness; to punish with a barbarous severity, and to rush headlong into battle, constituted, in his mind, all the functions of a general.

The president, Florida Blanca, eighty-one years of age, died at Seville, and the marquis of Astorga succeeded him, but the character of the junta was in no manner affected by the change. Some fleeting indications of vigour had been produced by the imminence of the danger during the flight from Aranjuez, but a large remittance of silver, from South America, having arrived at Cadiz, the attention of the members was absorbed by this object, and the public weal was blotted from their remembrance; even Mr. Frere, ashamed of their conduct, appeared to acquiesce in the just-

Appendix,
No. 13.
Vol. I.

Appendix,
No. 2,
section 2.

ness of sir John Moore's estimate of the value of Spanish co-operation.

The number of men to be enrolled for the defence of the country had been early fixed at five hundred thousand, but scarcely one-third had joined their colours ; nevertheless, considerable bodies were assembling at different points, because the people, especially those of the southern provinces, although dismayed, were obedient, and the local authorities, at a distance from the actual scene of war, rigorously enforcing the law of enrolment, sent the recruits to the armies ; hoping thereby either to stave the war off from their own districts, or to have the excuse of being without fighting men, to plead for quiet submission. The fugitive troops also readily collected again at any given point, partly from patriotism, partly because the French were in possession of their native provinces, partly that they attributed their defeats to the treachery of their generals, and partly that, being deceived by the gross falsehoods and boasting of the government, they, with ready vanity, imagined that the enemy had invariably suffered enormous losses. In fine, for the reasons mentioned in the commencement of this history, men were to be had in abundance, but, beyond assembling them and appointing some incapable person to command, nothing was done for defence. The officers, who were not deceived, had no confidence either in their own troops or in the government, nor were they themselves confided in or respected by their men : the latter starved, misused, ill-handled, possessed neither the compact strength of discipline nor the daring of enthusiasm.

Under such a system, the peasantry could not be rendered energetic soldiers, nor were they active supporters of the cause; but with a wonderful constancy they endured for it, fatigue, sickness, nakedness and famine, displaying in all their actions, and in all their sentiments, a distinct and powerful national character. This constancy, although rendered nugatory by the vices and follies of the juntas and leading men, hallowed the people's efforts, and the flagitious violence of the invasion almost justified their ferocity.

Palacios, on the receipt of the orders above mentioned, advanced, with five thousand men, to Vilharta, in La Mancha; and the duke of Infantado, anticipating the instructions of the junta, was already in motion from Cuença, his army, reinforced by the divisions of Cartoajal and Lilli and by fresh levies, being about twenty thousand men, of which two thousand were cavalry. To check the incursions of the French horsemen, he had, a few days after the departure of Napoleon from Madrid, detached general Senra and general Venegas with eight thousand infantry and all the horse to scour the country round Tarancon and Aranjuez, and the former entered Horcajada, while the latter endeavoured to cut off a French detachment, but was himself surprised and beaten by a very inferior force. Marshal Victor, nevertheless, withdrew his advanced posts, and, concentrating Ruffin's and Villatte's divisions of infantry and Latour Maubourg's cavalry, at Villa de Alorna, in the vicinity of Toledo, left Venegas in possession of Tarancon. But, among the Spanish generals, mutual recriminations succeeded their failure: the duke of Infantado possessed neither authority nor talents to repress their disputes, and in this untoward state of affairs receiving the orders of the junta, he projected a movement on Toledo, intending to seize that place and Aranjuez, break down the bridges, and maintain the line of the Tagus.

The 10th he quitted Cuença, with ten thousand men, intending to join Venegas, who, with the rest of the army, was at Tarancon.

The 13th, he met a crowd of fugitives near Carascosa, and heard, with equal surprise and consternation, that the division under Venegas was beaten, and the pursuers close at hand.

ROUT OF UCLES.

It appeared that Victor, ignorant of the exact situation and intentions of the Spanish generals, and yet uneasy at their movements, had marched from Toledo to Ocaña the 10th, and that Venegas then abandoned Tarancon and took post at Ucles. The French again advanced on the 12th in two columns, of which one, composed of Ruffin's division and a brigade of cavalry, lost its way, and arrived at Alcazar; the other, led by Victor in person, arrived in front of the Spanish position at Ucles early in the morning of the 13th. This meeting was unexpected by either party, but the French attacked without hesitation, and the Spaniards, making towards Alcazar, were cut off by Ruffin, and totally discomfited. Several thousands were taken, others fled across the fields, and one body preserving some order, marched towards Ocaña, where meeting the French parc, it received a heavy discharge of grape, and dispersed. Of the whole force, only one small detachment, under general Giron, forced a passage by the road of Carascosa, and so reached the duke of Infantado, who immediately retreated safely to Cuença, as the French cavalry was too much fatigued to pursue him briskly.

From Cuença he sent his guns towards Valencia by the road of Tortola, but marched his infantry and cavalry by Chinchilla, to Tobarra on the frontiers of Murcia, and then to Santa Cruz de Mudela, a town situated near the entrance to the defiles of the Sierra Morena. This place he reached in the beginning of February, having made a painful and circuitous retreat of more than two hundred miles, in a bad season; his artillery had been captured at Tortola, and his force was reduced by desertion and straggling, to a handful of discontented officers, and a few thousand men, worn out with fatigue and misery. Meanwhile, Victor, after scouring a part of the province of Cuença and disposing of his prisoners, made a sudden march upon Vilharta, intending to surprise Palacios, but that officer aware of Infantado's retreat had already effected a junction with the latter at Santa Cruz de Mudela; wherefore the French marshal relinquished the attempt and re-occupied his former position at Toledo.

The captives taken at Ucles were marched to Madrid; those who were weak and unable to walk, being, says Mr. Rocca, shot by order of Victor, because the Spaniards had hanged some French prisoners. If so, it was a barbarous and a shameful retaliation, unworthy of a soldier, for what justice or propriety is shewn in revenging the death of one innocent person by the murder of another?

Rocca's
Memoirs.

After the French had thus withdrawn, Infantado
and Palacios proceeded to re-organize their forces,
under the name of the Carolina Army, and when
the levies in Grenada and other parts came up,
the duke of Albuquerque, at the head of the cavalry, endeavoured to surprise a French regiment
of dragoons at Mora, but the latter rallied quickly,
fought stoutly, and effected a retreat with
scarcely any loss: Albuquerque then retired to
Consuegra, where he was attacked the next day
by superior numbers, and got off with difficulty.
The duke of Infantado was now displaced by
the junta, and general Urbina, Conde de Car-
taojal, the new commander, having restored some
discipline, advanced to Ciudad Real, and took
post on the left bank of the Upper Guadiana.
From thence he opened a communication with
Cuesta, whose army had been encreased to sixteen
thousand men, of which three thousand were cavalry; for the Spaniards suffered more in flight
than in action, and the horsemen escaping with
little damage, were more easily rallied, and in
greater relative numbers than the infantry. With
these forces, Cuesta had advanced to the Tagus,
when Moore's march upon Sahagun had drawn the
fourth corps across that river; the latter, however,
by fortifying an old tower, still held the bridge of
Arzobispo. Cuesta extended his line from the
mountains in front of that place, to the Puerto de
Mirabete, and broke down the bridge of Almaraz,
a magnificent structure, the centre arch of which
was above one hundred and fifty feet high.

In these positions both sides remained tranquil in
La Mancha, and in Estremadura, and so ended the

Spanish exertions to lighten the pressure upon the
British army; two French divisions of infantry,
and as many brigades of cavalry, had more than
sufficed to baffle them, and thus the imminent
danger of the southern provinces, when sir John
Moore's vigorous operations drew the emperor to
the north, may be justly estimated.

CHAPTER II.

CONTINUATION OF THE OPERATIONS IN ARAGON.

FROM the field of battle at Tudela, all the fugitives from O'Neil's, and a great part of those from
Castaños's army, fled to Zaragoza, and with such
speed as to bring the first news of their own disaster.
With the troops, also, came an immense number of
carriages, and the military chests, for the roads
were wide and excellent, and the pursuit was slack.
The citizens and the neighbouring peasantry
were astounded at this quick and unexpected
calamity. They had, with a natural credulity,
relied on the boasting promises of their chiefs, and
being necessarily ignorant of the true state of
affairs, never doubted that their vengeance would
be sated, by a speedy and complete destruction of
the French. When their hopes were thus suddenly blasted, when they beheld troops, from whom
they expected nothing but victory, come pouring
into the town with all the tumult of panic; when
the peasants of all the villages through which
the fugitives passed, came rushing into the city
along with the scared multitude of flying soldiers
and camp followers, every heart was filled with
consternation, and the date of Zaragoza's glory
would have ended with the first siege, if the
success at Tudela had been followed up by the
French with that celerity and vigour which the
occasion required.

Napoleon, foreseeing that this moment of confu- sion and terror would arrive, had, with his usual prudence, provided the means, and given directions for such an instantaneous and powerful attack, as would inevitably have overthrown the bulwark of the eastern provinces : but the sickness of marshal Lasnes, the difficulty of communication, the conse- quent false movements of Moncey and Ney, in fine, the intervention of fortune, omnipotent as she is in war, baffled the emperor's long-sighted calculations. The leaders had time to restore order amongst the multitude, to provide stores, to complete the defen- sive works, and, by a ferocious exercise of power, to insure implicit obedience : the danger of re- sisting the enemy appeared light when a suspi- cious word or gesture was instantly punished by death.

The third corps having missed the favour- able moment for a sudden assault, and being reduced by sickness, by losses in battle, and by detachments, to seventeen thousand four hundred men including the engineers and artillery, was too weak to invest the city in form, and, therefore, remained in observation on the Xalon river, while a battering train of sixty guns, with well-fur- nished parcs, which had been by Napoleon's orders previously collected in Pampeluna, was carried to Tudela and embarked upon the canal leading to Zaragoza. Marshal Mortier, with the fifth corps, was directed to assist in the siege, and he was in march to join Moncey, when his progress also, was arrested by sir John Moore's advance towards Burgos ; but the scope of that general's operation being determined by Napo- leon's counter-movement, Mortier resumed his

Muster roll of the French Army, MSS.

BOOK
V.
————
1808.
Dec.

Cavalhero.
Doyle's
Correspon-
dence,
MSS.

march to re-inforce Moncey, and, on the 20th
of December, 1808, their united corps, forming an army of thirty-five thousand men of all
arms, advanced against Zaragoza.   At this time,
however, confidence had been restored in the town,
and all the preparations necessary for a vigorous
defence were completed.

The nature of the plain in which Zaragoza is
situated, the course of the rivers, the peculiar
construction of the houses, and the multitude of
convents, have been already described, but the
difficulties to be encountered by the French troops
were no longer the same as in the first siege.   At
that time little assistance had been derived from
science ; now, instructed by experience, and inspired as it were by the greatness of their resolution, neither the rules of art. nor the resources of
genius were neglected by the defenders.

Zaragoza offered four irregular fronts.   The first,
reckoning from the right of the town, extended
from the Ebro to a convent of bare-footed Carmelites, and was about three hundred yards wide.

The second, twelve hundred yards in extent,
reached from the Carmelites to a bridge over the
Huerba.

The third, likewise of twelve hundred yards,
stretched from this bridge to an oil manufactory
built beyond the walls.

The fourth, being on an opening of four hundred yards, reached from the oil manufactory to
the Ebro.

Rogniat's
Siege of
Zaragoza.
Cavalhe-
ro'sSiege of
Zaragoza.
The first front, fortified by an ancient wall and
flanked by the guns on the Carmelite, was strength-
ened by new batteries and ramparts, and by the
Castle of Aljaferia, commonly called the Castle of

the Inquisition, which standing a little in advance, was a square fort, having a bastion and tower at each corner, and a good stone ditch, and it was connected with the body of the place by certain walls loop-holed for musketry.

The second front was defended by a double wall, the exterior one of recent erection, faced with sun-dried bricks, and covered by a ditch, with perpendicular sides, fifteen feet deep and twenty feet wide. The flanks of this front were formed from the convent of the Carmelites, by a large circular battery standing in the centre of the line, by a fortified convent of the Capuchins, called the Trinity, and by some earthen works protecting the head of the bridge over the Huerba.

The third front was covered by the river Huerba, the deep bed of which was close to the foot of the ramparts. Behind this stream a double entrenchment was carried from the bridge head to a large projecting convent of Santa Engracia. a distance of two hundred yards. Santa Engracia itself was very strongly fortified and armed, and, from thence to the oil manufactory, the line of defence was prolonged by an ancient Moorish wall, on which several terraced batteries were raised, to sweep all the space between the rampart and the Huerba. These batteries, and the guns in the convent of Santa Engracia, likewise overlooked some works raised to protect a second bridge, that crossed the river, about cannon-shot below the first.

Upon the right bank of the Huerba, and a little below the second bridge, stood the convent of San Joseph, the walls of which had been strengthened and protected by a deep ditch with a covered way and palisade. It was well placed, as an advanced work, to impede the enemy's approach, and to facilitate sallies on the right bank of the river, and it was open in the rear, to the fire from the works at the second bridge, both being overlooked by the terraced batteries, and by the guns of Santa Engracia.

The fourth front was protected, by the Huerba, by the continuation of the old city wall, by new batteries and entrenchments, and by several armed convents and large houses.

Beyond the walls, the Monte Torrero, which commanded all the plain of Zaragoza, was crowned by a large ill-constructed fort, raised at the distance of eighteen hundred yards from the convent of San Joseph. This work was covered by the royal canal, the sluices of which were defended by some field-works open to the fire of the fort itself.

On the left bank of the Ebro the suburb, built in a low marshy plain, was protected by a chain of redoubts and fortified houses, and, some gun-boats, manned by seamen from the naval arsenal of Carthagena, completed the circuit of defence. The artillery of the place was, however, of too small a calibre. There were only sixty guns carrying more than twelve-pound balls, and there were but eight large mortars: there was, however, no want of small arms, and colonel Doyle had furnished many English musquets.

Cavalhero.

These were the regular external defences of Zaragoza, most of which were constructed at the time, according to the skill and means of the engineers; but the experience of the former siege had taught the people not to trust to the ordinary

resources of art, and, with equal genius and resolution, they had prepared an internal system of defence infinitely more efficacious.

It has been already observed, that the houses of
Zaragoza were fire-proof, and, generally, of only
two stories, that, in all the quarters of the city, the
massive convents and churches rose like castles
above the low buildings, and that the greater streets,
running into the broad-way called the Cosso, divided
the town into a variety of districts, unequal in size,
but each containing one or more large structures.
Now, the citizens, sacrificing all personal convenience, and resigning all idea of private property,
gave up their goods, their bodies, and their houses
to the war, and, being promiscuously mingled with
the peasantry and the regular soldiers, the whole
formed one mighty garrison, well suited to the vast
fortress into which Zaragoza was transformed : for
the doors and windows of the houses were built
up, their fronts loop-holed, internal communications broken through the party walls, the streets
trenched and crossed by earthen ramparts mounted
with cannon, and every strong building turned
into a separate fortification. There was no weak
point, because there could be none in a town which
was all fortress, and where the space covered by
the city, was the measurement for the thickness of
the ramparts.

Nor in this emergency were the leaders un-
mindful of moral force. The people were cheered
by a constant reference to the former successful
resistance, their confidence was raised by the con-
templation of the vast works that had been executed, and it was recalled to their recollection
that the wet, usual at that season of the year, would

spread disease among the enemy's ranks, impairing,
if not entirely frustrating, his efforts. Neither was
the aid of superstition neglected: processions imposed upon the sight, false miracles bewildered the
imagination, and terrible denunciations of the divine
wrath shook the minds of men, whose former habits
and present situation rendered them peculiarly susceptible of such impressions. Finally, the leaders
were themselves so prompt and terrible in their pu-
nishments, that the greatest cowards were likely to
show the boldest bearing in their wish to escape
suspicion.

To avoid the danger of any great explosion, the
powder was made as occasion required, which was
the more easily effected, because Zaragoza contained a royal depôt and refinery for saltpetre, and
there were powder-mills in the neighbourhood,
which furnished workmen familiar with the process.
The houses and trees beyond the walls were all
demolished and cut down, and the materials carried
into the town. The public magazines contained six
months' provisions, the convents were well stocked,
the inhabitants had laid up their own stores for several
months, and General Doyle sent a convoy into the
town from the side of Catalonia; and there was abundance of money, because, in addition to the resources
of the town, the military-chest of Castaños's army,
which had been filled only the night before the battle
of Tudela, was, in the flight, carried to Zaragoza.
Doyle's
Correspon-
dence, MS.
Some companies of women were enrolled to attend
the hospitals and to carry provisions and ammunition
to the combatants; they were commanded by the
countess of Burita, a lady of an heroic disposition,
who is said to have displayed the greatest intelligence and the noblest character during both sieges.

There were thirteen engineer officers, eight hundred sappers and miners, composed of excavators
formerly employed on the canal, and from fifteen
hundred to two thousand cannoneers. The regular
troops that fled from Tudela, being joined by two
small divisions, which retreated, at the same time,
from Sanguessa and Caparosa, formed a garrison of
thirty thousand men, and, with the inhabitants and
peasantry, presented a mass of fifty thousand combatants, who, with passions excited almost to
phrensy, awaited an assault amidst those mighty
entrenchments, where each man's home was a fortress and his family a garrison. To besiege, with
only thirty-five thousand men, a city so prepared
was truly a gigantic undertaking!

SECOND SIEGE OF ZARAGOZA.

The 20th of December, the two marshals, Moncey
and Mortier, having established their hospitals and
magazines at Alagon on the Xalon, advanced in
three columns against Zaragoza.

The first, composed of the infantry of the third
corps, marched by the right bank of the canal.

The second, composed of general Suchet's division of the fifth corps, marched between the canal
and the Ebro.

The third, composed of general Gazan's division
of infantry, crossed the Ebro opposite to Tauste,
and from thence made an oblique march to the
Gallego river.

The right and centre columns arrived in front of
the town that evening. The latter, after driving
back the Spanish advanced guards, halted at a distance of a league from the Capuchin convent of the
Trinity; the former took post on both sides of the

Huerba, and, having seized the aqueduct by which
the canal is carried over that river, proceeded, in
pursuance of Napoleon's orders, to raise batteries,
and make dispositions for an immediate assault on
Monte Torrero. Meanwhile general Gazan, with
the left column, marching by Cartejon and Zuera,
reached Villa Nueva, on the Gallego river, without
encountering an enemy.

The Monte Torrero was defended by five thousand Spaniards, under the command of general St.
Marc; but, at day-break on the 21st, the French
opened their fire against the fort, and one column
of infantry having attracted the attention of the
Spaniards, a second, unseen, crossed the canal
under the aqueduct, and, penetrating between the
fort and the city, entered the former by the rear;
at the same time, a third column stormed the works
protecting the great sluices. These sudden attacks,
Cavalhero. and the loss of the fort, threw the Spaniards into
confusion, and they hastily retired to the town,
which so enraged the plebeian leaders that the
life of St. Marc was with difficulty saved by Palafox.

It had been concerted among the French that
general Gazan should assault the suburb, simultaneously with the attack on the Torrero, and that
officer, having encountered a body of Spanish and
Swiss troops placed somewhat in advance, drove
the former back so quickly that the Swiss, unable
to make good their retreat, were, to the number of
three or four hundred, killed or taken. But notwith-
Rogniat. standing this fortunate commencement, Gazan did
not attack the suburb itself, until after the affair at
Monte Torrero was over, and then only upon a
single point, without any previous examination of

the works; hence the Spaniards, recovering from their first alarm, reinforced this point, and Gazan was forced to desist, with the loss of four hundred men. This important failure more than balanced the success against the Monte Torrero; it restored the shaken confidence of the Spaniards at a most critical moment, and checking in the French, at the outset, that impetuous spirit, that impulse of victory, which great generals so carefully watch and improve, threw them back upon the tedious and chilling process of the engineer.

The 24th of December the investment of Zaragoza was completed on both sides of the Ebro. Gazan occupied the bridge over the Gallego with his left, and covered his front from sorties, by inundations and cuts, that the low, marshy plain where he was posted, enabled him to make without difficulty.

General Suchet occupied the space between the Upper Ebro and the Huerba.

Morlot's division of the 3d corps encamped in the broken hollow that formed the bed of that stream.

Meusnier's division crowned the Monte Torrero, and general Grandjean continuing the circuit to the Lower Ebro, communicated with Gazan's post on the other side. Several Spanish detachments that had been sent out to forage were thus cut off, and could never re-enter the town, and a bridge of boats constructed on the Upper Ebro completed the circle of investment, insuring a free intercourse between the different quarters of the army.

General Lacoste, an engineer of reputation, and

aid-de-camp to the Emperor, directed the siege.
His plan was, that one false and two real attacks
should be conducted by regular approaches on the
right bank of the Ebro, and he still hoped to take
the suburb by a sudden assault. The trenches
were opened the night of the 29th, the 30th
the place was summoned, and the terms dictated
by Napoleon when he was at Aranda de Duero,
being offered, the example of Madrid was cited
to induce a surrender. Palafox replied, that—
If Madrid had surrendered, Madrid had been sold:
Zaragoza would neither be sold nor surrender!
On the receipt of this haughty answer the attacks
were commenced, the right being directed against
the convent of San Joseph, the centre against the
upper bridge over the Huerba, the left, which was
the false one, against the castle of Aljaferia.

The 31st Palafox made sorties against all the
three attacks. From the right and centre he was
beaten back with loss, and he was likewise repulsed
on the left at the trenches; but some of his cavalry,
gliding between the French parallel and the Ebro,
surprised and cut down a post of infantry, stationed
behind some ditches that intersected the low ground
on the bank of that river. This trifling success
exalted the enthusiasm of the besieged, and Palafox
gratified his personal vanity by boasting proclamations, some of which bore the marks of genius, but
the greater part were ridiculous.

1809.   The 1st of January the second parallels of the
true attacks were commenced, and the next day Palafox caused the attention of the besiegers to be occupied on the right bank of the Ebro, by slight
skirmishes, while he made a serious attack from the

side of the suburb on Gazan's lines of contravallation. This sally was repulsed with loss, but, on the
right bank, the Spaniards obtained some success.

Marshal Moncey being called to Madrid, Junot
now assumed the command of the third corps, and,
about the same time, marshal Mortier was directed
to take post at Calatayud, with Suchet's division,
for the purpose of securing the communication with
Madrid. The gap in the circle of investment left
by this draft of eight thousand men, being but
scantily stopped by extending Morlot's division, a
line of contravallation was constructed at that
part to supply the place of numbers. Meanwhile
the besieged, hoping and expecting each day
that the usual falls of rain would render the besiegers' situation intolerable, continued their fire
briskly, and worked counter approaches to the right
of the French attacks: but the season was unusually
dry, and a thick fog rising each morning covered
the besiegers' advances and protected their workmen, both from the fire and from the sorties of the
Spaniards.

The 10th of January, thirty-two pieces of French
artillery battered in breach, both the convent of San
Joseph and the head of the second bridge on the
Huerba, and the town also was bombarded. San
Joseph was so much injured by this fire that the Spaniards, resolving to evacuate it, withdrew their guns;
nevertheless, two hundred of their men making a
vigorous sally at midnight, pushed close up to the
French batteries, but being taken in flank with a
discharge of grape, retired, with loss of half
their number.

The 11th, the besiegers' batteries having continued
to play on San Joseph, the breach became practicable,

and, at four o'clock in the evening, some companies
of infantry, with two field-pieces, attacked by the
right, while a column was kept in readiness to assail
the front, when this attack should have shaken the
defence, and two other companies of chosen men were
directed to search for an entrance by the rear, between the fort and the river.

The defences of the convent were now reduced to
a ditch eighteen feet deep, and a covered way,
which falling back on both flanks to the Huerba,
extended along the bank for some distance, and
was occupied by a considerable number of men,
but when some French guns raked it from the
right, the Spaniards, crossing the bed of the
river in confusion, took refuge in the town, and
at that moment the front of the convent was
assaulted. The depth of the ditch and the Spanish
fire checked the assailants a moment, yet the chosen
companies, passing round the works, found a small
bridge, crossed it, and entered by the rear, and the
next instant the front was stormed, and the defenders
were all killed or taken.

The French, who had suffered but little in this
assault, immediately lodged themselves in the
convent, raised a rampart along the edge of the
Huerba, and commenced batteries, against the body
of the place and against the works at the head of
the upper bridge, from whence, as well as from the
town, they were incommoded by the fire that played
into the convent.

The 15th, the bridge-head, in front of Santa
Engracia, was carried with the loss of only three
men; the Spaniards cut the bridge itself, and sprung
a mine under the works, but the explosion occasioned no mischief, and the third parallels being

soon completed, the trenches of the two attacks were united, and the defences of the besieged were confined to the town itsel f ;they could no longer make sallies on the right bank of the Huerba without overcoming the greatest difficulties. The passage of the Huerba was then effected by the French, and breaching and counter-batteries, mounting fifty pieces of artillery, were constructed against the body of the place, and as the fire also reached the bridge over the Ebro, the communication between the suburb and the town, was interrupted.

Unshaken by this aspect of affairs, the Spanish leaders, with great readiness of mind, immediately forged intelligence of the defeat of the emperor, and, with the sound of music, and amidst the shouts of the populace, proclaimed the names of the marshals who had been killed; asserting, also, that Palafox's brother, the marquis of Lazan, was already wasting France. This intelligence, extravagant as it was, met with implicit credence, for such was the disposition of the Spaniards throughout this war, that the imaginations of the chiefs were taxed to produce absurdities proportionable to the credulity of their followers; hence the boasting of the leaders and the confidence of the besieged, augmented as the danger increased, and their anticipations of victory seemed realized when the night-fires of a succouring force were discerned, blazing on the hills behind Gazan's troops.

The difficulties of the French were indeed fast increasing, for while enclosing Zaragoza, they were themselves encircled by insurrections, and their supplies so straitened that famine was felt in their camp. Disputes amongst the generals also dimi-

nished the vigour of the operations, and the bonds
of discipline being relaxed, the military ardour of
the troops naturally became depressed.   The soldiers
reasoned openly upon the chances of success, which,
in times of danger, is only one degree removed from
mutiny.

The nature of the country about Zaragoza was
exceedingly favourable to the Spaniards.   The town,
although situated in a plain, is surrounded at some
miles' distance by high mountains, and to the
south, the fortresses of Mequinenza and Lerida
afforded a double base of operations for any forces
that might come from Catalonia and Valencia.
The besiegers drew their supplies fram Pampeluna,
and their line of operation running through Alagon,
Tudela, and Caparosa, was harassed by the insurgents, who were in considerable numbers, on the side
of Epila and in the Sierra de Muela, threatening
Alagon; while others, descending from the mountains of Soria, menaced the important point of
Tudela.   The marquis of Lazan also, anxious to
assist his brother, had drafted five thousand men
from the Catalonian army, and taking post in the
Sierra de Liciñena, or Alcubierre, on the left of
the Ebro, drew together all the armed peasantry of
the valleys as high as Sanguessa.   Extending his
line from Villa Franca on the Ebro to Zuera on the
Gallego, he hemmed in the division of Gazan, and
sent detachments as far as Caparosa, to harass the
French convoys coming from Pampeluna.

To maintain their communications and to procure
provisions, the besiegers had placed between two
or three thousand men in Tudela, Caparosa, and
Tafalla, and some hundreds in Alagon and at
Montalbarra.   Between the latter town and the

investing army, six hundred and fifty cavalry were stationed; a like number were posted at Santa Fé to watch the openings of the Sierra de Muela; finally sixteen hundred cavalry and twelve hundred infantry, under the command of general Wathier, were pushed towards the south as far as Fuentes. Wathier, falling suddenly upon an assemblage of four or five thousand insurgents at Belchite, dispersed them, and then taking the town of Alcanitz, established himself there, in observation, for the rest of the siege. Lazan, however, still maintained himself in the Alcubierre.

In this state of affairs marshal Lasnes, having recovered from his long sickness, arrived before Zaragoza, and took the supreme command of both corps on the 22d of January. The influence of his firm and vigorous character was immediately perceptible; recalling Suchet's division from Calatayud, where it had been lingering without necessity, he sent it across the Ebro, ordered Mortier to Rogniat. attack Lazan, and at the same time directed a smaller detachment against the insurgents in Zuera, meanwhile, repressing all disputes, he restored discipline in the army, and pressed the siege with infinite resolution.

The detachment sent to Zuera defeated the insurgents, and took possession of that place and of the bridge over the Gallego. Mortier encountered the Spanish advanced guard at Perdeguera, and pushed it back to Nuestra Señora de Vagallar, where the main body, several thousand strong, was posted, and where, after a short fight, he defeated it, took four guns, and then spreading his troops in a half circle, extending, from Huesca, to Pina on the Ebro, awed the country between those places and Zaragoza, and checked further insurrection.

Before Lasnes arrived, the besieged had been much galled by a mortar battery, situated behind the second parallel of the centre attack, and one Mariano Galindo undertook, with eighty volunteers, to silence it. He surprised the guard of the trenches, and entered the battery, but the French reserve arrived in his front, the guard of the trenches rallied, and, thus surrounded, Galindo, fighting bravely, was wounded and taken, and his comrades perished, with as much glory as simple soldiers can attain to. After this, the armed vessels in the river, attempted to flank the batteries raised against the Aljaferia, but the French guns obliged them to retire, and the besiegers' works being carried over the Huerba, in the nights between the 21st and 26th of January, the third parallels of the true attack were completed. The oil manufactory, and other advantageous posts, on the left bank of that river, were then incorporated with the lines of approach, and the second parallel of the false attack was commenced at one hundred and fifty yards from the Aljaferia. These advantages were, however, not obtained without pain; for the Spaniards frequently sallied, spiked two guns, and burnt a post on the right of the besiegers' line.

The French fire now broke the walls rapidly; two practicable breaches were opened in front of the San Joseph, a third was commenced in the Santa Augustino, facing the oil manufactory, a broad way was made into the Santa Engracia, and at twelve o'clock on the 29th of January, four chosen columns rushing forth, from the trenches, burst upon the ruined walls of Zaragoza.

On the right, the assailants twice stormed an isolated stone house that defended the breach of Saint Augustin, and twice they were driven back with loss.

In the centre, regardless of two small mines that exploded at the foot of the walls, they carried the breach fronting the oil manufactory, and then endeavoured to break into the town; but the Spaniards retrenched within the place, opened such a fire, of grape and musquetry, that the French were finally content to establish themselves on the summit of the breach, and to connect their lodgement with the trenches by new works.

The third column was more successful; the breach was carried, and the neighbouring houses also, as far as the first large cross street; beyond that, the French could not penetrate, but they were enabled to establish themselves within the walls of the town, and immediately brought forward their trenches, so as to comprehend the lodgement within their works.

The fourth column, composed of the Polish soldiers of the Vistula, vigorously stormed the San Engracia and the convent adjoining it; and then, unchecked by the fire from the houses, and undaunted by the explosion of six small mines planted on their path, swept the ramparts to the left, as far as the first bridge on the Huerba. The guards of the trenches, excited by this success, now rushed forward tumultuously, mounted the walls, bayonetted the artillery men at the guns in the Capuchin, and then continuing their career, endeavoured, some

to reach the semicircular battery and the Misericordia, others to break into the city.

This wild assault was soon checked, by grape
from two guns planted behind a traverse on the
ramparts, and by a murderous fire from the houses,
and as the ranks of the assailants were thinned,
their ardour sunk, while the courage of their
adversaries increased. The French were driven
back upon the Capuchins, and the Spaniards were
already breaking into that convent in pursuit, when
two battalions, detached by general Morlot from
the trenches of the false attack, arrived, and
secured possession of that point, which was moreover untenable by the Spaniards, inasmuch as the
guns of the convent of Santa Engracia saw it in
reverse. The French lost, on this day, more than
six hundred men, but La Coste immediately abandoned the false attack against the castle, fortified
the Capuchin convent and a house situated at an
angle of the wall abutting upon the bridge over
the Huerba, and then joining them by works to his
trenches, the ramparts of the town became the
front line of the besiegers.

The walls of Zaragoza thus went to the ground,
but Zaragoza herself remained erect, and as the
broken girdle fell from the heroic city, the besiegers
started at the view of her naked strength. The
regular defences had, indeed, crumbled before the
skill of the assailants, but the popular resistance
was immediately called, with all its terrors, into
action! and, as if Fortune had resolved to mark
the exact moment when the ordinary calculations
of science should cease, the chief engineers on
both sides were simultaneously slain. The French

general, La Coste, a young man, intrepid, skilful,
and endowed with genius, perished like a brave
soldier. The Spanish colonel, San Genis, died,
not only with the honour of a soldier, but the glory
of a patriot. Falling in the noblest cause, his blood
stained the ramparts which he had himself raised
for the protection of his native place.

CHAPTER III.

THE war being now in the streets of Zaragoza, the sound of the alarm-bell was heard in every quarter; the people crowded into the houses nearest to the lodgements of the enemy, additional barricades were constructed across the principal thoroughfares, mines were prepared in the more open spaces, and the internal communications from house to house were multiplied, until they formed a vast labyrinth, the intricate windings of which, were only to be traced by the weapons and the dead bodies of the defenders. The junta, become more powerful from the cessation of regular warfare, urged the defence with redoubled energy, yet increased the horrors of the siege, by a ferocity pushed to the verge of frenzy ; every person who excited the suspicions of these furious men, or of those immediately about them, was instantly put to death. Amidst the noble bulwarks of war, a horrid array of gibbets was seen, on which crowds of wretches were each night suspended, because their courage sunk under accumulating dangers, or that some doubtful expression, some gesture of distress, had been misconstrued by their barbarous chiefs.

Cavalhero.

Rogniat.
From the height of the walls which he had conquered, Lasnes contemplated this terrific scene, and judging that men so passionate, and so prepared, could not be prudently encountered in open battle, he resolved to proceed by the slow, certain process of the mattock and the mine : this also was in unison with the emperor's instructions, and hence

until the 2d of February, the efforts of the French
were only directed to the enlargement of their
lodgements on the ramparts. This they effected
with severe fighting and by means of explosions,
working through the nearest houses, and sustaining
many counter-assaults, of which the most noted and
the fiercest was made by a friar on the Capuchins'
convent.

It has been already observed, that the large
streets divided the town into certain small districts, or islands of houses. To gain possession of
these, it was necessary not only to mine but to
fight for each house; and to cross the great intersecting
streets it was indispensable to construct traverses
above, or to work by underground galleries; a
battery raked each street, and each house was defended by a garrison that, generally speaking, had
only the option, of repelling the enemy in front or
dying on the gibbet erected behind. As long
as the convents and churches remained in possession
of the Spaniards, the progress of the French among
the islands of small houses was of little advantage to them; the strong garrisons in the greater
buildings, enabled the defenders, not only to make
continual and successful sallies, but to countermine
their enemies, whose superior skill in that kind of
warfare, was often frustrated by the numbers and
persevering energy of the besieged.

To overcome these obstacles, the batteries opposite the fourth front, had breached the convents of
Augustin and Santa Monica, and the latter had been
taken the 31st of January; for while the attack
was hot, a part of the wall in another direction was
blown in by a petard, and the besiegers pouring
through took the main breach in rear, cleared the

convent and several houses behind it. Nevertheless the Spaniards opened a gallery from the Augustins and worked a mine that night under Santa Monica, but the French discovered it and stifled the miners. The next day the breach in the Augustin becoming practicable, the attention of the defenders was drawn to it, while the French springing a mine, which they had carried under the wall, from the side of Santa Monica, entered by the opening, and the Spaniards thus again unexpectedly taken in the rear were easily driven out. Rallying a few hours after, they vainly attempted to retake the structure, and the besiegers then broke into the neighbouring houses, and at one push, reached the point where the Quemada-street joined the Cosso; but the Spaniards renewed the combat with such a fury, that the French were beaten out of the houses again, and lost more than two hundred men.

On the side of San Engracia a contest still more severe took place; the houses in the vicinity were blown up, yet the Spaniards fought so obstinately for the ruins, that the Polish troops were scarcely able to make good their lodgement—although two successive and powerful explosions had, with the buildings, destroyed a number of the defenders.

The experience of these attacks induced a change in the mode of fighting on both sides. Hitherto the play of the French mines had reduced the houses to ruins, leaving the soldiers exposed to the fire from the next Spanish posts; the engineers, therefore, diminished the quantity of powder, that the interior only might fall and the outward walls stand, and this method was found successful. Whereupon the Spaniards, with ready ingenuity, saturated the timbers of the houses with rosin and pitch, and setting fire to those which could no longer be maintained, interposed a burning barrier, which often delayed the assailants for two days, and always prevented them from pushing their successes during the confusion that necessarily followed the bursting of the mines. The fighting was, however, incessant; a constant bombardment, the explosion of mines, the crash of falling buildings, clamorous shouts, and the continued echo of musquetry deafened the ear, while volumes of smoke and dust clouding the atmosphere, lowered continually over the heads of the combatants, as hour by hour, the French, with a terrible perseverance, pushed forward their approaches to the heart of the miserable but glorious city.

Their efforts were chiefly directed from two points, namely, San Engracia, which may be denominated the left attack, and Saint Augustin, which constituted the right attack. At San Engracia they laboured on a line perpendicular to the Cosso, from which they were only separated by the large convent of the Daughters of Jerusalem, and by the hospital for madmen, which was entrenched, although in ruins since the first siege; the line of this attack was protected on the left by the convent of the Capuchins, which La Coste had fortified to repel the counter-assaults of the Spaniards. The attack from the Augustin was more diffused, because the localities presented less prominent features to determine the direction of the approaches. But the French having mounted a number of light six-inch mortars, on peculiar carriages, drew them from street to street, and house to house, as occasion offered; on the other hand the Spaniards continually plied their enemies with hand grenades, which seem to have produced a surprising effect. In this manner the never-ceasing combat was prolonged until the 7th of February, when the besiegers, by dint of alternate mines and assaults, had worked their perilous way at either attack to the Cosso, yet not without several changes of fortune and considerable loss; and they were unable to obtain a footing on that public walk, for the Spaniards still disputed every house with undiminished resolution. Meanwhile, Lasnes having caused trenches to be opened on the left bank of the Ebro, played twenty guns against an isolated structure called the Convent of Jesus, which covered the right of the suburb line; on the 7th of February this convent was carried by storm, with so little difficulty, that the French, supposing the Spaniards to be panic stricken, entered the suburb itself, but were quickly driven back, they, however, made good their lodgement in the convent.

On the town side the 8th, 9th, and 10th were wasted by the besiegers in vain attempts to pass the Cosso. They then extended their flanks; to the right with a view to reach the quay, and so connect this attack with that against the suburb; to the left to obtain possession of the large and strongly built convent of St. Francisco, in which, after exploding an immense mine and making two assaults they finally established themselves.

The 11th and 12th, mines, in the line of the right attack, were exploded under the university, a large building on the Spanish side of the Cosso, yet their play was insufficient to open the walls, and the storming party was beaten, with the loss of fifty men. Nevertheless, the besiegers continuing their labours during the 13th, 14th, 15th, 16th, and 17th, passed the Cosso by means of traverses, and prepared fresh mines under the university, yet deferred their explosion until a simultaneous effort could be combined on the side of the suburb. At the left attack also, a number of houses, bordering on the Cosso, being gained, a battery was established that raked that great thoroughfare above ground, while under it, six galleries were carried, and six mines loaded to explode at the same moment.

But the spirit of the French army was now exhausted. They had laboured and fought without intermission for fifty days; they had crumbled the walls with their bullets, burst the convents with their mines, and carried the breaches with their bayonets;—fighting above and beneath the surface of the earth, they had spared neither fire nor sword, their bravest men were falling in the obscurity of a subterranean warfare, famine pinched them, and Zaragoza was still unconquered!

" Before this siege," they exclaimed, " was it ever known, that twenty thousand men should besiege fifty thousand? Scarcely a fourth of the town is won, and we are already exhausted. We must wait for reinforcements, or we shall all perish among these cursed ruins, which will become our own tombs, before we can force the last of these fanatics from the last of their dens " Rogniat.

Marshal Lasnes, unshaken by these murmurs, and obstinate to conquer, endeavoured to raise the soldiers' hopes. He told them that the losses of the besieged so far exceeded their own, that the Spaniards' strength would soon be exhausted and their courage sink, that the fierceness of their defence

was already abating; and that if contrary to expectation, they should renew the example of Numantia,
their utter destruction must quickly be effected, by
the united evils of battle, pestilence, and misery.
His exhortations were successful, and on the 18th
of February, all combinations being completed, a
general assault took place.

The French at the right attack opened a party-
wall by the explosion of a petard, made a sudden
rush through some burning ruins, and then carried,
without a check, the whole island of houses leading
down to the quay, with the exception of two
buildings; the Spaniards were thus forced to
abandon all the external fortifications between Saint
Augustin and the Ebro, which they had preserved
until that day. During this assault the mines
under the university containing three thousand
pounds of powder were sprung, and the walls
tumbling with a terrific crash,—a column of the
besiegers entered the place, and after one repulse
secured a lodgement. Meanwhile fifty pieces of
artillery thundered upon the suburb, ploughed up
the bridge over the Ebro, and by midday opened
a practicable breach in the great convent of Saint
Lazar, which was the principal defence on that
side. Lasnes, observing that the Spaniards seemed
to be shaken by this overwhelming fire, ordered an
assault there also, and Saint Lazar being carried forth-
with, the retreat to the bridge was thus intercepted,
and the besieged falling into confusion, and their
commander, Baron Versage, being killed, were all
destroyed or taken, with the exception of three
hundred men, who, braving the terrible fire to which
they were exposed, got back into the town.
General Gazan immediately occupied the abandoned

works, and having thus cut off more than two thousand men that were stationed on the Ebro, above the suburb, forced them also to surrender.

This important success being followed on the 19th, by another fortunate attack on the right bank of the Ebro, and by the devastating explosion of sixteen hundred pounds of powder, the constancy of the besieged was at last shaken. An aid-de-camp of Palafox came forth to demand certain terms, before offered by the marshal, adding thereto, that the garrison should be allowed to join the Spanish armies, and that a certain number of covered carriages should follow them. Lasnes rejected these proposals, and the fire continued, but the hour of surrender was come! Fifty pieces of artillery on the left bank of the Ebro, laid the houses on the quay in ruins. The church of Our Lady of the Pillar, under whose especial protection the city was supposed to exist, was nearly effaced by the bombardment, and the six mines under the Cosso loaded with many thousand pounds of powder, were ready for a simultaneous explosion, which would have laid a quarter of the remaining houses in the dust. In fine, war had done its work, and the misery of Zaragoza could no longer be endured.

The bombardment which had never ceased since the 10th of January, had forced the women and children to take refuge in the vaults, with which the city abounded: there the constant combustion of oil, the closeness of the atmosphere, unusual diet, and fear and restlessness of mind, had combined to produce a pestilence which soon spread to the garrison. The strong and the weak, the daring soldier and the shrinking child, fell before it alike,

BOOK
V.
———
1809.
February.

Cavalhero.
Rogniat.
Suchet.

and such was the state of the atmosphere and the predisposition to disease, that the slightest wound gangrened and became incurable. In the beginning of February the daily deaths were from four to five hundred; the living were unable to bury the dead; and thousands of carcases, scattered about the streets and court-yards, or piled in heaps at the doors of the churches, were left to dissolve in their own corruption, or to be licked up by the flames of the burning houses as the defence became contracted. The suburb, the greatest part of the walls and one-fourth of the houses were in the hands of the French; sixteen thousand shells thrown during the bombardment, and the explosion of forty-five thousand pounds of powder in the mines had shaken the city to its foundations, and the bones of more than forty thousand persons of every age and sex, bore dreadful testimony to the constancy of the besieged.

Palafox was sick, and of the plebeian chiefs, the curate of St. Gil, the lemonade seller of the Cosso, and the Tios, Jorge, and Marin, having been slain in battle, or swept away by the pestilence, the obdurate violence of the remaining leaders was so abated, that a fresh junta was formed, and after a stormy consultation, the majority being for a surrender, a deputation waited upon Marshal Lasnes on the 20th of February, to negotiate a capitulation. They proposed that the garrison should march out with the honours of war; that the peasantry should not be considered as prisoners; and at the particular request of the clergy, they also demanded that the latter should have their full revenues guaranteed to them, and punctually paid. This last article was rejected with indignation, and, according to the French writers, the place surrendered at discretion; but the Spanish writers assert, that Lasnes granted certain terms, drawn up by the deputation at the moment, the name of Ferdinand the 7th being purposely omitted in the instrument, which in substance ran thus:—

The garrison to march out with the honours of war; to be constituted prisoners, and marched to France; the officers to retain their swords, baggage, and horses; the men their knapsacks; persons of either class, wishing to serve Joseph, to be immediately enrolled in his ranks; the peasants to be sent to their homes; property and religion to be guaranteed.

With this understanding the deputies returned to the city, where fresh commotions had arisen during their absence. The party for protracting the defence, although the least numerous, were the most energetic; they had before seized all the boats on the Ebro, fearing that Palafox and others, of whom they entertained suspicions, would endeavour to quit the town; and they were still so menacing and so powerful, that the deputies not daring to pass through the streets, retired outside the walls to the castle of Aljaferia, and from thence sent notice to the junta of their proceedings. The dissentient party would, however, have fallen upon the others the next day, if the junta had not taken prompt measures to enforce the surrender; the officer in command of the walls near the castle, by their orders, gave up his post to the French during the night, and on the 21st of February, from twelve to fifteen thousand sickly beings, laid down those arms which they were scarcely able to handle, and this cruel and memorable siege was finished.

OBSERVATIONS.—1°.—When the other events of the Spanish war shall be lost in the obscurity of time, or only traced by disconnected fragments, the story of Zaragoza, like some ancient triumphal pillar standing amidst ruins, will tell a tale of past glory, and already men point to the heroic city, and call her Spain, as if her spirit were common to the whole nation; yet it was not so, nor was the defence of Zaragoza itself the effect of unalloyed virtue. It was not patriotism, nor was it courage, nor skill, nor fortitude, nor a system of terror, but all these combined under peculiar circumstances, that upheld the defence; and this combination, and how it was brought about, should be well considered; for it is not so much by catching at the leading resemblances, as by studying the differences of great affairs, that the exploits of one age can be made to serve as models for another.

2°.—The defence of Zaragoza may be examined under two points of view; as an isolated event, and as a transaction bearing on the general struggle in the Peninsula. With respect to the latter, it was a manifest proof, that neither the Spanish people, nor the government, partook of the Zaragozan energy. It would be absurd to suppose that, in the midst of eleven millions of people animated by an ardent enthusiasm, fifty thousand armed men could for two months be besieged, shut in, destroyed, they and their works, houses and bodies, mingled in one terrible ruin, by less than thirty-five thousand adversaries, without one effort being made to save them! Deprive the transaction of

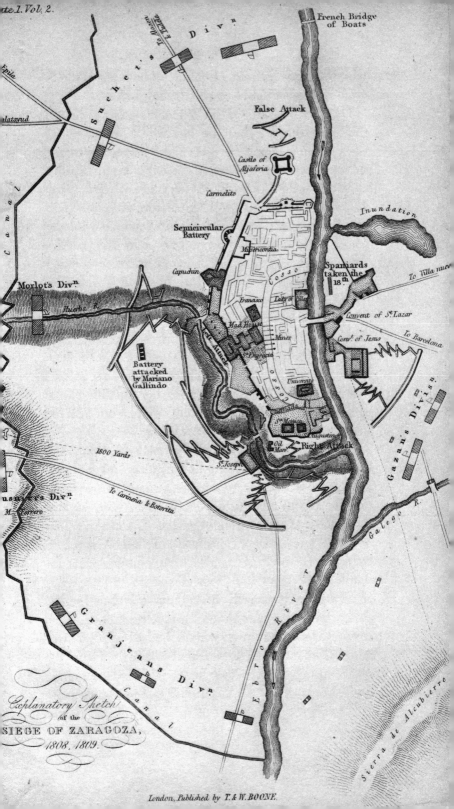

Plate 1. Vol. 2.

French Bridge of Boats

To Alagon

Suchet's Divⁿ

False Attack

Egila

Calatayud

Castle of Aljaferia

Carmelite

Inundation

Semicircular Battery

Misericordia

Spaniards taken the 18th

To Villa nueva

Morlot's Divⁿ

Capuchin

Cosso

Huerba R.

Francisco

Lady of Pillar

Convent of St. Lazar

To Barcelona

Mad House

Mines

Conv^{t.} of Jesus

Battery attacked by Mariano Gallindo

Left Attack

Quemada

Gazan's Divⁿ

University

1800 Yards

St. Augustin

Oil Man^s

Right Attack

Musner's Divⁿ

St. Joseph

Galego R.

M. Guerero

To Carineña & Botorita

Ebro River

Granjean's Divⁿ

Canal

Sierra de Alcubierre

Explanatory Sketch of the

SIEGE OF ZARAGOZA,

1808, 1809.

London, Published by T. & W. BOONE.

its dazzling colours, and the outline comes to this: Thirty-five thousand French, in the midst of insurrections, did, in despite of a combination of circumstances peculiarly favourable to the defence, reduce fifty thousand of the bravest and most energetic men in Spain. It is true, the latter suffered nobly; but was their example imitated? Gerona, indeed, although less celebrated, rivalled, and perhaps more than rivalled, the glory of Zaragoza; elsewhere her fate spoke, not trumpet-tongued to arouse, but with a wailing voice, that carried dismay to the heart of the nation.

3d.—As an isolated transaction, the siege of Zaragoza is very remarkable, yet it would be a great error to suppose, that any town, the inhabitants of which were equally resolute, might be as well defended. Fortune and bravery will do much, but the combinations of science are not to be defied with impunity. There are no miracles in war! If the houses of Zaragoza had not been nearly incombustible, the bombardment alone would have caused the besieged to surrender, or to perish with their flaming city.

4th.—That the advantages offered by the peculiar structure of the houses, and the number of convents and churches, were ably seized by the Spaniards, is beyond doubt. General Rogniat, Lacoste's successor, treats his opponents' skill in fortification with contempt; but colonel San Genis' talents are not to be judged of by the faulty construction of a few out-works, at a time when he was under the control of a disorderly and ferocious mob; he knew how to adapt his system of defence to the circumstances of the moment, and no stronger proof of real genius can be given. "Do not consult me about a capi-

tulation," was his common expression. " *I shall
never be of opinion that Zaragoza can make no further defence.*" Yet neither the talents of San Genis,
nor the construction of the houses, would have
availed, if the people within had not been of a
temper adequate to the occasion ; and to trace the
passions by which they were animated to their true
causes is a proper subject for historical and military
research. That they did not possess any superior
courage is evident from the facts ; the besieged,
although twice the number of the besiegers, never
made any serious impression by their sallies, and
they were unable to defend the breaches. In large
masses, the standard of courage which is established by discipline, may be often inferior to that
produced by fanaticism or any other peculiar excitement ; but the latter never lasts long, neither is it
equable, because men are of different susceptibility,
following their physical and mental conformation ;
hence a system of terror has always been the resource of those leaders who, being engaged in great
undertakings, were unable to recur to discipline.
Enthusiasm stalked in front of their bands, but
punishment brought up the rear, and Zaragoza was
no exception to this practice.

5th.—It may be said that the majority of the besieged, not being animated by any peculiar fury,
a system of terror could not be carried to any great
length ; a close examination explains this seeming
mystery. The defenders were composed of three
distinct parties,—the regular troops, the peasantry
from the country, and the citizens ; the citizens,
who had most to lose, were naturally the fiercest,
and, accordingly, amongst them, the system of
terror was generated. The peasantry followed the

example, as all ignorant men, under no regular control, will do. The soldiers meddled but little in the
interior arrangements, and the division of the town
into islands of posts rendered it perfectly feasible
for violent persons, already possessed of authority,
to follow the bent of their inclinations : there was
no want of men, and the garrison of each island
found it their own interest to keep those in front of
them to their posts, that the danger might be the
longer staved off from themselves.

6th.—Palafox was only the nominal chief of Zaragoza, the laurels gathered in both sieges should
adorn plebeian brows, but those laurels dripped
with kindred as well as foreign blood. The energy
of the real chiefs, and the cause in which that
energy was exerted, may be admired ; the acts perpetrated were, in themselves, atrocious, and
Palafox, although unable to arrest their savage
proceedings, can claim but little credit for his own
conduct. For more than a month preceding the
surrender, he never came forth of a vaulted building, which was impervious to shells, and in which,
there is too much reason to believe, that he and
others, of both sexes, lived in a state of sensuality,
forming a disgusting contrast to the wretchedness
that surrounded them.

OBSERVATIONS ON THE FRENCH OPERATIONS.

1°. Before the arrival of marshal Lasnes, these
operations were conducted with little vigour. The
want of unity, as to time, in the double attack of
the Monte Torrero and the suburb, was a flagrant
error, which was not redeemed by any subsequent
activity ; after the arrival of that marshal, the
siege was pursued with singular intrepidity and

firmness ; and although General Rogniat appears to disapprove of Suchet's division having been sent to Calatayud, it seems to have been a judicious measure, inasmuch as it was necessary,— 1°. To protect the line of correspondence with Madrid. 2°. To have a corps at hand, lest the duke of Infantado should quit Cuença, and throw himself into the Guadalaxara district, a movement that would have been extremely embarrassing to the king. Suchet's division, while at Calatayud, fulfilled these objects, without losing the power of succouring Tudela, or of intercepting the duke of Infantado if he attempted to raise the siege of Zaragoza ; but, when the Spanish army at Cuença was directed to Ucles, and that the marquis of Lazan was gathering strength on the left bank of the Ebro, it was undoubtedly proper to recal Suchet.

2°.—It may not be misplaced here to point out the errors of Infantado's operations. If, instead of bringing on a battle with the first corps, he had marched to the Ebro, established his depôts and places arms at Mequinenza and Lerida, opened a communication with Murcia, Valencia, and Catalonia, and joined the marquis of Lazan's troops to his own ; he might have formed an entrenched camp in the Sierra de Alcubierre, and from thence have carried on a methodical war with, at least, twenty-five thousand regular troops. The insurrections on the French flanks and line of communication with Pampeluna would then have become formidable, and, in this situation, having the fortresses of Catalonia behind him, with activity and prudence he might have raised the siege.

3°.—From a review of all the circumstances

attending the siege of Zaragoza, we may conclude
that fortune was extremely favourable to the French. ——
They were brave, persevering, and skilful, and they
did not lose above four thousand men, but their
success partly resulting from the errors of their opponents, was principally due to the destruction
caused by the pestilence within the town ; for, of Rogniat.
all that multitude said to have fallen, six thousand
Spaniards only were slain in battle; and although
thirteen convents and churches had been taken;
yet, when the town surrendered, forty remained to
be forced !

Such were the principal circumstances of this
memorable siege. I shall now relate the contemporary operations in Catalonia.

CHAPTER IV.

OPERATIONS IN CATALONIA.

BOOK V.

1808.

It will be remembered, that when the second siege of Gerona was raised, in August, 1808, general Duhesme returned to Barcelona, and general Reille to Figueras, after which, the state of affairs obliged those generals to remain on the defensive. Napoleon's measures to aid them were as prompt as the occasion required; for while the siege of Gerona was yet in progress, he had directed troops to assemble at Perpignan in such numbers, as to form with those already in Catalonia, an army of more than forty thousand men, to be called the " *7th corps*," and to be commanded by general Gouvion St. Cyr, to whom he gave this short but emphatic order: " *Preserve Barcelona for me. If that place be lost, I cannot retake it with* 80,000 *men.*"

St. Cyr's Journal of Operations

The troops assembled at Perpignan were, the greatest part, raw levies; Neapolitans, Etruscans, Romans, and Swiss, mixed, however, with some old regiments; but as the preparations for the grand army under the emperor absorbed the principal attention of the administration in France, general St. Cyr was straightened in the means necessary to take the field, and his undisciplined troops, suffering severe privations, were depressed in spirit, and inclined to desert. On the 1st of November, Napoleon, who was at Bayonne, sent orders to the " *7th corps*" to commence

operations; St. Cyr, therefore, put his divisions in motion on the 3d, and crossing the frontier, established his head-quarters at Figueras on
the 5th.

Meanwhile in Catalonia, as in other parts of Spain,
lethargic vanity, and abuses of the most fatal kind,
had succeeded the first enthusiasm and withered the
energy of the people. The local junta had, indeed,
issued abundance of decrees, and despatched agents
to the supreme junta, and to the English commanders
in the Mediterranean and Portugal, all charged with
the same instructions, namely, to demand arms, ammunition, and money, and although the central junta
treated their demands with contempt, the English
authorities answered them generously and freely.
Lord Collingwood lent the assistance of his fleet; from
Malta and Sicily arms were obtained, and sir Hew
Dalrymple having completely equipped the Spanish
regiments released by the convention of Cintra,
despatched them to Catalonia in British transports.
Yet it may be doubted if the conduct of the central
junta were not the wisest, for the local government
established at Tarragona had already become so
neglected, or so corrupt, that the arms thus sup- Lord Col-
plied were, instead of being used in defence of the Correspon-
country, sold to foreign merchants! Such being the dence.
political state of Catalonia, it naturally followed
that the military affairs should be ill conducted.

The count of Caldagues, after having relieved Gerona, returned by Hostalrich, and resumed the line of
the Llobregat; fifteen hundred men, drawn from the Cabanes.
garrison of Carthagena, reached Taragona, and
the marquis of Palacios, accompanied by the junta,
quitted the latter town, and fixed his quarters at
Villa Franca, within twenty miles of Caldagues, and

the latter then disposed his troops, five thousand in number, on different points between Martorel and San Boy, covering a line of eighteen miles, along the left bank of the river.

Meanwhile Duhesme who had rested but a few days, marched in the night from Barcelona with six thousand men, and having arrived the 2d of September at day-break on the Llobregat, attacked Caldagues' line on several points, but principally at San Boy and Molino del Rey. The former post was carried, and the Spaniards were pursued to Vegas, a distance of seven or eight miles, but at Molino del Rey the French were repulsed, and Duhesme then returned to Barcelona.

It was the intention of the British ministers, that an auxiliary force should have sailed from Sicily about this period, to aid the Catalans, and doubtless it would have been a wise and timely effort, but Napoleon's foresight prevented the execution. He directed Murat to menace Sicily, and that prince, feigning to collect forces on the coast of Calabria, spread many reports of armaments being in preparation, while, as a preliminary measure, general Lamarque carried the island of Capræ; here sir Hudson Lowe first became known to history, by losing, in a few days, a post that, without any pretensions to celebrity, might have been defended for as many years. Murat's demonstrations sufficed to impose upon sir John Stuart, and from ten to twelve thousand British troops were thus paralysed at a most critical period; and such will always be the result of a policy which has no fixed, definite object in view. When statesmen cannot see their own way clearly, the executive officers will seldom act with vigour.

During September the Spanish army daily increased, the tercios of Migueletes were augmented, and a regiment of hussars, that had been most absurdly kept in Majorca ever since the beginning of the insurrection, arrived at Taragona. Palacios however remained at Villa Franca, Caldagues continued to guard the Llobregat, and Mariano Alvarez commanded the advanced guard, composed of the garrisons of Gerona and Rosas, the corps of Juan Claros, and other partizan chiefs. Francisco Milans and Milans de Bosch, with six thousand Migueletes, kept the mountains, northward and eastward of Barcelona; the latter hemming in the French right, the former covering the district of El Vallés, and watching, like a bird of prey, the enemy's foragers in the plain of Barcelona. The little port of Filieu de Quixols, near Palamos Bay, was filled with privateers, and the English frigates off the coast, besides aiding the Spanish enterprizes, carried on a littoral warfare in the gulf of Lyons with great spirit and success. Many petty skirmishes happened between the Migueletes and the French; but on the 10th of October, Duhesme attacked Milans de Bosch at St. Gerony beyond the Besos, and completely dispersed his corps, and the 11th, sent colonel Devaux, with two thousand men, against Granollers, which the Spaniards deserted, although it was their chief depôt. Devaux having captured and destroyed a considerable quantity of stores returned the 12th to Mollet, where a column of equal strength was stationed in support, and then occupied the pass of Moncada, while general Millossewitz proceeded with the second column to forage El Vallés. Meanwhile, Caldagues drawing together three thousand infantry,

BOOK
V.
———
1808.
October.

Lafaille
campagne
de Cata'.o-
nia.

Vacani.

two squadrons of cavalry, and six guns, marched
by the back of the hills towards Moncada, hoping
to intercept the French on their return to Barcelona,
thus Millossewitz and he met unexpectedly at
San Culgat.   In the confused action which ensued
the French were beaten, and retreated across the
mountains to Barcelona, while Caldagues, justly
proud of his soldier-like movement, returned to his
camp on the Llobregat.

The 28th of October, Palacios was ordered to take
the command of the levies then collecting in the
Sierra Morena, and general Vives succeeded him in
Catalonia. The army was now reinforced with more
infantry from Majorca; the Spanish troops, released
by the convention of Cintra, arrived at Villa
Franca; seven or eight thousand Grenadian levies
were brought up to Taragona by general Reding,
and, at the same time, six thousand men drafted
from the army of Arragon, reached Lerida, under
the command of the marquis of Lazan.   The whole
were organized in six divisions: the troops in the
Ampurdan forming one, and including the garrisons
of Hostalrich, Gerona, and Rosas, this *army of the
right*, as it was called, amounted to thirty-six thousand men, of which twenty-two thousand foot and
twelve hundred horse were near Barcelona or in
march for it.

Vives seeing himself at the head of such a power
and in possession of all the hills and rivers surrounding Barcelona, resolved to storm that city,
and all things seemed to favour the attempt.   The
inhabitants were ready to rise, a battalion of the
Walloon guards who had been suffered to remain in
the city in a species of neutrality plotted to seize one
of the gates, and the French were so uneasy that

Duhesme actually resolved to abandon the town and
confine his defence to the citadel and Montjouik;
a resolution from which he was only diverted by the
remonstrances of the chief engineer Lafaille. In
this state of affairs, Vives transferring his quarters
to Martorel, directed a general attack on the French
outposts, but he was repulsed at every point, and returned to the mountains; the Walloon guards were
then disarmed, the inhabitants awed, and the defences
of the town increased. From that period to the
raising of the blockade the warfare of the
Spanish general was contemptible, although disputes amongst his adversaries had arisen to such
a height, that Duhesme was advised to send Lecchi
a prisoner to France.

Catalonia was now a prey to innumerable disorders.
Vives, a weak, indolent man, had been the friend
of Godoy, and was not popular; he had, when
commanding in the islands, retained the troops
in them with such tenacity as to create doubts
of his attachment to the cause, yet the supreme
junta while privately expressing their suspicions,
and requesting lord Collingwood to force him to Lord Collingwood's
an avowal of his true sentiments, wrote publicly Correspondence.
to Vives in the most flattering terms, and, finally,
appointed him captain-general of Catalonia. By
the people, however, he and others were vehemently
suspected, and, as the mob governed throughout
Spain, the authorities, civil and military, were more
careful to avoid giving offence to the multitude,
than anxious to molest the enemy, and hence although Catalonia was full of strong places, they
were neither armed nor provisioned, for all persons
were confident that the French only thought of
retreating.

BOOK
V.
—————
1808.
Nov.

Muster
rolls of the
French
army,
MSS.
St. Cyr.

Such was the state of the province and of the armies, when Napoleon, being ready to break into the northern parts of Spain, ordered St. Cyr to commence operations. His force (including a German division of six thousand men, not yet arrived at Perpignan) amounted to more than thirty thousand men; ill-composed, however, and badly provided, and St. Cyr himself was extremely discontented with his situation. The Emperor had given him discretionary powers to act as he judged fitting, only bearing in mind the importance of relieving Barcelona, but marshal Berthier neglected the equipment of the troops, and Duhesme declared that his magazines would not hold out longer than December. To march directly to Barcelona was neither an easy nor an advantageous movement. That city could only be provisioned from France, and, until the road was cleared by the taking of Gerona and Hostalrich, no convoys could pass except by sea. To attack those places with prudence, it was essential to get possession of Rosas; not only to secure an intermediate port for French vessels passing with supplies to Barcelona, but to deprive the English of a secure harbour, and the Spaniards of a point from whence they could, in concert with their allies, intercept the communications of the French army and even blockade Figueras, which, from the want of transport, could not be provisioned at this period. These considerations having determined St. Cyr to commence by the siege of Rosas, he repaired to Figueras, in person, the 6th of November, and, on the 7th, general Reille being charged to conduct the operation, after a sharp action, drove in the Spaniards before that place and completed the investment.

SIEGE OF ROSAS.

This town was but a narrow slip of houses built along the water's edge, at the head of the gulf of the same name. The citadel, a large irregular pentagon, stood on one side, and, on the other, the mountains that skirt the flat and swampy plain of the Ampurdan, ˉrose, bluff and rocky, at the distance of half a mile. An old redoubt was built at the foot of the hills, and, from thence to the citadel,˗ an entrenchment had been drawn to cover the houses, hence, Rosas, looking towards the land, had the citadel on the left hand, the mountains on the right, and the front covered by this entrenchment. The roadstead permitted ships of the line to anchor within cannon-shot of the place, and on the right hand, coming up the gulf, a star fort, called the Trinity, crowned a rugged hill about a mile and a quarter distant from the citadel ; the communication between it and the town being by a narrow road carried between the foot of the mountain and the water's edge.

The garrison of Rosas consisted of nearly three thousand men ; two bomb-vessels, and an English seventy-four (the Excellent), were anchored off the town, and captain West, the commodore, reinforced the garrisons of the Trinity and the citadel with marines and seamen from these vessels ; but the damages sustained in a former siege had been only partially repaired ; both places were ill-found in guns and stores, and the Trinity was commanded at the distance of pistol-shot from a point of the mountains called the Puig Rom.

The force under Reille, consisting of his own
and Pino's Italian division, skirmished daily with
the garrison; but the rain flooded the Ampurdan,
the roads became impassable for the artillery, and
the opening of the trenches was delayed. Meanwhile Souham's division took post between the
Fluvia and Figueras, to cover the siege on the side
of Gerona, and general Chabot's Italian brigade
was sent to Rabos and Espollas, to keep down the
Somatenes. Before Chabot's arrival, Reille had
detached a battalion to that side, and being uneasy
for its safety sent three more to its assistance,
but too late, for two companies had been cut off by
the Somatenes This loss however proved bene-
ficial, it enraged the Italians and checked a disposition to desert; and St. Cyr, unwilling to pursue
the system of burning villages and yet desirous to
repress the insidious hostility of the peasants,
seized, in reprizal for the loss of his companies,
an equal number of villagers, whom he sent to
France.

St. Cyr.

At Rosas the inhabitants embarked or took refuge
in the citadel, leaving the houses and the entrenchment covering them, to the French; the latter were
however prevented by the fire of the English
ships from making any permanent lodgement, and
in a few days, a mixed detachment of soldiers and
townsmen re-established a post there. This done,
on the 8th captain West, in conjunction with the
governor, made a sally but was repulsed, and on
the 9th several yards of the citadel's ramparts
crumbled away. Fortunately the enemy did not
perceive the accident which was repaired in the
night, and on the 15th an obstinate assault made

Captain
West's
despatch.

on the Trinity was repulsed, the English seamen bearing a principal share in the success.

The 16th the roads became passable, and the French battering-train was put in motion. The way leading up to the Puig Rom was repaired, two battalions were posted there, on the point commanding the Trinity, and on the 19th three guns were mounted. The trenches were then opened at the distance of four hundred yards from the citadel, and the 20th the fire of the French mortars obliged the vessels of war to anchor beyond the range of the shells.

During this time, Souham was harassed by the Migueletes from the side of Gerona, and the French cavalry, unable to find forage, were sent back to France. Napoleon, meanwhile rendered uneasy by the reports of general Duhesme, directed the seventh corps to advance to Barcelona, so as to arrive there by the 26th of November, yet St. Cyr refused to abandon the siege of Rosas without a more positive order. On the other side the assistance afforded to the besieged by captain West was represented to the Catalonian government as an attempt to possess himself of the place, and the junta readily believing the tale, entered into an angry correspondence with don Pedro O'Daly, the governor, relative to the supposed treachery, yet took no measures to raise the siege. Pending the correspondence, however, the Excellent sailed from Rosas, and was succeeded by the Fame, captain Bennet, who immediately landed some men under the Trinity, and endeavoured, but ineffectually, to take the battery opposed to that fort.

The 27th the besiegers assaulted the Spaniards,

BOOK
V.

1809.
Nov.

Doyle's
Correspon-
dence,
MSS.

who had entrenched themselves in the deserted houses of the town ; a hundred and sixty were taken, fifty escaped into the citadel, and the rest were slain. Breaching batteries were then commenced among the ruins of the houses, and the communication with the shipping rendered so unsafe, that Lazan, who had come from Lerida to Gerona with six thousand men, and had collected provisions and stores at the mouth of the Fluvia, with the intention of supplying Rosas by sea, abandoned his design.

Reille observing the dilapidated state of the citadel now sent another summons, but the governor was firm, and meanwhile as the engineers reported the breach in the Trinity to be practicable, an assault there was ordered for the 30th of November. An Italian officer, who had formerly served in the fort, being appointed to lead the storming party, asserted that the breach was a false one ; his remonstrance was unheeded, and indeed the Spanish commandant thought the post so untenable, that two days before, the marines of the Fame had been withdrawn by captain Bennet. But at this moment lord Cochrane, a man of infinite talent in his profession, and of surpassing courage and enterprise, threw himself with eighty seamen into the fort. He found the breach really practicable, yet broken into an old gallery, which he immediately filled with earth and hammocks, and so cut off the opening ; hence the unfortunate Italian could do nothing, and fell with all his followers, except two who escaped to their own side, and two, who being spared by the seamen, were drawn up with ropes. A second assault, made a few days after, was likewise repulsed.

CHAP.
IV.

1808.
Dec.

While this passed at the Trinity, the breaching batteries opened against the citadel, and a false attack was commenced on the opposite side; the next night the garrison made a sally with some success, but the walls were completely broken by the French fire, and the 5th of December O'Daly, hopeless of relief, surrendered with two thousand four hundred men: lord Cochrane then abandoned the Trinity, first blowing up the magazine.

St. Cyr observes that the garrison of Rosas might have been easily carried off, at night, by the British shipping. To embark two thousand five hundred men, in the boats of two ships, and under a heavy fire, whether by night or day, is not an easy operation, yet the censure seems well founded, because sufficient preparation might have been previously made. Nor can the defence of the place (with the exception of lord Cochrane's exploit) be deemed brilliant, whether with relation to the importance of the place, the assistance that might have been rendered from the sea, or the number of the garrison compared with that of the besiegers. It held out, however, thirty days, and, if that time had been well employed by the Spaniards outside, the loss of the garrison would have been amply repaid; but Vives, wholly occupied with Barcelona, was indifferent to the fate of Rosas; a fruitless attack on Souham's posts, by Mariano Alvarez, was the only effort made to interrupt the siege, or to impede the farther progress of the enemy: Lazan, although at the head of six or seven thousand men, could not rely upon more than three thousand, and his applications to Vives for a reinforcement were unheeded.

Doyle's
Correspon-
dence,
MS.

The fall of Rosas enabled St. Cyr to march to the relief of Barcelona, and he resolved to do so, although the project, at first sight, appeared rather insane than hardy; for the roads, by which Gerona and Hostalrich were to be turned, being mere paths impervious to carriages, no artillery, and little ammunition, could be carried, and the country was full of strong positions. The Germans had not yet arrived at Perpignan, it was indispensable to leave Reille in the Ampurdan, to protect Rosas and Figueras, and these deductions being made, less than eighteen thousand men, including the cavalry, which had been recalled from France, remained disposable for the operation: but, on the Spanish side, Reding having come up, there were twenty-five thousand men in the camp before Barcelona, and ten thousand others, under Lazan and Alvarez, were at Gerona. The Spanish troops were, however, exceedingly ill organized. Two-thirds of the

Cabanes.

Migueletes carried pikes, and many were without any arms at all; there was no sound military system; the Spanish generals were ignorant of the French movements and strength, and their own indolence and want of vigilance drew upon them the contempt and suspicion of the people.

The 8th of December St. Cyr united his army on the left bank of the Fluvia. The 9th he passed that river, and driving the Spaniards over the Ter, established his head-quarters at Mediña, ten miles from Gerona. He wished, before pursuing his own march, to defeat Lazan, lest the latter should harass the rear of the army, but, finding that the marquis would not engage in a serious affair, he made a show of sitting down before Gerona on the 10th,

hoping thereby to mislead Vives, and render him
slow to break up the blockade of Barcelona: this
succeeded, the Spaniard remained in his camp, irresolute and helpless, while his enemy was rapidly
passing the defiles and rivers between Gerona and
the Besos.

The nature of the country between Figueras and
Barcelona has been described in the first volume, and
referring to that description, the reader will find
that the only carriage routes by which St. Cyr
could march were, one by the sea-coast, and one
leading through Gerona and Hostalrich. The first,
exposed to the fire of the English vessels, had
been broken up by lord Cochrane, in August; and
to use the second, it was necessary either, to take
the fortresses, or to turn them by marching for three
days through the mountains. St. Cyr adopted the
last plan, trusting that rapidity and superior knowledge of war would enable him to separate Lazan
and Alvarez from Vives, and so defeat them all in
succession.

The 11th of December he crossed the Ter and
reached La Bisbal; here he left the last of his carriages, delivered out four days' biscuit and fifty
rounds of ammunition to the soldiers, and with this
provision, a drove of cattle, and a reserve of only ten
rounds of ammunition for each man, he commenced
his hardy march, making for Palamos. On the
route he encountered and beat some Migueletes that
Juan Claros had brought to oppose him, and, when
near Palamos, he suffered a little from the fire of
the English ships, but he had gained a first step,
and his hopes were high.

The 13th, he turned his back upon the coast, and,
by a forced march, reached Vidreras and Llagostera,

thus placing himself between Vives and Lazan, for
the latter had not yet passed the heights of Casa
de Selva.

The 14th, marching by Mazanet de Selva and
Martorel, he reached the heights above Hostalrich,
and encamped at Grions and Masanas. During
this day's journey, his rear was slightly harassed
by Lazan and Claros, but he was well content to
find the strong banks of the Tordera undefended by
Vives. His situation was, however, extremely
critical; Lazan and Claros had, the one on the
11th, the other on the 12th, informed Vives of the
movement, hence the bulk of the Spanish force
before Barcelona might be expected, at any moment, in some of the strong positions in which
the country abounded; the troops from Gerona
were, as we have seen, close in the rear, the Somatenes were gathering thickly on the flanks, Hostalrich was in front, and the French soldiers had only
sixteen rounds of ammunition.

St. Cyr's design was to turn Hostalrich, and get
into the main road again behind that fortress. The
smugglers of Perpignan had affirmed that there
was no pathway, but a shepherd assured him
that there was a track by which it could be effected,
and, when the efforts of the staff-officers to trace
it failed, St. Cyr himself discovered it, but nearly
fell into the hands of the Somatenes during the
search.

The 15th, at day-break, the troops being put in
motion, turned the fortress and gained the main
road, and the garrison of the place, endeavouring
to harass their rear, was repulsed; yet the Somatenes on the flanks, emboldened because the
French, to save ammunition, did not return their

CHAP.
IV.

1808.
Dec.

fire, became exceedingly troublesome, and near
San Celoni, the head of the column encountered
some battalions of Migueletes, which Francisco
Milans had brought up from Arenas de Mar, by
the pass of Villa Gorguin.

Milans, not being aware of St. Cyr's approach,
was soon beaten, and his men fell back, part to
Villa Gorguin, part to the heights of Nuestra Señora de Cordera: the French thus gained the defile
of Treintapasos, but they were now so fatigued
that all desired to halt, save the general, who insisted
upon the troops clearing that defile, and reaching a
plain on the other side, which was not effected before ten o'clock. Lazan's troops did not appear
during the day, but Vives' army was in front, and
its fires were seen on the hills between Cardadeu
and Llinas.

Information of St. Cyr's march, as I have already
observed, had been transmitted to Vives on the
11th, and there was time for him to have carried
the bulk of his forces to the Tordera, before the
French could pass that river; but intelligence of
the battle of Tudela, and of the appearance of the
French near Zaragoza, arrived at the same moment, Cabanes.
and the Spanish general betrayed the greatest
weakness and indecision; at one moment resolving
to continue before Barcelona, at another designing Doyle's Correspon-
to march against St. Cyr. He had, on the 9th, dence, MS.
sent Reding with six guns, six hundred cavalry,
and one thousand infantry, to take the command in
the Ampurdan, and, the 12th, after receiving Lazan's
report, he reinforced Reding, who was still at Granollers, and directed him upon Cardadeu. The
14th, he ordered Francisco Milans to march by
Mattaro and Arenas de Mar, to examine the coast

road, and, if the enemy was not in that line, to repair also to Cardadeu. The 15th, Milans, as we have seen, was beaten at St. Celoni, but, in the night, he rallied his whole division on the heights of Cordera, thus flanking the left of the French forces at Llinas.

A Spanish council of war had been held on the 13th. Caldagues advised that four thousand Migueletes should be left to observe Duhesme, and that the rest of the army should march at once to fight St. Cyr; good and soldier-like counsel; but Vives was loth to abandon the siege of Barcelona, and adopting half-measures, left Caldagues, with the right wing of the army, to watch Duhesme, and carried the centre and the left, by the route of Granollers, to the heights between Cardadeu and Llinas, where, exclusive of Milans' division, he united, in the night of the 15th, about eight thousand regulars, besides several thousand Somatenes. Duhesme immediately occupied the posts abandoned by Vives, and thus separated him from Caldagues; yet St. Cyr's position, on the morning of the 16th, would have been very dangerous, if he had been opposed by any but Spanish generals and Spanish troops.

Vives and those about him, irresolute and weak as they were in action, were not deficient in boasting words; they called the French army, in derision, " *the succour;*" and, in allusion to the battle of Baylen, announced that a second " *bull-fight,*" in which Reding was again the " *matador,*" would be exhibited. Dupont and St. Cyr were, however, men of a different temper: the latter knowing that the Spaniards were not troops to stand the shock of a good column, united his army in one solid mass at day-break on the 16th, and without hesitation

marched against the centre of the enemy, ordering
the head of the column to go headlong on, without
either firing or forming line.

BATTLE OF CARDADEU.

The hills occupied by the Spanish army were
high and wooded. Vives, in person, commanded
on the left; the other wing was under Reding,
and the Somatenes clustered upon a lofty ridge
which was separated from the right of the position
by the little river Mogent. The main road from
Llinas led through the centre of the line, and a
second road branching off from the first, and running between the Mogent and Reding's ground,
went to Mattaro.

The flank of the French attacking column was
galled by the Somatenes, and halted, general Pino,
who led it, instead of falling on briskly, sent for
fresh instructions, and meanwhile extended his
first brigade in a line to his left. St. Cyr reiterated
the order to fight in column; but he was sorely
troubled at Pino's error, for Reding advancing
against the front and flank of the extended brigade,
obliged it to commence a fire, which it could not
nourish from the want of ammunition.

In this difficulty the French general acted with
great ability and vigour; Pino's second brigade was
directed to do that which the first should have
done, two companies were sent to menace the left
of the Spaniards, and St. Cyr himself rapidly carried
Souham's division, by the Mattaro road, against
Reding's extreme right. The effect was instantaneous and complete, the Spaniards overthrown
on their centre and right, and charged by the
cavalry, were beaten, and dispersed in every direc-

tion, leaving their artillery, ammunition, and two thousand prisoners behind.

Vives escaped on foot across the mountain to Mattaro, where he was taken on board an English vessel, but Reding fled on horseback by the main road, and the next day, having rallied some of the fugitives at Monmalo, retreated by the route of San Culgat to Molino del Rey. The loss of the French was only six hundred men, and the battle, which lasted one hour, was so decisive, that St. Cyr resolved to push on to Barcelona immediately, without seeking to defeat Milans or Lazan, whom he judged too timid to venture an action: moreover, he hoped that Duhesme, who had been informed, on the 7th, of the intended march, and who could hear the sound of the artillery, would intercept and turn back the flying troops.

The French had scarcely quitted the field of battle when Milans arrived, and, finding how matters stood, retired to Arenas de Mar, giving notice to Lazan, who retreated to Gerona; St. Cyr's rear was thus cleared. Meanwhile Duhesme, heedless of what was passing at Cardadeu, instead of inter-cepting the beaten army, sent Lecchi to attack Caldagues, who having concentrated his division on the evening of the 16th, repulsed Lecchi, and then retired behind the Llobregat, leaving behind some artillery and the large magazines which Vives had collected for the siege. Thus St. Cyr reached Barcelona without encountering any of Duhesme's troops, and, in his Memoirs of this campaign, he represents that general as astonishingly negligent; seeking neither to molest the enemy nor to meet the French army; treating every thing belonging to the service with indifference; making false

returns, and conniving at gross malversation in
his generals. Duhesme, however, has not wanted
defenders.

St. Cyr, now reflecting upon the facility with
which his opponents could be defeated, and the
difficulty of pursuing them, resolved to rest a few
days at Barcelona, in hopes that the Spaniards, if
unmolested, would re-assemble in numbers behind
the Llobregat, and enable him to strike an effectual
blow, for his design was to disperse their forces so
as they should not be able to interrupt the sieges
which he meditated ; nor was he deceived in his
calculations. Reding joined Caldagues, rallied
from twelve to fifteen thousand men behind the
Llobregat, and Vives who had relanded at Sitjes,
sent orders to Lazan and Milans to join him there
by the way of Vallés; the arrival of the latter
was, however, so uncertain that the French general, who knew of these orders, judging it better
to attack Reding at once, united Chabran's division
to his own, and on the 20th, advanced to St. Felieu
de Llobregat.

The Spaniards were drawn up on the heights
behind the village of San Vincente, and their position
lofty and rugged, commanded a free view of the
approaches from Barcelona ; the Llobregat covered
the front, and the left was secured from attack,
except at the bridge of Molino del Rey, which was
entrenched, guarded by a strong detachment, and
protected by heavy guns. Reding's cavalry
amounted to one thousand, and he had fifty pieces
of artillery, the greatest part of which were in battery at the bridge of Molino del Rey; his right
was, however, accessible, because the river was
fordable in several places. The main road to Villa

Franca led through this position, and, at the distance of ten or twelve miles in the rear, the pass of
Ordal offered another post of great strength.

Vives was at San Vincente on the 19th, but returned to Villa Franca the same day; hence, when the
French appeared on the 20th, the camp was thrown
Cabanes. into confusion, and a council of war being held,
one party was for fighting, another for retreating to
Ordal; finally an officer was sent to Vives for orders,
and he returned with a message, that Reding might
retreat if he could not defend his post, but the
latter fearing that he should be accused, and perhaps sacrificed for returning without reason, resolved to fight, although he anticipated nothing but
disaster. The season was extremely severe, snow
was falling, and both armies suffered from cold and
wet; but the Spanish soldiers were dispirited by past
defeats, and the despondency and irresolution of
their generals could not escape observation, while
the French and Italian troops were confident in their
commander, and flushed with success. In these
dispositions the two armies passed the night.

BATTLE OF MOLINO DEL REY.

St. Cyr observing that Reding's attention was
principally directed to the bridge of Molino, ordered
Chabran's division to that side, with instructions to
create a diversion by opening a fire from some artillery, and then retiring as if his guns could not
resist the weight of the Spanish metal; in short, to
persuade the enemy that a powerful effort would be
made there; but when the centre and right of the
Spaniards should be attacked, Chabran was to force
the passage of the bridge, and assail the heights

beyond it. This stratagem succeeded; Reding accumulated troops on his left, and neglected his right, which was the real point of attack.

The 21st, Pino's division crossing the Llobregat at daylight, by a ford in front of St. Felieu, marched against the right of the Spanish position; Chabot's division followed; Souham's which had passed at a ford lower down, and then, ascended by the right bank, covered Pino's passage; the light cavalry were held in reserve behind Chabot's division, and a regiment of cuirassiers was sent to support Chabran at Molino del Rey.

The Spanish position consisted of two mountain heads, separated by a narrow ravine and a torrent, and as the troops of the right wing were exceedingly weakened, they were immediately chased off their headland by the leading brigade of Pino's division. Reding then seeing his error, changed his front, drawing up on the other mountain, on a new line, nearly perpendicular to the Llobregat, but he still kept a strong detachment at the bridge of Molino, which was thus in rear of his left. The French divisions formed rapidly for a fresh effort, Souham was on the right, Pino in the centre, Chabot on the left; and the latter gained ground in the direction of Villa Franca, endeavouring to turn the Spaniards' right, and cut off their retreat, while the light cavalry making way between the mountain and the river, sought to connect themselves with Chabran at Molino. The other two columns, having crossed the ravine that separated them from the Spaniards, ascended the opposite mountain. The Catalans forming quickly, opposed their enemies with an orderly but ill directed fire, and their front line advancing, offered to charge with an appearance of great in-

trepidity, but their courage sinking, they turned as
the hostile masses approached, and the reserve immediately opened a confused volley upon both parties; in this disorder, the road to Villa Frana
being intercepted by Chabot, the right was forced
upon the centre, the centre upon the left, and the
whole pushed back in confusion upon Molino del
Rey. Meantime a detachment from Chabran's division, passing the Llobregat above Molino, blocked
the road to Martorel, and in this miserable situation
the Spaniards being charged by the light cavalry,
scarcely a man would have escaped if Chabran had
obeyed his orders, by pushing across the bridge of
Molino upon their rear. But that general, at all
times feeble in execution, remained a tranquil spec-
tator of the action, until the right of Souham's
division reached the bridge; thus the routed troops
escaped by dispersion, throwing away every thing
that could impede their flight across the mountains.
Vives reached the field of battle just as the route
was complete, and was forced to fly with the rest.
The victorious army pursued in three columns; Chabran's in the direction of Igualada; Chabot's by the
road of San Sadurni, which turned the pass of
Ordal; Souham's by the royal route of Villa Franca,
at which place the head-quarters were established
on the 22d. The posts of Villa Nueva and Sitjes
were immediately occupied by Pino, while Souham
pushed the fugitives to the gates of Tarragona.

The loss of the Spaniards, owing to their swiftness, was less than might have been expected; not
more than twelve hundred fell into the hands of the
French, but many superior officers were killed or
wounded, and, on the 22d, the count de Caldagues
was taken, a man apparently pedantic in military

affairs, and wanting in modesty, but evidently possessed of both courage and talent. The whole of
the artillery, vast quantities of powder, and a magazine of English muskets, quite new, were captured, yet many of the Migueletes were unarmed,
and the junta were unceasing in their demands for
succours of this nature ! but the history of any one
province was the history of all Spain.

CHAPTER V.

BOOK
V.
————
1809.
January.
BARCELONA was now completely relieved, and the captured magazines supplied it for several months; there was no longer a Spanish army in the field, and in Tarragona, where some eight or nine thousand of the Spanish fugitives, from this and the former battle, had taken refuge, there was terrible disorder.

Cabanes.
The people rose tumultuously, broke open the public stores, and laying hands on all the weapons they could find, rushed from place to place, as if searching for something to vent their fury upon; they called aloud for the head of Vives, and to save his life he was cast into prison by Reding, who was proclaimed general-in-chief. The regular officers were insulted by the populace, and there was as usual a general cry to defend the city, mixed with furious menaces against traitors; but there were neither guns, nor ammunition, nor provisions, and during the first moment of

St. Cyr.
anarchy, St. Cyr might certainly have rendered himself master of Tarragona by a vigorous effort. The opportunity soon passed away; the French general seeking only to procure subsistence, occupied himself in forming a train of field artillery, while Reding, who had been almost without hope, proceeded to rally the army, and place the town in a state of defence.

Doyle's
Correspon-
dence,
MSS.
The 1st of January eleven thousand infantry and eight hundred cavalry re-assembled at Tarragona and Reus; a Swiss regiment from Majorca, and two

Spanish regiments from Grenada, increased this
force, and the 5th three thousand four hundred
men arrived from Valencia, from whence also five
thousand musquets, ammunition in proportion, and
ten thousand pikes fresh from England, were forwarded to Tarragona, and a supply of money, obtained from the British agents at Seville, completed
the list of fortuitous events following the disaster of
Molino del Rey. These fortunate circumstances
and in the inactivity of St. Cyr, who seemed paralyzed, restored the confidence of the Catalans, yet
their system remained unchanged, for in Spain
confidence often led to insubordination, but never to
victory.

A part of the fugitives from Molino had taken
refuge at Bruch, where, being joined by the Somatenes, they chose major Green, an English military
agent, for their general, thinking to hold that post
which was considered impregnable ever since the
defeats of Chabran and Swartz. St. Cyr, glad of this
opportunity to retrieve the honour of the French arms,
detached Chabran himself the 11th January to take
his own revenge, but as that general was still depressed by the recollection of his former defeat,
to encourage him, Chabot was directed from San
Sadurni upon Igualada, by which the defile of
Bruch was turned, and a permanent defence rendered impossible. Green made little or no resistance; eight guns were taken, a considerable number
of men were killed, the French pursued to Igualada,
and a detachment, without orders, even assailed and
took Montserrat itself, and rejoined the main body
without loss. Chabot was then recalled to San
Sadurni, and Chabran was quartered at Martorel.

While these events were passing beyond the

Llobregat, the marquis of Lazan advanced, with seven or eight thousand men, towards Castellon de Ampurias. The 1st of January he drove back a battalion of infantry upon Rosas with considerable loss, but the next day general Reille, having assembled about three thousand men, intercepted his communications, and attacked him in his position behind the Muga; the victory seems to have been undecided, and in the night, Lazan regaining his communications, returned to Gerona.

The battle of Molino del Rey having abated, for a time, the ardour of the Catalans, Reding was enabled to avoid serious actions, while the Somatenes harassed the enemy; and this plan being followed during the months of January and February, was exceedingly troublesome to St. Cyr, because he was obliged to send small parties continually to seek for provision, which the country people hid with great care, striving hard to protect their scanty stores. In the beginning of February the country between the Llobregat and Tarragona was almost exhausted of food; the English ships continued to vex the coast-line, and the French, besides deserters, lost many men, killed and wounded, in the innumerable petty skirmishes sustained by the marauding parties. Still St. Cyr maintained his positions, until the country people, tired of a warfare in which they were the chief sufferers, clamoured against Reding, that he, with a large regular force, should look calmly on, until the last morsel of food was discovered, and torn from their starving families; the townspeople, also feeling the burden of supporting the troops, impatiently urged the general to fight, nor was this insubordination confined to the rude multitude. Lazan, although at the head of nine thousand men, remained perfectly inactive after the skirmish at Castellon de Ampurias; but when Reding required him to leave a suitable garrison in Gerona, and bring the rest of his troops to Igualada, he would not obey, and their dispute was only terminated by Lazan's marching, with five thousand men, to the assistance of Zaragoza. His operations there have been related in the narrative of that siege.

CHAP. V.

1809. January.

The army immediately under Reding was very considerable, the Swiss battalions were numerous and good, and some of the most experienced of the Spanish regiments were in Catalonia; every fifth man of the robust population had been called out after the defeat of Molino del Rey, and, although the people, averse to serve as regular soldiers, did not readily answer the call, the force under Reding was, in the beginning of February, not less than twenty-eight thousand men. The urban guards were also put in activity, and above fifteen thousand Somatenes assisted the regular troops; but there was more show than real power, for Reding was incapable of wielding the regular troops skilfully, and the Migueletes being ill armed, without clothing and insubordinate, devastated the country equally with the enemy. The Somatenes, who only took arms for local interests, would not fight, except at the times, in the manner, and in the place that suited themselves; they neglected the advice of the regular officers, reviled all who would not adopt their own views, and caused many to be removed from their commands. The Spanish generals never obtained from them good information of the enemy's movements; yet their own plans were always

made known to the French, for at Reding's head-
quarters, as at those of Castaños before the battle of
Tudela, every project was openly and ostentatiously
discussed. Reding himself was a man of no military talent, his activity was of body, not of mind;
but he was brave and honourable; and popular,
because, being without system, arrangement, or
deep design, and easy in his nature, he thwarted
no man's humours, and thus floated in the troubled
waters until their sudden reflux left him on the rocks.

The Catalonian army was now divided into four
distinct corps.

Alvarez, with four thousand men, held Gerona
and the Ampurdan.

Lazan, with five thousand, was near Zaragoza.

Don Juan Castro, an officer, accused by the
Spaniards of treachery, and who afterwards did
attach himself to Joseph's party, occupied, with
sixteen thousand men, a line extending from Olesa,
on the upper Llobregat, to the pass of San Cristina, near Tarragona; this line running through
Bruch, Igualada, and Llacuna, was above sixty
miles long.

The remainder of the army, amounting to ten or
twelve thousand men under Reding himself, was
quartered at Tarragona, Reus, and the vicinity
of those places.

The troops were fed from Valencia and Aragon,
the convoys from the former being conveyed in
vessels along the coast; but the magazines being
accumulated on one or two points of the line,
and chosen without judgement, fettered Reding's
movements and regulated those of the French,
whose only difficulty, in fact, was to procure food.

Early in February, St. Cyr, having exhausted

the country about him, and finding his communications much vexed by the Somatenes and by descents
from the English ships, concentrated his divisions
in masses at Vendril, Villa Franca, San Sadurni,
and Martorel. The seventh corps having been reinforced by the German division, and by some
conscripts, amounted at this period to forty-eight
thousand men, of which forty-one thousand were
under arms, but the force immediately with St.
Cyr did not exceed twenty-three thousand combatants. The relative position of the two armies
was, however, entirely in favour of the French
general; his line extending from Vendril, by Villa
Franca, to Martorel, was not more than thirty miles,
and he had a royal road by which to retreat on
Barcelona; whereas the Spanish posts covering an
extent of above sixty miles, formed a half-circle
round the French line, and their communications
were more rugged than those of St. Cyr. Nevertheless, it is not to be doubted that, by avoiding
any serious action, the Catalans might have obliged
the French to abandon the country between the
Llobregat and Tarragona; famine and the continued
drain of men, in a mountain warfare, would have
forced the latter away, nor could they have struck
any formidable blow to relieve themselves, seeing
that all the important places were fortified towns
requiring a regular siege. The never-failing arrogance of the Spanish character, and the unstable
judgement of Reding, induced him to forego these
advantages. The closing of the French posts and
some success in a few petty skirmishes were magnified, the last into victories, and the first into a
design on the part of the enemy to fly; and an intercourse opened with some of the inhabitants of

Barcelona gave hopes of regaining that city by
means of a conspiracy within the walls. The
Catalans had before made proposals to general
Lecchi to deliver up the citadel of that place, nor is
there any thing that more strongly marks the absurd
self-sufficiency of the Spaniards, during this war,
than the repeated attempts they made to corrupt
the French commanders. As late as the year 1810,
Martin Carrera, being at the head of about two
thousand ragged peasants, half-armed, and only
existing under the protection of the English outposts, offered to Marshal Ney, then investing Ciudad
Rodrigo, rank and honours in the Spanish army if
he would desert!

Reding, swayed by the popular clamour, which
this state of affairs produced, resolved to attack, and
in this view directed Castro to collect his sixteen
thousand men to fall upon the right flank and rear of
St. Cyr, by the routes of Llacuna and Igualada; and
to send a detachment to seize the pass of Ordal,
to cut off the French line of retreat to Barcelona;
meanwhile, advancing with eight thousand by the
road of Vendril and St. Cristina, he, himself, was
to attack the enemy in front. All the Migueletes
and Somatenes between Gerona and the Besos were
to aid in these operations, the object being to surround the French, a favourite project with the
Spaniards at all times; and as they publicly announced this intention, the joy was universal, the
destruction of the hostile army being as usual
anticipated with the utmost confidence.

The Catalans were in motion on the 14th of
February, but St. Cyr had kept his army well
in hand and seeing the Spaniards were ready
to break in upon him, resolved to strike first.

Wherefore leaving Souham's division at Vendril, to hold Reding in check, on the 16th St. Cyr marched from Villa Franca, with Pino's division, and overthrew Castro's advanced posts which were at Lacuña and Saint Quinti. The Spanish centre was thus pierced, their wings completely separated, and Castro's right was thrown back upon Capellades.

The 17th, the French general continuing his movement with Pino's division, reached Capellades, where he expected to unite with Chabot and Chabran, who had orders to concentrate there,—the one from San Sadurni, the other from Martorel. By this skilful movement he avoided the pass of Bruch, and concentrated three divisions on the extreme right of Castro's left wing and close to his magazines, which were at Igualada.

Chabot arrived the first, and, being for a little time unsupported, was attacked and driven back with loss, but when the other divisions came up, the action was restored, and the Spaniards put to flight. They rallied again at Pobla de Claramunt, between Capellades and Igualada, a circumstance agreeable to St. Cyr, because he had sent Maz- zuchelli's brigade from Llacuna direct upon Igualada, and if Chabot had not been so hard pressed, the action at Capellades was to have been delayed until Mazzuchelli had got into the rear; scarcely however was the head of that general's column descried, when Castro, who was at Igualada with his reserves, recalled the troops from Pobla de Claramunt. The French were close at their heels, and the whole passed through Igualada, fighting and in disorder, after which, losing all courage, the Spaniards threw away their arms, and fled by the three routs of Cervera, Calaf, and Manresa. They were pursued all the 17th, yet the French returned the next day with few prisoners, because, says St. Cyr, *" the Catalans are endowed by nature with strong knees."*

Having thus broken through the centre of the Spanish line, defeated a part of the left wing and taken the magazines, St. Cyr posted Chabot and Chabran at Igualada, to keep the beaten troops in check, while himself, with Pino's division, marched on the 18th to fight Reding, whose extreme left was now at St. Magi. Souham also had been instructed, when by preconcerted signals he should know that the attack at Igualada had succeeded, to force the pass of Cristina, and push forward to Villa Radoña, upon which town St. Cyr was now marching.

The position of St. Magi, being attacked at four o'clock in the evening of the 18th, was carried without difficulty, but it was impossible to find a single peasant to guide the troops, on the next day's march to the abbey of Santa Creus. In this perplexity, a wounded Spanish captain, who was prisoner, having

St. Cyr.   demanded to be allowed to go to Tarragona, St. Cyr assented, offering to carry him to the Creus, and thus the prisoner unconsciously acted as a guide to his enemies. The march was long and difficult, and it was late ere they reached the abbey, which was a strong point occupied in force by the troops that had been beaten from San Magi the evening before, wherefore the French, after a fruitless demonstration of assaulting it, took a position for the night. Meanwhile, Reding hearing of Castro's defeat, made a draft of men and guns from the right wing and was marching by Pla and the pass of Cabra, intending to rally his left;

his road run just behind St. Creus, and he was passing at the moment when the French appeared before that place, but as neither general was aware of the other's presence, each continued his particular movement.

The 20th St. Cyr crossing the Gaya river under a fire from the abbey, continued his rapid march upon Villa Radoña, near which place he dispersed a small corps, but finding that Souham was not come up, he sent an officer, escorted by a battalion, to hasten that general, whose non-arrival gave reason to believe that the staff-officers and spies, sent with the previous instructions, had all been intercepted. This caused the delay of a day and a half, which would otherwise have sufficed to crush Reding's right wing, surprised as it would have been, without a chief, in the plain of Tarragona.

While the French rested at Villa Radoña, Reding pursued his march to St. Coloma de Querault, where he rallied many of Castro's fugitives, and thus the aspect of affairs was totally changed; for Souham, after forcing the pass of San Cristina, reached Villa Radoña the 21st, and, at the same time, the weakly men, who had been left at Villa Franca, also arrived; hence more than two-thirds of the whole French army were concentrated at Villa Radoña at the moment when the Spanish commander, being joined by the detachment beaten from San Cristina and by the troops from the abbey of Creus, had also rallied the greatest part of his forces, at St. Coloma de Querault. Each general could now, by a rapid march, overwhelm his adversary's right wing; but the troops left by Reding, in the plain of Tarragona, could retire upon that fortress, while those left by

St. Cyr at Igualada, were without support. When,
therefore, the French general, who, continuing his
movement on Tarragona, had reached Valls the 22d,
heard of Reding's march, he immediately returned
with Pino's division to Pla, resolved, if the Spanish
general should advance towards Igualada, to follow
him with a sharp spur.

The 23d the French halted ; Souham at Valls to
watch the Spanish troops in the plain of Tarragona ; Pino's division at Pla, but sending detachments to the abbey of Creus and towards Santa
Coloma to feel for Reding. In the evening these
detachments returned with some prisoners ; the one
reported that the abbey was abandoned ; the other
that the Spanish general was making his way back
to Tarragona, by the route of Sarreal and Momblanch. St. Cyr, therefore, retaining Pino's division
at Pla, pushed his advanced posts on the right to
the abbey, and in front to the defile of Cabra, designing to encounter the Spaniards, if they returned by either of these roads ; and he ordered
Souham to take post in front of Valls, with his left
on the Francoli river, his right towards Pla, and
his advanced guard at Pixa Moxons, to watch for
Reding by the road of Momblanch.

The 24th the Spanish general, being in St.
Coloma, called a council of war, at which colonel
Doyle, the British military agent, assisted. One
party was for fighting St. Cyr, another for retreating
to Lerida, a third for attacking Chabran at Igualada, a fourth for regaining the plain of Tarragona.
There were many opinions, but neither wisdom nor
resolution, and finally, Reding, leaving general
Wimpfen, with four thousand men, at San Coloma,
decided to regain Tarragona, and took the route of

Momblanch with ten thousand of his best troops, following the Spanish accounts, but St. Cyr says with fifteen thousand. The Catalan general knew that Valls was occupied, and his line of march intercepted; but he imagined the French to be only five or six thousand, for the exact situation and strength of an enemy were particulars that seldom troubled Spanish commanders.

BATTLE OF VALLS.

While in full march without any scouts, at daybreak on the 25th of February, the head of Reding's column was suddenly fired upon at Pixa Moxons by Souham's detachment, which was immediately driven in upon the main body; and this attack being vigorously followed, the whole of that general's division gave way. Under cover of this fight the Spanish baggage and artillery passed the Francoli river, and the road to Tarragona being thus opened, Reding might have effected his retreat without difficulty; but he continued to press Souham until St. Cyr, who had early intelligence of what was passing, came down from Pla upon the left flank of the Spanish army. When the French dragoons, which preceded their infantry, appeared in Souham's line, Reding re-crossed the Francoli and took a position behind that river intending to retreat from thence in the evening, but his able opponent obliged him again to fight.

At three o'clock the action recommenced. The banks of the Francoli were steep and rugged, and the position beyond strong and difficult of access, yet the French general wishing, as he himself states, to increase the moral ascendancy of his soldiers, forbad the artillery, although well placed for execution, to play on Reding's battalions, lest they should fly before the infantry could reach them! Under this curious arrangement the action was begun by the light troops.

The French, or rather Italian infantry, were superior in number to the Spaniards, and the columns, covered by the skirmishers, passed the river with great alacrity, and ascended the heights under an exceedingly regular fire, which was continued until the attacking troops had nearly reached the summit of the position; then both Swiss and Catalans wavered, and breaking ere the infantry could close with them, were instantly charged by the French cavalry. Reding, after receiving several sabre wounds, saved himself at Tarragona, where the greatest number of the vanquished also took refuge, while the remainder fled in the greatest disorder by the routes of Tortosa and Lerida; the count of Castel d'Orius and many other superior officers, the artillery and the baggage were taken, and four thousand men were killed or wounded. During all these movements and actions, Reding received no assistance from the Somatenes; nor is this surprising, for it may be received as an axiom in war, that armed peasants are only formidable to stragglers and small detachments: when the regular forces engage, the poor countryman, sensible of his own weakness, wisely quits the field.

St. Cyr lost only a thousand men, and on the 26th Souham entered the rich town of Reus, where, contrary to the general custom, the inhabitants remained; Pino then occupied Pla, Alcover, and Valls, detachments were sent to Salou and Villa Seca, on the sea-coast west of Tarragona, and Chabot, recalled from Igualada, was posted at the

Santa Creuz, to watch Wimpfen, who still remained at Santa Coloma de Querault.

The battle of Valls finished the regular warfare in Catalonia. Those detachments, which by the previous movements had been cut off from the main body of the army, joined the Somatenes, and as partizan corps, troubled the communications of the French; but St. Cyr had no longer a regular army to deal with in the field, and Tortosa, which was in a miserably defenceless condition, without provisions, must have fallen, if after the battle any attempt had been made against it. Lazan, indeed, after his defeat near Zaragoza, carried a few men to Tortosa, where he declared himself independent of Reding's command, but this battle and the fall of Zaragoza had stricken terror far and wide, the neighbouring provinces fearing and acting each for its own safety, had no regard to any general plan, and the confusion was universal.

Meanwhile, the fugitives from Valls, joined to the troops already in Tarragona, crowded the latter place, and an infectious disorder breaking out, a great mortality ensued; wherefore, St. Cyr, satisfied that sickness should do the work of the sword, begirt the city with a resolution to hold his positions while food could be procured. In this policy he remained stedfast until the middle of March, although Wimpfen attacked and drove Chabran in succession from Igualada, Llacuna, and St. Quinti, to Villa Franca; and although the two Milans and Claros, acting between the Besos and the Llobregat, had cut his communication with Barcelona, and in conjunction with the English squadron, renewed the blockade of that city. This plan appears injudicious; the sickness in Tarragona did not cause it to surrender, and the subjugation of Catalonia was certainly retarded by the cessation of offensive operations. The object of the French general should have been to seize some strong places, such as Tortosa, Tarragona, Gerona, or Lerida, while the terror of defeat was fresh ; his inactivity after the battle of Molino del Rey and at this period, enabled the Catalonians to recover confidence, and to put those towns in a state of defence; thus he gained nothing but the barren glory of victory.

Towards the middle of March the resources of the country being all exhausted, he at last determined to abandon the plains of Tarragona, and take some position where he could feed his troops, cover the projected siege of Gerona, and yet be at hand to relieve Barcelona. The valleys about Vich alone offered all these advantages, but as Claros and the Milans were in force at Molino del Rey, he ordered Chabran to drive them from that point, that the sick and wounded men might be first transferred from Valls to Barcelona.

The 10th of March, Chabran sent a battalion with one piece of artillery on that service, and the Migueletes thinking it was the advanced guard of a greater force, abandoned the post, but being undeceived, returned, beat the battalion, and took the gun. The 12th, Chabran received orders to march with his whole division, consisting of eight battalions and three squadrons, and he reached the bridge, yet he returned without daring to attack. St. St. Cyr. Cyr repeated his orders, and on the 14th the troops, apparently ashamed of their general's irresolution, fell on vigorously, carried the bridge and established themselves on the heights at both sides of the river.

The communication thus opened, it was found that Duhesme, pressed by the Migueletes without, was also extremely fearful of conspiracies within the walls; his fears, and the villainous conduct of his police, had at last excited the inhabitants to attempt that which their enemies seemed so much to dread. In March, an insurrection was planned in concert with the Migueletes and the English squadron, and the latter coming close in cannonaded the town on the 10th, expecting that Wimpfen, the Milans, and Claros would have assaulted the gates, which was to have been the signal for the insurrection within. The inhabitants were sanguine of success, because there were above two thousand Spanish prisoners in the city, and outside the walls there were two tercios secretly recruited and maintained by the citizens; and these men being without uniforms, constantly passed in and out of the town, yet Duhesme was never able to discover or to prevent them. This curious circumstance is illustrative of the peculiar genius of the Spaniards, which in all matters of surprise and stratagem is unrivalled. The project against the city was, however, baffled by Chabran's actions at Molino del Rey, which occupied the partizan corps outside the walls, and the British squadron exposed to a heavy gale, and disappointed in the co-operation from the landside, sailed away the 11th.

St. Cyr intended to commence his retrograde movement the 18th, but the 17th a cannonade was heard on the side of Momblanch, which was ascertained to proceed from a detachment of six hundred men, with two guns, under the command of Colonel Briche. This officer being sent by Mortier

CHAP.
V.

1809.
March.

St. Cyr.

to open the communication after the fall of Zaragoza, had forced his way through the Spanish
partizan corps, and to favour his return the army
halted two days; but the enterprize, after a trial,
appeared so dangerous, that he relinquished it,
and attached himself to the seventh corps.

Meanwhile the inactivity that succeeded the battle
of Valls, and the timidity displayed by Chabran in
the subsequent skirmishes, had depressed the spirits
of the troops; they contemplated the approaching
retreat with great uneasiness, and many officers
infected with fear advised the general to hide his
movements from the enemy; but he, anxious to
restore their confidence, took the part of giving the
Spaniards a formal notice of his intentions, desiring
Reding to send proper officers to take over the hospitals which had been fitted up at Valls, as well as
some French, wounded, that could not be moved.
This done, the army commenced its retreat, reached
Villa Franca the 21st of March, and the 22d passed
the Llobregat, followed, but not molested, by some
feeble Spanish detachments. The 23d Wimpfen,
who had rallied the Migueletes of Claros and the
Milans, at Tarrasa after the affair of the 24th, was
beaten by general Pino, who pursued him to near
Manresa, and then foraging the country, returned
with provisions sufficient to feed the army without
drawing on the magazines of Barcelona.

During these proceedings, Reding died in Tarragona of his wounds. He had been received there
with such dissatisfaction after the battle of Valls,
that the interference of the British consul was necessary, to save him from the first fury of the populace, who were always ready to attribute a defeat to

the treachery of the general. His military conduct
was, by his own officers, generally and justly con-
demned and his skill in war was slight, but his courage and honesty were unquestionable, and he was of
distinguished humanity; at this unhappy period,
when the French prisoners in every part of Spain
were tortured with the most savage cruelty, and when
to refrain from such deeds was to incur suspicion,
Reding had the manliness, not only to repress all
barbarities within the range of his command, but
even to conclude a convention with St. Cyr, under
which the wounded men on both sides were to receive decent treatment, and to be exchanged as
soon as their hurts were cured. In his last moments he complained that he had been ill-served as
a general; that the Somatenes had not supported
him; that his orders were neglected, his plans disclosed to the enemy, and that he could never
get true intelligence; complaints which the experience of Moore, Baird, Cradock, Murray, and,
above all, of Wellington, proved to be applicable to
every part of Spain, at every period of the war.
Coupigny succeeded Reding, but was soon superseded by Blake, who was appointed captain
general of the Coronilla, or little crown, a title
given to the union of Valencia, Aragon, and
Catalonia. The warfare in Aragon being thus ul-
timately connected with that in Catalonia, a short
account of what was passing in the former province
will be useful.

When Zaragoza fell, Lasnes returned to France,
and Mortier, who succeeded him, sent detachments
against Monzon, Jaca, Mequinenza and Lerida.
The fort of Monzon commanding a passage over the
Cinca river, was abandoned by the Spaniards, and

Jaca surrendered, by which a new and important line of communication was opened with France; but the demonstration against Mequinenza failed, and the summons to Lerida was fruitless. Mortier then quartered his troops on both sides of the Ebro, from Barbastro to Alcanitz, and sent colonel Briche, as we have seen, to open a communication with the seventh corps. This was in March, and in April Mortier moved with the fifth corps to Castile, leaving Junot with the third corps to hold Aragon; but that officer being sick, soon returned to France, and was replaced by general Suchet. The third corps was now very much reduced, one brigade was employed to protect the communication with Navarre, another was escorting the prisoners from Zaragoza to Bayonne, and many artillery-men and non-commissioned officers had been withdrawn to serve in Germany: thus the number of disposable troops in Aragon did not exceed twelve thousand men under arms.

The weakness of the army gave the new general great uneasiness, which was not allayed when he found that men and officers were discontented and dispirited. Suchet was, however, no ordinary man; with equal vigour and prudence he commenced a system of discipline in his corps, and of order in his government, that afterwards carried him, with scarcely a check, from one success to another, until he obtained for himself the rank of a marshal; and for his troops the honour of belonging to the only French army in Spain that never suffered any signal reverse. He at first hoped that the battle of Valls, and other defeats sustained by the Spaniards at this period, would give him time to re-organize his corps in tranquillity—but this hope soon vanished. The

peasantry, observing the weakness of the third
corps, only waited for a favourable opportunity to
rise, and the Migueletes and Somatenes of the
mountains about Lerida and Mequinenza, were,
under the command of Pereña and Baget, already
in activity.

While Junot still held the command, Blake drawing troops from Valencia and Tarragona, had joined
Lazan, and fixed his quarters at Morella, on the
frontier of Aragon. Designing to operate in that
province rather than in Catalonia, he endeavoured
to re-kindle the fire of insurrection; nor was fortune adverse to him, for a part of the garrison of
Monzon having made an unsuccessful marauding
excursion beyond the Cinca, the citizens fell upon
those who remained, and obliged them to abandon
that post, which was immediately occupied by Pereña. The duke of Abrantes then sent eight companies of infantry and thirty cuirassiers to retake
the place, but Baget reinforced Pereña, the French
were repulsed, and the Cinca suddenly overflowing
behind them, cut off their retreat; the cavalry,
plunging with their horses into the river, escaped
by swimming; the infantry finding the lower passages guarded by the garrison of Lerida, and the
upper cut off by the partizan corps, after three days
marching and skirmishing surrendered. The prisoners were carried to Tarragona, and soon afterwards exchanged, in pursuance of a convention
made by Reding and St. Cyr.

This slight success excited the most extravagant
hopes, and the garrison of Mequinenza having contrived to burn the bridge of boats which the French
had thrown over the Ebro at Caspe, Blake drove
the French from Beceyta and Val de Ajorfa, and

entered Alcanitz. The beaten troops retired with
loss to Samper and Ixar; and it was at this moment
when the quarters on both sides of the Ebro were
harassed, and the wings of the third corps separated
by the destruction of the bridge at Caspe, that
Suchet arrived to take the command of the third
corps. Finding his troops spread over a great tract
of country, and in danger of being beaten in detail,
he immediately ordered general Habert to abandon
the left bank of the Ebro, cross that river at Fuentes,
and follow in reserve upon Ixar, where Suchet
himself rallied all the rest of the troops, with the
exception of a small garrison left in Zaragoza.

BATTLE OF ALCANITZ.

The French battalions were fearful and disorderly:
but the general, anxious to raise their spirits,
Suchet's   marched towards Blake on the 23d of May. The
Memoirs.   latter was in position in front of Alcanitz; a bridge
over the Guadalupe was immediately behind his
centre, which was covered by a hill, and his left was
well posted near some pools of water, but his right
was rather exposed. The French had about eight
thousand infantry and seven hundred cavalry in the
field, and the Spaniards about twelve thousand of
all arms.

Suchet, observing Blake's dispositions, judged,
that if he could carry the hill in the centre and so
separate the Spanish wings, the latter would be cut
off from the bridge of Alcanitz, and obliged to surrender. In this design he directed a column against
each wing to draw Blake's attention to his flanks,
and when the skirmishers were well engaged, three
thousand men, pushing rapidly along the main
road attacked the hillock; but a brisk fire of musketry

CHAP.
V.

1809.
May.

and artillery checked their progress, the Spaniards stood firm, and the French, after a feeble effort to ascend the hill, began to waver, and finally fled outright. Suchet, who was himself slightly wounded, rallied them in the plain, and remained there for the rest of the day, but without daring to renew the action. In the night, he retreated, but, although not pursued, his troops were seized with panic, and, at day-light, came pouring into Samper with all the tumult and disorder of a rout. Blake's inactivity enabled the French general to restore order, and he caused the man who first commenced the alarm to be shot; then encouraging the troops, that they might not seem to fly, he rested in position two whole days, after which he retreated to Zaragoza.

This action at Alcanitz was a subject of triumph and rejoicing all over Spain; the supreme junta conferred an estate upon Blake; the kingdom of Murcia was added to his command, his army rapidly augmented, and he, greatly elated, and confirmed in a design he had formed to retake Zaragoza, turned his whole attention to Aragon, and totally neglected Catalonia. To the affairs of that province it is now time to return.

St. Cyr remained in Barcelona for a considerable period, during which he endeavoured to remedy the evils of Duhesme's government, and to make himself acquainted with the political disposition of the inhabitants. He also filled the magazines with three months' provisions, and, as the prisoners within the walls were an incumbrance on account of their subsistence, and a source of uneasiness from their numbers, he resolved to send them to France. The 15th of April, having transferred his sick and weakly men to the charge of Duhesme, and ex-

changed Chabran's for Lecchi's division, he marched
to Granollers, giving out that he was returning to
the frontier of France, lest the Catalans should
remove their provisions from Vich, and thus frus-
trate his principal object.

The Migueletes, under Milans and Claros, had
taken post on each side of the long and narrow
defile of Garriga, in the valley of the Congosto,
which they barricadoed with trees and pieces of rock,
and mined in several places ; Wimpfen with his
corps was also at a little distance, ready to join
them at the first alarm.   Hence, when on the 16th
Lecchi's division, escorting two thousand prisoners,
appeared at the head of the defile, an action commenced, but in an hour the Migueletes fled on all
sides ; for St. Cyr, fully aware of the strength of
the position, had secretly detached Pino to attack
Wimpfen, and, while Lecchi was engaged at the
entrance, Souham and Chabot, traversing the mountains, arrived, the one upon the flank, the other at
the further end of this formidable pass.

The 18th, the French were established at Vich ;
the inhabitants had fled to the hills with their
effects, but left their provisions behind.   Chabot's
and Pino's division were immediately posted at
Centellas, San Martin, Tona, and Col de Sespino,
to guard the entrances into the valley, but Souham's
division remained near the town, his right being at
Roda and Manlieu on the Ter, and his advanced
posts at Gurp, St. Sebastian, and St. Eularia.
General Lecchi then marched with the prisoners by
Filieu de Pallerols to Besalu, and although he was
attacked several times on the march, delivered
his charge to general Reille, and returned without
loss, bringing news of Napoleon's arrival in Paris,

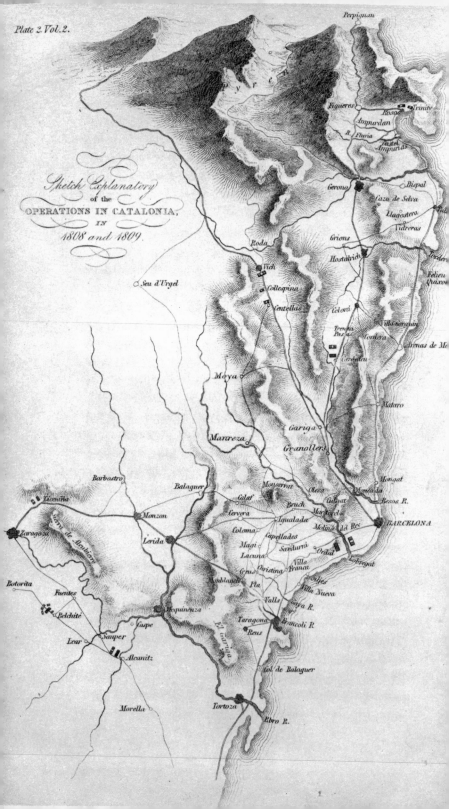

Plate 2.Vol.2.

Sketch Explanatory
of the
OPERATIONS IN CATALONIA,
IN
1808 and 1809.

and of the approaching war with Austria. On the other side, a moveable column sent to Barcelona brought back the pleasing intelligence that admiral Cosmao's squadron, baffling the extreme vigilance of Lord Collingwood, had reached that city with ample supplies. Thus, in May, what may be called the irregular movements in Catalonia terminated, and the more methodical warfare of sieges commenced; but this part was committed to other hands; general Verdier had succeeded Reille in the Ampurdan, and marshal Augereau was on the road to supersede St. Cyr.

OBSERVATIONS.—1°. Although his marches were hardy, his battles vigorous, and delivered in right time and place; St. Cyr's campaign may be characterised as one of great efforts without corresponding advantages. He himself attributes this to the condition of the seventh corps, destitute and neglected, because *the emperor disliked and wished to ruin its chief;* a strange accusation, and unsustained by reason or facts. What! Napoleon wilfully destroy his own armies! sacrifice forty thousand men, to disgrace a general, whom he was not obliged to employ at all. St. Cyr acknowledges, that when he received his instructions from the emperor, he observed the affliction of the latter at the recent loss of Dupont's force, yet he would have it believed, that, in the midst of this regret, that monarch, with a singular malice, was preparing greater disasters for himself, merely to disgrace the commander he was talking to, and why? because the latter had formerly served with the army of the Rhine! Yet St. Cyr met with no reverses in Catalonia, and was afterwards made a marshal by this implacable enemy.

2°.—That the seventh corps was not well supplied, and its commander thereby placed in a difficult situation, is not to be disputed in the face of the facts stated by St. Cyr; but if war were a state of ease and smoothness, the fame which attends successful generals would be unmerited. Napoleon selected St. Cyr because he thought him a capable commander; in feeble hands, he knew the seventh corps would be weak, but, with St. Cyr at its head, he judged it sufficient to overcome the Catalonians, nor was he much mistaken. Barcelona, the great object of solicitude, was saved; Rosas was taken; and if Tarragona and Tortosa did not also fall, the one after the battle of Molino del Rey, the other after that of Valls, it was because the French general did not choose to attack them. Those towns were without the slightest preparation for defence, moral or physical, and must have surrendered; nor can the unexpected and stubborn resistance of Gerona, Zaragoza, and Valencia be cited against this opinion; these cities were previously prepared and expectant of a siege, yet, in two instances, there was a moment of dismay and confusion, not fatal, only because the besieging generals wanted that ready vigour which is the characteristic of great captains.

3°.—St. Cyr, aware that a mere calculation of numbers and equipment, is but a poor measure of the strength of armies, exalts the enthusiasm and the courage of the Catalans, and seems to tremble at the danger which, owing to Napoleon's suicidal jealousy, menaced, at that period, not only the seventh corps but even the south of France. In answer to this, it may be observed that M. de St. Cyr did not hesitate, with eighteen thousand men,

having no artillery and carrying only sixty rounds
of musket-ammunition, to plunge into the midst of
those terrible armies; to march through the mountains for whole weeks; to attack the strongest positions with the bayonet alone, nay, even to dispense
with the use of his artillery, when he did bring it
into action, lest his men should not have a sufficient
contempt for their enemies. And who were these
undaunted soldiers, so high in courage, so confident, so regardless of the great weapon of modern
warfare? Not the select of the imperial guards,
the conquerors in a hundred battles, but raw levies;
the dregs and scrapings of Italy, the refuse of Naples
and of Rome; states which to name as military was
to ridicule. With such soldiers, the battles of Cardadeu, Molino, Igualada, and Valls, were gained; yet
St. Cyr does not hesitate to call the Migueletes,
who were beaten at those places, the best light
troops in the world. The best *light troops* are
neither more nor less than the best troops in the
world; but if, instead of fifteen thousand Migueletes, the four thousand men composing Wellington's
light division had been on the heights of Cardadeu,
St. Cyr's sixty rounds of ammunition would scarcely
have carried him to Barcelona. The injurious force
with which personal feelings act upon the judgement are well known, or it might excite wonder,
that so good a writer and so able a soldier should
advance such fallacies.

4°.—St. Cyr's work, admirable in many respects,
bears, nevertheless, the stamp of carelessness.
Thus, he affirms that Dupont's march to Andalusia
encouraged the tumults of Aranjues, yet the tumults
of Aranjues happened in the month of March,
nearly three months previous to Dupont's move-

ment, which took place in May and June.   Again,
he says, that, Napoleon, to make a solid conquest
in the Peninsula, should have commenced with
Catalonia, instead of over-running Spain by the
northern line of operations; an opinion quite un-
sustainable.   The progress of the seventh corps was
impeded by the want of provisions, not by the enemy's
force ; twenty thousand men could beat the Spaniards in the field, but they could not subsist.   To
have increased the number would only have increased
the difficulty.   Would it have given a just idea of
Napoleon's power, to employ the strength of his empire
against the fortified towns in Catalonia?   In what
would the greater solidity of this plan have consisted?
While the French were thus engaged, the patriots
would have been organizing their armies ; England
would have had time to bring all her troops into
line, and two hundred thousand men placed between
Zaragoza and Tortosa, or breaking into France by
the western Pyrenees, while the Austrians were
advancing to the Rhine, would have sorely shaken
the solidity of general St. Cyr's plan.

5°.—The French emperor better understood what
he was about.   He saw a nation intrinsically powerful and vehemently excited, yet ignorant of war and
wanting the aid which England was eager to give.
All the elements of power existed in the Peninsula,
and they were fast approximating to a centre, when
Napoleon burst upon that country, and as the
gathering of a water-spout is said to be sometimes
prevented by the explosion of a gun, so the rising
strength of Spain was dissipated by his sudden and
dreadful assault ; if the war was not then finished,
it was because his lieutenants were tardy and
jealous of each other.   St. Cyr also appears to have

fallen into an error, common enough in all times, and one very prevalent among the French generals in Spain. He considered his task as a whole in itself, instead of a constituent part of a greater system. He judged very well what was wanting for the seventh corps, to subjugate Catalonia in a solid manner, but he did not discern that it was fitting that the seventh corps should forget Catalonia, to aid the general plan against the Peninsula. Rosas surrendered at the very moment when Napoleon, after the victories of Baylen, Espinosa, Tudela, and the Somosierra, was entering Madrid as a conqueror; the battles of Cardadeu and Molino del Rey may, therefore, be said to have completely prostrated Spain, because the English army was isolated, the Spanish armies destroyed, and Zaragoza invested. Was that a time to calculate the weight of powder and the number of pick-axes required for a formal siege of Tarragona? The whole Peninsula was shaken to the centre, the proud hearts of the Spaniards sunk with terror, and in that great consternation, to be daring, was, on the part of the French generals, to be prudent. St. Cyr was not in a condition to besiege Tarragona formally, but he might have assaulted it with less danger than he incurred by his march to Barcelona. The battle of Valls was another epoch of the same kind; the English army had re-embarked, and the route of Ucles had taken place; Portugal was invaded and Zaragoza had just fallen. That was a time to render victory fruitful, yet no attempt was made against Tortosa.

6°.—St. Cyr, who justly blames Palacios and Vives for remaining before Barcelona instead of carrying their army to the Ter and the Fluvia,

seems inclined to applaud Reding for conduct
equally at variance with the true principles of war.
It was his own inactivity after the battle of Molino
that produced the army of Reding, and the impatient folly of that army, and of the people, produced
the plan which led to the route of Igualada and
the battle of Valls. Instead of disseminating
thirty thousand men on a line of sixty miles, from
Tarragona to the Upper Llobregat, Reding should
have put Tarragona and Tortosa into a state of
defence, and leaving a small corps of observation
near the former, have made Lerida the base of his
operations. In that position, keeping the bulk
of his force in one mass, he might have acted on
St. Cyr's flanks and rear effectually, by the lines
of Cervera and Momblanch—and without danger to
himself; nor could the French general have attempted aught against Tarragona.

But it is not with reference to the seventh corps
alone that Lerida was the proper base of the
Spanish army. Let us suppose that the supreme
junta had acted for a moment upon a rational
system; that the Valencian troops, instead of remaining at Morella, had been directed on Lerida,
and that the duke of Infantado's force had been
carried from Cuença to the same place instead
of being routed at Ucles. Thus, in the beginning
of February, more than fifty thousand regular troops
would have been assembled at Lerida, encircled by
the fortresses of Monzon, Balaguer, Mequinenza,
Tarragona, and Tortosa. Its lines of operations
would have been as numerous as the roads.
The Seu d'Urgel, called the granary of Catalonia,
would have supplied corn, and the communication
with Valencia would have been direct and open.

From this central and menacing position, such a CHAP.
V.
force might have held the seventh corps in check, ———
and even raised the siege of Zaragoza; nor could
the first corps have followed Infantado's movements
without uncovering Madrid and abandoning the
system of the emperor's operations against Portugal
and Andalusia.

7°.—The French general praises Reding's project
for surrounding the French, and very gravely observes that the *only method* of defeating it was by
taking the offensive himself. Nothing can be juster;
but he should have added that it was a *certain
method;* and, until we find a great commander acting
upon Reding's principles, this praise can only be
taken as an expression of civility towards a brave
adversary. His own movements were very different;
he disliked Napoleon personally, but he did not
dislike his manner of making war. Buonaparte's
campaign in the Alps against Beaulieu, was not
unheeded by his lieutenant. For one proceeding of
St. Cyr's, however, there is no precedent, nor is it
likely that it will ever be imitated. He stopped the
fire of his artillery, when it was doing infinite execution, the better to establish the moral ascendancy of his troops. What a sarcasm on the courage of his enemies! What a complete answer
to his own complaints that Napoleon had mali-
ciously given him a hopeless task! But, he says,
his adversaries were numerous and fought bravely!
Surely he could not have commanded so long
without knowing *that there is in all battles a decisive moment, when every weapon, every man, every
combination of force that can be brought to bear, is
necessary to gain the victory.* Wilfully to neglect
the means of reducing the enemy's strength, pre-

vious to that critical period of an action, is a gross
folly.

8°.—If general St. Cyr's own matches and battles did not sufficiently expose the fallacy of his
opinions relative to the vigour of the Catalans, lord
Collingwood's correspondence would supply the
deficiency. That able and sagacious man, writing
at this period, says,—

" In Catalonia, every thing seems to have gone
wrong since the fall of Rosas. The Spaniards are
in considerable force, yet are dispersed and panic-
struck whenever the enemy appears."—" The applications for supplies are unlimited ; they want
money, arms, and ammunition, of which no use
appears to be made when they get them."—" In
the English papers, I see accounts of successes, and
convoys cut off, and waggons destroyed, which are
not true. What has been done in that way has
been by the boats of our frigates, which have, in
two or three instances, landed men and attacked
the enemy with great gallantry. The Somatenes
range the hills in a disorderly way, and fire at a
distance, but retire on being approach."—" The multitudes of men do not make a force."

Add to this the Spanish historian Cabanes' statements that the Migueletes were always insubordinate, detested the service of the line, and were
many of them armed only with staves, and we
have the full measure of the Catalans' resistance.

It was not the vigour of the Catalans, but
of the English, that in this province, as in every
part of the Peninsula, retarded the progress of the
French. Would St. Cyr have wasted a month before Rosas ? Would he have been hampered in his
movements by his fears for the safety of Barcelona ?

Would he have failed to besiege and take Tarragona and Tortosa, if a French fleet had attended
his progress by the coast, or if it could even have
made two runs in safety? To lord Collingwood,
who, like the Roman Bibulus, perished of sickness
on his decks rather than relax in his watching,—to
his keen judgement, his unceasing vigilance, the
resistance made by the Catalans was due. His fleet
it was, that interdicted the coast-line to the French,
protected the transport of the Spanish supplies from
Valencia, assisted in the defence of the towns, aided
the retreat of the beaten armies; in short, did that
which the Spanish fleets in Cadiz and Carthagena
should have done. But the supreme junta, equally
disregarding the remonstrances of lord Collingwood,
the good of their own country, and the treaty with
England, by which they were bound to prevent
their ships from falling into the hands of the enemy,
left their fleets to rot in harbour, although money
was advanced, and the assistance of the British
seamen offered to fit them out for sea.

Having now related the principal operations that
took place in the eastern and central provinces of
Spain, which were so suddenly overrun by the
French emperor; having shown that, however rest-
less the Spaniards were, under the yoke imposed
upon them, they were unable to throw it off; I
shall turn to Portugal, where the tide of invasion
still flowing onward although with diminished
volume, was first stayed, and finally forced back,
by a counter flood of mightier strength.

BOOK VI.

CHAPTER I.

TRANSACTIONS IN PORTUGAL.

BOOK VI.
1808.

WHEN sir John Moore marched from Portugal, the regency, established by sir Hew Dalrymple, nominally governed that country; but the weak characters of the members, the listless habits engendered by the ancient system of misrule, the intrigues of the Oporto faction, and the general turbulence of the people soon produced an alarming state of anarchy. Private persons usurped the functions of government, justice was disregarded, insubordination and murder were hailed as indications of patriotism, and war was the universal cry; yet military preparations were wholly neglected, for the nation, in its foolish pride, believed that the French had neither strength nor spirit for a second invasion.

Appendix, No. 3, section 1.

In Lisbon there was a French faction, the merchants were apprehensive, the regency unpopular, and the public mind unsettled; in Oporto, the violence of both people and soldiers was such, that sir Harry Burrard sent two British regiments there, by sea, to preserve tranquillity; in fine, the seeds of disorder were widely cast and sprouting vigorously, before the English cabinet though fit to accredit a responsible diplomatist near the government, or to place a permanent chief at the head of the forces left by sir John Moore. The convention of Cintra was known in England in September; the regency was established and the frontier fortresses occupied by British troops in the same month; yet it was not until the middle of December that Mr. Villiers and sir John Cradock, charged with the conduct of the political and military proceedings in Portugal, reached Lisbon; thus the important interval, between the departure of Junot and their arrival, was totally neglected by the English cabinet.

Sir Hew Dalrymple, who had nominated the regency; sir Arthur Wellesley, who, to local knowledge and powerful talents, added the influence of a victorious commander, Burrard, Spencer, were all removed from Portugal at the very moment when the presence of persons acquainted with the real state of affairs, was essential to the well-being of the British interests in that country. And this error was the offspring of passion and incapacity; for, if the convention of Cintra had been rightly understood, the ministers, appreciating the advantages of that treaty, would have resisted the clamour of the moment, and the generals would not have been withdrawn from the public service abroad, to meet unjust and groundless charges at home.

It may be disputed whether Portugal was the fittest theatre for the first operations of a British army; but, when that country was actually freed from the presence of an enemy; when the capital and the frontier fortresses were occupied by English troops; when sir John Moore leaving his hospitals, baggage, and magazines there, as in a place of arms, had marched to Spain, the question was no longer doubtful. The ancient relations between

England and Portugal, the greatness of the port of
Lisbon, the warlike disposition of the Portuguese,
above all, the singularly-happy circumstance, that
there was neither court nor monarch to balance the
English influence, and that even the nomination
of the regency was the work of an English general,
offered such great and obvious advantages as could
no where else be obtained. It was a miserable
policy that, neglecting such an occasion, retained
sir Arthur Wellesley in England, while Portugal,
like a drunken man, at once weak and turbulent,
was reeling on the edge of a precipice.

The 5th of December, 1808, sir John Cradock,
being on his voyage to Lisbon, touched at Coruña.
Fifteen hundred thousand dollars had just arrived
there in the Lavinia frigate, but sir John Moore's
intention to retreat upon Portugal being known,
Cradock divided this sum, and carried away eight
hundred thousand dollars; proposing to leave a
portion at Oporto, and to take the remainder to
Lisbon, that Moore might find, on whatever line he
retreated, a supply of money.

From Coruña he proceeded to Oporto, where
he found that sir Robert Wilson had succeeded in
organizing, under the title of the Lusitanian Legion,
about thirteen hundred men, and that others were
on their way to reinforce him; but this excepted,
nothing, civil or military, bespoke either arrangement or common sense. The bishop, still intent
upon acquiring supreme rule, was deeply engaged with secret intrigues, and, under him, a
number of factious and designing persons, instigated the populace to violent actions with a view
to profit from their excesses.

The formation of this Lusitanian Legion was ori-

Appendix,
No. 3.
section 2d.

ginally a project of the chevalier da Souza, Portuguese minister in London; he was one of the bishop's faction, and this force was raised not so much to repel the enemy, as to support that party against the government. The men were promised higher pay than any other Portuguese soldiers, to the great discontent of the latter; and they were clad in uniforms differing in colour from the national troops. The regency, who dreaded the machinations of the turbulent priest, entertained the utmost jealousy of this legion, which, in truth, was a most anomalous force, and as might be expected from its peculiar constitution, was productive of much embarrassment.

Sir John Cradock left three hundred thousand dollars at Oporto, and directed the two British battalions which were in that neighbourhood to march to Almeida, then taking on board a small detachment of German troops, he set sail for Lisbon. Before his departure, he strongly advised sir Robert Wilson to move such of his legionaries as were sufficiently organized to Villa Real, in Tras os Montes, a place appointed by the regency for the assembly of the forces in the north; Sir Robert, tired of the folly and disgusted with the insolence and excesses of the ruling mob, readily adopted this advice, so far as to quit Oporto, but having views of his own, went to Almeida instead of Villa Real.

The state of the capital was little better than that of Oporto. There was arrangement neither for present nor for future defence, and the populace, albeit less openly encouraged to commit excesses, were quite uncontrolled by the government. The regency had a keener dread of domestic insurrection than of the return of the French, whose operations

Appendix,
No. 3,
section 5.

they regarded with even less anxiety than the bishop did, as being further removed than he was from the immediate theatre of war. Their want of system and vigilance was evinced by the following fact. Sattaro and another person, having contracted for the supply of the British troops, demanded, in the name of the English general, all the provisions in the public stores of Portugal, and then sold them to the English commissaries for his own profit.

Sir John Cradock's instructions directed him to reinforce Moore's army, and not to interfere with that general's command if the course of events brought him back to Portugal. In fact, his operations were limited to the holding of Elvas, Almeida, and the capital; for, although he was directed to encourage the formation of a native army upon a good and regular system, and even to act in concert with it on the frontier, he was debarred from political interference; even his relative situation as to rank, was left unsettled until the arrival of Mr. Villiers, to whose direction all political and many military arrangements were entrusted.

It is evident that the influence of a general thus fettered, and commanding only a small scattered force, must be feeble and insufficient to produce any real amelioration in the military situation of the country; yet the English ministers, attentive only to the false information obtained from interested agents, still imagined that not only the Spanish, but the Portuguese armies were numerous, and to be relied upon; and they confidently expected, that the latter would be able to take an active part in the Spanish campaign. Cradock, feeling the danger of this illusion, made it his first object to

transmit home exact information of the real strength
and efficiency of the native regular troops. They
were nominally twenty thousand; but Miguel Pereira
Forjas, military secretary to the regency, and the
ablest public man Portugal possessed, acknowledged
that this force was a nullity, and that there were
not more than ten thousand stand of serviceable
arms in the kingdom, the greatest part of which
were English. The troops themselves were undisciplined and unruly; the militia and the "*ordenanza*," or armed peasantry, animated by a spirit
of outrage rather than of enthusiasm, evinced no
disposition to submit to regulation; neither was
there any branch of administration free from the
grossest disorder.

The Spanish dollar had a general acceptance in
Portugal. The regency, under the pretence that a
debased foreign coin would drive the Portuguese
coin out of circulation, deprived the dollar of its
current value. This regulation, true in principle,
and applicable, as far as the Portuguese gold coin
(which is of peculiar fineness) was concerned, had,
however, a most injurious effect. The Spanish
dollar was in reality finer than the Portuguese silver
cruzado-nova, and would finally have maintained
its value, notwithstanding this decree, if the slur
thus thrown upon it by the government, had not
enabled the money changers to run its value down
for the moment; a matter of infinite importance, for
the English soldiers and sailors being all paid in
these dollars, at four shillings and sixpence, which
was the true value, were thus suddenly mulcted
fourpence in each, by the artificial depreciation of
the moment. The men attributed this to fraud in
the shopkeepers, the retail trade of Lisbon was

CHAP.
I.

1808.
Dec.

Cradock's
Correspon-
dence,
MSS.

interrupted, and quarrels between the tradesmen and the soldiers took place hourly. To calm this effervescence, a second decree was promulgated, directing that the dollar should be received at the mint and in the public offices at its real value; it then appeared that the government could profit by coining the dollar of four shillings and sixpence into cruzado-novas, a circumstance which gave the whole affair the appearance of an unworthy trick to recruit the treasury. This happened in October, and as the financial affairs were ill managed, and the regency destitute of vigour or capacity, the taxes were unpaid, the hard cash exhausted, and the treasury paper at a heavy discount when Cradock arrived.

Upon the scroll thus unfolded he could only read confusion, danger and misfortune; such being the fruits of victory, what could be expected from disaster, and at this period (the middle of December) sir John Moore was supposed to be in full retreat upon Portugal, followed by the emperor with one French army, while another threatened Lisbon by the line of the Tagus. The English troops in the kingdom did not amount to ten thousand men, including the sick, and they were ill equipped and scattered; moreover, the capital was crowded with women and children, with baggage and non-combatants, belonging as well to the army in Spain as to that in Portugal. There were in the river three Portuguese ships of the line, two frigates, and eight other smaller vessels of war, but none were in a state for sea, and the whole likely to fall into the hands of the enemy, for in the midst of this confusion sir Charles Cotton was recalled, without a successor being appointed. The zeal and talents of captain

Halket, the senior officer on the station, amply compensated for the departure of the admiral, as far as professional duties were concerned, but he could not aid the general, nor deal with the regency, as vigorously as an officer of higher rank, and formally accredited, could have done.

Sir John Cradock, although fully sensible of his own difficulties, with a very disinterested zeal, resolved to make the reinforcing of sir John Moore's army his first care, but his force at this time was, as I have already said, less than ten thousand men of all arms. It consisted of eight British and four German battalions of infantry, four troops of dragoons, and thirty pieces of artillery, of which, however, only six were horsed so as to take the field. There was, also, a battalion of the 60th regiment, composed principally of Frenchmen recruited from the prison ships, but it had been sent back from Spain, as the soldiers could not be trusted near their countrymen. Of these thirteen battalions two were in Abrantes, one in Elvas, three at Lamego on the Duero, one in Almeida, and the remaining six at Lisbon. Three of the four battalions in the north were immediately directed to join sir John Moore by the route of Salamanca, and of those in the south, two, accompanied by a demi-brigade of artillery, were sent to him from Abrantes, by the road of Castello Branco and Ciudad Rodrigo.

Sir J. Cradock's Papers, MSS.

Meanwhile Mr. Villiers arrived, and sir John Cradock forwarded to the regency a strong representation of the dangerous state of Portugal. He observed that there was neither activity in the government nor enthusiasm among the people; that the army, deficient in numbers,

and still more so in discipline, was scattered and
neglected, and, notwithstanding that the aspect of
affairs was so threatening, the regency were apparently without any system, or fixed principle of
action. He proposed, therefore, that a general
enrolment of all the people should take place, and
from the British stores he offered a supply of a
thousand muskets and ten thousand pikes. This
giving of pikes to the people, which appears to have
been in compliance with Mr. Villiers' wishes, betrayed more zeal than prudence ; a general levy,
and arming with pikes of the turbulent populace of
a capital city, at such a conjuncture, was more
likely to lead to confusion and mischief than to any
effectual defence. The main objects pressing upon
the general's attention were however sufficiently
numerous and contradictory, to render it difficult
for him to avoid errors.

It was a part of his instructions, and of manifest
importance, to send reinforcements to sir John
Moore; yet it was equally necessary to keep a
force towards the frontier on the line of the Tagus,
seeing that the fourth French corps had just passed
that river at Almaraz, had defeated Galluzzo's army
and menaced Badajos, which was without arms,
ammunition, or provisions; moreover, the populace there, were in commotion and slaying the
chief persons. Now, sir John Cradock's instructions directed him to keep his troops in a position
that would enable him to abandon Portugal, if a
very superior force should press him; but as, in
such a case, he was to carry off the British
army, and the Portuguese navy and stores, destroying what he could not remove, and to receive on
board his vessels all the natives who might be de-

CHAP.
I.

1808.
Dec.

Appendix,
No. 4, sec-
tion 1.

sirous of escaping, it was of pressing necessity to
ship the women, children, baggage, and other
encumbrances belonging to Moore's army, immediately, that his own rear might be clear for a
sudden embarkation. In short, he was to send his
troops to Spain, and yet defend Portugal; to excite
confidence in the Portuguese, and yet openly to
carry on the preparations for abandoning that
country.

The populace of Lisbon were, however, already
uneasy at the rumours of an embarkation, and it
was doubtful if they would permit even the British
non-combatants to get on board quietly, much less
suffer the forts to be dismantled, and the ships of
war to be carried off, without a tumult, which, at
such a conjuncture, would have been fatal to all
parties. Hence it was imperative to maintain a
strong garrison in Lisbon and in the forts commanding the mouth of the river, and this draft, together
with the troops absorbed by the fortresses of Almeida
and Elvas, reduced the fighting men in the field to
insignificance.

The regency, knowing the temper of the people,
and fearing to arm them, were not very eager to
enforce the levy; anxious, however, to hide their
weakness, they promised, at the urgent solicitations
of the English general, to send six thousand troops
to Alcantara, on the Spanish frontier, with a view
to observe the march of the fourth corps,—a promise
which they never intended, and indeed were unable, to perform. Forjas, who was supposed to
be very inimical to the British influence, frankly
declared that they neither could nor would move
without an advance of money, and sir John Cradock,

BOOK
VI.

1808.
Dec.

Sir J. Cra-
dock's Cor-
respon-
dence,
MSS.

although he recommended that this aid should be given, had no power to grant it himself.

Letters from sir John Moore, dated at Salamanca, now reached Lisbon; they increased the anxiety to reinforce the army in Spain, but, as they clearly showed that reverses were to be expected, Cradock, although resolved to maintain himself in Portugal as long as it was possible to do so without a breach of his instructions, felt more strongly that timely preparation for an embarkation should be made; especially as the rainy season, in which south-west winds prevail, had set in, and rendered the departure of vessels from the Tagus very uncertain. Meanwhile the internal state of Portugal was in no wise amended, or likely to amend.

The government had, indeed, issued a decree, on the 23d of December, for organizing the population of Lisbon in sixteen legions, but only one battalion of each was to parade at the same moment for exercise, and those only on Sundays, nor were the legions, at any time, to assemble without the order of the general commanding the province; this regulation, which rendered the whole measure absurd, was dictated by the fears of the regency. A proposal to prepare the Portuguese vessels for sea was acceded to, without any apparent dissatisfaction, but the government secretly jealous of their allies, fomented or encouraged discontent and suspicion among the people. No efforts were made to improve the regular force, none to forward the march of troops to Alcantara, and so inactive or so callous were the regency to the rights of humanity, that a Appendix,
No. 3, sec-
tion 4. number of French prisoners, captured at various periods by the Portuguese, and accumulated at Lis-

bon, were denied subsistence; sir John Cradock,
after many fruitless representations, was forced to
charge himself with their supply, to avert the hor-
ror of seeing them starved to death. The provisions necessary for Fort La Lippe were also withheld, and general Leite, acting upon the authority
of the regency, strenuously urged that the British
troops should evacuate that fortress.

The march of the reinforcements for sir John
Moore left only three hundred dragoons and seven
battalions available for the defence of Portugal, of
which four were necessarily in garrison, and the
remainder were unable to take the field in default
of mules, of which animal the country seemed
bereft; yet, at this moment, as if in derision, Mr.
Frere, the central junta, the junta of Badajos, and
the regency of Portugal, were, with common and
characteristic foolishness, pressing sir John Cradock
to march into the south of Spain, although there
was scarcely a Spanish soldier there in arms to
assist him; and such a movement, if it had been
either prudent or practicable, was directly against
his instructions.

Towards the end of December, the communication with sir John Moore was suddenly interrupted,
and the line of the Tagus acquired great importance. The troops going from Elvas to the army in
Spain were therefore directed to halt at Castello
Branco, and general Richard Stewart, who commanded them, being reinforced with two hundred
cavalry, was ordered, for the moment, to watch the
roads by Salvatierra and the two Idanhas, and to
protect the flying bridges at Abrantes and Vilha
Velha from the enemy's incursions. At the same
time, a promise was obtained from the regency that

BOOK
VI.

1808.
Dec.

Sir J. Cra-
dock's Cor-
respon-
dence,
MSS.

all the Portuguese troops in the Alemtejo should be collected at Campo Mayor and Portalegre.

Sir John Cradock fixed upon Sacavem as the position in which his main body should be concentrated, intending to defend that point as long as he could with so few troops ; and as he knew that Almeida, although full of British stores, and important in every way, was, with respect to its own defence, utterly neglected by the regency, who regarded with jealousy even the presence of a British force there ; he sent brigadier-general A. Cameron, with instructions to collect the convalescents of Moore's army, to unite them with the two battalions still at Almeida, and then to make his way to the army in Spain ; but if that should be judged too dangerous, he was to return to Lisbon. In either case, the stores and the sick men lying at Almeida were to be directed upon Oporto.

The paucity of cavalry was severely felt on the frontier ; it prevented the general from ascertaining the real strength and objects of the enemy's parties, and the Portuguese reports were notoriously contradictory and false. The 14th dragoons, seven hundred strong, commanded by major-general Cotton, had been disembarked since the 22d of December, and were destined for the army in Spain. But the commissary doubted if he could forward that small body even by detachments, such was the penury of the country, or rather the difficulty of drawing forth its resources ; many debts of sir John Moore's army were also still unpaid, and a want of confidence prevented the country people from bringing in supplies upon credit.

In the midst of these difficulties, rumours of re-

verses in Spain became rife, and acquired importance, when it became known that four thousand
infantry, and two thousand cavalry, the advanced
guard of thirty thousand French troops, were
actually at Merida, on the road to Badajos; the
latter town being, not only in a state of anarchy,
but destitute of provisions, arms, and ammunition.
Had the Portuguese force been assembled at Alcantara, sir John Cradock would have supported it
with the British brigades, from Abrantes and Castello Branco, but not a man had been put in motion,
and he, feeling no confidence either in the troops
or promises of the regency, resolved to concentrate
his own army near Lisbon. General Stewart was,
therefore, directed to destroy the bridges of Vilha
Velha and Abrantes, and fall back to Sacavem.
Meanwhile, the Lisbon populace, supposing that
the English general designed to abandon them
without necessity, were violently excited. The
regency, either from fear or folly, made no effort
to preserve tranquillity, and the people proceeded
from one excess to another, until it became evident
that, in a forced embarkation, the British would
have to fight their allies as well as their enemies.
At this gloomy period when ten marches would
have brought the French to Lisbon, when a stamp
of Napoleon's foot would have extinguished that
spark of war which afterwards blazed over the
Peninsula, sir John Moore made his daring movement upon Sahagun, and Portugal, gasping as in
a mortal agony, was instantly relieved.

CHAPTER II.

BOOK
VI.

1808.
Dec.

IT was the advanced guard of the fourth corps that had approached Merida with the intention of proceeding to Badajos, and the emperor was, as we have seen, preparing to follow; but, in the night of the 26th of December, an officer carrying the intelligence of Moore's movement, reached Merida, and, next morning, the French marching hastily to the Tagus, crossed it, and rejoined their main body, from which another powerful detachment was immediately directed upon Placentia. This retrograde movement obviated the immediate danger, and sir John Cradock endeavoured to pacify the people of Lisbon. Ordering Stewart's brigade, which had been strengthened by two German battalions, to halt at Santarem, he explained his own motives to the Portuguese, and urged the regency to a more frank and vigorous system, than they had hitherto followed ; for like the Spanish juntas, they promised every thing, and performed nothing; neither would they, although consenting, verbally, to all the measures proposed, ever commit themselves by writing, having the despicable intention of afterwards disclaiming that which might prove disagreeable to the populace, or even to the French. Sir John Cradock, however, had no power beyond his own personal influence to enforce attention to his wishes ; no successor to sir Charles Cotton had yet arrived, and Mr. Villiers seems to have wanted the decision and judgement required to meet such a momentous crisis.

Appendix,
No. 2, Sec-
tions 1 and
2.

Appendix,
No. 3, Sec-
tion 5.

In the north, general Cameron, having sent the sick men and part of the stores from Almeida towards Oporto, gave up that fortress to sir Robert Wilson, and on the 5th of January, marched, with two British battalions and a detachment of convalescents, by the Tras os Montes to join the army in Spain. On the 9th, hearing of sir John Moore's retreat to Coruña, he would have returned to Almeida, but Lapisse, who had taken Zamora, threatened to intercept his line of march, whereupon he made for Lamego, and advised sir R. Wilson to retire to the same place. Colonel Blunt, with seven companies, escorting a convoy for Moore's army, was likewise forced to take the road to Oporto, and on that city all the British stores and detachments were now directed.

Notwithstanding the general dismay, sir R. Wilson, who had been reinforced by some Spanish troops, Portuguese volunteers, and straggling convalescents of the British army, rejected Cameron's advice, and proceeded to practise all the arts of an able partizan—that is to say, enticing the French to desert, spreading false reports of his own numbers, and, by petty enterprizes and great activity, arousing a spirit of resistance throughout the Ciudad Rodrigo country.

The continued influx of sick men and stores at Oporto, together with the prospect of general Cameron's arrival there, became a source of uneasiness to sir John Cradock. Oporto, with a shifting-bar and shoal water, is the worst possible harbour for vessels to clear out, and one of the most dangerous for vessels to lie off, at that season of the year; hence, if the enemy advanced in force, a great loss, both of men and stores, was to be anticipated. The departure of sir Charles Cotton had diminished

BOOK
VI.

1809.
Jan.

Sir John
Cradock's
Correspon-
dence,
MSS.

the naval means, and, for seventeen successive days, such was the state of the wind that no vessel could leave the Tagus; captain Halket, however, contrived at last to send to Oporto tonnage for two thousand persons, and undertook to keep a sloop of war off that place. Sir Samuel Hood also despatched some vessels from Vigo, but the weather continued for a long time so unfavourable that these transports could not enter the harbour, and the encumbrances hourly increasing, at last produced the most serious embarrassments.

Sir John Moore having now relinquished his communications with Portugal, sir John Cradock had to consider how, relying on his own resources, he could best fulfil his instructions and maintain his hold of that country, without risking the utter destruction of the troops intrusted to his care. For an inferior army Portugal has no defensible frontier. The rivers, generally running east and west, are fordable in most places, subject to sudden rises and falls, offering but weak lines of resistance, and with the exception of the Zezere, presenting no obstacles to the advance of an enemy penetrating by the eastern frontier. The mountains, indeed, afford many fine and some impregnable positions, but such is the length of the frontier line and the difficulty of lateral communications, that a general who should attempt to defend it against superior forces would risk to be cut off from the capital if he concentrated his troops; and if he extended them his line would be immediately broken. The possession of Lisbon constitutes, in fact, the possession of Portugal, south of the Duero, and an inferior army can only protect Lisbon by keeping close to the capital.

Sensible of this truth, sir John Cradock adopted the French colonel Vincente's views for the defence of Lisbon, and proceeded, on the 4th of January, with seventeen hundred men, to occupy the heights behind the creek of Sacavem—leaving, however, three thousand men in the forts and batteries at Lisbon. At the earnest request of the regency, who in return promised to assemble the native troops at Thomar, Abrantes, and Vilha Velha, he ordered general Stewart's brigade, two thousand seven hundred strong, to halt at Santarem; but the men had been marching for a month under incessant rain, their clothes were worn out, their equipments ruined, and in common with the rest of the army they wanted shoes.

Sir John
Cradock's
Correspon-
dence,
MSS.

Cameron being now on the Douro, Kemmis with the 40th regiment at Elvas, and the main body under Cradock between Santarem and Lisbon, this army not exceeding ten thousand men, but with the encumbrances of an army of forty thousand, was placed on the three points of a triangle, the shortest side of which was above a hundred and fifty miles. The general commanding could not bring into the field above five thousand men, nor could that number be assembled in a condition for service at any one point of the frontier, under three weeks or a month; moreover, the uncertainty of remaining in the country at all, rendered it difficult to feed the troops, for the commissioners being unable to make large contracts for a fixed time, were forced to carry on, as it were, a retail system of supply.

At this moment of extreme weakness, Mr. Frere, with indefatigable folly, was urging sir John Cradock to make a diversion in Spain, by the line of the Tagus, and Mr. Villiers was as earnest that he

should send a force by sea to Vigo. His own instructions prescribed the preservation of Lisbon,
Elvas, and Almeida; the assembling, in concert with
the native government, of an Anglo-Portuguese
army on the frontier, and the sending of succours
to sir John Moore. Cradock's means were so scanty
that the attainments of any one of those objects
was scarcely possible, yet Mr. Canning writing
officially to Mr. Villiers at this epoch, as if a mighty
and well furnished army was in Portugal, enforced
the " *necessity of continuing to maintain possession
of Portugal, as long as could be done with the force
intrusted to sir John Cradock's command, remember-
ing always that not the defence of Portugal alone,
but the employment of the enemy's military force,
and the diversion which would be thus created in
favour of the south of Spain, were objects not to be
abandoned, except in case of the most extreme necessity.*" The enemy's military force! It was three
hundred thousand men, and this despatch was a
pompous absurdity. The ministers and their agents
eternally haunted by the phantoms of Spanish and
Portuguese armies, were incapable of perceiving
the palpable bulk and substance of the French
hosts; the whole system of the cabinet was one of
shifts and expedients, every week produced a fresh
project, and minister and agent, alike, followed his
own views, without reference to any fixed principle;
the generals were the only persons not empowered
to arrange military operations.

The number of officers employed to discover the
French movement, enabled Cradock, although his
direct communications were interrupted, to obtain
intelligence of Moore's advance towards Sahagun;
wherefore, he again endeavoured to send a rein-

forcement into Spain by the way of Almeida. The
difficulty of getting supplies, however, finally induced him to accede to Mr. Villiers' wishes, and on
the 12th of January he shipped six hundred cavalry and thirteen hundred infantry, meaning to
send them to Vigo; but while they were still in the
Tagus, intelligence of the retreat upon Coruña was
received, and the troops were disembarked.

The 14th of January the Conqueror line-of-battle-
ship, having admiral Berkeley on board, reached
Lisbon, and for the first time since sir John Cradock took the command of the troops in Portugal,
he received a communication from the ministers in
England. It now appeared that their thoughts were
less intently fixed upon the defence of Portugal
than upon getting possession of Cadiz. Their
anxiety upon this subject had somewhat subsided
after the battle of Vimeira, but it revived with greater
vigour when sir John Moore, contemplating a movement in the south, suggested the propriety of
securing Cadiz as a place of arms, and in January
an expedition was prepared to sail for that town,
with the design of establishing a new base of operations for the English army. This project failed,
but the following particulars of the transaction
afford ample proof of the perplexed unstable nature
of the minister's policy.

NEGOTIATION FOR THE OCCUPATION OF CADIZ.

While it was still unknown in England that the
supreme junta had fled from Aranjuez, sir George
Smith, who had conducted Spencer's negotiation
in 1808, was again sent to Cadiz to prepare the
way for the reception of an English garrison. Four

thousand men destined for this service were then embarked at Portsmouth, general Sherbrooke who commanded them, was first directed to touch at Lisbon on his way to Cadiz; he was afterwards desired to make for Coruña to be at the order of sir J. Moore, yet finally, his force being increased to five thousand men, he sailed on the 14th of January for Cadiz, under his first instructions. Mr. Frere was then directed to negotiate for the admission of these troops into Cadiz, as the only condition upon which a British army could be employed to aid the Spanish cause in that part of the Peninsula.

As the reverses in the north of Spain became known, the importance of Cadiz increased, and the importance of Portugal decreased in the eyes of the English ministers. Sir John Cradock was *Appendix, No. 8.* made acquainted with Sherbrooke's destination, and was himself commanded to obey any requisition *Appendix, No. 5.* for troops that might be made by the Spanish junta; and so independent of the real state of affairs were the ministerial arrangements, that Cradock, whose despatches had been one continued complaint of his inability to procure horses for his own artillery, was directed to furnish them for Sherbrooke's.

Sir George Smith, a man somewhat hasty, but of remarkable zeal and acuteness, left England about the middle of December; and, on his arrival at Cadiz, at once discovered that there, as in every other part of the Peninsula, all persons being engaged in theories or intrigues, nothing useful for defence was executed. The ramparts of the city were in tolerable condition, but scarcely any guns were mounted, while, two miles in front of the town, an outwork had been commenced upon such a scale that it could not possibly be finished under four months, and, after the slow mode of Spanish proceedings, would have taken as many years to complete.

For a solid defence of all the fortifications, sir George Smith judged that twenty thousand good troops would be requisite, but that ten thousand would suffice for the city, there were, however, only five thousand militia and volunteers in the place, and not a regular soldier under arms, neither any within reach. The number of guns mounted and to be mounted exceeded four hundred ; to serve them, two hundred and fifty peasants and volunteers were enrolled, and, being clothed in uniforms were called artillery-men.

Knowing nothing of sir John Moore's march to Sahagun, sir George Smith naturally calculated upon the immediate approach of the French ; wherefore seeing the helpless state of Cadiz, and being assured that the people would willingly admit an English garrison, he wrote to sir John Cradock for troops. The latter, little thinking that, at such a conjuncture, the supreme junta would be more jealous of their allies than fearful of their enemies ; judging also, from the tenor of his latest instructions, that obedience to this requisition would be consonant to the minister's wishes ; immediately ordered colonel Kemmis to proceed from Elvas with the fortieth regiment, by the route of Seville, and, at the same time, embarking three thousand of the best troops at Lisbon, sent them to Cadiz. This force, commanded by major-general Mackenzie, sailed the 2d February, and reached their destination the 5th of the same month.

Meanwhile, Mr. Frere, although acquainted with

Sir J. Cradock's Correspondence, MSS.

Parl. Papers, 1810.

the sailing of Mackenzie's armament, was ignorant
that sir George Smith had applied to the governor

of Cadiz for permission to take military possession
of that town ; for Smith had no instructions to
correspond with Mr. Frere, and the latter had opened
a separate negotiation with the central junta at

Seville, in which he endeavoured to pave the
way for the occupation by proposing to have the
troops admitted as guests, and he sent Mr. Stuart
to arrange this with the local authorities. Mr.
Frere had, however, meddled much with the
personal intrigues of the day, he was, moreover,
of too slender a capacity to uphold the dignity and
just influence of a great power on such an occasion,
and the flimsy thread of his negotiation snapped
under the hasty touch of sir George Smith. The
supreme junta, averse to every thing that threatened
to interrupt their course of sluggish indolence, had
sent the marquis de Villel, a member of their own
body, to Cadiz, avowedly to prepare the way for
the admission of the troops, but, in reality, to
thwart that measure ; hence the circumstance of
Mackenzie's arrival, with an object different from
that announced by Mr. Frere, was instantly taken
advantage of to charge England with treachery.
The junta, knowing Mr. Frere to be their own

dupe, believed, or affected to believe, that he was
also the dupe of the English minister, and that the
whole transaction was an artifice, on the part of
the latter, to get possession of the city with a
felonious intent. The admission of the British troops

was nevertheless earnestly desired by the inhabitants of Cadiz, and of the neighbouring towns ; and
this feeling was so well understood by Mr. Stuart
and sir George Smith, that they would, notwith-

standing the reluctance of the supreme junta, have brought the affair to a good conclusion; but, at the most critical period of the negotiation, the former was sent on a secret mission to Vienna, by the way of Trieste, and the latter, who was in bad health, died about the same period; thus the negotiation failed for want of a head to conduct it.

General Mackenzie, like sir George Smith, thought that the object might be attained: he observed, indeed, that the people, far from suspecting any danger, were ignorant of, or incredulous of the reverses in the north, that nothing had been done towards equipping the fleet for sea, and that, notwithstanding the earnest remonstrances of admiral Purvis and Mr. Stuart, the Spaniards would neither work themselves nor permit the English sailors to work for them; but he also saw that the public feeling was favourable to the British troops and the good will of the people openly expressed. The affair was, however, now in the hands of Mr. Frere.

In the course of the negotiations carried on by that minister, the supreme junta had proposed,

1°. That the troops should land at Port St. Mary's, to be quartered there and in the neighbouring towns.—2°. That they should join Cuesta's army.—3°. That they should go to Catalonia.—4°. That they should be parcelled out in small divisions, to be attached to the different Spanish armies. Nay, untaught by their repeated disasters, and pretending to hold the English soldiery cheap, those self-sufficient men proposed that the British should garrison the minor fortresses on the coast, in order to release an equal number of Spaniards for the field.

Mr. Frere wished to accept the first of these proposals, but general Mackenzie, sir George Smith, and Mr. Stuart agreed that it would be injurious for many reasons; not the least urgent of which was, that as the troops could not have been embarked again without some national dishonour, they must have marched towards Cuesta, and thus have been involved in the campaign without obtaining that which was their sole object, *the possession of Cadiz as a place of arms.*

Mr. Frere then suggested a modification of the second proposal, namely, to leave a small garrison in Cadiz, and to join Cuesta with the remainder of the troops. At this time sir G. Smith was dead; Mr. Stuart had embarked for Trieste; and general Mackenzie, reluctant to oppose Mr. Frere's wishes, consented to march, if the necessary equipments for his force could be procured; but he observed, that the plan was contrary to his instructions, and to the known wishes of the English government, and liable, in part, to the same objections as the first proposition. This was on the 18th of February; on the 22d, a populur tumult commenced in Cadiz.

The supreme junta, desirous to shew that the city did not require an English garrison for its protection, had sent there two regiments, composed of Poles, Germans, and Swiss, deserters or prisoners. The people, aware that the junta disliked and intended to disarm the volunteers of Cadiz, were justly offended that deserters should be trusted in preference to themselves; they stopped the courier, opened the despatches from Seville, and imprisoned the marquis of Villel, who was obnoxious, because, while mild to persons suspected of favouring the French, he had harshly or rather brutally punished some ladies of rank. Proceeding from one violence to another, the populace endeavoured to kill the state prisoner, and being prevented in that, committed other excesses, and murdered don Joseph Heredia, the collector of public rents. During the tumult, which lasted two days, the disembarkation of the English troops was repeatedly called for by the mob, and two British officers being sent on shore as mediators, were received with enthusiasm, and obeyed with respect, a manifest proof of the correct view taken by sir George Smith.

The 24th, tranquillity was restored; the 25th, general Mackenzie, not having received from Mr. Frere an answer to his letter of the 18th, suggested that of the three English battalions then in the harbour, two should be placed in Cadiz, and that the third, proceeding to Seville, should there unite with the 40th regiment, and both together march to join Cuesta. Mr. Frere, however, instead of addressing the junta with an authority and dignity becoming the representative of a great nation, on whose support the independence of the whole Peninsula rested, had been endeavouring to gain his end by subtlety. The object was one that England had a right to seek, the Spanish rulers no right to refuse, for the people wished to further it, and the threat of an appeal to them would soon have silenced the feeble negative of such a despicable and suspected government. Mr. Frere, incapable of taking a single and enlarged view, pressed a variety of trifling points, and discussed them with the secretary of the junta, with more regard to epistolary dexterity than to useful diplo-

Appendix,
No. 9.

macy; and when his opponent conceded the great point of admitting troops at all, broke off the negotiation, upon the question, whether the number to be admitted should be one or two thousand men; as if the way to drive a wedge was with the broad end foremost.

Self-baffled in that quarter, the British plenipotentiary, turning towards Cuesta, the avowed enemy of the junta, and one much feared by them, sought to secure his assistance by holding out the lure of having a British force added to his command, but the sarcastic old general derided the diplomatist. " Although I do not," said he, " discover any great difficulty in the actual state of things, which should Parl. Papers, 1810. prevent his British majesty's troops from garrisoning Cadiz under such terms, and for the purpose which your excellency proposes, I am far from supposing that the supreme junta, which is fully persuaded of the importance of our union with England, is not grounded in its objections; and your excellency knows that it is sufficient that they should have them, to prevent my giving any opinion on so important a measure, *unless they should consult me.* With regard to the 4,300 men, which your excellency is pleased to mention, there is no doubt that I stand in need of them; but I flatter myself, England, sensible of the importance of Estremadura, will even lend me much greater assistance, particularly if, from any change of circumstances, the supreme junta should no longer manifest the repugnance we speak of."

This answer having frustrated the projected intrigue, Mr. Frere, conscious perhaps of diplomatic incapacity, returned with renewed ardour to the task of directing the military affairs, in every part of the

Peninsula.   He had seen an intercepted letter of
Soult's, addressed to the king, in which the project
of penetrating into Portugal was mentioned ; and
immediately concluding that general Mackenzie's
troops would be wanted for the defence of that kingdom, counselled him to abandon Cadiz and return to
Lisbon; but the general, who knew that, even
should he return, a successful defence of Portugal
with so few troops would be impossible, and that
every precaution was already taken for an embarkation in the last extremity, observed, that " the
danger of Lisbon rendered the occupation of Cadiz
more important."

General Mackenzie's reply was written the 26th
of February.   On the 3d of March he received
another despatch from Mr. Frere.   Cadiz, and the
danger of Portugal, seemed to have passed from Appendix,
No. 9.
the writer's mind, and were unnoticed; entering
into a minutely inaccurate statement of the situation
of the French and Spanish armies, he observed, that
Soult having failed in an attempt to penetrate Portugal by the Minho, *it was impossible from the position of the Spanish forces, assisted as they were by
the Portuguese, that he could persevere in his plan.*
Wherefore, he proposed that the British force then
in the harbour of Cadiz should proceed immediately
to Tarragona, to aid Reding, and this wild scheme
was only frustrated by an unexpected despatch from Appendix,
No. 3,
sir John Cradock, recalling the troops to Lisbon.
They arrived there on the 12th of March; and
thus ended a transaction clearly indicating an unsettled policy, shallow combinations, and a bad
choice of agents on the part of the English cabinet,
and a most unwise and unworthy disposition in the
supreme junta.

General Mackenzie attributed the jealousy of the latter to French influence; Mr. Frere to the abrupt proceedings of sir George Smith, and to fear, lest the junta of Seville, who were continually on the watch to recover their ancient power, should represent the admission of the British troops as a treasonable proceeding on the part of the supreme government. It is, however, evident that the true cause was the false position in which the English ministers had originally placed themselves, by inundating Spain with arms and money, without at the same time asserting a just influence, and making their assistance the price of good order and useful exertion.

CHAPTER III.

THE effort made to secure Cadiz was an act of disinterested zeal on the part of sir John Cradock. The absence of his best troops exposed him to the most galling peevishness from the regency, and to the grossest insults from the populace; with his reduced force, he could not expect to hold even a contracted position at the extremity of the rock of Lisbon against the weakest army likely to invade Portugal; and as there was neither a native force nor a government to be depended upon, there remained for him only the prospect of a forced and, consequently, disgraceful embarkation, and the undeserved obloquy that never fails to follow disaster.

In this disagreeable situation, as Elvas and Almeida no longer contained British troops, his attention was necessarily fixed upon Lisbon and upon Oporto, which the violence of the gales had rendered a sealed port; meanwhile, the hospitals and magazines of Almeida, and even those of Salamanca being sent to Lamego, had crowded that place with fifteen hundred sick men, besides escorts and hourly accumulating stores. The Douro had overflowed, the craft could not ply, one large boat attempting to descend was overset, and eighty persons, soldiers and others, had perished. General Cameron also, hearing of this confusion, relinquished the idea of embarking at Oporto, and, re-crossing the Douro, made for Lisbon, where he arrived the beginning of February, with two thousand men, who were worn with fatigue, having marched eight hundred miles

BOOK.
VI.
——
1809.
January.

Appendix,
No. 6,
sect. 1.

Appendix,
No. 6,
sect. 1.

Appendix,
No. 10,
sect. 1.

under continued rains.　Sir Robert Wilson had sent his guns to Abrantes, by the road of Idanha Nova; but, partly from a spirit of adventure, partly from an erroneous idea that sir John Cradock wished him to defend the frontier, he remained with his infantry in the neighbourhood of Ciudad Rodrigo. His force had been increased by a Spanish detachment under Don Carlos d'España, and by some volunteers, but it was still weak, and his operations were necessarily confined to a few trifling skirmishes: yet, like many others, his imagination so far outstripped his judgment, that, when he had only felt the advanced post of a single division, he expressed his conviction that the French were going to abandon Spain altogether.

Sir John Cradock entertained no such false expectations, he was informed of the battle of Coruña and the death of Moore, and he knew too well the vigour and talent of that general to doubt that he had been oppressed by an overwhelming force; he knew also that Zaragoza had fallen, and that twenty-five thousand French troops were thus free to act in other quarters; he knew that Soult, with at least twenty thousand men, was on the Minho; that Romana was incapable of making any head; that Portugal was one wide scene of helpless confusion, and that a French army was again in the neighbourhood of Merida, threatening Lisbon by the line of the Tagus; in fine, that his own embarrassments were hourly increasing, and that the moment was arrived when the safety of his troops was the chief consideration.　The tenor of the few despatches he had received from England led him to suppose that the ministers designed to abandon Portugal; but, as their intentions on that head

were never clearly explained, he resolved to abide
by the literal interpretation of his first instructions,
and to keep his hold of the country as long as it
was possible to do so without risking the utter
destruction of his army.   To avoid that danger, he
put every incumbrance at Lisbon on board the
transports in the Tagus; proceeded to dismantle
the batteries at the mouth of the river, and in concert with the admiral, made preparations for carrying away or destroying the military and naval
stores in the arsenal.   At the same time, he renewed his efforts to embark the sick men and stores
at Oporto; but the weather continued so unfavourable that he was finally obliged to remove the
invalids and stores by land, yet he could not procure carriages for the whole.

After the arrival of Cameron's detachment, the
effective British force under arms, including convalescents and fifteen hundred stragglers from sir
John Moore's army, was about eight thousand men, Appendix,
No. 11.
yet when the security of the forts and magazines,
and the tranquillity of Lisbon, was provided for,
only five thousand men, and those not in the best
order, could be brought into the field.   As this
force was infinitely too weak to cover such a town
as Lisbon, the general judged that it would be
unwise to take up a position in advance, whence
he should be obliged to retreat through the midst
of a turbulent and excited population, which had
already given too many indications of ill-temper to
leave any doubt of its hostility under such circumstances.   He, therefore, came to the resolution of
withdrawing from Saccavem and Lisbon, to concentrate his whole force on a position at Passa D'Arcos Appendix,
No.10,sect.
near the mouth of the river, where he could embark 2 and 3.

with least danger, and where he had the best chance of defending himself, if necessary, against superior numbers.

This reasoning was sound, and Cradock's intention was, undoubtedly, not to quit Portugal, unless driven from it by force, or in pursuance of orders from England, his arrangements, however, seem to have carried more the appearance of alarm than was either politic or necessary; the position of Passa D'Arcos might have been prepared, and the means necessary for an embarkation secured, and yet the bulk of the troops kept in advance until the last moment. To display a bold and confident front in war is, of all things, the most essential, as well to impose upon friends as upon enemies; sir John Cradock did not fail to experience the truth of this maxim. The population of Lisbon, alarmed by the reverses in Spain, yet, like all the people in the Peninsula, confident in their own prowess and resolution until the very moment of attack, became extremely exasperated; the regency, partly from their natural folly and insincerity, but more from the dread of the lower orders, countenanced, if they did not instigate, the latter to commit excesses, and to interrupt the proceedings of the British naval and military authorities. The measures of precau-

Appendix,
No.3, sec-
tion 5. tion relative to the forts had originated with the regency, yet they now formally protested against them, and, with a view to hamper the general, encouraged their subalterns to make many false and even ridiculous charges against the British executive officers; and it would appear that the remonstrances of the admiral and generals were but imperfectly supported by Mr. Villiers.

In this manner the people's violence was nourished

until the city was filled with tumult; mobs, armed
with English pikes and muskets, collected night and
day in the streets and on the high-roads, and under
the pretext of seeking for and killing Frenchmen,
attacked indiscriminately all foreigners, even those Appendix,
No. 3, sec-
tion 6.
in the British service wearing the British uniform.
The guards, who endeavoured to protect the victims
of this ferocity, were insulted; couriers, passing
with despatches, were intercepted and deprived of
their papers; English officers were outraged in the
streets, and such was the audacity of the people that
the artillery was placed in the squares, in expectation of an affray. The state of Lisbon was similar
to what it had been at the period of Junot's convention, and if the British had abandoned the
country at this time, they would have been assailed
with as much obloquy by the Portuguese; for such
has been, and will be, the fate of all unsuccessful
auxiliaries: a reflection that should render histo-
rians cautious of adopting accusations upon the
authority of native writers on the like occasions.

This spirit was not confined to Lisbon. In
Oporto the disposition to insult the British was
more openly encouraged than in the capital, the
government of the multitude was more decidedly
pronounced; from the cities it spread to the villages. The people of the Alemtejo frontier were, Appendix,
No. 3, sec-
tion 6.
indeed, remarkably apathetic, but, from the Minho
to the Tagus, the country was in horrible confusion;
the soldiers were scattered, without regard to mili- Appendix,
No. 3, sec-
tion 6.
tary system, and being unpaid lived at free quarters; the peasantry of the country assembling in
bands, and the populace of the towns in mobs,
intercepted the communications, appointed or displaced the generals at their pleasure, and massacred

all persons of whom they were suspicious ; the ammunition which had been supplied from England was wasted, by constant firing in token of insubordination, and as if the very genius of confusion was abroad, some of the British troops, principally *malingerers*,* of sir John Moore's army,
added their quota of misconduct, to increase the general distress.

The leading instigator of the excesses at Oporto was one Raymundo, a coadjutor and creature of the bishop's, a turbulent and cruel fellow, who by taking a share in the first insurrection against the French obtained a momentary influence, and has since been elevated, by a very credulous writer, into a patriotic hero. He was, however, a worthless coward, fitted for secret villany, and incapable of a noble action.

This state of affairs, productive of so much misery and danger, continuing, without intermission, caused many of the upper classes to despair of their country's safety by war, and increased the number of those who, wishing to attach themselves to the fortune of France, were ready to accept of a foreign prince for their sovereign, if with him they could obtain tranquillity and an ameliorated constitution : and when soon afterwards, the edge of the enemy's sword, falling upon the senseless multitude, filled the streets of Oporto with blood, there was a powerful French party in Portugal. The bulk of the people were, however, stanch in their country's cause ; they were furious and disorderly, but imbued with hatred of the French, ready at the call of honour, and

---

* An appellation given among soldiers to men who, under pretence of sickness, shrink from the performance of their duties in the field.

susceptible of discipline, without any loss of
energy.

The turbulence of the citizens, the remonstrances of the regency, and the representations of Mr. Villiers, who was in doubt for the personal safety of the British subjects residing in Lisbon, convinced sir John Cradock that political circumspection and adroitness, were as important as military arrangements to prevent a catastrophe at this critical period; hence, as contrary to what might have been expected, the enemy had not yet made any actual movement across the frontier, he suspended his design of falling back to Passa D'Arcos.

In this unsettled state, affairs remained until March, when intelligence arrived that the French fleet was at sea, whereupon two of the line-of-battle ships in the Tagus were despatched to reinforce sir Thomas Duckworth's squadron, and the batteries at mouth of the river were again armed. Meanwhile, Soult was making progress in the north, the anarchy at Oporto was continually increasing, and the English government had certainly come to the resolution of abandoning Portugal if the enemy advanced; for, although sir John Cradock was not informed of their views, an officer in England, well acquainted with Portuguese customs, actually received orders, and was embarking, to aid the execution of this measure, when suddenly, the policy of the cabinet once more changed, and it was resolved to reinforce the army. This resolution, which may be attributed partly to the Austrian war, partly to the failure at Cadiz, partly to the necessity of satisfying public opinion in England, was accompanied by a measure, which laid the first solid basis on which to build a reasonable hope of success.

BOOK
VI.
———
1809.
March.

Appendix,
No. 6.

The Portuguese Government, either sponta-
neously, or brought thereto by previous negotiation,
had offered the command of their troops, with the
title of marshal, to an English general, and the British ministers accepted this offer, promised supplies
of arms, ammunition, clothing, and a subsidy for
the payment of a certain number of regular soldiers ;
thus obtaining a firm hold of the military resources
of Portugal, and gaining for the first time a position in the Peninsula suitable to the dignity of England and the contest in which she was engaged.
The Portuguese desired to have sir Arthur Wellesley, but he refused the offer, and it is said that
sir John Murray, (he who afterwards failed at
Taragona,) sir John Doyle, and even the marquis
of Hastings, a man undoubtedly well qualified,
sought for the office, but that powerful parliamentary
interest prevailing, Major-general Beresford was
finally chosen, and at the same time received the local
rank of lieutenant-general ; to the great discontent
of several officers of superior rank, who were displeased that a man without any visible claim to
superiority should be placed over their heads.

Information of this change was immediately sent
to sir John Cradock, and general Sherbrooke was
ordered to repair to Lisbon. The latter was close
to Cadiz harbour when the orders overtook him,
and his and Mackenzie's divisions arrived together in
the Tagus on the 12th of March, thus the fate
of Portugal was again fixed by England. But if
Mr. Frere's plan had been followed—if Mackenzie
had proceeded to Taragona, and nothing but foul
weather prevented him—if Sherbrooke's voyage
had not been delayed by storms, and that sailing
about from port to port, he had, as is most pro-

bable, been engaged in some other enterprize—if
Victor, obeying his orders, had marched to Abrantes
—if any of these events had happened, sir John
Cradock must have abandoned Portugal, and then
how infinitely absurd the proceedings of the English ministers would have appeared, and how justly
their puerile combinations would have excited the
scorn of Europe.

Marshal Beresford reached Lisbon early in March,
and after some negotiation, received from the
regency, power to appoint British officers to the
command of regiments, and to act without control
in any manner he should judge fitting to ameliorate
the condition and discipline of the Portuguese
forces; and this was the more important, as the military polity of Portugal, although fallen into disuse,
was severe, precise, and admirably calculated to
draw forth the whole strength of the nation. The army
could be completed by coercion ; the militia were
bound to assemble by regiments, and liable to any
service within the frontiers ; and the whole of the
remaining male population could be enrolled under
the name of *ordenanças*, numbered by battalions in
their different districts, and obliged under very
severe penalties to assemble, at the orders of the
local magistrates, either to work, to fight, to escort
convoys, or in any manner to aid the operations of
the army.

This affair arranged, Beresford fixed his quarters
at Thomar, collected the Portuguese troops in
masses, and proceeded to recast their system on the
model of the British army ; commencing, with stern
but wholesome rigour, a reform that, in process of
time, raised out of chaos an obedient, well disciplined, and gallant force, worthy of a high place

among the best in Europe ; for the Portuguese people, though easily misled and excited to wrath, are
of a docile orderly disposition, and very sensible of
just and honourable conduct in their officers. This
reform was, however, not effected at once, nor
without many crosses and difficulties being raised
by the higher orders and by the government—difficulties that general Beresford could never have
overcome, if he had not been directed, sustained,
and shielded, by the master spirit under whom he
was destined to work. The plan of giving to English officers the command of the Portuguese troops
was at first proceeded on with caution ; but after a
time, the ground being supposed safe, it was
gradually enlarged, until almost all the military
situations of importance were held by Englishmen,
which combined with other causes, gave rise to
numerous intrigues, not confined to the natives,
and as we shall find, in after times, seriously
threatening the power of the marshal, the existence of the British influence, and the success
of the war.

Sir John Cradock's situation was now materially
alleviated. The certainty of the Austrian war produced a marked change in the disposition of the
regency ; the arrival of Sherbrooke's and Mackenzie's divisions increased the British force to fourteen
thousand men, and the populace became more
cautious of offering insults. About the middle
of March, two thousand men being left to maintain
tranquillity in Lisbon, the remainder of the army
was encamped at Lumiar and Saccavem, and while
these things were passing at Lisbon, the aspect of
affairs changed also in other parts of the kingdom.
The bulk of the Portuguese regular troops,

amounting to ten or twelve thousand men, was collected by marshal Beresford, between the Tagus and the Mondego. Beyond the valley of the Mondego, colonel Trant had assembled a small corps of volunteers, students from the university, and general Vittoria was at the head of two regular battalions in Upper Beira. The bishop of Oporto was preparing to defend that town, with a mixed, but ferocious and insubordinate multitude. General Silveira, with four or five thousand men, had taken post in the Tras os Montes, and Romana, who had collected seven or eight thousand at Monterey, was in communication with him. Sir Robert Wilson, who was at the head of about three thousand men, had withdrawn the legion from Almeida, and sent a detachment to Bejar, but remained himself on the Agueda, watching the advanced posts of Lapisse. A few Portuguese regiments were extended from Salvatierra and Idanha to Alcantara. A permanent bridge of boats was laid over the Tagus at Abrantes, and there were small garrisons in that town and at Elvas.

All these forces united would not, however, with the exception of the British, have been capable of sustaining the shock of ten thousand French soldiers for half an hour, and the whole mass of the latter, then hanging on the frontier of Portugal, was above fifty thousand; gathering like clouds on the horizon, they threatened many points, but gave no certain indication of where the storm would break. Soult, indeed, with about twenty thousand men, was endeavouring to pass the Minho; but Lapisse, although constantly menacing Ciudad Rodrigo, kept his principal masses at Salamanca and Ledesma, and Victor had concentrated his between the Al-

berche and the Tietar. Hence Lapisse might join
either Soult or Victor, and the latter could march
by Placentia against Ciudad Rodrigo, while Soult
attacked Oporto; or he might draw Lapisse to him,
and penetrate Portugal by Alcantara; he might
pass the Tagus, attack Cuesta, and pursue him to
Seville; or, after defeating him, he might turn
short to the right, and enter the Alemtejo.

In this uncertainty, sir John Cradock, keeping
the British concentrated at Lumiar and Saccavem,
waited for the enemy to develope his plans, and, in
the mean time, endeavoured to procure the necessary
equipments for an active campaign. He directed
magazines to be formed at Coimbra and Abrantes;
urged the regency to exertion, took measures to
raise money, and despatched officers to Barbary to
procure mules. But while thus engaged, intelligence arrived that Victor having suddenly forced
the passage of the Tagus at Almaraz, was in pursuit of Cuesta on the road to Merida; that Soult,
having crossed the Minho, and defeated Romana
and Silveira, was within a few leagues of Oporto,
and that Lapisse had made a demonstration of
assaulting Ciudad Rodrigo. The junta of Oporto
now vehemently demanded aid from the regency,
and the latter, although not much inclined to the
bishop's party, proposed that sir John Cradock
uniting a part of the British forces to the Portuguese troops under marshal Beresford, should
march to the succour of Oporto. Beresford was
averse to trust the Portuguese under his immediate
command, among the disorderly multitude of that
city, but he thought the whole of the British army
should move in a body to Leiria, and from thence
either push on to Oporto, or return, according to

Sir J.
Cradock's
Correspon-
dence,
MSS.

the events that might occur in the latter town, and he endeavoured to persuade Cradock to follow this plan.

It was doubtful, he said, if Victor and Soult intended to co-operate in a single plan, but, on the supposition that it was so, he considered it essential to drive back or to overcome one before the other could come to his assistance. Victor was then in pursuit of Cuesta; if he continued that pursuit, it must be to enter Seville, or to cripple his opponent previous to the invasion of Portugal; in either case he would be in the Sierra Morena before he could hear of the march from Leiria, and, as Cradock had daily intelligence of his movements, there would be full time to relieve Oporto, and return again to the defence of Lisbon. If, however, Soult depended on the co-operation of Victor, he would probably remain on the right of the Duero until the other was on the Tagus, and Lapisse also would be contented for the present with capturing Ciudad Rodrigo and Almeida.

This unsound reasoning did not weigh with sir John Cradock, who resolved to preserve his central position, covering the capital at such a distance as to preclude the danger of being cut off from it by one army while he was engaged with another. Portugal, (he observed,) was in a state of anarchy equally incompatible with firm resistance and rapid movements; the peasantry were tumultuous and formidable to everybody but the enemy; Beresford himself acknowledged that the regular forces were mutinous, disregarding their officers, chosing when and where to rest, when to fight, when to remain in quarters, and altogether unfit to be trusted within the circle of the Oporto mischief. The British

Appendix, No. 12, section 1.

Appendix, No. 12, section 2.

troops, therefore, were the only solid resource; but they were too few to divide, and must act in a body, or not at all. Lisbon and Oporto were the enemy's objects; which was it most desirable to protect?—the former was of incomparably greater importance that the latter; the first was near, the second two hundred miles off; and, although the utmost exertions had been made, the army was not yet equipped for an active campaign. The troops were ill-clothed, and wanted shoes; the artillery was unhorsed; the commissariat possessed only a fourth part of the transport necessary for the conveyance of provisions and ammunition, and no activity could immediately supply these deficiencies, inasmuch as some of the articles required were not to be had in the country; to obtain others, the interference of the regency was necessary, but hitherto all applications to that quarter had been without any effect. Was it wise then to commence offensive operations in the north? The troops of Soult and Lapisse united were estimated at thirty thousand men, of which above five thousand were cavalry; the British could only bring fifteen guns and twelve thousand men, of all arms, into the field; yet, if they marched with the avowed intention of relieving Oporto, they must accomplish it, or be dishonoured!

Was it consistent with reason to march two hundred miles in search of a combat, which the very state of Oporto would render it almost impossible to gain, and for an object perhaps already lost? Suspicion was alive every where, if Oporto was already taken, the army must come back; that would be the signal for fresh tumults—for renewed cries that the country was to be abandoned; Lisbon would instantly be in a state of insurrection, and would be even more formidable to the British than the enemy; besides, it was impossible to reckon upon Cuesta's aid in keeping Victor employed. He was personally inimical to the English, and his principal object was to gain time for the increase and discipline of his own force. Victor was apparently pursuing Cuesta, but his parties had already appeared in the neighbourhood of Badajos, and there was nothing but a weak Portuguese garrison in Elvas to impede his march through the Alemtejo. To cover Lisbon and the Tagus was the wisest plan: fixed in some favourable position, at a prudent distance from that capital, he could wait for the reinforcements he expected from England. He invited the Portuguese troops to unite with him; a short time would suffice to establish subordination; and then the certainty that the capital could not be approached, except in the face of a really formidable army, would not only keep the enemy in check, but, by obliging him to collect in greater numbers for the attempts, would operate as a diversion in favour of Spain.

The general soundness of this reasoning is apparent, and it must not be objected to sir John Cradock that he disregarded the value of a central position, which might enable him to forestall the enemy; if the latter should march on his flank against Lisbon, the difficulty of obtaining true intelligence from the natives and his own want of cavalry rendered it utterly unsafe for him to divide his army, or to trust it any distance from the capital. Marshal Beresford's plan, founded on the supposition that Cradock could engage Soult at

Oporto, and yet quit him and return at his pleasure
to Lisbon, if Victor advanced, was certainly falla-
cious ; the advantages rested on conjectural, the
disadvantages on positive data : it was conjectural
that they could relieve Oporto, it was positive that
they would endanger Lisbon. The proposition was,
however, not made upon partial views ; but at this
period, other men, less qualified to advise, pestered
sir John Cradock with projects of a different stamp,
yet deserving of notice, as showing that the mania
for grand operations, which I have before marked
as the malady of the time, was still raging.

To make a suitable use of the British army was
the object of all these projectors, but there was a
marvellous variety in their plans. The regency
desired that the Portuguese and British troops
should co-operate for the relief of Oporto, and yet
protect Lisbon, objects which were incompatible.
Beresford advised that the whole English army should
march. The bishop was importunate to have some
British soldiers placed under his command, and he
recalled sir Robert Wilson to the defence of Oporto.
It appeared reasonable that the legion should defend
the city in which it was raised, but Mr. Frere wrote
from Seville, that sir Robert would do better to
remain ; he therefore accepted Spanish rank, and
refusing obedience to the prelate's orders, retained
his troops. The regency, glad of the opportunity,
approved of this proceeding, and adopted the legion
as a national corps. Meanwhile Romana was
earnest with Cradock for money, and wanted to
have a thousand British soldiers sent to aid the insurrection at Vigo ; but at the same time, Mr. Frere,
and colonel D'Urban, a corresponding officer placed

Cradock's
Correspon-
dence,
MSS.

by Cradock at Cuesta's head-quarters, proposed
other plans of higher pretensions.

Zaragoza, said the latter, has fallen, and ten
thousand French troops being thus released, are
marching towards Toledo; this is the moment to
give a fatal blow to Marshal Victor! It is one of
those critical occasions that seldom recur in war!
In a day or two sir Robert Wilson will be on the
Tietar with two thousand five hundred men; augment his force with a like number of Portuguese,
who may be drawn from Sobreira, Idanha, and Salvatierra, he shall thus turn the right and rear of
Victor's army, and his movement cannot be interrupted by the French force now at Salamanca and
Alva, because the communication from thence to
the Tagus by the passes of Banos and Tornevecas
is sealed up; while sir Robert Wilson thus gets
in the rear of Victor with five thousand men, Cuesta,
with twelve thousand infantry and two thousand
cavalry, shall attack the latter in front; a matter of
easy execution, because Cuesta can throw a pontoon
bridge over the Tagus, near Almaraz, in an hour
and a half, and the Conde de Cartoajal, who is at
Manzanares in La Mancha, with ten thousand
infantry and two thousand horse, will keep Sebastiani in check. The hope is great, the danger
small, and if a few British troops can be added
to the force on the Tietar, the success will be infallible!

There were, however, some grave objections to
this infallible plan. General Cuesta was near Almaraz, sir John Cradock was at Lisbon, and sir
Robert Wilson was at Ciudad Rodrigo. Their circuitous line of correspondence was thus above four
hundred miles long, and it is not very clear how the
combination was to be effected with that rapidity,

which was said to be essential to the success; neither is it very evident, that operations to be combined at such a distance, and executed by soldiers of different nations, would have been successful at all. On the one side, twenty thousand raw Portuguese and Spanish levies were to act on double external lines of operation ; on the other, twenty-five thousand French veterans waited in a central position, with their front and flanks covered by the Tagus and the Tietar. In such a contest it is possible to conceive a different result from that anticipated by colonel D'Urban.

Mr. Frere's plans were not less extensive, or less sanguine. When his project for assisting Catalonia had been frustrated, by the recal of general Mackenzie from Cadiz, he turned his attention to the north. Soult, he wrote to Sir John Cradock, tired of the resistance he has met with, will probably desist from his " *unaccountable project of entering Portugal, and occupying Gallicia at the same time.*" Let the British army, therefore, make a push to drive the enemy out of Salamanca and the neighbouring towns, while the Asturians, on their side, shall take possession of Leon and Astorga, and thus open the communication between the northern and southern provinces. Fearing, however, that if this proposal should not be adopted, the English general might be at a loss for some enterprise, Mr. Frere also recommended that the British army should march to Alcantara, and that the fortieth regiment, which hitherto he had retained at Seville, contrary to sir John Cradock's wishes, should join it at that place ; and then, said he, the whole operating by the northern bank of the Tagus, may, in concert with Cuesta, " *beat the French out of Toledo, and consequently out of Madrid.*"

Appendix,
No. 7.

Now, with respect to the first of these plans, Soult never had the intention of holding Gallicia, which was Marshal Ney's province; but he did propose to penetrate into Portugal, and he was not likely to abandon his purpose, because the only army capable of opposing him was quitting that kingdom, and making a " *push* " of four hundred miles to drive Lapisse out of Salamanca; moreover, the Asturians were watched by general Bonnet's division on one side, and by Kellerman on the other, and the fifth corps, not ten but fifteen thousand strong, having quitted Zaragoza, were at this time in the Valladolid country, close to Leon and Astorga.

Muster-
rolls of the
French
Army,
MSS.

With respect to the operations by the line of the Tagus, which were to drive Joseph out of Madrid, and consequently to attract the attention of all the French corps, it is to be observed, that sir John Cradock could command about twelve thousand men, Cuesta sixteen thousand, Cartoajal twelve thousand, making a total of forty thousand. But Soult had twenty-three thousand, Lapisse nine thousand, Victor was at the head of twenty-five thousand, Sebastiani could dispose of fifteen thousand, Mortier of a like number, the King's guards and the garrison of Madrid were twelve thousand, making a total of nearly a hundred thousand men. Hence while Mr. Frere and colonel D'Urban, confiding in Soult's inactivity, were thus plotting the destruction of Victor and Sebastiani, the first marshal stormed Oporto; the second, unconscious of his danger, crossed the Tagus, and defeated Cuesta's army at Medellin, and at the same moment Sebastiani routed Cartoajal's at Ciudad Real.

BOOK VII.

CHAPTER I.

HAVING described the unhappy condition of
Portugal and given a general view of the transactions in Spain, I shall now resume the narrative of
Soult's operations; thus following the main stream
of action; for the other marshals were appointed to
tranquillize the provinces already overrun by the
emperor, or to war down the remnants of the
Spanish armies, but the duke of Dalmatia's task
was to push onward in the course of conquest. Nor
is it difficult to trace him through the remainder of
a campaign, in which, traversing all the northern
provinces, fighting in succession the armies of three
different nations, and enduring every vicissitude of
war, he left broad marks of his career, and certain
proofs that he was an able commander and of a
haughty resolution in adversity.

It has been observed, in a former part of this
work, that the inhabitants of Coruña honourably
maintained their town until the safety of the fleet
which carried sir John Moore's army from the Spanish shores was secure; they were less faithful to
their own cause. Coruña might have defied irregular operations, and several weeks must have
elapsed before a sufficient battering train could have
been brought up to that corner of the Peninsula;
yet, a short negotiation sufficed to put the French
in possession of the place on the 19th of January,

and the means of attacking Ferrol were immediately organized from the resources of Coruña.

The harbour of Ferrol contained eight sail of the line, and some smaller ships of war. The fortifications were regular, there was an abundance of artillery, ammunition, and a garrison of seven or eight thousand men, consisting of soldiers, sailors, citizens, and armed countrymen, but their chiefs were treacherous. After a commotion in which the admiral Obregon was arrested, his successor Melgarejo surrendered upon somewhat better terms than those granted to Coruña, and thus in ten days were reduced two regular fortresses, which with more resolution might have occupied thirty thousand men for several months.

While yet before Ferrol the duke of Dalmatia received the following despatch, prescribing the immediate invasion of Portugal:—

"Before his departure from this place, (Valladolid,) the emperor forseeing the embarkation of the English army, drew up instructions for the ultimate operations of the duke of Elchingen and yourself." He orders that when the English army shall be embarked you will march upon Oporto with your four divisions, that is to say, the division of Merle, Mermet, Delaborde, and Heudelet, the dragoons of Lorge, and La Houssaye, and Franceschi's light cavalry, with the exception of two regiments that his majesty desires you to turn over to the duke of Elchingen, in order to make up his cavalry to four regiments."

" Your ' *corps d'armée*,' composed of seventeen regiments of infantry and ten regiments of cavalry, is destined for the expedition of Portugal, in combi-

nation with a movement the duke of Belluno is
going to effect. General Loison, some engineers,
staff and commissiarat officers, and thirteen Portuguese, all of whom belonged to the army formerly
in Portugal under the duke of Abrantes, have received instructions to join you immediately, and
you can transmit your orders for them to Lugo.
This is the 21st of January, and it is supposed you
cannot be at Oporto before the 5th of February, or
at Lisbon before the 16th. Thus, at that time,
namely, when you shall be near Lisbon, the ' corps
d'armée' of the duke of Belluno, composed of his
own three divisions, of the division Leval, and of
ten or twelve regiments of cavalry, forming a body
of thirty thousand men, will be at Merida, to make a
strong diversion in favour of your movement, and in
such a mode, as that he can push the head of a
column upon Lisbon if you find any great obstacles
to your entrance, which it is, however, presumed
will not be the case."

" General Lapisse's division of infantry, which
is at this moment in Salamanca, and general Maupetit's brigade of cavalry, will, when you shall be
at Oporto, receive the duke of Istria's orders to
march upon Ciudad Rodrigo and Abrantes, where
this division will again be under the command of
the duke of Belluno, who will send it instructions to
join him at Merida: I let you know this that you
may be aware of the march of Lapisse, on your
left flank, as far as Abrantes. Such are the last
orders I am charged to give you in the name of the
emperor: you will have to report to the king and
to receive his orders for your ulterior operations.
The emperor has unlimited confidence in your

talents for the fine expedition that he has charged
you with."

ALEXANDER,

Prince of Neufchatel, &c.

It was further intended, by Napoleon, that when
Lisbon fell, marshal Victor should invade Andalusia, upon the same line as Dupont had moved
the year before; and like Dupont, he was to have
been assisted by a division of the second corps,
which was to cross the Guadiana and march on
Seville. Meanwhile, the duke of Elchingen, whose
corps, reinforced by two regiments of cavalry and by
the arrival of stragglers, amounted to near twenty
thousand men, was to maintain Gallicia, confine the
Asturians within their own frontier line, and keep
open the communication with the second corps.
Thus, nominally eighty thousand, and in reality
sixty thousand men, were disposed for the conquest
of Lisbon, and in such a manner that forty thousand
would, after that had been accomplished, have
poured down upon Seville and Cadiz, at a time
when neither Portugal nor Andalusia were capable
of making any resistance. It remains to shew from
what causes this mighty preparation failed.

The gross numbers of the second corps amounted
to forty-seven thousand; but general Bonnet's division remained always at St. Ander, in observation
of the eastern Asturian frontier, eight thousand
were detached for the service of the general communications, and the remainder had, since the 9th
of November, been fighting and marching incessantly among barren and snowy mountains; hence,
stragglers were numerous, and twelve thousand men
were in hospital. The force, actually under arms,

Muster-
rolls of the
French ar-
my, MSS.

BOOK
VII.
_____
1809.
Jan.

S.
Journal of
Operations
of the se-
cond corps,
MSS.

did not exceed twenty-five thousand men, worn down with fatigue, barefooted, and without ammunition. They had outstripped their commissariat, the military chest was not come up, the draft animals were reduced in number, and extenuated by fatigue, the gun-carriages were shaken by continual usage, the artillery parc was still in the rear; and as the sixth corps had not yet passed Lugo, two divisions of the second corps were required to hold Coruña and Ferrol. Literally to obey the emperor's orders was consequently impossible, wherefore Soult taking quarters at St. Jago di Compostella, proceeded to re-organize his army.

Ammunition was fabricated from the loose powder found in Coruña; shoes were obtained partly by requisition, partly from the Spanish magazines, filled as they were with stores supplied by England; the artillery were soon refitted and the greatest part of the stragglers were rallied. In six days, the márshal thought himself in a condition to obey his orders, and, although his troops were still suffering from fatigue and privation, marched, on the 1st of February, with nineteen thousand infantry, four thousand cavalry, and fifty-eight pieces of artillery; but, to understand his operations, the state of Gallicia and the previous movements of Romana must be described.

When the Spanish army, on the 2d of January, crossed the line of sir John Moore's march, it was already in a state of disorganization. Romana, with the cavalry, plunged at once into the deep valleys of the Syl and the Minho, but the artillery and a part of his infantry were overtaken and cut up by Franceschi's cavalry; the remainder wandered in bands from one place to another, or dispersed to seek food and shelter among the villages in the mountains. General Mendizabel, with a small body, halted in the Val des Orres, and placing guards at the Puente de Bibey, a point of singular strength of defence, he purposed to cover the approaches to Orense on that side; but Romana himself, after wandering for a time, collected two or three thousand men, and took post, on the 15th, at Toabado, a village about twenty miles from Lugo. Meanwhile Ney arrived at that place, having detached some cavalry from Villa Franca to scour the valleys on his left, and also sent Marchand's division by the road of Orense to St. Jago and Coruña. Marchand dispersed Mendizabel's troops on the 17th, and after halting some days at Orense, where he established an hospital, continued his march to St. Jago.

The defeat of Mendizabel and the subsequent movements of Marchand's division completed the dispersion of Romana's army; the greatest part throwing away their arms, returned to their homes, and he himself, with his cavalry, and the few infantry that would follow him, crossed the Minho, passed the mountains, and, descending into the valley of the Tamega, took refuge, on the 21st, at Oimbra, a place on the frontier of Portugal, close to Monterey, where there was a small magazine, collected for the use of sir John Moore's army. In this obscure situation, unheeded by the French, he entered into communication with the Portuguese general Silveira, and with sir John Cradock, demanding money and arms from the latter; he endeavoured also to reassemble a respectable body of troops, but Blake and other officers deserted him, and these events and the general want of patriotic spirit drew from him the following observation :—

" I know not wherein the patriotism, so loudly
" vaunted, consists ; any reverse, any mishap pros-
" trates the minds of these people, and, thinking
" only of saving their own persons, they sacrifice
" their country and compromise their commander."

The people of Gallicia, poor, scattered, living
hardly, and, like all mountaineers, very tenacious
of the little property they possess, disregarded
political events which did not immediately and
visibly affect their interests. They were, with the
exception of those of the sea-port towns, but
slightly moved by the aggression of the French, as
long as that aggression did not extend to their
valleys, and hence, at first, they treated the English
and French armies alike. Sir David Baird's division, in its advance, paid generously for supplies,
yet it was regarded with jealousy and defrauded.
Soult's and Moore's armies, passing like a whirl-
wind, were beheld with terror, and the people fled
from both. The British and German troops that
marched to Vigo being conducted without judgement, were licentious, and as their number was
small, the people murdered stragglers, and showed
without disguise their natural hatred of strangers.
On several occasions, parties sent to collect cars
for the conveyance of the sick, had to sustain a
skirmish before the object could be obtained, and
five officers, misled by a treacherous guide, were
scarcely saved from death by the interference of an
old man, whose exertions, however, were not successful until one of the officers had been severely
wounded in the head. On the other hand, general
Marchand discovered so little symptoms of hostility, during his march to Orense, that he left his
hospital at that town without a guard, under the

joint care of Spanish and French surgeons, and the
duties of humanity were faithfuly discharged by
the former without hindrance from the people.

This quiescence did not last long : the French
generals were obliged to subsist their troops, by
requisitions extremely onerous to a people whose
property chiefly consisted of cattle. The many
abuses and excesses which always attend this mode
of supplying an army soon created a spirit of
hatred that Romana laboured incessantly to increase,
and he was successful; for, although a bad general,
he possessed intelligence and dexterity suited to the
task of exciting a population. Moreover, the monks
and friars laboured to the same purpose; and, while
Romana denounced death to those who refused to
take arms, the clergy menaced eternal perdition;
and all this was necessary, for the authority of the
supreme junta was only acknowledged as a matter
of necessity—not of liking. Gallicia, although
apparently calm, was, therefore, ripe for a general
insurrection, at the moment when the duke of
Dalmatia commenced his march from St. Jago di
Compostella.

From that town several roads lead to the Minho;
the principal one running by the coast line crosses
the Ulla, the Umia, the Vedra, and the Octaven,
and passes by Pontevedra and Redondela, to Tuy a
dilapidated fortress, situated on the Spanish side
of the Minho. The second, crossing the same rivers
nearer to their sources, passes by the Monte de
Tenteyros, and, entering the valley of the Avia,
follows the course of that river to Ribidavia, a
considerable town, situated at the confluence of the
Avia with the Minho, having a stone bridge over
the former, and a barque ferry on the latter river.

The third, turning the sources of the Avia, connects
St. Jago with Orense, and from Orense another
road passes along the right bank of the Minho,
and connects the towns of Ribidavia, Salvatierra,
and Tuy, ending at Guardia, a small fortress at the
mouth of the Minho.

As the shortest route to Oporto, and the only one
convenient for the artillery, was that leading by
Redondela and Tuy, and from thence by the coast,
the duke of Dalmatia formed the plan of passing the
S.
Journal of
Operations
MSS.
Minho between Salvatierra and Guardia ; wherefore
on the 1st of February, Franceschi, followed by
the other divisions in succession, took the Pontevedra
road, and at Redondela defeated a small body of
insurgents, and captured four pieces of cannon,
after which Vigo surrendered to one of his detachments, while he himself marched upon Tuy, and
took possession of that town and Guardia.   During
these operations La Houssaye's dragoons, quitting
Mellid, had crossed the Monte de Tenteyro,
passed through Ribidavia, and taken possession
of Salvatierra, on the Minho ; and general Soult,
the marshal's brother, who had assembled three
thousand stragglers and convalescents, between
Astorga and Carrion, received orders to enter
Portugal by Puebla de Senabria, and thus join the
main body.

The rainy season was in full torrent, every stream
and river overflowed its banks, the roads were deep,
and the difficulty of procuring provisions great.
These things, and the delivering over to marshal
Ney the administration of Ferrol and Coruña, where
the Spanish government and Spanish garrisons were
not only retained but paid by the French, delayed
the rear of the army so long that it was not until

the 15th or 16th that the whole of the divisions were assembled on the Minho, between Salvatierra, Guardia, and Redondela.

The Minho, from Melgaço to the mouth, forms the frontier of Portugal, the banks on both sides being guarded by a number of fortresses, originally of considerable strength, but at this time all in a dilapidated condition. The Spanish fort of Guardia fronted the Portuguese fort of Caminha; Tuy was opposed by Valenza; which was garrisoned, and the works in somewhat a better condition than the rest; Lapella, Moncao, and Melgaço, completed the Portuguese line. But the best defence at this moment was the Minho itself, which, at all times a considerable river, was now a broad and raging flood, and the Portuguese *ordenanzas* and militia who were in arms on the other side had removed all the boats. Nevertheless Soult, after examining the banks with care, decided upon passing at Campo Saucos, a little village where the ground was flatter, more favourable, and so close to Caminha that the army, once across, could easily seize that place, and the same day reach Viana on the Lima, from whence to Oporto was only three marches.

To attract the attention of the Portuguese, La Houssaye, who was at Salvatierra, spread his dragoons along the Minho, and attempted to push small parties across that river, above Melgaço; but the bulk of the army was concentrated in the neighbourhood of Campo Saucos, and a detachment seized the small sea-port of Bayona, in the rear. A division of infantry, and three hundred French marines released at Coruña and attached to the second corps, were then employed to transport some large fishing boats and some heavy guns from the harbour and fort of Guardia overland to Campo Saucos. This was effected by the help of rollers over more than two miles of rugged and hilly ground; it was a work of infinite labour, but from the 11th to the 15th, the troops toiled unceasingly, and the craft was launched in a small lake at the confluence of the Tamuga river with the Minho.

In the night of the 15th the heavy guns were placed in battery, and three hundred soldiers being embarked, the boats manned by the marines, dropped silently down the Tamuga into the Minho, and endeavoured to reach the Portuguese side of the latter river during the darkness; yet whether from the violence of the flood, or want of skill in the men, the landing was not effected before day-break, and the *ordenança* fell with great fury upon the first who got on shore, the foremost being all slain, the others pulled back, and regained their own side with great difficulty. This action was infinitely creditable to the Portuguese, and it had a surprising influence on the issue of the campaign. It was a gallant action, because it might reasonably have been expected that a tumultuous assemblage of half-armed peasants, collected on the instant, would have been dismayed at the sight of many boats filled with soldiers, some pulling across and others landing under the protection of a heavy battery that thundered from the midst of a multitude of troops, who clustered on the heights, or thronged to the edge of the opposite bank in eager expectation. It was an event of leading importance, inasmuch as it baffled an attempt that, being successful, would have ensured the fall of Oporto by the 21st of February, which was precisely the

period when general Mackenzie's division being at
Cadiz, sir John Cradock's troops were reduced to
almost nothing ; when the English ministers only
waited for an excuse to abandon Portugal ; when
the people of that country were in the very extremity of disorder ; when the Portuguese army was a
nullity, and when the regency was evidently preparing to receive the French with submission. It
was the period, also, when Soult was expected to
be at Lisbon, following the Emperor's orders, and,
consequently, Lapisse and Victor could not have
avoided to fulfil their part of the plan for the subjugation of Portugal.

The duke of Dalmatia's situation was now, al- See Plan 4.
though not one of imminent danger, extremely embarrassing, and more than ordinary quickness and
vigour were required to conduct the operations with
success. Posted in a narrow, contracted position,
he was hemmed in on the left by the Spanish insurgents, who had assembled immediately after La
Houssaye passed Orense, and who, being possessed
of a very rugged and difficult country, were, moreover, supported by the army of Romana, which
was said to be at Orense and Ribidavia. In the
French general's front was the Minho, broad, raging,
and at the moment impassable, while heavy rains
forbad the hope that its waters would decrease. To
collect sufficient means for forcing a passage would
have required sixteen days, but long before that
period, the subsistence for the army would have
entirely failed, and the Portuguese, being alarmed,
would have greatly augmented their forces on the
opposite bank. There remained then only to retrace his steps to St. Jago, or breaking through the

Spanish insurgents, to ascend the Minho, and open a way into Portugal by some other route.

Soult's attempt to pass the river had been baffled on the 15th of February, and on the 16th he was in full march towards Ribidavia upon a new line of operations, and this promptitude of decision was supported by an equally prompt execution. La Houssaye, with his dragoons, quitted Salvatierra, and, keeping the edge of the Minho, was galled by the fire of the Portuguese from the opposite bank, but before evening, he twice broke the insurgent bands, and, in revenge for some previous excesses of the peasantry, burnt the villages of Morentan and Cobreira : meanwhile the main body of the army, passing the Tea river, at Salvatierra and Puente d'Arcos, marched, by successive divisions, along the main road from Tuy to Ribidavia.

Between Franquera and Canizar the route was cut by the streams of the Morenta and Noguera rivers, and, behind those torrents, eight hundred Gallicians, having barricadoed the bridges and repulsed the advanced parties of cavalry, stood upon their defence. The 17th, at daybreak, the leading brigade of Heudelet's division forced the passage, and pursued the Spaniards briskly, but, when within a short distance of Ribidavia, the latter rallied upon eight or ten thousand insurgents, arrayed in order of battle, on a strong hill, covering the approaches to that town. At this sight the advanced guard halted until the remainder of the division and a brigade of cavalry were come up, and then, under the personal direction of Soult, the French assailed and drove the Gallicians, fighting, through the town and across the Avia. The loss of the van-

quished was very considerable, the bodies of twenty
priests were found amongst the slain, and either
from fear or patriotism, every inhabitant had quitted Ribidavia.

The 18th, a brigade of infantry scouring the valley
of the Avia, dispersed three or four thousand of
the insurgents, who were disposed to make a second
stand on that side; a second brigade, pushing on
to Barbantes, seized a ferry-boat on the Minho,
close to that place, and being joined, the same
evening, by the infantry who had scoured the
valley of the Avia, and by Franceschi's cavalry, on
the 19th entered Orense in time to prevent the
bridge over the Minho from being cut; La Houssaye's dragoons then took post at Maside, while the
remainder of the horse and Laborde's infantry united
at Ribidavia; the artillery were however still between Tuy and Salvatierra, under the protection of
Merle's and Mermet's divisions.   Thus, in three
days, the duke of Dalmatia had, with admirable
celerity and vigour, extricated his army from a contracted unfavourable country, strangled a formidable
insurrection in its birth, and at the same time opened
a fresh line of communication with St. Jago, and an
easy passage into Portugal.

The 20th, a regiment being sent across the
Minho, by the ferries of Barbantes and Ribidavia,
defeated the insurgents of the left bank, advanced
to the Arroyo river, and took post on the heights of
Merea.   The army with the exception of the division
guarding the guns was concentrated the same day
at Orense; but the efforts of the artillery had been
baffled by the difficulties of the road from Tuy to
Ribidavia, and this circumstance viewed in conjunction with the precarious state of the communica-

tion, a daily increasing sick-list, and the number of
small detachments required to protect the rear,
seemed to forbid the invasion of Portugal.   A man
of ordinary genius would have failed.   The duke of
Dalmatia with ready boldness resolved to throw the
greatest part of his artillery and the whole of his
other incumbrances into Tuy, as a place of arms,
then relinquishing all communication with Gallicia,
for the moment, to march in one mass directly upon
Oporto; from whence, if successful, he proposed to
re-open his communication with Tuy, by the line
of the coast, recover his artillery and re-establish a
regular system of operations.

In pursuance of this resolution, sixteen of the
lightest guns and six howitzers, with a proportion
of ammunition-waggons, were, with infinite labour
and difficulty, transported to Ribidavia; the remaining thirty-six pieces and a vast parc of carriages,
carrying ammunition, and hospital, and commissariat
stores, were put into Tuy, where general La Martiniere was left with an establishment of artillery and
engineer officers, a garrison of five hundred men fit
to carry arms, and nine hundred sick.   All the
stragglers, convalescents, and detachments, coming
from St. Jago, and the military chest, which was
still in the rear, guarded by six hundred infantry,
were likewise directed upon Tuy, the gates were
shut, and La Martiniere was abandoned to his
own resources.

The men in hospital at Ribidavia were now forwarded to Orense, and the marshal's quarters were
established at the latter town on the 24th, but other
obstacles were to be vanquished before the army
could commence the march into Portugal.   The
gun-carriages had been so shaken in the transit from

Tuy to Ribidavia that three days were required to
repair them; it was extremely difficult to obtain
provisions, and numerous bands of the peasants
were still in arms, nor were they quelled until
combats had taken place at Gurzo, on the Monte
Blanco, in the Val d'Ornes, and up the valley of
Avia, in which the French wasted time, lost men,
and expended ammunition that could not be replaced. Soult endeavoured to soften the people's
feelings by kindness and soothing proclamations;
and as he enforced a strict discipline among his
troops, his humane and politic demeanour, joined
to the activity of his moveable columns, abated the
fierceness of the peasantry. The inhabitants of
Ribidavia soon returned to their houses, those of
Orense had never been very violent, and now becoming friendly, even lent assistance to procure provisions. It was not, however, an easy task to
restrain the soldiers within the bounds of humanity :
the frequent combats, the assassination, the tor-
turing of isolated men, and the privations endured,
had so exasperated the French troops, that the
utmost exertions of their general's authority could
not always control their revenge.

Appendix,
No. 13.

While the duke of Dalmatia was thus preparing
for a formidable inroad, his adversaries were a prey
to the most horrible anarchy. The bishop, always
intent to increase his own power, had assembled
little short of fifty thousand armed persons in
Oporto, and commenced a gigantic line of entrenchment on the hills to the northward of that city.
This worse than useless labour so completely occupied all persons, that the defence of the strong
country lying between the Duero and the Minho
was totally neglected, and when the second corps

appeared on the bank of the latter river, the
northern provinces were struck with terror; then it
was that the people, for the first time, understood
the extent of their danger; then it was that the
bishop, aroused from his intrigues, became sensible
that the French were more terrible enemies than
the regency. Once impressed with this truth, he
became clamorous for succour; he recalled Sir
Robert Wilson from the Agueda, he hurried on the
labour of the entrenchments, and he earnestly pressed
sir John Cradock for assistance, demanding arms,
ammunition, and a reinforcement of British soldiers.
Sir Robert Wilson, as I have already related,
disregarded his orders; but the British general,
although he refused to furnish him with troops,
supplied him with arms, and very ample stores of
powder, sending artillery and engineer officers to
superintend the construction of the defensive works,
and to aid in the arrangements for a reasonable
system of operations.

Appendix,
No. 3, sec-
tion 6.

The people were, however, become too headstrong
and licentious to be controlled, or even advised, and
the soldiers being drawn into the vortex of insubordination, universal and hopeless confusion prevailed.
Don Bernadim Friere was the legal commander-in-
chief of the Entre Minho e Douro, but all the
generals claimed equal and independent authority,
each over his own force; and this was, perhaps, a
matter of self-preservation, for general and traitor
were, at that period, almost synonymous; to obey
the orders of a superior against the momentary
wishes of the multitude was to incur instant death.
Nor were there men wanting who found it profitable
to inflame the passions of the mob, and direct its
blind vengeance against innocent persons adverse

Appendix,
No. 3, sec-
tion 1.

to the prelate's faction, which was not without opponents even in Oporto.

Such was the unhappy state of affairs, when the undisciplined gallantry of the peasants, baffling the efforts of the French to cross the Minho at Campo Saucos, obliged Soult to march by Orense. A part of the regular troops were immediately sent forward to the Cavado river, where they were joined by the *ordenanzas* and the militia of the district, but all in a state of fearful insubordination, and there were no arrangements made for the regular distribution of provisions, or of any one necessary supply. Among the troops despatched from Oporto was the second battalion of the Lusitanian legion, nine hundred strong, well armed, well equipped, and commanded by baron Eben, a native of Prussia, who, without any known services to recommend him, had suddenly attained the rank of major in the British service. This man destined to act a conspicuous part in Portuguese tragedy, had been left at Oporto when sir Robert Wilson marched to Almeida; his orders were to follow with the second battalion of the legion, when its clothing and equipment should be completed, but he retained the troops, to push his own fortune under the prelate's auspices.

General Freire having reached the Cavado, was joined by fourteen or fifteen thousand militia and *ordenanzas;* fixing his head-quarters at Braga, he sent detachments to occupy the posts of Salamonde and Ruivaens in his front, and, unfortunately for himself, endeavoured to restrain his troops from wasting their ammunition by wanton firing in the streets and on the roads. This exertion of command was heinously resented; Freire, being willing

Appendix,
No. 3, sec-
tion 6.

to uphold the authority of the regency, had been
for some time obnoxious to the bishop's faction;
already he was pointed to as a suspected person, and
the multitude were inimically disposed towards him.

Meanwhile, general Silveira, assuming the command of the Tras os Montes, advanced to Chaves,
and put himself in communication with the marquis
of Romana, who, having remained tranquil at
Oimbra and Monterey since the 21st of January,
had been joined by his dispersed troops, and was
again at the head of nine or ten thousand men.
Silveira's force was about four thousand, half
regulars half militia, and he was accompanied by
many of the *ordenanças;* but here, as elsewhere, all
were licentious, insubordinate, and disdainful of their
general; moreover the national enmity between them
and the Spaniards having overcome their sense of a
common cause and common danger, the latter were
Appendix, evilly treated, and a deadly feud subsisted between
No. 6, sec-
tion 3. the two armies.   The generals, indeed, agreed to
act in concert, offensively and defensively, yet
neither of them were the least acquainted with the
numbers, intention, or even the position of their
antagonists: and it is a proof of Romana's unfitness
for command that he, having the whole population
at his disposal, was yet ignorant of every thing,
relating to his enemy that it behoved him to know.
The whole of the French force in Gallicia, at this
period, was about forty-five thousand men, Romana
estimated it at twenty-one thousand; the number
under Soult was above twenty-four thousand, Romana supposed it to be twelve thousand; and
among these he included general Marchand's division of the sixth corps, which he always imagined
to be a part of the duke of Dalmatia's army.

The Spanish general was so elated at the spirit
of the peasants about Ribidavia, that he anticipated
nothing but victory; he knew also that on the Arosa, an estuary, running up towards St. Jago de Compostella, the inhabitants of Villa Garcia had risen, and, being joined by all the neighbouring districts, were preparing to attack Vigo and Tuy; hence, partly from his Spanish temperament, partly from his extreme ignorance of war, he was convinced that the French only thought of making their escape out of Gallicia, and that even in that Appendix, No. 6, section 3. they would be disappointed. To effect their destruction more certainly, he also, as we have seen, pestered sir John Cradock for succours in money Cradock's Correspondence, MSS. and ammunition, and desired that the insurgents on the Arosa might be assisted with a thousand British soldiers. Cradock anxious to support the cause, although he refused the troops, sent ammunition, and five thousand pounds in money, but before it arrived Romana was beaten, and in flight.

The combined Spanish and Portuguese forces, amounting to sixteen thousand regulars and militia, besides *ordenanças*, were posted in a straggling unconnected manner along the valley of the Tamega, extending from Monterey, Verim, and Villaza, to near Chaves, a distance of more than fifteen miles. This was the first line of defence for Portugal. Freire and Eben, with fourteen guns and twenty-five thousand men, were at Braga, in second line, their outposts being on the Cavado and at the strong passes of Ruivaens and Venda Nova; but of these twenty-five thousand only six thousand were armed with muskets, and it is to be observed that the militia and troops of the line differed from the armed peasantry only in name, save that their faulty discipline and mutinous disposition rendered them less active and intelligent as skirmishers, without making them fitter for battle. The bishop, with his disorderly and furious rabble, formed the third line, occupying the entrenchments that covered Oporto. Such was the state of affairs, and such were the depositions made to resist the duke of Dalmatia; but his army, although galled and wearied by continual toil, and, when halting, disturbed and vexed by the multitude of insurrections, was, when in motion, of a power to overthrow and disperse these numerous bands, even as a great ship feeling the wind, breaks through and scatters the gun-boats that have gathered round her in the calm.

CHAPTER II.

SECOND INVASION OF PORTUGAL.

THE Entre Minho e Douro and the Tras os Montes lying together, form the northern part of Portugal; the extreme breadth of either, when measured from the frontier to the Douro, does not exceed seventy miles. The river Tamega, running north and south, and discharging itself into the Douro, forms the boundary line between them; but there is, to the west of this river, a succession of rugged mountain ridges, which, under the names of Sierra de Gerez, Sierra de Cabrera, and Sierra de Santa Catalina, form a second barrier, nearly parallel to the Tamega, and across some part of these ridges, an invader coming from the eastward, must pass to arrive at Oporto.

Other Sierras, running also in a parallel direction with the Tamega, cut the Tras os Montes in such a manner, that all the considerable rivers flowing north and south tumble into the Douro. But as the western ramifications of the Sierras de Gerez and Cabrera shoot down towards the sea, the rivers of the Entre Douro e Minho discharge their waters into the ocean, and consequently flow at right angles to those of Tras os Montes. Hence it follows, that an enemy penetrating to Oporto, from the north, would have to pass the Lima, the Cavado, and the Ave, to reach Oporto; and if, coming from the east, he invaded the Tras os Montes, all the rivers and intervening ridges of that province must be crossed, before the Entre Minho e Douro could be reached.

The duke of Dalmatia was, however, now in such a position, near the sources of the Lima and the Tamega rivers, that he could choose whether to penetrate by the valley of the first into the Entre Minho e Douro, or by the valley of the second into the Tras os Montes, and there was also a third road, leading between those rivers through Montalegre upon Braga; but this latter route, passing over the Sierra de Gerez, was impracticable for artillery.

The French general had, therefore, to consider—

1°. If, following the course of the Lima, he should disperse the insurgents between that river and the Minho, and then recovering his artillery from Tuy, proceed against Oporto by the main road leading along the sea coast.

2°. If he should descend the Tamega, take Chaves, and then continuing his route to Villa Real, near the Douro, take the defences of Tras os Montes in reverse; or, turning to the right, cross the Sierra de Cabrera by the pass of Ruivaens, enter Braga, and so go against Oporto.

The first project was irregular, and hazardous, inasmuch as Romana and Silveira could have fallen upon the flank and rear of the French during their march through a difficult country; but as the position of those generals covered Chaves, to attack them was a preliminary measure to either plan, and with this object, Soult moved on the 4th of March. The 5th, his van being at Villa Real and Penaverde, he sent a letter by a flag of truce to Romana in which after exposing all the danger of

CHAP.
II.

1809.
March.
Sir J. Cra-
dock's pa-
pers, MSS.

the latter's situation, he advised him to submit; no answer was returned, nor would the bearer have been suffered to pass the outposts, but that Romana himself was in the rear, for he dreaded that such an occurrence would breed a jealousy of his conduct, and, perhaps, cause his patriotism to be undervalued.

This failing, three divisions of infantry and one of cavalry marched the next morning against Monterey, while La Houssaye's dragoons, taking the road of Laza, covered the left flank, and pushed parties as far La Gudina, on the route to Puebla de Senabria. The fourth division of infantry remained at Villa del Rey, to cover the passage of the sick and wounded men from Orense, for the duke of Dalmatia, having no base of operations, transported his hospitals, and other incumbrances, from place to place as the army moved; acting in this respect after the manner of the Roman generals, when invading a barbarous country.

As the French advanced, the Spaniards abandoned their positions in succession, spiked the guns in the dilapidated works of Montery, and after a slight skirmish at Verim, took the road to Puebla de Senabria; but Franceschi followed close, and overtaking two or three thousand as they were passing a rugged mountain, assailed their rear with a battalion of infantry, and at the same time leading his horsemen round both flanks, headed the column, and obliged it to halt. The Spaniards, trusting to the rough ground, drew up in one large square to receive the charge. Franceschi had four regiments of cavalry, each regiment settled itself against the face of a square, and then the whole, with loud

cries, bore down swiftly upon their opponents; the
latter unsteady, irresolute, dismayed, shrunk from
the fierce assault, and were instantly trampled down
in heaps. Those who escaped the horses' hoofs
and the edge of the sword became prisoners, but
twelve hundred bodies were stretched lifeless on the
field of battle, and Franceschi continued his movements on La Gudina.

Romana was at Semadems, several miles in the
rear of Verim, when his vanguard was attacked, and
there was nothing to prevent him from falling back
to Chaves with his main body, according to a plan
before agreed upon between him and Silveira; but

Appendix,
No. 6, sec-
tion 3.
either from fear, or indignation at the treatment his
soldiers had received at the hands of the Portuguese, he left Silveira to his fate, and made off
with six or seven thousand men towards Bragança;
from thence passing by Puebla de Senabria, he regained the valley of the Syl. Meanwhile, two
thousand Portuguese infantry, with some guns,
issuing from the side of Villaza, cut the French
line of march at the moment when Franceschi and
Heudelet having passed Monterey, Laborde was
approaching that place; a slight combat ensued,
the Portuguese lost their guns, and were driven
down the valley of the Tamega as far as the village

S.
Journal of
Operations
MSS.
of Outeiro, within their own frontier. This defeat,
and the flight of Romana, had such an effect upon
the surrounding districts that the Spanish insurgents returned in crowds to their habitations
and delivered up their arms. Some of the clergy,
also, changing their opinions, exhorted the people
to peace, and the prisoners taken on the 6th,
being dissatisfied with Romana's conduct, and

moved by their hatred of the Portuguese, entered
the French service.

These affairs occupied Soult until the 9th, during
which period his outposts were pushed towards
Chaves, Montalegre, and La Gudina, but the main
body remained at Verim to cover the arrival of the
sick at Monterey, while Silveira, thus beaten at
Villaza, and deserted by Romana, fell back on the
7th to a strong mountain position, one league behind
Chaves, from whence he could command a view of
all the French movements as far as Monterey; his
ground was advantageous, but his military talents
were moderate, his men, always insubordinate,
were now mutinous, and many of the officers were
disposed to join the French. He wished to abandon Chaves, but his troops resolved to defend it,
and three thousand five hundred men actually did
throw themselves into that town, in defiance of him;
for he was already, according to the custom of the
day, pronounced a traitor and declared worthy of that
death which he would inevitably have suffered, but Appendix,
No. 6, sec-
that some of his soldiers still continued to respect tion 3.
his orders.

The 10th, the convoy of French sick was close to s.
Journal of
Monterey, and as Romana's movement was known Operations
MSS.
to be a real flight, and not made with a design to
create fresh insurrections in the rear, the French
troops were again put in motion towards Chaves;
Merle's division however remained at Verim to
protect the hospital, and Franceschi's took the road
of La Gudina, as if he had been going towards
Salamanca. A report that he had actually entered
that town reached Lisbon, and was taken as an
indication that Soult would not pass the Portuguese
frontier at Chaves, but Franceschi quickly returned,

by Osonio and Feces de Abaxa, and being assisted
by Heudelet's division, invested Chaves on the left
bank of the Tamega, while Laborde, Mermet, La
Houssaye, and Lorge, descending the right bank,
beat the Portuguese outposts, and getting possession
of a fort close under the walls, completed the investment of the town. The place was immediately
summoned to surrender, but no answer was returned,
and the garrison, like men bereft of their wits and
fighting with the air, kept up a continual fire of
musketry and artillery until the 12th, when they
surrendered on receiving a second summons, more
menacing than the first. The 13th the French
entered the town, and Silveira retired to Villa
Real.

The works of Chaves were in a bad state; few
of the fifty guns mounted on the ramparts were fit
for service, but there was a stone-bridge, and the
town was in many respects more suitable for a
place of arms than Monterey; wherefore the sick
were brought down from the latter place, and an
hospital was established for twelve hundred men,
the number now unfit to carry arms. The fighting
men were reduced to twenty-one thousand, and
Soult, partly from the difficulty of guarding his prisoners, partly from a desire to abate the hostility
of the Portuguese, permitted the militia and
ordenanças to return to their homes, after taking an
oath not to resume their arms; to some of the
poorest he also gave money and clothes, and he
enrolled, at their own request, the few regular troops
taken in Chaves.

This wise and gentle proceeding was much
blamed by some of his officers, especially by those
who had served under Junot. They desired that

Chaves might be assaulted, and the garrison put to
the sword, for they were embued with a personal
hatred of the Portuguese, and being averse to serve
in the present expedition, endeavoured, as it would
appear, to thwart their general, yet the prudence
of his conduct was immediately visible in the
softened feelings of the country people, and the
scouting parties being no longer molested spread
themselves, some on the side of Bragança and Villa Journal of
Operations
MSS.
Real, others in the Entre Minho e Douro. The
former reported that there was no enemy in a condition to make head in the Tras os Montes, but the
latter fell in with the advanced guard of Freire's
army at Ruivaens, on the road to Braga.

From Chaves Soult could operate against Oporto, Journal of
Operations
MSS.
either by the Tras os Montes or the Entre Minho e
Douro, the latter presented the strongest position,
but the road was shorter and more practicable for
guns, than that by the valley of the Tamega, and the
communication with Tuy could be sooner recovered;
hence, when the scouts brought intelligence that a
Portuguese army was at Braga, the French general
decided to penetrate by that line.

The road from Chaves to Braga entered a deep
and dangerous defile, or rather a succession of defiles, which extended from Venda Nova to Ruivaens,
and re-commenced after passing the Cabado river;
Freire's advanced guards, composed of *ordenanças*,
occupied those places, and he had also a detachment
under Eben on the road of Montalegre; he however recalled the latter on the 14th, on the 16th
Franceschi forced the defile of Nova; and the remainder of the French army being formed in alternate masses of cavalry and infantry, began to pass
the Sierra de Cabrera; meanwhile Lorge's dragoons

descending the Tamega, ordered rations for the whole army along the road to Villa Real, and then, suddenly retracing their steps, rejoined the main body.

The 17th, Franceschi, being reinforced with some infantry, won the bridge of Ruivaens, and entered Salamonde; the Portuguese, covered by Eben's detachment, which had arrived at St. Joa de Campo, then fell back on the Pico de Pugalados, close to Braga, and Franceschi took post at Carvalho Este, two leagues in front of that city.

Soult now expecting to reach Braga without further opposition, caused his artillery, guarded by Laborde's division, to enter the pass of Venda Nova; but the *ordenanças*, reinforced by some men from the side of Guimaraens, immediately re-assembled, and clustering on the mountains to the left of the column of march, attacked it with great fierceness and subtlety.

The peasants of the northern provinces of Portugal, unlike the squalid miserable population of Lisbon and Oporto, are robust, handsome, and exceedingly brave; their natural disposition is open and obliging, and they are, when rightly handled as soldiers, docile, intelligent, and hardy. They are, however, vehement in their anger; and being now excited by the exhortations and personal example of their priests, they came rushing down the sides of the hills, and many of them, like men deprived of reason, broke furiously into the French battalions, and were there killed. The others, finding their efforts unavailing, fled, and were pursued a league up the mountain by some battalions sent out against them; yet they were not abashed, and making a circuit behind the hills, fell upon the rear of the line of march, killed fifty of the stragglers, and plundered the baggage. Thus galled, the French slowly, and with much trouble, passed the long defiles of Venda Nova, Ruivaens, and Salamonde, and gathered by degrees in front of Freire's position.

That general was no more; and his troops, reeking from the slaughter of their commander, were raging, like savage beasts, at one moment congregating near the prisons to murder some wretch within, at another rushing tumultuously to the outposts, with a design to engage the enemy. The *ordenanças* of the distant districts also came pouring into the camp, dragging with them suspected persons, and adding to the general distraction.

The unfortunate Freire, unable to establish order in his army, had resolved to retreat, and in pursuance of that design, recalled Eben on the 14th, giving directions to the officers at the different outposts in front of Braga to retire at the approach of the enemy. This, and his endeavour to prevent the waste of ammunition, gave effect to a plan which had been long prepared by the bishop's faction for his destruction. In passing through Braga, he was openly reviled in the streets by some of the *ordenanças;* and as the latter plainly discovered their murderous intention, he left the army; he was however seized on the 17th, at a village behind Braga, and brought back: what followed is thus described by baron Eben, in his official report to sir John Cradock:—

" I did not reach Braga until nine o'clock in the morning of the 17th. I found every thing in the greatest disorder; the houses shut, the people flying

in all directions, and part of the populace armed
with guns and pikes. Passing through the streets,
I was greeted with loud *vivas*. Though the people
knew me, I could not guess the meaning of this.
At the market-place, I was detained by the rapidly-
increasing populace, who took the reins of my
horse, crying out loudly, that they were ready to
do any thing to defend the city; requesting me
to assist them, and speaking in the lowest terms of
their general. I promised them to do all in my
power to aid their patriotic zeal; but said that I
must first speak to him. Upon this, they suffered
me to proceed, accompanied by about a hundred
of them: but I had not got far on my way to his
quarters, when I saw him on foot, conducted by a
great armed multitude, who suffered no one to pass,
and on my attempting it, threatened to fire. I
was, therefore, obliged to turn my horse, and this
the people applauded. Two men had hold of the
general's arms, his sword was taken from him, and
the people abused him most vehemently. On my
way back to the market-place, they wanted to shoot
me, taking me for general Freire; but I was saved
by a soldier of the legion, who explained the
mistake. When I reached the market-place, I
found about a thousand men drawn up: I communicated to them my determination to assist them in
their laudable endeavours to defend themselves,
provided they would first permit me to speak to the
general, for whose actions I promised to be answerable as long as I should be with him. I had
ordered a house to be got ready for my reception,
where the general arrived, accompanied as before;
I saluted him with respect, at which they plainly

discovered their disapprobation. I repeated my
proposal, but they would not listen to it. I perceived the danger of the general, and proposed to
take him to my quarters. My adjutant offered him
his arm: when I spoke to him, he only replied,
' save me !'

   " At the entrance of my house, I was surrounded
by thousands, and heard the loud cry of ' kill ! kill !'
I now took hold of him, and attempted to force
my way into the house, and a gentleman slightly
wounded him with the point of his sword, under
my arm. He collected all his strength, rushed
through them, and hid himself behind the door of
the house. The people surrounded me, and forced
me from the house. To draw the attention of the
people from the general, I ordered the drummers
to beat the alarm, and formed the *ordenanças* in
ranks ; but they kept a constant fire upon my house,
where the general still was. As a last attempt to
save him, I now proposed that he should be conducted to prison, in order to take a legal trial ;
this was agreed to, and he was conducted there in
safety. I now hoped that I had succeeded, as the
people demanded to be led against the enemy, now
rapidly advancing, in number about two thousand.
I again formed them, and advanced with them ;
but soon after, I heard the firing again, and was
informed that the people had put the general to
death with pikes and guns. I was now proclaimed
general."

   When this murder was perpetrated, the people
seemed satisfied, and Eben announcing the approach
of a British force from Oporto, sent orders to the
outposts to stand fast, as he intended to fight; but
another tumult arose, when it was discovered that

BOOK
VII.

1809.
March.
Eben's Re-
ports, MS.

an officer of Freire's staff, one Villaboas, was in Eben's quarters. Several thousand *ordenanças* instantly gathered about the house, and the unhappy man was haled forth and stabbed to death at the door, the mob all the time shouting and firing volleys in at the windows. Yet, when their fury was somewhat abated, they obliged their new general to come out and show that he had not been wounded, and expressed great affection for him.

In the course of the night the legion marched in from Pico de Pugalados, and the following morning a reinforcement of six thousand *ordenanças* came up in one mass. Fifty thousand dollars also arrived in the camp from Oporto; for the Portuguese, like the Spaniards, commonly reversed the order of military arrangements, leaving their weapons in store, and bringing their encumbrances to the field of battle. In the evening the corregidor and two officers of rank, together with many persons of a meaner class, were brought to the town as prisoners and put in jail, the armed mob being with difficulty restrained from slaying them on the way thither. In this distracted manner they were proceeding when Franceschi arrived at Carvalho on the 17th, and, surely, if that bold and enterprising soldier could have obtained a glimpse of what was passing, or known the real state of affairs, he would have broke into the midst of them with his cavalry; for, of the twenty-five thousand men composing the

Cradock's
Papers,
MSS.
S.
Journal of
Operations
MSS.

whole of the Portuguese force, eighteen thousand were only armed with pikes, the remainder had wasted the greatest part of their ammunition, and the powder in store was not made up in cartridges. But Braga, situated in a deep hollow, was hidden from him, and the rocky and wooded hills surrounding it were occupied by what appeared a formidable multitude; hence Franceschi, although reinforced by a brigade of infantry, was satisfied by feints and slight skirmishes to alarm his opponents, and to keep them in play until the other divisions of the French army could arrive.

While these events were passing at Braga, Silveira again collected a considerable force of militia and *ordenanças* in the Tras os Montes, and captain Arentschild, one of the officers sent by sir John Cradock to aid the bishop, also rallied a number of fugitives at Guimaraens and Amarante. In Oporto, however, the multitude, obeying no command, were more intent upon murder than upon defence.

Eben's posts extended from Falperra, on the route of Guimaraens to the Ponte Porto, on the Cavado river; but his principal force was stationed on a lofty ridge called the Monte Adaufé, which, at the distance of six or seven miles from Braga, crossed the road to Chaves. The left, or western, end, overhanging the river Cavado, covered the detachment guarding the Ponte Porto. The right was wooded and masked by the head of a deep ravine, but beyond this wood the ridge, taking a curved and forward direction, was called the Monte Vallonga, and a second mass of men was posted there, but separated from those on the Monte Adaufé by an interval of two miles, and by the ravine and wood before mentioned. A third body, being pushed still more in advance, crowned an isolated hill, flanking the Chaves road, being intended to take the French in rear when the latter should attack the Monte Adaufé.

Behind the Monte Vallonga, and separated from it by a valley three miles wide, the ridge of Falperra was guarded by detachments from Guimaraens and from Braga.

The road to Braga, leading directly over the centre of the Monte Adaufé, was flanked on the left by a ridge shooting perpendicularly out from that mountain, and ending in a lofty mass of rocks which overhangs Carvalho Esté. But the Portuguese neglected to occupy either these rocks or the connecting ridge, and Franceschi seized the former on the 17th.

The 18th, Soult arrived in person, and, wishing to prevent a battle, released twenty prisoners, and sent them in with a proclamation couched in conciliatory language, and offering a capitulation; the trumpeter who accompanied them was however detained, and the prisoners were immediately slain. The next day Eben brought up all his reserves to the Adaufé, and the Portuguese on the isolated hill in front of Monte Vallonga took possession of Lanhoza, a village half-way between that hill and the rocky height occupied by Franceschi on the 17th.

Two divisions of French infantry being now up, Soult caused one of them and the cavalry to attack Lanhoza, from whence the Portuguese were immediately driven, and, being followed closely, lost their own hill also. The other French division took post, part in Carvalho, part on the rocky headland, and six guns were carried to the latter during the night; in this position the French columns were close to the centre of the Portuguese, and could, by a slight movement in advance, separate Eben's wings. The rest of the army was at hand, and a general attack was arranged for the next morning.

BATTLE OF BRAGA.

The 20th, at nine o'clock, the French were in motion : Franceschi and Mermet, leaving a detachment on the hill they had carried the night before, endeavoured to turn the right of the people on the Monte Vallonga.

Laborde, supported by La Houssaye's dragoons, advanced against the centre by the ridge connecting Carvalho with the Monte Adaufé.

S.
Journal of
Operations
MSS.

Heudelet, with a part of his division and a squadron of cavalry, attacked Eben's left, with the view of seizing the Ponte Porto.

The Portuguese opened a straggling fire of musketry and artillery in the centre, but after a few rounds, the bursting of a gun created a confusion, from which Laborde's rapidly-advancing masses gave them no time to recover. By ten o'clock the whole of the centre was flying in disorder down a narrow wooded valley leading from the Adaufé to Braga : the French followed hard, and having discovered one of their men, who had been a prisoner, mutilated in a dreadful manner, and still alive, they gave no quarter. Braga was abandoned, and the victorious infantry passing through, took post on the other side, while the cavalry continued the havoc for some distance on the road to Oporto ; yet, so savage was the temper of the fugitives that, in passing through Braga, they stopped to murder the corregidor and other prisoners in the jail, then, casting the mangled bodies into the street, continued their flight. Meanwhile the centre was forced, and Heudelet, breaking over the left of the Monte Adaufé, descended upon Ponte Porto, and, after a sharp skirmish, carried that

Eben's Re-
port, MS.

S.
Journal of
Operations
MS.

bridge and the village on the other side of the Cavado.

Franceschi and Mermet found considerable difficulty in ascending the rugged sides of the Monte Vallonga, but having, at last, attained the crest, the whole of their enemies fled, and the two generals crossed the valley to gain the road of Guimaraens, and cut off that line of retreat; but they fell in with the three thousand Portuguese posted above Falperra, and these men, seeing the cavalry approach, drew up with their backs to some high rocks, and opened a fire of artillery. Franceschi immediately placed his horsemen on either flank, a brigade of infantry against the front, and, as at Verim, making all charge together, strewed the ground with the dead. Nevertheless, the Portuguese fought valiantly at this point, and Franceschi acknowledged it. The vanquished lost all their artillery and above four thousand men, of which four hundred only were made prisoners. Some of the fugitives crossing the Cavado river, made for the Ponte de Lima, others retired to Oporto, but the greatest number took the road of Guimaraens, during the fight at

Sir J. Cra-
dock's Pa-
pers, MSS. Falperra. Eben appears, by his own official report, to have been at Braga when the action commenced, and to have fled among the first, for he makes no mention of the fight at Falperra, nor of the skirmish at Ponte Porto, and his narrative bears every mark of inaccuracy.

Braga was at first abandoned by the inhabitants, they returned however the next day, and when the French outposts were established, general Lorge, crossing the Cavado, entered Bacellos; he was well received by the corregidor, for which the latter was a few days afterwards hanged by the Portu-

guese general, Botilho, who commanded between
the Lima and the Minho. At Braga provisions
were found, and a large store of powder, which was
immediately made up in cartridges for the use of
the French; the gun-carriages and ammunition-
waggons, which had been very much damaged,
were again repaired, and an hospital was established
for eight hundred sick and wounded : hence it may
be judged, that the loss sustained in action since
the 15th, was not less than six hundred men.

The French general having thus broken through
the second Portuguese line of defence could either
march directly upon Oporto, or recover his communication with Tuy. He resolved upon the former,
1°. because he knew through his spies and by intercepted letters that Tuy, although besieged, was
in no distress; that its guns overpowered those of
the Portuguese fortress of Valença on the opposite
bank of the Minho, and that the garrison made
successful sallies. 2°.—Because information reached
him that sixty thousand men, troops of the line,
militia, and *ordenança*, were assembled in the entrenched camp covering Oporto, and his scouts
reported also that the Portuguese were in force
at Guimaraens, and had broken the bridges along the
whole course of the Ave. It was essential to crush
these large bodies before they could acquire any
formidable consistency; wherefore Soult put his army
again in march, leaving Heudelet's division at Braga
to protect his hospitals against Botilho. Meanwhile Silveira struck a great blow, for being reinforced from the side of Beira he remounted the
Tamega, invested Chaves on the day of battle at
Braga, and the 28th forced the garrison, consisting
of one hundred fighting men and twelve hundred

sick, to capitulate, after which he took post at Amarante, while Soult, ignorant of the event, continued his march against Oporto in three columns.

The first, composed of Franceschi's and Mermet's divisions, marched by the road of Guimaraens and San Justo, with orders to force the passage of the Upper Ave, andscour the country towards Pombeiro. The second, consisting of Merle's, Laborde's and La Houssaye's divisions, was commanded by Soult in person, and moved upon Barca de Trofa, the third, under general Lorge, quitting Bacellos, made way by the Ponte d'Ave.

The passage of the Ave was fiercely disputed, and the left column was fought with in front of Guimaraens, and at Pombeiro, and again at Puente Negrellos. The last combat was rough, and the French general Jardon was killed. The march of the centre column was arrested at Barca de Trofa, by the cutting of the bridge, but the marshal, observing the numbers of the enemy, ascended the right bank, and forced the passage at San Justo; not however without the help of Franceschi, who came down the opposite side of the river, after the fight at Ponte Negrellos.

When the left and centre had thus crossed, colonel Lallemand was detached with a regiment of dragoons to assist Lorge, who was still held in check at the Ponte Ave; Lallemand was at first beaten back, but, being reinforced with some infantry, finally succeeded, when the Portuguese, enraged at their defeat, brutally murdered their commander, general Vallonga, and dispersed. The whole French army was now in communication on the left bank of the Ave, the way to Oporto was opened, and, on the 27th, the troops were finally concentrated in front of the entrenchments covering that city.

The action of Monterey, the taking of Chaves, and the defeat at Braga, had so damped the bishop's ardour that he was, at one time, inclined to abandon the defence of Oporto; but this idea was relinquished when he considered the multitudes he had drawn together, and that the English army was stronger than it had been at any previous period since Cradock's arrival; Beresford, also, was at the head of a considerable native force behind the Mondego, and, with the hope of their support, he resolved to stand the brunt. He had collected, in the entrenched camp, little short of forty thousand men, and among them were many regular troops, of which two thousand had lately arrived under the command of general Vittoria. This officer had been sent by Beresford to aid Silveira, but when Chaves surrendered, he entered Oporto. The hopes of the people, also, were high, for they could not believe that the French were a match for them; the preceding defeats were attributed, each to its particular case of treason, and the murder of innocent persons followed as an expiation. No man but the bishop durst thwart the slightest caprice of the mob, and he was little disposed to do so, while Raymundo, and others of his stamp, fomented their fury, and directed it to gratify personal enmities. Thus, the defeat of Braga being known in Oporto, caused a tumult on the 22d, in which Louis D'Olivera, a man of high rank, who had been cast into prison, was, with fourteen other persons, haled forth, and despatched with many stabs; the bodies were then mutilated, and dragged in triumph through the streets.

The entrenchments extending, as I have said, from the Douro to the coast, were complete, and armed with two hundred guns. They consisted of a number of forts of different sizes, placed on the top of a succession of rounded hills, and where the hills failed, the defences were continued by earthen ramparts, loopholed houses, ditches, and felled trees. Oporto itself is built in a hollow, and a bridge of boats, nearly three hundred yards in length, formed the only communication between the city and the suburb of Villa Nova; this bridge was completely commanded by fifty guns, planted on the bluff and craggy heights that overhung the river above Villa Nova, and over-looked, not only the city, but a great part of the entrenched camp beyond it. Within the lines, tents were pitched for even greater numbers than were assembled, and the people running to arms, manned their works with great noise and tu-mult, when the French columns, gathering like heavy thunder clouds, settled in front of the camp.

The duke of Dalmatia arrived on the 27th. While at Braga he had written to the bishop, calling on him to calm the popular effervescence; now, be-holding the extended works in his front, and reading their weakness even in the multitudes that guarded them, he renewed his call upon the prelate, to spare this great and commercial city the horrors of a storm. A prisoner, employed to carry this sum-mons, would have been killed, but that it was pre-tended he came with an offer from Soult to sur-render his army; and notwithstanding this in-genious device, and that the bishop commenced a negotiation, which was prolonged until evening, the

firing from the entrenchments was constant and
general during the whole of the 28th.

The parley being finally broken off, Soult made
dispositions for a general action on the 29th. To
facilitate this, he caused Merle's division to approach
the left of the entrenchments in the evening of the
28th, intending thereby to divert attention from the
true point of attack ; a prodigious fire was immediately opened from the works, but Merle, having
pushed close up, got into some hollow roads and
enclosures, where he maintained his footing. At
another part of the line, however, some of the
Portuguese pretending a wish to surrender, general
Foy, with a single companion, imprudently approached them, when the latter was killed, and Foy
himself made prisoner, and carried into the town.
He was mistaken for Loison, and the people called
out to kill " *Maneta*," but with great presence of mind
he held up his hands, and the crowd, convinced
of their error, suffered him to be cast into the jail.

The bishop, having brought affairs to this awful
crisis, had not resolution to brave the danger himself. Leaving generals Lima and Pareiras to command the army, he, with an escort of troops, quitted
the city, and, crossing the river, took his station in
the Sarea convent, built on the top of the rugged hill
which overhung the suburb of Villa Nova, from
whence he beheld in safety the horrors of the next
day. The bells in Oporto continued to ring all
night, and about twelve o'clock a violent thunder
storm arising, the sound of the winds was mistaken
in the camp for the approach of enemies ; at once
the whole line blazed with a fire of musketry, the
roar of two hundred pieces of artillery was heard
above the noise of the tempest, and the Portuguese

calling to one another with loud cries, were agitated
at once with fury and with terror. The morning,
however, broke serenely, and a little before seven
o'clock the sound of trumpets and drums, and the
glitter of arms, gave notice that the French army
was in motion for the attack.

BATTLE AND STORMING OF OPORTO.

s.
Journal of
Operations
MS.

The feint made the evening before against the
left, which was the weakest part of the line, had
perfectly succeeded, the Portuguese generals placed
their principal masses on that side ; but the duke of
Dalmatia was intent upon the strongest points of
the works, being resolved to force his way through
the town, and seize the bridge during the fight, that
he might secure the passage of the river. His army
was divided into three columns ; of which the first,
under Merle, attacked the left of the Portuguese
centre ; the second, under Franceschi and Laborde,
assailed their extreme right ; the third, composed
of Mermet's division, sustained by a brigade of
dragoons, was in the centre. General Lorge was
appointed to cut off a body of ordenança, who were
posted with some guns, in front of the Portuguese
left, but beyond the works on the road of Villa de
Conde.

The battle was commenced by the wings ; for
Mermet's division was withheld, until the enemy's
generals, believing the whole of the attack was
developed, had weakened their centre to strengthen
their flanks. Then the French reserves, rushing
violently forwards, broke through the entrenchments, and took the two principal forts, entering by the embrasures, and killing or dispersing
all within them. Soult instantly rallied his troops,

and sent two battalions to take the Portuguese left wing in the rear, while two other battalions were ordered to march straight into the town, and make for the bridge. The Portuguese army, thus cut in two, was soon beaten on all points. Laborde carried in succession a number of forts, took fifty pieces of artillery, and reaching the edge of the city, halted until Franceschi, who was engaged still more to the left, could join him. By this movement a large body of the Portuguese were driven off from the town, and forced back to the Douro, being followed by a brigade under general Arnaud.

Merle, seeing that the success of the centre was complete, brought up his left flank, carried all the forts to his right in succession, killed a great number of the defenders, and drove the rest towards the sea. These last dividing, fled for refuge, one part to the fort of St. Joa, the other towards the mouth of the Douro, where, maddened by terror, as the French came pouring down upon them, they strove, some to swim across, others to get over in small boats; their general, Lima, called out against this hopeless attempt, but they turned and murdered him, within musket-shot of the approaching enemy, and then, renewing the attempt to cross, nearly the whole perished. The victory was now certain, for Lorge had dispersed the people on the side of Villa de Conde, and general Arnaud hemming in those above the town prevented them from plunging into the river also, as in their desperate mood they were going to do.

Nevertheless the battle continued within Oporto, for the two battalions sent from the centre having burst the barricades at the entrance of the streets, penetrated, fighting, to the bridge, and here all

the horrid circumstances of war seemed to be accumulated, and the calamities of an age compressed
into one doleful hour. More than four thousand
persons, old and young, and of both sexes, were
seen pressing forward with wild tumult, some
already on the bridge, others striving to gain it, all
in a state of phrenzy. The batteries on the opposite
bank opened their fire when the French appeared,
and at that moment a troop of Portuguese cavalry
flying from the fight came down one of the streets,
and remorseless in their fears, bore, at full gallop,
into the midst of the miserable helpless crowd,
trampling a bloody pathway to the river. Suddenly
the nearest boats, unable to sustain the increasing
weight, sunk and the foremost wretches still
tumbling into the river, as they were pressed from
behind, perished, until the heaped bodies rising
above the surface of the waters, filled all the space
left by the sinking of the vessels.

The first of the French that arrived, amazed at
this fearful spectacle, forgot the battle, and hastened to save those who still struggled for life—
and while some were thus nobly employed, others
by the help of planks, getting on to the firmer parts
of the bridge, crossed the river and carried the batteries on the heights of Villa Nova. The passage
was thus secured, but this terrible destruction did
not complete the measure of the city's calamities;
two hundred men, who occupied the bishop's palace, fired from the windows and maintained that
post until the French, gathering round them in
strength, burst the doors, and put all to the sword.
Every street and house then rung with the noise of
the combatants and the shrieks of distress; for the
French soldiers, exasperated by long hardships,

and prone like all soldiers to ferocity and violence
during an assault, became frantic with fury, when,
in one of the principal squares, they found several
of their comrades who had been made prisoners,
fastened upright, and living, but with their eyes
burst, their tongues torn out, their other members mutilated and gashed. Those that beheld the
sight spared none who fell in their way. It was in
vain that Soult strove to stop the slaughter; it was
in vain that hundreds of officers and soldiers opposed, at the risk of their lives, the vengeance of
their comrades, and by their generous exertions
rescued vast numbers that would otherwise have
fallen victims to the anger and brutality of the
moment. The frightful scene of rape, pillage, and
murder, closed not for many hours, and what with
those who fell in battle, those who were drowned,
and those sacrificed to revenge, it is said that ten
thousand Portuguese died on that unhappy day!
The loss of the French did not exceed five hundred
men.

CHAP. III.

BOOK VII.

1809.
Jan.

THE dire slaughter at Oporto was followed up by a variety of important operations; but before these are treated of, it is essential to narrate the contemporaneous events on the Tagus and the Guadiana, for the war was wide and complicated, and the result depended more upon the general combinations than upon any particular movements.

OPERATIONS OF THE FIRST AND FOURTH CORPS.

Page 15.

It has been already related that Marshal Victor, after making a futile attempt to surprise the marquis of Palacios, had retired to his former quarters at Toledo; that the conde de Cartoajal, who succeeded the duke of Infantado, had advanced to Ciudad Real with about fourteen thousand men; that Cuesta having broken the bridge of Almaraz, guarded the line of the Tagus with fourteen thousand infantry and two thousand five hundred cavalry. The 4th corps remained at Talavera and Placentia, but held the bridge of Arzobispo by a detachment. The remainder of the French army was in Catalonia, at Zaragoza, or on the communication; the reserve of heavy cavalry had been suppressed, and the regiments dispersed among the *corps d'armée;* the whole army, exclusive of the king's guards, was about two hundred and seventy thousand men, with forty thousand horses, shewing a decrease of sixty-five thousand men since the 15th of November. But this included the imperial guards,

Imperial Muster-rolls, MSS.

the reserve of infantry, and many detachments drafted from the corps—in all forty thousand men, who had been struck off the rolls of the army in Spain, with a view to the war in Germany. The real loss of the French by sword, sickness, and captivity, in the four months succeeding Napoleon's arrival in the Peninsula, was therefore about twenty-five thousand—a vast number, but not incredible, when it is considered that two sieges, twelve pitched battles, and innumerable combats had taken place during that period.

Such was the state of affairs when the duke of Belluno, having received orders to aid Soult in the invasion of Portugal, changed places with the fourth corps. Sebastiani was then opposed to Cartoajal, and Victor stood against Cuesta. The former fixed his head-quarters at Toledo, the latter at Talavera de la Reyna, the communication between them being kept up by Montbrun's division of cavalry, while the garrison of Madrid, composed of the king's guards, and Dessolle's division, equally supported both. But to understand the connection between the first, second, and fourth corps, and Lapisse's division, it is necessary to have a clear idea of the nature of the country on both sides of the Tagus.

That river, after passing Toledo, runs through a deep and long valley, walled up on either hand by lofty mountains. Those on the right bank are always capped with snow, and ranging nearly parallel with the course of the stream, divide the valley of the Tagus from Old Castile and the Salamanca country; the highest parts being known by the names of the Sierra de Gredos, Sierra de Bejar, and Sierra de Gata. In these sierras the

Alberche, the Tietar, and the Alagon, take their rise, and, ploughing the valley in a slanting direction, fall into the Tagus.

The principal mountain on the left bank is called the Sierra de Guadalupe; it extends in a southward direction from the river, dividing the upper part of La Mancha from Spanish Estremadura.

The communications leading from the Salamanca country into the valley of the Tagus are neither many nor good; the principal passes are—

1st. The way of Horcajada, an old Roman road, which, running through Pedrahita and Villa Franca, crosses the Sierra de Gredos at Puerto de Pico, and then descends by Montbeltran to Talavera.

2d. The pass of Arenas, leading nearly parallel to, and a short distance from, the first.

3d. The pass of Tornevecas, leading upon Placentia.

4th. The route of Bejar, which, crossing the Sierra de Bejar at the pass of Baños, descends likewise upon Placentia.

5th. The route of Payo or Gata, which crosses the Sierra de Gata by the Pass of Perales, and afterwards dividing, sends one branch to Alcantara, the other to Coria and Placentia. Of these five passes the two last only are, generally speaking, practicable for artillery.

The royal roads, from Toledo and Madrid to Badajos, unite near Talavera and follow the course of the Tagus by the right bank as far as Naval Moral, but then, turning to the left, cross the river at the bridge of Almaraz. Now, from Toledo, westward, to the bridge of Almaraz, a distance of above fifty miles, the left bank of the Tagus is so crowded by the rugged shoots of the Sierra de Guadalupe, that it may be broadly stated as impassable for an army, and this peculiarity of ground gives the key to the operations on both sides. For Cuesta and Cartoajal, by reason of this impassable Sierra de Guadalupe, had no direct military communication; but Victor and Sebastiani, occupying Toledo and Talavera, could unite on either line of operations by the royal roads above mentioned, or by a secondary road which running near Yebenes crosses the Tagus by a stone bridge near Puebla de Montalvan, half way between Toledo and Talavera.

The rallying point of the French was Madrid, and their parallel lines of defence were the Tagus, the Alberche, and the Guadarama.

The base of Cartoajal's operations was the Sierra de Morena.

Cuesta's first line was the Tagus, and his second the Guardiana, from whence he could retreat by a flank march to Badajos, or by a direct one to the defiles of Monasterio in the Sierra Morena.

The two Spanish armies, if they had been united, would not have furnished more than twenty-six thousand infantry and five thousand cavalry, and they had no reserve. The two French corps, united, would have exceeded thirty-five thousand fighting-men, supported by the reserve under the king. The French, therefore, had the advantage of numbers, position, and discipline.

Following the orders of Napoleon, marshal Victor should have been at Merida before the middle of February. In that position he would have confined Cuesta to the Sierra Morena, and with his twelve regiments of cavalry he could easily have kept all the flat country, as far as Badajos, in subjection. That fortress itself had no means of resist-

ance, and, certainly, there was no Spanish force in
the field capable of impeding the full execution of
the emperor's instructions, which were also reiterated
by the king.　Nevertheless, the duke of Belluno
remained inert at this critical period, and the
Spaniards, attributing his inactivity to weakness,
endeavoured to provoke the blow so unaccountably
withheld; for Cuesta was projecting offensive movements against Victor, and the duke of Albuquerque
was extremely anxious to attack Toledo from the
side of La Mancha.　Cartoajal opposed Albuquerque's plans, but offered him a small force with
which to act independently.　The duke complained
to the junta of Cartoajal's proceedings, and Mr.
Frere, whose traces are to be found in every intrigue, and every absurd project broached at this
period, having supported Albuquerque's complaints,
Cartoajal was directed by the junta to follow the
duke's plans; but the latter was himself ordered
to join Cuesta, with a detachment of four or five
thousand men.

ROUT OF CIUDAD REAL.

Cartoajal, in pursuance of his instructions,
marched with twelve thousand men, and twenty
guns, towards Toledo; his advanced guard attacked
a regiment of Polish lancers, near Consuegra, but
the latter retired without loss.　Hereupon, Sebastiani, with about ten thousand men, came up against
him, and the leading divisions encountering at
Yebenes, the Spaniards were pushed back to Ciudad
Real, where they halted, leaving guards on the
river in front of that town.　The French immediately forced the passage, and a tumultuary action
ensuing, Cartoajal was totally routed, with the loss

of all his guns, a thousand slain, and several thou-

sand prisoners; the vanquished fled by Almagro,
and the French cavalry pursued even to the foot of
the Sierra Morena. This action, fought on the
27th of March, and commonly called the battle of
Ciudad Real, was not followed up with any great
profit to the victors. Sebastiani gathered up the
spoils, sent his prisoners to the rear, and held his
troops concentrated on the Upper Guadiana, to
await the result of Victor's operations; thus enabling
the Spanish fugitives to rally at Carolina, where they
were reinforced by levies from Grenada and Cordova.

While these events were passing in La Mancha,
Estremadura was also invaded, for the king, having
received a despatch from Soult, dated Orense and
giving notice that the second corps would be at
Oporto about the 15th of March, had reiterated the
order for Lapisse to move on Abrantes, and for the
duke of Belluno to pass the Tagus and drive Cuesta
beyond the Guadiana. Marshal Victor, who appears
to have been, for some reason unknown, averse to
aiding the operations of the second corps at all,
remonstrated, and especially urged that the order
to Lapisse should be withdrawn, lest his division
should arrive too soon, and without support, at
Abrantes; but this time the king was firm, and,
on the 14th of March, the duke of Belluno, having
collected five days' provisions, made the necessary
dispositions to pass the Tagus.

The amount of the Spanish force immediately on
that river was about sixteen thousand men, and Cuesta General
Semelé's
Journal
of Opera-
tions,
MS.
had also several detachments and irregular bands
in his rear, which may be calculated at eight thousand more. The Duke of Belluno, however, estimated the troops in position before him at thirty

thousand, a great error for so experienced a commander to make.   On the other hand, Cuesta was as ill informed; for this was the moment when, with his approbation, colonel D'Urban proposed to sir John Cradock, that curiously combined attack against Victor, already noticed, in which the Spaniards were to cross the Tagus, and sir Robert Wilson was to come down upon the Tietar.   This, also, was the period that Mr. Frere, apparently ignorant that there were at least twenty-five thousand fighting men in the valley of the Tagus, without reckoning the king's or Sebastiani's troops, proposed, that the twelve thousand British under sir John Cradock, should march from Lisbon to " drive the fourth French corps from Toledo," and " consequently," as he phrased it, " from Madrid." The first movement of Marshal Victor awakened Cuesta from these dreams.

The bridges of Talavera and Arzobispo were, as we have seen, held by the French, and their advanced posts were pushed into the valley of the Tagus, as far as the Barca de Bazagona.

The Spanish position extended from Garbin, near the bridge of Arzobispo, to the bridge of Almaraz, the centre being at Meza d'Ibor, a position of surprising strength, running at right angles from the Tagus to the Guadalupe.   The head-quarters and reserves were at Deleytosa, and a road, cut by the troops, afforded a communication between that place and Meza d'Ibor.

On the right bank of the Tagus there was easy access to the bridges of Talavera, Arzobispo, and Almaraz; but on the left bank no road existed, by which artillery could pass the mountains except that of Almaraz, which was crossed at the distance

of four or five miles from the river by the almost
impregnable ridge of Mirabete.

The Duke of Belluno's plan was, to pass the Tagus
at the bridges of Talavera and Arzobispo, with his
infantry and part of his cavalry, and to operate in
the Sierra de Guadalupe against the Spanish right;
while the artillery and grand parc, protected by
the remainder of the cavalry, were to be united op- Journal of
Operations
posite Almaraz, having with them a raft bridge to of the First
Corps,
throw across at that point. This project is MS.
scarcely to be reconciled with the estimate made of
Cuesta's force; for surely nothing could be more
rash than to expose the whole of the guns and field
stores of the army, with no other guard than some
cavalry and one battalion of infantry, close to a
powerful enemy, who possessed a good pontoon
train, and who might, consequently, pass the river
at pleasure.

The 15th, Laval's division of German infantry,
and Lasalle's cavalry, crossed at Talavera, and,
turning to the right, worked a march through the
rocky hills; the infantry to Aldea Nueva, on a line
somewhat short of the bridge of Arzobispo; the
cavalry higher up the mountain towards Estrella.
The 16th, when those troops had advanced a few
miles to the front, the head-quarters, and the other
divisions of infantry, passed the bridge of Arzobispo;
while the artillery and the parcs, accompanied by a
battalion of grenadiers, and the escorting cavalry,
moved to Almaraz, with orders to watch, on the 17th
and 18th, for the appearance of the army on the
heights at the other side, and then to move down
to the point before indicated for launching the raft
bridge.

Alarmed by these movements, Cuesta hastened

in person to Mirabete, and directing general Henestrosa to defend the bridge of Almaraz, with eight
thousand men, sent a detachment to reinforce
his own right wing, which was posted behind the
Ibor, a small river, but at this season running
with a full torrent from the Guadalupe to the
Tagus.

The 17th, the Spanish advanced guards were
driven, with some loss, across the Ibor. They attempted to re-form on the high rocky banks of that
river, but being closely followed, retreated to the
camp of Meza d'Ibor, the great natural strength of
which was increased by some field-works. Their
position could only be attacked in front, and this
being apparent at the first glance, Laval's division was instantly formed into columns of attack,
which pushed rapidly up the mountain, the inequalities of ground covering them in some sort from
the effects of the enemy's artillery. As they arrived
near the summit, the fire of musketry and grape
became murderous, but at this instant the Spaniards,
who should have displayed all their vigour, broke
and fled to Campillo, leaving behind them baggage,
magazines, seven guns, and a thousand prisoners,
besides eight hundred killed and wounded. The
French had only seventy killed, and five hundred
wounded; and while this action was taking place
at Meza d'Ibor, Villatte's division, being higher up
the Sierra, to the left, overthrew a smaller body of
Spaniards, at Frenedoso, making three hundred
prisoners, and capturing a large store of arms.

The 18th, at day-break, the duke of Belluno, who
had superintended in person the attack at Meza
d'Ibor, examined from that high ground all the remaining position of the Spaniards. Cuesta, he

observed, was in full retreat to Truxillo, but Henestrosa was still posted in front of Almaraz; wherefore Villatte's division was detached after Cuesta,
to Deleytosa, and Laval's Germans were led against
Henestrosa, and the latter, aware of his danger
and already preparing to retire, was driven hastily
over the ridge of Mirabete.

In the course of the night, the raft bridge was
thrown across the Tagus; the next day the French
dragoons passed to the left bank, the artillery followed, and the cavalry immediately pushed forward
to Truxillo, from which town Cuesta had already
fallen back to Santa Cruz, leaving Henestrosa to
cover the retreat. The 20th, after a slight skirmish,
the latter was forced over the Mazarna, and the
whole French army, with the exception of a regiment of dragoons (left to guard the raft bridge) was
poured along the road to Merida.

The advanced guard, consisting of a regiment of
light cavalry, under general Bordesoult, arrived the
21st in front of Miajadas, where the road dividing,
sends one branch to Merida, the other to Medellin.
A party of Spanish horsemen were posted near the
town, they appeared in great alarm, and by their
hesitating movements invited a charge; the French
incautiously galloped forward, and, in a moment,
twelve or fourteen hundred Spanish cavalry, placed
in ambush, came up at speed on the flanks.
General Lasalle, who from a distance had observed
the movements of both sides, immediately rode forward with a second regiment, and arrived just as
Bordesoult had extricated himself from a great peril,
by his own valour, but with the loss of seventy
killed and a hundred wounded.

After this well-managed combat, Cuesta retired
to Medellin without being molested, and Victor

BOOK
VII.
———
1809.
March.

Journal of
Operations
MSS.

spreading his cavalry posts on the different routes to gain intelligence and to collect provisions, established his own quarters at Truxillo, a town of some trade, and advantageously situated for a place of arms. It had been deserted by the inhabitants and pillaged by the first French troops that entered, but it still offered great resources for the army, and there was an ancient citadel, capable of being rendered defensible, which was immediately armed with the Spanish guns, and provisioned from the magazines taken at Meza d'Ibor. Meanwhile, the flooding of the Tagus and the rocky nature of its bed injured the raft-bridge near Almaraz, and delayed the passage of the artillery and stores; wherefore directions were given to have a boat-bridge prepared, and a field-fort constructed on the left bank of the Tagus, to be armed with three guns, and garrisoned with a hundred and fifty men to protect the bridge. These arrangements and the establishment of an hospital, for two thousand men, at Truxillo, delayed the first corps until the 24th of March.

The light cavalry reinforced by twelve hundred *voltigeurs* being posted at Miajadas, had covered all the roads branching from that central point with their scouting parties, and now reported that a few of Cuesta's people had retired to Medellin; that from five to six thousand men were thrown into the Sierra de Guadalupe on the left of the French; that four thousand infantry and two thousand cavalry were behind the river Garganza, in front of Medellin, and that every thing else was over the Guadiana. Thus the line of retreat chosen by Cuesta uncovered Merida, and, consequently, the great road between Badajos and Seville was open to the French. But Victor was not disposed to profit from this, for he was aware that Albuquerque was coming from La Mancha to Cuesta, and believed that he brought nine thousand infantry and two thousand cavalry; he therefore feared that Cuesta's intention was either to draw him into a difficult country, by making a flank march to join Cartoajal in La Mancha; or by crossing the Guadiana above Naval Villar, where the fords are always practicable, to rejoin his detachments in the Sierra de Guadalupe, and so establish a new base of operations on the left flank of the French army. This reasoning was misplaced; neither Cuesta nor his army were capable of such operations; his line of retreat was solely directed by a desire to join Albuquerque, and to save his troops, by taking to a rugged instead of an open country. The duke of Belluno lost the fruits of his previous success, by thus over-rating his adversary's skill; instead of following Cuesta with a resolution to break up the Spanish army, he, after leaving a brigade at Truxillo and Almaraz, to protect the communications, was contented to advance a few leagues on the road to Medellin with his main body; sending his light cavalry to Merida, and pushing on detachments towards Badajos and Seville, while other parties explored the roads leading into the Guadalupe.

The 27th, however, he marched in person to Medellin, at the head of two divisions of infantry, and a brigade of heavy cavalry. Eight hundred Spanish horse posted on the right bank of the Guadiana, retired at his approach, and crossing that river, halted at Don Benito, where they were reinforced by other squadrons, but no infantry were to be discovered. The duke of Belluno then passing the river took post on the road leading to Mingabril and Don Benito, and the situation of the French army in the evening was as follows :—

The main body, consisting of two divisions of infantry, and one incomplete brigade of heavy cavalry in position on the road leading from Medellin to Don Benito and Mingabril.

The remainder of the dragoons, under Latour Maubourg, at Zorita, fifteen miles on the left, watching the Spaniards in the Guadalupe.

The light cavalry at Merida, eighteen miles to the right, having patrolled all that day on the roads to Badajos, Seville, and Medellin.

Ruffin's division at Miajadas eighteen miles in the rear.

But in the course of the evening intelligence arrived that Albuquerque was just come up with eight thousand men ; that the combined troops, amounting to twenty-eight thousand infantry and seven thousand cavalry, were in position on the table land of Don Benito, and that Cuesta, aware of the scattered state of the French army, was preparing to attack the two divisions on their march the next day. Upon this, Victor, notwithstanding the strength of the Spanish army, resolved to fight, and immediately sent orders to Lasalle, to Ruffin, and to Latour Maubourg, to bring their divisions down to Medellin ; the latter was also directed to leave a detachment at Miajadas to protect the route of Merida, and a brigade at Zorita, to observe the Spaniards in the Sierra de Guadalupe.

Cuesta's numbers were greatly exaggerated ; that general blaming every body but himself, for his failure on the Tagus, had fallen back to Campanarios, rallied all his scattered detachments, and then returned to Villa Nueva de Serena, where he

was joined on the 27th by Albuquerque, who
brought up, not a great body of infantry and cavalry
as supposed, but less than three thousand infantry
and a few hundred horse. This reinforcement,
added to some battalions drawn from Andalusia,
increased Cuesta's army to about twenty-five thousand foot, four thousand horse, and eighteen or
twenty pieces of artillery; and with this force, he,
fearing for the safety of Badajos, retraced his steps
and rushed headlong to destruction.

Medellin, possessing a fine stone-bridge, is situated in a hollow on the left bank of the Guadiana,
and just beyond the town is a vast plain, or table
land, the edge of which, breaking abruptly down,
forms the bed of the river. The Ortigosa, which cuts
this plain, is a rapid torrent, rushing perpendicularly
on to the Guadiana, and having steep and rugged
banks, yet in parts passable for artillery. Two
roads branch out from Medellin, the one leading to
Mingrabil on the right, the other to Don Benito on
the left, those places being about five miles apart.

BATTLE OF MEDELLIN.

The French army, with the exception of the
troops left to cover the communications and those at
Zorita, was concentrated in the town at ten o'clock, and
at one, about fourteen thousand infantry, two thousand five hundred cavalry, and forty-two pieces of
artillery, went forth to fight. The plain on the side
of Don Benito was bounded by a high ridge of
land, behind which Cuesta kept the Spanish infantry concealed, showing only his cavalry and some
guns in advance. To make him display his lines
of infantry the French general sent Lasalle's light
cavalry, with a battery of six guns and two batta-

lions of German infantry, towards Don Benito,
while Latour Maubourg, with five squadrons of
dragoons, eight guns, and two other battalions,
keeping close to the Ortigosa, advanced towards a
point of the enemy's ridge called the Retamosa.
The rest of the army were kept in reserve, the
division of Villatte and the remainder of the Germans, being, one-half on the road of Don Benito,
the other half on the road of Mingabril. Ruffin's
division was a little way in rear, and a battalion
was left to guard the baggage at the bridge of
Medellin.

As the French squadron advanced, the artillery
on both sides opened, and the Spanish cavalry
guards in the plain retired slowly to the higher
ground. Lasalle and Latour Maubourg then pressed
forward, but just as the latter, who had the shortest
distance to traverse, approached the enemy's position, the whole Spanish line of battle was suddenly
descried in full march over the edge of the ridge,
and stretching from the Ortigosa to within a mile of
the Guadiana,—a menacing but glorious apparition.
Cuesta, Henestrosa, and the duke del Parque,
with the mass of cavalry, were on the left; Francisco Frias, with the main body of infantry, in the
centre; Equia and Portazgo on the right, which
was prolonged to the Guadiana by some scattered
squadrons under Albuquerque, who flanked the
march of the host as it descended with a rapid pace
into the plain.

Cuesta's plan was now disclosed; his line overlapped the French left, and he was hastening to cut
their army off from Medellin, but his order of battle
was on a front of three miles, and he had no reserve. The Duke of Belluno, seeing this, instantly

brought his centre a little forward, and then, reinforcing Latour Maubourg with ten guns and a battalion of grenadiers, and detaching a brigade of
infantry as a support, ordered him to fall boldly on
the advancing enemy; at the same time Lasalle,
who was giving way under the pressure of his
antagonist, was directed to retire towards Medellin,
always refusing his left.

The Spaniards marched briskly forward into the
plain, and a special body of cavalry, with three
thousand infantry, running out from their left, met
Latour Maubourg in front, while a regiment of hussars fell upon the French columns of grenadiers
and guns in his rear. The hussars being received
with grape, a pelting fire of musketry, and a charge
in flank by some dragoons, were beaten at once;
but the Spanish infantry, closely followed by the
rest of their own cavalry, came boldly up to Latour
Maubourg's horsemen, and with a rough discharge,
forced them back in disorder. The French, however, soon rallied, and smashing the Spanish ranks
with artillery, and fighting all together, broke
in and overthrew their enemies, man and horse.
Cuesta was wounded and fell, but, being quickly
remounted, escaped.

While this was passing on the French right, Lasalle's cavalry, continually refusing its left, was
brought fighting close up to the main body of the
French infantry, which was now disposed on a new
front, having a reserve behind the centre. Meanwhile Latour Maubourg's division was being re-
formed on the ridge from whence the Spaniards had
first descended, and the whole face of the battle
was changed; for the Spanish left being put to
flight, the French right wing overlapped the centre

of their antagonist, and the long attenuated line of the latter wavering, disjointed, and disclosing wide chasms, was still advancing without an object.

The duke of Belluno, aware that the decisive moment of the battle had arrived, was on the point of commanding a general attack, when his attention was arrested by the appearance of a column coming down on the rear of his right wing from the side of Mingabril. A brigade from the reserve, with four guns, was immediately sent to keep this body in check, while Lasalle's cavalry, taking ground to its left, unmasked the infantry in the centre, and the latter advancing, poured a heavy fire into the Spanish ranks ; Latour Maubourg, sweeping round their left flank, then fell on the rear, and, at the same moment, Lasalle also galloped in upon the dismayed and broken bands. A horrible carnage ensued, for the French soldiers, while their strength would permit, continued to follow and strike, until three-fifths of the Spanish army wallowed in blood. Six guns and several thousand prisoners were taken ; General Frias, deeply wounded, fell into the hands of the victors ; and so utter was the discomfiture, that for several days after, Cuesta could not rally a single battalion of infantry, and his cavalry was only saved by the speed of the horses.

Following general Semelé's journal, of which, however, I only possess an unauthenticated copy, the French loss did not exceed three hundred men ; a number so utterly disproportionate to that of the vanquished as to be scarcely credible, and if correct, discovering a savage rigour in the pursuit by no means commendable; for it does not appear that any previous cruelties were perpetrated by the Spaniards to irritate the French soldiers. The right to slaughter an enemy in battle can neither be disputed nor limited; but a brave soldier should always have regard to the character of his country, and be sparing of the sword towards beaten men.

The main body of the French army passed the night of the 28th near the field of battle; but Latour Maubourg marched with the dragoons by the left bank of the Gaudiana to Merida, leaving a detachment at Torre Mexia to watch the roads of Almendralego and Villa Franca, and to give notice if the remains of Cuesta's army should attempt to gain Badajos, in which case the dragoons had orders to intercept them at Loboa. The 29th, Villatte's division advanced as far as Villa Nueva de Serena, and the light cavalry were pushed on to Campanarios; yet, as all the reports agreed that Cuesta, with a few horsemen, had taken refuge in the Sierra Morena, and that the remnants of his army were dispersed and wandering through the fields and along the bye-roads, without any power of reuniting, the duke of Belluno relinquished the pursuit. Having fixed his head-quarters at Merida, and occupied that place and Medellin with his infantry, he formed with his cavalry a belt extending from Loboa on the right to Mingrabil on the left; but from all this tract of country the people had fled, and even the great towns were deserted. Merida, situated in a richly-cultivated basin, possessed a fine bridge and many magnificent remains of antiquity, Roman and Moorish; amongst others, a castle built on the right bank of the river, close to the bridge, was so perfect that, in eight days, it was rendered capable of resisting any sudden assault; six

guns were mounted on the walls, an hospital for a
thousand men was established there, and a garrison
of three hundred men, with two months' stores and
provisions for eight hundred, was put into it.

The king now repeated his orders, that the duke
of Belluno should enter Portugal, and that general
Lapisse should march upon Abrantes. The former
again remonstrated, on the ground that he could
not make such a movement and defend his communications with Almaraz, unless the division of
Lapisse was permitted to join him by the route of
Alcantara. Nevertheless as Badajos, although more
capable of defence than it had been in December,
when the fourth corps was at Merida, was still far
from being secure; and as many of the richer
inhabitants, disgusted and fatigued with the violence
of the mob government, were more inclined to be-
tray the gates to the French than to risk a siege;
Victor, whose battering train (composed of only
twelve pieces, badly horsed and provided) was still
at Truxillo, opened a secret communication with
the malcontents. The parties met at the village of
Albuera, and everything was arranged for the surrender, when the peasants giving notice to the
junta that some treason was in progress, the latter
arrested all the persons supposed to be implicated,
and the project was baffled. The duke of Belluno
then resigned all further thoughts of Badajos, and
contented himself with sending detachments to
Alcantara to get intelligence of general Lapisse,
of whose proceedings it is now time to give some
account.

OPERATIONS OF GENERAL LAPISSE.

This general, after taking Zamora in January,

te 3. Vol. 2.

MADRID

Aranjues

Mora

Consuegra

To Sierra

Guadarama R.

Yebenes

Guadiana R.

Toledo

Ciudad Real

Torijos

Puebla Montalvar
S. Ollalla

Cazalegos

Monbeltran

Vera de Plasencia

Puerto Arenas

Talavera
la Reyna

Sierra Guadalupe

Oropeza

Arzobispo

Puente Conde

Tietar R.

Navalmoral

Fresel Ibor

Deleytoza

Zorita

To Campan
La Ser

Toril

Almaraz

Bazagona

Pass of Perales

Plasensia

Truxillo

Miajadas

Benito

Ortije

Mingral

Medelin

Burdalo R.

Pass of Baños

Sierra Bejar

Puente Cardena

Torre Mocha

Merida

Coria

Alagon R.

Moraleja

Torre Me.
to Almer

Pass of Perales

Sierra Gatta

Lobos

Albuer

Tagus R.

Guadiana R.

Elgo R.

Alcantara

Salvatierra

Badajos

Sketch Explanatory
of
Mr. VICTOR'S OPERATIONS
AGAINST CUESTA.
in March 1809.

▭▬ French
▬▬ Spanish

occupied Ledesma and Salamanca, where he was joined by general Maupetit's brigade of cavalry; sir Robert Wilson's legion and the feeble garrisons in Ciudad Rodrigo and Almeida were the only bodies in his front, and universal terror prevailed; yet he, although at the head of ten thousand men, with a powerful artillery, remained inactive from January to the end of March, and suffered sir Robert, with a few hundred Portuguese, to vex his outposts, to intercept his provisions, to restrain his patroles, and even to disturb his infantry in their quarters. This conduct brought him into contempt, and enabled Wilson to infuse a spirit into the people which they were far from feeling when the enemy first appeared.

Don Carlos d'España, with a small Spanish force, being after a time placed under sir Robert's command, the latter detached two battalions to occupy the pass of Baños, and Lapisse was thus deprived of any direct communication with Victor. In this situation the French general remained without making any vigorous effort, either to clear his front, or to get intelligence of the duke of Dalmatia's march upon Oporto, until the beginning of April, when he advanced towards Bejar; but, finding the passes occupied, turned suddenly to his right, dissipated Wilson's posts on the Ecla, and forced the legion, then commanded by colonel Grant, to take refuge under the guns of Ciudad Rodrigo. He summoned that town to surrender on the 6th, and, after a slight skirmish close to the walls, took a position between the Agueda and Ledesma. This event was followed by a general insurrection, from Ciudad Rodrigo to Alcantara and from Tamames to Bejar; for Lapisse, who had been again ordered

by the king to fulfil the emperor's instructions, and
advance to Abrantes, instead of obeying, suddenly
quitted his positions on the Agueda, and, without
regarding his connexion with the second corps,
abandoned Leon, and made a rapid march, through
the pass of Perales, upon Alcantara, followed
closely by sir Robert Wilson, don Carlos d'España,
the two battalions from Bejar, and a multitude of
peasants, both Portuguese and Spanish.

At Alcantara, a corps of Spanish insurgents endeavoured to defend the passage of the river, but
the French broke through the entrenchments on
the bridge, and, with a full encounter carried the
town, which they pillaged and then joined the first
corps at Merida on the 19th of April. This false
movement greatly injured the French cause. From
that moment the conquering impulse given by Napoleon was at an end, and his armies, ceasing to
act on the offensive, became stationary or retro-
graded, while the British, Spanish, and Portuguese
once more assumed the lead. The duke of Dalmatia, abandoned to his own resources, and in total
ignorance of the situation of the corps by which
his movements should have been supported, was
forced to remain in Oporto; and at the moment
when the French combinations were thus paralyzed,
the arrival of English reinforcements at Lisbon and
the advance of sir John Cradock towards Leiria,
gave a sudden and violent impetus both to the
Spaniards and Portuguese along the Beira frontier.
The insurrection, no longer kept down by the
presence of an intermediate French corps, connecting Victor's and Soult's forces, was thus put into
full activity, from Alcantara on the Tagus, to Amarante on the Tamega.

During this time Cuesta was gathering another host in the Morena. The simultaneous defeat of the armies in Estremadura and La Mancha had at first produced the greatest dismay in Andalusia; yet the Spaniards, when they found such victories as Ciudad Real and Medellin only leading to a stagnant inactivity on the part of the French, concluded that extreme weakness was the cause, and that the Austrian war had, or would, oblige Napoleon to abandon his projects against the Peninsula. This idea was general, and upheld the people's spirit and the central junta's authority, which could not otherwise have been maintained after such a succession of follies and disasters.

The misfortunes of the two Spanish generals had been equal; but Cartoajal, having no popular influence, was dismissed, while Cuesta was appointed to command what remained of both armies; and the junta, stimulated for a moment by the imminent danger in which they were placed, drew together all the scattered troops and levies in Andalusia, to reinforce him. To cover Seville, Cuesta took post in the defiles of Monasterio, and was there joined by eight hundred horse and two thousand three hundred infantry, drafted from the garrison of Seville; these were followed by thirteen hundred old troops from Cadiz; and by three thousand five hundred Grenadian levies; and finally, eight thousand foot, and two thousand five hundred horsemen, taken from the army of La Mancha, contributed to swell his numbers, until, in the latter end of April, they amounted to twenty-five thousand infantry, and six thousand cavalry. General Venegas, also, being recalled from Valencia, repaired to La Carolina, and proceeded to organize another army of La Mancha. Meanwhile Joseph, justly displeased at the false disposition made of Lapisse's division, directed that Alcantara should be immediately re-occupied. This however could not be done without an action, which belongs to another combination, and shall be noticed hereafter; it is now proper to return to the operations on the Douro, which were intimately connected with those on the Guadiana.

CHAPTER IV.

WHEN the bishop of Oporto beheld, from his station at Sarea, the final overthrow of his ambitious
schemes in the north of Portugal, he fled to Lisbon.
There he reconciled himself to the regency, became a member of that body, was soon after created
patriarch, and, as I shall have occasion to shew,
used his great influence in the most mischievous
manner; discovering, on every occasion, the untamed violence and inherent falseness of his disposition.

The fall of Oporto enabled marshal Soult to
establish a solid base of operations, and to commence a regular system of warfare. The immediate fruit of his victory was the capture of immense
magazines of powder; of a hundred and ninety-seven
pieces of artillery, every gun of which had been
used in the action, and of thirty English vessels,
wind-bound in the river, loaded with wine and
provisions for a month, which fell into his hands.
Having repressed the disorders attendant on the
battle, he adopted the same conciliatory policy
which had marked his conduct at Chaves and Braga,
and endeavoured to remedy, as far as it was possible, the deplorable results of the soldiers' fury;
recovering and restoring a part of the plunder, he
caused the inhabitants remaining in the town to be
treated with respect, and invited, by proclamation,
all those who had fled to return. He demanded no

contribution, and restraining with a firm hand the
violence of his men, contrived, from the captured
public property, to support the army and even to
succour the poorest and most distressed of the
population.

But his ability in the civil and political administration of the Entre Minho e Douro produced an
effect which he was not prepared for. The prince
regent's desertion of the country was not forgotten.
The national feeling was as adverse to Portugal
being a dependency on the Brazils, as it was to the
usurpation of the French, and the comparison between Soult's government and the horrible anarchy
which preceded it, was all in favour of the former.
His victories, and the evident vigour of his character, contrasted with the apparent supineness of the
English, promised permanency for the French power,
and the party, formerly noticed as being inimical to
the house of Braganza, revived. The leaders,
thinking this a favourable opportunity to execute
their intention, waited upon the duke of Dalmatia,
and expressed their desire for a French prince and
an independent government. They even intimated
their good wishes towards the duke himself, and
demanded his concurrence and protection, while,
in the name of the people, they declared that the
Braganza dynasty was at an end.

Although unauthorized by the emperor to accede
to this proposition, Soult was yet unwilling to
reject a plan from which he could draw such immediate and important military advantages. Napoleon
was not a man to be lightly dealt with on such an
occasion, but the marshal, trusting that circumstances would justify him, encouraged the design,
appointed men to civil employments and raised a Por-

CHAP.
IV.

1809.
April.

Appendix,
No. 13.

tuguese legion of five battalions. He acted with so much dexterity that in fifteen days, the cities of Oporto and Braga, and the towns of Bacellos, Viana, Villa de Conde, Povoa de Barcim, Feira, and Ovar, sent addresses, containing the expression of their sentiments, and bearing the signatures of thirty thousand persons, as well of the nobles, clergy, and merchants, as of the people. These addresses were burnt when the French retreated from Oporto, but the fact that such a project was in agitation has never been denied; the regency even caused inquest to be made on the matter, and it was then asserted that very few persons were found to be implicated. That many of the signatures were forged by the leaders may readily be believed; but the policy of lessening the importance of the affair is also evident, and the inquisitors, if willing, could not have probed it to the bottom.

This transaction formed the ground-work of a tale, generally credited even by his own officers, that Soult perfidiously aimed at an independent crown. The circumstances were certainly such as might create suspicion; but that the conclusion was false, is shewn, by the mode in which Napoleon treated both the rumour and the subject of it. Slighting the former, he yet made known to his lieutenant that it had reached his ears, adding, " *I remember nothing but Austerlitz,*"* and at the same time largely increased the duke of Dalmatia's command. On the other hand, the policy of Soult's conduct on this occasion, and the great influence, if not the numbers of the Portuguese malcontents, were abundantly proved by the ameliorated rela-

* Soult distinguished himself in that battle.

tions between the army and the peasantry. The fierceness of the latter subsided; and even the priests abated of their hostility in the Entre Minho e Douro. The French soldiers were no longer assassinated in that province; whereas, previous to this intrigue, that cruel species of warfare had been carried on with infinite activity, and the most malignant passions called forth on both sides.

Among other instances of Portuguese ferocity, and of the truculent violence of the French soldiers, the death of colonel Lameth and the retaliation which followed, may be cited. That young officer, when returning from the marshal's quarters to his own, was waylaid, near the village of Arrifana, and murdered; his body was then stripped, and mutilated in a shocking manner. This assassination, committed within the French lines, and at a time when Soult enforced the strictest discipline, was justifiable neither by the laws of war nor by those of humanity. No general could neglect to punish such a proceeding. The protection due to the army, and even the welfare of the Portuguese within the French jurisdiction, demanded a severe example; for the violence of the troops had hitherto been with difficulty restrained by their commander, and if, at such a moment, he had appeared indifferent to their individual safety, his authority would have been set at nought, and the unmeasured indiscriminating vengeance of an insubordinate army executed.

Impressed with this feeling, and afflicted at the unhappy death of a personal friend, Soult directed general Thomieres to march, with a brigade of infantry, to Arrifana, and punish the criminals. Thomieres was accompanied by a Portuguese civilian, and, after a judicial inquiry, shot five or six persons whose guilt was said to have been proved; but it is certain that the principal actor, a Portuguese major of militia, and some of his accomplices, escaped across the Vouga to colonel Trant, who, disgusted at their conduct, sent them to marshal Beresford. It would also appear, from the statement of a peasant, that Thomieres, or those under him, exceeded Soult's orders; for, in that statement, attested by oath, it is said that twenty-four innocent persons were killed, and that the soldiers, after committing many atrocious excesses, burnt the village.

These details have been related partly because they throw a light upon the direful nature of this contest, but chiefly because the transaction has been adduced by other writers as proof of cruelty in Soult; a charge not to be sustained by the facts of this case, and belied by the general tenor of his conduct, which even his enemies, while they attributed it to an insidious policy, acknowledged, at the time, to be mild and humane. And now, having finished this digression, in which the chronological order of events has been anticipated, I shall resume the narrative of military operations at that part where the disorders attendant on the battle of Oporto having been repressed, a fresh series of combinations were commenced, not less important than those which brought the French army down to the Douro.

The heavy blow struck on the 29th of March was followed up with activity. The boat-bridge was restored during the night; the forts of Mazinho and St. Joa de Foz surrendered; Franceschi's cavalry crossed the Douro, and taking post ten

Appendix,
No. 13.

miles in advance on the Coimbra road, pushed
patroles as far as the Vouga river. To support this
cavalry, general Mermet's division occupied a position somewhat beyond the suburb of Villa Nova;
Oporto itself was held by three brigades; the dragoons of Lorge were sent to Villa da Conde, a
walled town, situated at the mouth of the Ave; and
general Caulaincourt was directed up the Douro
to Peñafiel, with a brigade of cavalry, having orders
to clear the valley of the Tamega. Another brigade of cavalry was posted on the road leading to
Barca de Trofa, to protect the rear of the army,
and general Heudelet was directed to forward the
hospitals from Braga to Oporto, but to hold his
troop in readiness to open the communication with
Tuy.

These dispositions being made, Soult had leisure
to consider his general position. The flight of the
bishop had not much abated the hostility of the
people, nor relieved the French from their difficulties; the communication with the Minho was
still intercepted; the Tras os Montes was again in
a state of insurrection; and Silveira, with a corps
of eight thousand men, not only commanded the
valley of the Tamega, but had advanced, after re-
taking Chaves, into the Entre Minho e Douro;
posting himself between the Sierra de Catalina and
the Douro. Lisbon, the ultimate object of the
campaign, was two hundred miles distant, and
covered by a British army, whose valour was to be
dreaded, and whose numbers were daily increasing.
A considerable body of natives were with Trant
upon the Vouga, and Beresford's force between the
Tagus and the Mondego, its disorderly and weak
condition being unknown, appeared formidable at a

distance. The day on which the second corps, following the emperor's instructions, should have reached Lisbon was overpassed by six weeks, the line of correspondence with Victor was uncertain, and his co operation could scarcely be calculated upon. Lapisse's division was yet unfelt as an aiding force, nor was it even known to Soult that he still remained at Salamanca: finally, the three thousand men expected from the Astorga country, under the conduct of the marshal's brother, had not yet been heard of.

On the other hand, the duke of Dalmatia had conquered a large and rich city; he had gained the military command of a very fertile country, from whence the principal supplies of the British army and of Lisbon were derived; he had obtained a secure base of operations and a prominent station in the kingdom; and if the people's fierceness was not yet quelled, they had learned to dread his talents, and to be sensible of their own inferiority in battle. In this state of affairs, judging that the most important objects were to relieve the garrison of Tuy and to obtain intelligence of Lapisse's division, Soult entrusted the first to Heudelet, and the second to Franceschi.

The last-named general had occupied Feira and Oliveira, and spread his posts along the Vouga; but the inhabitants fled to the other side of that river, and the rich valleys beyond were protected by colonel Trant. This officer, well known to the Portuguese as having commanded their troops at Roriça and Vimiero, being at Coimbra when intelligence of the defeat at Braga arrived, had taken the command of all the armed men in that town, among which was a small body of volunteers, stu-

dents at the university. The general dismay and
confusion being greatly increased by the subsequent
catastrophe at Oporto, the fugitives from that town
and other places, accustomed to violence, and attributing every misfortune to treachery in the generals, flocked to Trant's standard; and he, as a
foreigner, was enabled to assume an authority that
no native of rank durst either have accepted or refused without imminent danger. He soon advanced
with eight hundred men to Sardao and Aveiro,
where Eben and general Vittoria joined him, and
the conde de Barbacena brought him some cavalry.
But as the people regarded these officers with suspicion Trant retained the command, and his force was
daily increased by the arrival of ordenança and even
regular troops, who abandoned Beresford's army to
join him.

When Franceschi advanced, Trant sent a detachment by Castanheira to occupy the bridge of the
Vouga; but the men, seized with a panic, dispersed,
and this was followed by the desertion of many
thousand *ordenança*,—a happy circumstance, for
the numbers that had at first collected behind the
Vouga exceeded twelve thousand men, and their
extreme violence and insubordination exciting the
utmost terror, impeded the measures necessary for
defence. Trant, finally, retained about three thousand men, with which imposing upon the French,
he preserved a fruitful country from their incursions; he was however greatly distressed for money,
because the bishop of Oporto, in his flight, laid
hands on all that was at Coimbra and carried it to
Lisbon.

Franceschi, although reinforced with a brigade
of infantry, contented himself with chasing some

insurgents that infested his left flank, while his
scouts, sent forward on the side of Viseu, endeavoured to obtain information of Lapisse's division;
but that general, as we have seen, was still beyond
the Agueda; and while Franceschi was thus employed in front of the French army, Caulaincourt's
cavalry on the Tamega was pressed by Silveira.
And although Loison marched with a brigade of
infantry to his assistance on the 9th of April,
Silveira was too strong for both; on the 12th,
advancing from Canavezes, obliged Loison, after a
slight action, to take post behind the Souza.

Meanwhile, Heudelet was hastening towards Tuy
to recover the artillery and depôts, from which the
army had now been separated forty days. He was
joined on the 6th of April, at Bacellos, by Lorge,
who had taken Villa de Conde and cleared the
coast line. The 7th they marched to Ponte de
Lima, but the Portuguese resisted the passage vigorously, and it was not forced until the 8th. The
10th the French arrived in front of Valença, on the
Minho. This fortress had been maltreated by the
fire from Tuy, and the garrison, amounting to two
hundred men, having only two days' provisions left,
capitulated, on condition of being allowed to retire
to their homes, and before the French could take
possession, deserted the town. The garrison in
Tuy, never having received the slightest intelligence of the army since the separation at Ribidavia,
marvelled that the fire from Valença was discontinued, and their surprise was extreme when they
beheld the French colours flying in that fort, and
observed French videttes on the left bank of the
Minho.

La Martiniere's garrison, by the arrival of strag-

glers and a battalion of detachments that followed
the army from St. Jago, had been increased to three
thousand four hundred men; twelve hundred were
in hospital, and two-thirds of the artillery-horses
had been eaten in default of other food; the Portuguese had passed the Minho, and, in conjunction
with the Spaniards, attacked the place on the 15th
of March; yet the French general, by frequent
sallies, obliged them to keep up a distant blockade.
The 22d of March, the defeat at Braga being
known, the Portuguese repassed the Minho, the
Spaniards dispersed, and La Martiniere immediately
sent three hundred men to bring off the garrison of
Vigo; it was too late, that place was taken, and
the detachment with difficulty regained Tuy.

The peasants on the Arosa Estuary had, as I
have before noticed, risen, the 27th of February,
while Soult was still at Orense; they were headed,
at first, by general Silva and by the count de Me-
zeda, and, finally, a colonel Barrois, sent by the
central junta, took the command. As their numbers were very considerable, Barrois with one part
attacked Tuy, and Silva assisted by the Lively and
Venus, British frigates on that station, invested
Vigo. The garrison of the latter place was at first
small, but the paymaster-general of the second
corps, instead of proceeding to Tuy, entered Vigo,
with the military chest and an escort of eight hundred men, and was blockaded there; nevertheless,
after some slight attacks had been repulsed, the
French governor negotiated for a capitulation on
the 23d of March; distrustful however of the peasantry, he was still undecided on the 26th, and
meanwhile, some of Romana's stragglers coming
from the Val des Orres, collected between Tuy and

Vigo; and Pablo Murillo, a regular officer, assembling fifteen hundred retired soldiers, joined the blockading force. His troops acting in concert with Captain Mackinley, of the Lively, obliged the garrison to surrender on terms. The 27th, thirteen hundred men and officers, including three hundred sick, marched out with the honours of war, and, having laid down their arms on the glacis, were embarked for an English port, according to the articles agreed upon. Four hundred and forty-seven horses, sixty-two covered waggons, some stores, and the military chest, containing five thousand pounds, fell into the victor's hands. The Spaniards then renewed their attack on Tuy; the Portuguese once more crossed the Minho, and the siege continued until the 10th of April, when the place was relieved by Heudelet.

The depôts and the artillery were immediately transported across the river, and directed upon Oporto. The following day general Maucune, with a division of the sixth corps, arrived at Tuy, with the intention of carrying off the garrison, but seeing that the place was relieved, returned. Heudelet, after taking Viana, and the fort of Insoa, at the mouth of the Minho, placed a small garrison in the former, and blowing up the works of Valença, retired to Braga and Bacellos, sending Lorge again to Villa de Conde. The French sick were transported in boats along shore, from the mouth of the Minho to Viana, Villa de Conde, and thence to Oporto, and while these transactions were taking place on the Minho, La Houssaye, with a brigade of dragoons and one of infantry, scoured the country between the Lima and the Cavado, and so protected the rear of Heudelet.

All resistance in the Entre Minho e Douro had now ceased, because the influence of the *Anti-Braganza* party was exerted in favour of the French ; but, on the Tras os Montes side, Silveira was advancing, and being joined by Botilho, from the Lima, boasted that he would be in Oporto the 15th. This unexpected boldness was explained by the news of Chaves having fallen, which now, for the first time, reached Soult. He then perceived that while Silveira was in arms, the tranquillity of the Entre Minho e Douro could only be momentary, and therefore directed Laborde with a brigade of infantry, to join Loison and attack the Portuguese general by Amarante, while La Houssaye crossing the Cavado, should push through Guimaraens for the same point.

The 15th, Laborde reached Peñafiel, and Silveira, hearing of La Houssaye's march, retired to Villamea. The 18th, Laborde drove back the Portuguese without difficulty, and their retreat soon became a flight. Silveira himself passed the Tamega at Amarante, and was making for the mountains, without a thought of defending that town, when colonel Patrick, a British officer in the Portuguese service, encouraging his battalion, faced about, and rallying the fugitives, beat back the foremost of the enemy. This becoming act obliged Silveira to return, and while Patrick defended the approaches to the bridge on the right bank with obstinate valour, the former took a position, on the left bank, on the heights overhanging the suburb of Villa Real.

The 19th, La Houssaye arrived, the French renewed their attack on the town, and Patrick again baffled their efforts ; but when that gallant man being mortally wounded, was carried across the

bridge, the defence slackened, and the Portuguese
went over the Tamega: the passage of the river
was, however, still to be effected. The bridges of
Mondin and Cavez above, and that of Canavezas
below Amarante, were destroyed ; the Tamega was
in full flood, with a deep rocky bed; the bridge in
front of the French mined was barred with three
rows of pallisades, and commanded by a battery of
ten guns; the Portuguese were in position on the
heights beyond, and could from thence discern all
that passed on the bridge, and reinforce their advanced guard which was posted in the suburb.

PASSAGE OF THE TAMEGA, AT AMARANTE.

Laborde at first endeavoured to work a way over
by the flying sap. He reached the barricade the
20th of April, but the Portuguese fire was so deadly
that he soon relinquished this method and sought to
construct a bridge of tressels half a mile below;
which failed, and the efforts against the stone bridge
were renewed. The 27th, the centre barricade was
burned by captain Brochard, an engineer, who then
devised a method of forcing a passage so singularly
bold, that all the generals and especially Foy, were
opposed to it. Nevertheless it was transmitted to
Oporto, and Soult despatched general Hulot to
examine its merits on the spot, who approved of it.

It appeared that the Portuguese mine was so constructed that while the muzzle of a loaded musket
was in the chamber, a string tied to the trigger passed
over the trenches and secured the greatest precision
for the explosion. Brochard therefore proceeded
in the following manner. In the night of the 2d of
May, the French troops were conveniently disposed
as near the head of the bridge as the necessity of

keeping them hidden would permit; at eight o'clock although the moon shone bright, twenty men were sent a little below the bridge to open an oblique fire against the entrenchments, and this being replied to and the attention of the Portuguese diverted to that side, a sapper, dressed in dark grey, crawled out, pushing with his head a barrel of powder, which was likewise enveloped in grey cloth to deaden the sound, along that side of the bridge which was darkened by the shadow of the parapet; when he had placed his barrel against the entrenchment covering the Portuguese mine, he retired in the same manner. Two others followed in succession, and retired without being discovered, but the fourth, after placing his barrel, rose to run back, and was immediately shot at and wounded. The fire of the Portuguese was then directed on the bridge itself, but as the barrels were not discovered, it soon ceased, and a fifth sapper advancing like the others, attached a sausage seventy yards long to the barrels. At two o'clock in the morning the whole was completed, the French kept very quiet, and the Portuguese remained tranquil and unsuspicious.

Brochard had calculated that the effect of four barrels exploding together would destroy the Portuguese entrenchments, and burn the cord attached to their mine. The event proved that he was right, for a thick fog arising about three o'clock in the morning, the sausage was fired, and the explosion made a large breach. Brochard, with his sappers, instantly jumped on to the bridge, threw water into the mine, cut away all obstacles, and, followed by a column of grenadiers, was at the other side before the smoke cleared away. The grenadiers being supported by other troops, not only the suburb, but the camp on the height behind were carried without a check, and the Portuguese dispersing, fled over the mountains. The execution of this bold, ingenious, and successful project, cost only seven or eight men killed; while in the former futile attempts above a hundred and eighty men, besides many engineer and artillery officers, had fallen. It is, however, a singular fact that there was a practicable ford near the bridge, unguarded, and apparently unknown to both sides.

A short time after the passage of the Tamega, Heudelet, marching from Braga by Guimaraens, entered Amarante; Laborde occupied the position abandoned by Silveira, and sent detachments up the left bank of the river to Mondin, while Loison pursued the fugitives. The Portuguese, at the bridge of Canavesas, hearing of the action, destroyed the ammunition, and retired across the Douro. Over that river also went the inhabitants of Mezamfrio and Villa Real, when Loison, on the 6th of May, appeared in their vicinity.

This being made known to Soult, he reinforced Loison, and directed him to scour the right bank of the Douro as high as Pezo de Ragoa; to complete the destruction of Silveira's army, and with a view to the reduction of the Tras os Montes, to patrole towards Braganza, on which side Bessieres had been asked to co-operate. That marshal was however, gone to France, and the reply of his successor Kellerman being intercepted, it appeared that he was unable or unwilling to afford any aid.

Laborde was now recalled to Oporto, with two regiments of infantry, another regiment and a brigade of dragoons were left to guard the communi-

cations with Amarante, and meanwhile Loison, meeting with resistance at Pezo de Ragoa, and observing
a considerable movement on the opposite bank of
the Douro, became alarmed, and fell back to Mezamfrio. The 8th he returned to Amarante, but
his march was harassed by the peasantry, with
a vigour and boldness that indicated the vicinity of some powerful support, and in truth a new
actor had appeared; the whole country was in
commotion, and the Duke of Dalmatia felt himself
suddenly pushed backward by a strong and eager hand.

OBSERVATIONS.—SPANISH OPERATIONS.

1°.—The great pervading error of the Spaniards
in this campaign was the notion that their armies
were capable of taking the lead in offensive movements, and fighting the French in open countries;
whereas, to avoid general actions should have been
with them a vital principle.

2°.—The resolution to fight the French having
been unfortunately adopted, the second great error
was the attaching equal importance to the lines of
operation in La Mancha and Estremadura; the one
should have been considered only as an accessory.
It is evident that the first rank belonged to La
Mancha, because it was in a more open country;
because it more immediately threatened Madrid;
and because a defeat there endangered Seville more
than a defeat in Estremadura would have done. In
La Mancha the beaten Spanish army must have
fallen back upon Seville, in Estremadura it might
have retired upon Badajos. But the latter place
being defensible, and to the Spaniards of infinitely
less importance than Madrid was to their opponents,
the lead in the campaign must always have belonged

to the army of La Mancha, which could, at any
time, have obliged the French to fight a battle for
the capital. The army of Estremadura might,
therefore, have been safely reduced to fifteen thousand men, provided the army of La Mancha had
been increased to forty or fifty thousand, and it
would appear that, with a very little energy, the
junta could have provided a larger force. It is true
that they would have been beaten just the same,
but that is only an argument against fighting great
battles, which was, certainly, the worst possible
plan for the Spaniards to pursue.

3°.—The third great error was the inertness of
Valencia and Murcia, or rather their hostility, for
they were upon the verge of civil war with the
supreme junta. Those provinces, so rich and
populous, had been unmolested for eight months;
they had suffered nothing from Moncey's irruption, they had received large succours from the
English government, and Valencia had written her
pretensions to patriotism in the bloody characters
of assassination; yet were it not for the force under
Llamas, which, after the defeat of Tudela, helped
to defend Zaragoza, Valencia and Murcia might
have been swallowed up by the ocean without any
sensible effect upon the general cause. Those countries were however admirably situated to serve as a
support to Aragon, Catalonia, Andalusia, and La
Mancha, and they could, at this time, have paralyzed
a large French force, by marching an army to San
Clemente. It was the dread of their doing so that
made the king restrain Sebastiani from pursuing Parl. Papers, 1810.
his victory at Ciudad Real; and assuredly, the
Valencians should have moved; for it is not so
much in their numbers as in the variety of their

lines of operation that a whole people find their advantage in opposing regular armies. This, the observation of that profound and original writer, general Lloyd, was confirmed by the practice of Napoleon, in Spain.

FRENCH OPERATIONS.

1°.—To get possession of Seville and Cadiz was certainly as great an object with Napoleon as to seize Lisbon, but the truth of the maxim quoted above regulated the emperor's proceedings. If Victor had been directed at once upon Andalusia, the Portuguese and Valencians could have carried their lines of operations upon his flanks and rear; if Badajos and Lisbon had been the objects of his march, the Andalusians could have fallen on his left flank and cut his communications. Now all such dangers were avoided by the march of Soult and Lapisse; their direction was not only concentric, but a regular prolongation of the great line of communication with France. Ney protected the rear of one, Bessieres the rear of the other, and those two marshals, also, separated and cut off the Asturias from the rest of Spain; thus, all that was formidable was confined to the south of the Tagus. For the same reason the course of conquest was to have proceeded from Portugal to Andalusia, which would then have been assailed both in front and flank, while the fourth corps held the Valencians in check. By this plan the French would never have lost their central position, nor exposed their grand line of communication to a serious attack.

2°.—That this plan, so wisely conceived in its general bearing, should fail, without any of the different corps employed having suffered a defeat, nay, when they were victorious in all quarters, is surprising, but not inexplicable. It is clear that Napoleon's orders were given at a time when he did not expect that a battle would have been fought at Coruña, or that the second corps would have suffered so much from the severity of the weather and the length of the marches ; neither did he anticipate the resistance, made by the Portuguese, between the Minho and the Douro. The last error was a consequence of the first, for his plans were calculated upon the supposition that the rapidity of Soult's movements would forestal all defence ; yet the delay cannot be charged as a fault to that marshal, his energy was conspicuous.

3°.—Napoleon's attention, divided between Asturia and Spain, must have been somewhat distracted by the multiplicity of his affairs. He does not seem to have made allowance for the very rugged country through which Soult had to march, at a season when all the rivers and streams were overflowing; and as the combinations of war are continually changing, the delay thus occasioned rendered Lapisse's instructions faulty ; for, although it be true, that if the latter had marched by Guarda upon Abrantes while Soult advanced to Lisbon by Coimbra and Victor entered the Alemtejo, Portugal would have been conquered without difficulty ; yet the combination was so wide, and the communications so uncertain, that unity of action could not be insured. Soult, weakened by the obstacles he encountered, required reinforcements after the taking of Oporto, and if Lapisse attaching himself to Soult's instead of Victor's incursion, had then marched upon Viseu, the duke of Dalmatia would have been enabled to win his way without regard to the co-operation in the Alemtejo.

4°.—The first error of the French, if the facts are correctly shewn, must therefore be attributed to Napoleon, because he overlooked the probable chances of delay, combined the operations on too wide a scale, and gave Ciudad Rodrigo and Abrantes, instead of Lamego and Viseu, for the direction of Lapisse's march. I say, if the facts are correctly shewn, for it is scarcely discreet to censure Napoleon's military dispositions however erroneous they may *appear* to have been, and it is certain that, in this case, his errors, if errors they were, although sufficient to embarrass his lieutenants, will not account for their entire failure. Above sixty thousand men were put in motion by him, upon good military principles, for the subjugation of Lisbon; we must therefore search in the particular conduct of the generals for the reason why a *project of Napoleon's, to be executed by sixty thousand French veterans, should have ended as idly and ineffectually as if it had been concocted by the Spanish junta.*

OBSERVATIONS ON THE SEPARATE OPERATIONS OF LAPISSE, VICTOR, SOULT, ROMANA, SILVEIRA, AND CUESTA.

LAPISSE.

1°.—An intercepted letter of general Maupetit, shews the small pains taken by Lapisse to communicate with Soult. He directs that *even so many* as three hundred men should patrole towards Tras os Montes, to obtain information of the second corps, at a time when the object was so important that his whole force should have moved in mass rather than have failed of intelligence.

2°.—The manner in which he suffered sir Robert Wilson to gather strength and to insult his outposts was inexcusable. He might have marched straight upon Ciudad Rodrigo and Almeida, and dispersed every thing in his front; one of those fortresses would probably have fallen, if not both, and from thence a strong detachment pushed towards La-mego, would not only have ascertained the situation of the second corps, but would have greatly aided its progress by threatening Oporto and Braga. It cannot be urged that Salamanca required the pre-sence of a large force, because, in that open country, the people were at the mercy of Bessieres' cavalry, and so sensible were the local junta of this, that both Salamanca and Ledesma refused assistance from Ciudad Rodrigo, when it was offered, and preferred a quiet submission.

3°.—When, at last, the king's reiterated orders obliged Lapisse to put his troops in motion, he made a demonstration against Ciudad Rodrigo, so feeble that it scarcely called the garrison to the ramparts, and then as if all chance of success in Portugal was at an end, he broke through the pass of Perales, reached Alcantara and rejoined the first corps, a movement equally at variance with Napoleon's orders and with good military discretion; for the first directed him upon Abrantes, and the second would have carried him upon Viseu. The march to the latter place, while it insured a junction with Soult, would not have prevented an after movement upon Abrantes; the obstacles were by no means so great as those which awaited him on the march to Alcantara, and the great error of abandoning the whole country, between the Tagus and the Douro, to the insurgents, would have been avoided. Here then was one direct cause of failure; yet the error, although great, was not irreparable. If Soult was abandoned to his own resources, he had also obtained a firm and important position in the north, while Victor, reinforced by ten thousand men, was enabled to operate against Lisbon by the Alemtejo, more efficaciously than before; he, however, seems to have been less disposed than Lapisse to execute his instructions.

VICTOR.

1°.—The inactivity of this marshal after the rout of Ucles has been already mentioned. It is certain that if the fourth and first corps had been well handled, neither Cuesta nor Cartoajal could have ventured beyond the defiles of the Sierra Morena, much less have bearded the French generals and established a line of defence along the Tagus. Fifty thousand French troops should in two months have done something more than maintain fifty miles of country on one side of Madrid.

2°.—The passage of the Tagus was successful, but can hardly be called a skilful operation, unless the duke of Belluno calculated upon the ignorance of his adversary. Before an able general and a moveable army, possessing a pontoon train, it would have scarcely answered to separate the troops in three divisions in an extent of fifty miles, leaving the artillery and parc of ammunition, protected only by some cavalry and one battalion of infantry, within two hours' march of the enemy for three days. If Cuesta had brought up all his detachments, the Meza d'Ibor might have been effectually manned, and ten thousand infantry and all the Spanish cavalry spared, to cross the Tagus at Almaraz on the 17th; in this case Victor's artillery would probably have been captured, and his project certainly baffled.

3°.—When the passage of the Tagus was effected, Victor not only permitted Cuesta to escape, but actually lost all traces of his army; an evident fault, and not to be excused by pleading the impediments arising from the swelling of the river, the necessity of securing the communications, &c. If Cuesta's power was despised before the passage of the river, when his army was whole and his position strong, there could be no reason for such great circumspection after his defeat, a circumspection, too, not supported by skill, as the dispersed state of the French army the evening before the battle of Medellin proves.

4°. That Victor was enabled to fight Cuesta, on the morning of the 28th, with any prospect of success, must be attributed rather to fortune than to talent. It was a fault to permit the Spaniards to retake the offensive after the defeat on the Tagus, nor can the first movement of the duke of Belluno in the action be praised. He should have marched into the plain in a compact order of battle. The danger of sending Lasalle and Latour Maubourg to such a distance from the main body I shall have occasion to show in my observations on Cuesta's operations; the after-movements of the French in this battle were well and rapidly combined and vigorously executed, and the success was proportionate to the ability displayed.

5°.—The battles of Medellin and Ciudad Real, which utterly destroyed the Spanish armies and

laid Seville and Badajos open; those battles, in
which blood was spilt like water, produced no
result to the victors, for the French generals, as if
they had touched a torpedo, never stretched forth
their hands a second time. Sebastiani, indeed,
wished to penetrate the Sierra Morena, but the
king, fearful of the Valencians, restrained him.
On the other hand Joseph urged Victor to invade
the Alemtejo, and the latter would not obey, even
when reinforced by Lapisse's division. This last was
the great and fatal error of the whole campaign,
for nearly all the disposable British and Portuguese
troops were thus enabled to move against the duke
of Dalmatia, while the duke of Belluno contrived
neither to fulfil the instructions of Napoleon, nor
the orders of the king, nor yet to perform any
useful achievement himself.

He did not assist the invasion of Portugal, he
did not maintain Estremadura, he did not take
Seville, nor even prevent Cuesta from twice renewing the offensive; yet he remained in an unhealthy
situation until he lost more men, by sickness, than
would have furnished three such battles as Medellin. Two months so unprofitably wasted by a
general, at the head of thirty thousand good troops,
can scarcely be cited. The duke of Belluno's reputation has been too hardly earned to attribute
this inactivity to want of talent. That he was
averse to aid the operations of marshal Soult is
evident, and, most happily for Portugal, it was so;
but, whether this aversion arose from personal
jealousy, from indisposition to obey the king, or
from a mistaken view of affairs, I have no means of
judging.

CUESTA.

1°.—Cuesta's peculiar unfitness for the lead of an
army has been remarked more than once. It remains to shew that his proceedings, on this occasion,
continued to justify those remarks.

To defend a river, on a long line, is generally
hopeless, and especially when the defenders have
not the means of passing freely, in several places,
to the opposite bank. Alexander, Hannibal, Cæsar,
Gustavus, Turenne, Napoleon, Wellington, and
hundreds of others have shown how the passage of
rivers may be won. Eumenes, who prevented Antigonus from passing the Coprates, is, perhaps, the
only example of a general baffling the efforts of
a skilful and enterprising enemy in such an attempt.

2°.—The defence of rivers having always proved
fruitless, it follows that no general should calculate
upon success, and that he should exert the greatest
energy, activity, and vigilance to avoid a heavy
disaster; that all his lines of retreat should be kept
free and open, and be concentric; and that to bring
his magazines and depôts close up to the army, in
such a situation, is rashness itself. Now Cuesta
was inactive, and, disregarding the maxim which
forbids the establishment of magazines in the first
line of defence, brought up the whole of his to
Deleytosa and Truxillo. His combinations were
ill-arranged; he abandoned Mirabete without an
effort; his depôts fell into the hands of the enemy;
his retreat was confused; and eccentric, inasmuch as part of his army retired into the Guadalupe, while others went to Merida and he himself
to Medellin.

3°.—The line of retreat upon Medellin and Campanarios, instead of Badajos; being determined by the necessity of uniting with Albuquerque, cannot be blamed; the immediate return to Medellin was bold and worthy of praise but its merit consisted in recovering the offensive immediately after a defeat, wherefore, Cuesta should not have halted at Medellin, thus giving the lead again to the French general; he should have continued to advance, and falling upon the scattered divisions of the French army, endeavoured to beat them in detail, and rally his own detachments in the Sierra de Guadalupe. The error of stopping short at Medellin would have been apparent, if Victor, placing a rear-guard to amuse the Spanish general, had taken the road to Seville by Almendralejos and Zafra.

4°. Cuesta's general design for the battle of Medellin was well imagined; that is, it was right to hide his army behind the ridge, and to defer the attack until the enemy had developed his force and order of battle in the plain; but the execution was on the lowest scale. If, instead of advancing in one long and weak line without a reserve, Cuesta had held the greatest part of his troops in solid columns, and thrust them between Lassalle and Latour Maubourg's divisions, which were pushed out like horns from the main body of the French, those generals would have been cut off, and the battle commenced by dividing the French army into three unconnected masses, while the Spaniards would have been compact, well in hand, and masters of the general movements. Nothing could then have saved Victor, except hard fighting, whereas Cuesta's dispositions rendered it impossible for the Spaniards to win the battle by courage, or to escape the pursuit by swiftness.

5°. It is remarkable that the Spanish general seems never to have thought of putting Truxillo, Guadalupe, Merida, Estrella, or Medellin in a state of defence, although most if not all of those places had some castle or walls capable of resisting a sudden assault. There was time to do it, for Cuesta remained unmolested, on the Tagus, from January to the middle of March, and every additional point of support thus obtained for an undisciplined army would have diminished the advantages derived by the French from their superior facility of movement; the places themselves might have been garrisoned by the citizens and peasantry, and a week's, a day's, nay, even an hour's, delay was of importance to a force like Cuesta's, which, from its inexperience, must have always been liable to confusion.

SOULT.

1°. The march of this general in one column, upon Tuy, was made under the impression that resistance would not be offered; otherwise, it is probable that a division of infantry and a brigade of cavalry would have been sent from St. Jago or Mellid direct upon Orense, to insure the passage of the Minho; it seems to have been also an error in Ney, arising, probably, from the same cause, not to have kept Marchand's division of the sixth corps at Orense until the second corps had effected an entrance into Portugal.

2°. Soult's resolution to place the artillery and stores in Tuy, and march into Portugal, trusting to victory for re-opening the communication, would increase the reputation of any general. Three times

HISTORY OF THE

254

BOOK VII.

1809.

before he reached Oporto he was obliged to halt, in order to fabricate cartridges for the infantry, from the powder taken in battle, and his whole progress from Tuy to that city was energetic and able in the extreme.

3°. The military proceedings, after the taking of Oporto, do not all bear the same stamp. The administration of the civil affairs appears to have engrossed the marshal's attention, and his absence from the immediate scene of action sensibly affected the operations. Franceschi shewed too much respect for Trant's corps; Loison's movements were timid and slow; even Laborde's genius seems to have been asleep. The importance of crushing Silveira was obvious, and there is nothing more necessary in war than to strike with all the force you can at once; but here Caulaincourt was first sent, being too weak, Loison reinforced him, Laborde reinforced Loison, and all were scarcely sufficient at last to do that which half would have done at first. But the whole of these transactions are obscure. The great delay that took place before the bridge of Amarante, and the hesitation and frequent recurrence for orders to the marshal, indicate want of zeal, or a desire to procrastinate, in opposition to Soult's wishes. Judging from Mr. Noble's history of the campaign, this must be traced to a conspiracy in the French army, which shall be touched upon hereafter.

4°. The resistance made by the Portuguese peasantry was infinitely creditable to their courage, but there cannot be a stronger proof of the inefficacy of a like defence, when unsupported by good troops. No country is more favourable to such a warfare than the northern provinces of Portugal; the people

were brave, they had the assistance of the organized
forces under Romana, Silveira, Eben, and the
bishop; yet Soult, in the very worst season of the
year, overcoming all resistance, penetrated to Oporto,
without an actual loss, in killed, wounded, and
prisoners, of more than two thousand five hundred
men, including the twelve hundred sick, captured
at Chaves.

ROMANA.

1°. Romana remained at Oimbra and Monterey,
unmolested, from the 21st of January to the 6th of
March; he had therefore time to reorganise his
forces, and he had, in fact, ten thousand regular
troops in tolerable order. He knew, on the 11th or
12th, that Soult was preparing to pass the Minho,
between Tuy and Guardia. He knew, also, that
the people of Ribidavia and Orense were in arms;
that those on the Arosa were preparing to rise, and
that, consequently, the French must, were it only
from want of food, break out of the contracted position they occupied, either by Ribidavia and Orense,
or by crossing the Minho, or by retreating to
St. Jago. With these guides, the path of the
Spanish general was as plain as the writing on the
wall; he was at the head of ten thousand regular
troops, and two marches would have brought him
to Ribidavia; in front of that town he might have
occupied a position close on the left flank of the
French, rallied all the insurgents about him, and
organized a formidable warfare. The French durst
not have attempted the passage of the Minho while
he was in front of Ribidavia, and if they turned
against him, the place was favourable for battle, the
retreat open by Orense and Monterey; and the

difficulty of bringing up artillery would have hampered the pursuit.   On the other hand, if Soult had
retreated, that alone would have been tantamount to
a victory, and Romana would have been well placed
to follow, connecting himself with the English vessels
of war upon that coast as he advanced.

2°. So far from contemplating operations of this
nature, Romana did not even concentrate his force ;
but keeping it extended, in small parties, along
fifteen miles of country, indulged himself in specu-
lations about his enemy's weakness, and the prospect
of their retreating altogether from the Peninsula.
He was only roused from his reveries, by finding his
divisions beaten in detail, and himself forced either
to join the Portuguese with whom he was quarrelling, or to break his promises to Silveira and fly by
cross roads over the mountain on his right : he
adopted the latter, thus proving, that whatever
might be his resources for raising an insurrection,
he could not direct one, and that he was, although
brave and active, totally destitute of military talent.
At a later period of the war, the duke of Wellington, after a long and fruitless military discussion,
drily observed, that either Romana or himself had
mistaken their profession !

SILVEIRA.

1₀. This Portuguese general's first operations were
as ill conducted as Romana's ; his posts were too
extended, he made no attempt to repair the works
of Chaves, none to aid the important insurrection of
Ribidavia ; but these errors cannot be fairly charged
upon him, as his officers were so unruly, that they
held a council of war per force, where thirty voted
for fighting at Chaves, and twenty-nine against it ;

the casting voice being given by the voter calling
on the troops to follow him. The after-movement,
by which Chaves was recaptured, whether devised
by Silveira himself, or directed by marshal Beresford, was bold and skilful; but the advance to
Penafiel, while La Houssaye and Heudelet could
from Braga pass by Guimaraens, and cut him off
from Amarante, was as rash as his subsequent flight
was disgraceful: yet, thanks to the heroic courage
of colonel Patrick, Silveira's reputation as a general was established among his countrymen, by the
very action which should have ruined him in their
estimation.

BOOK VIII.

CHAPTER I.

BOOK
VIII.
————
1809.
March.
It will be remembered that the narrative of sir John Cradock's proceedings was discontinued, at the moment when that general, nothing shaken by the importunities of the regency, the representations of marshal Beresford, or the advice of Mr. Frere, resolved to await at Lumiar for the arrival of the promised reinforcements from England. While in this position, he made every exertion to obtain
Appendix,
No. 5.
transport for the supplies, remounts for the cavalry, and draught animals for the artillery; but the Porguese government gave him no assistance, and an attempt to procure horses and mules in Morocco proving unsuccessful, the army was so scantily furnished that, other reasons failing, this alone would have prevented any advance towards the frontier.

The singular inactivity of Victor surprised Cradock, but did not alter his resolution; yet, being continually importuned to advance, he, when assured that five thousand men of the promised rein-
Sir John
Cradock's
Correspon-
dence,
MSS.
forcements were actually off the rock of Lisbon, held a council of war on the subject. All the generals were averse to marching on Oporto, except Beresford, and he admitted that its propriety depended on Victor's movements: meanwhile, that marshal approached Badajos, Lapisse came down upon the Agueda, and Soult, having stormed Oporto, pushed his advanced posts to the Vouga.

A cry of treason was instantly heard throughout
Portugal, and both the people and the soldiers
evinced a spirit truly alarming. The latter, disregarding the authority of Beresford, and menacing
their own officers, declared that it was necessary to
slay a thousand traitors in Lisbon; and the regiments in Abrantes even abandoned that post, and
marched to join Trant upon the Vouga. But, when
these disorders were at the worst, and when a vigorous movement of Victor and Lapisse would have
produced fatal consequences, general Hill landed
with about five thousand men and three hundred
artillery horses. Cradock, then, resolved to advance,
moved thereto chiefly by the representations of
Beresford, who thought such a measure absolutely
necessary to restore confidence, to ensure the obedience of the native troops, and to enable him to
take measures for the safety of Abrantes. Thus,
about the time that Tuy was relieved by the French,
and that Silveira was attacked at Penafiel by Laborde, the English army was put in motion, part
upon Caldas and Obidos, part upon Rio Mayor;
the campaign was, therefore, actually commenced
by Cradock, when that general, although his measures had been all approved of by his government,
was suddenly and unexpectedly required to surrender his command to sir Arthur Wellesley, and
proceed himself to Gibraltar.

It would appear that this arrangement was adopted
after a struggle in the cabinet, and, certainly, neither the particular choice nor the general principle
of employing men of talent without regard to seniority can be censured; nevertheless, sir John
Cradock was used unworthily. A general of his
rank would never have accepted a command on

such terms, and it was neither just nor decent to expose him to an unmerited mortification.

Before the arrival of his successor, Cradock had assembled the army at Leiria, and established his magazines at Abrantes, Santarem, and Peniché; but as the admiral fearing the difficult navigation at that season, would not send victuallers to the latter place, the magazines there were but scantily supplied. Meanwhile Lapisse made way by Alcantara to Merida, the re-capture of Chaves became known, and the insurrection in Beira and Tras os Montes took its full spring. Trant's force also increased on the Vouga, and Beresford, who had succeeded in restoring order among the Portuguese battalions, was more than ever urgent for an attack upon Soult; nevertheless Cradock, unprovided with a due proportion of cavalry, unable to procure provisions or forage, and fearful for the safety of Lisbon, refused, and the 24th of April, hearing that his successor had arrived, resigned the command and repaired to Gibraltar.

Sir Arthur Wellesley landed the 22d of April. On the 24th he signified to the British ministers that, affairs being in the condition contemplated by them, it was his intention to assume the command of the army; a circumstance worthy of attention, as indicating that the defence of Portugal was even then considered a secondary object, and of uncertain promise. The deliverance of the Peninsula was never due to the foresight and perseverance of the English ministers, but to the firmness and skill of the British generals, and to the courage of troops whom no dangers could daunt and no hardships dishearten, while they remedied the eternal errors of the cabinet.

Appendix,
No. 15.

The unexpected arrival of a man known only as a victorious commander created the greatest enthusiasm in Portugal. The regency immediately nominated him marshal-general of their troops; the people, always fond of novelty, hailed his presence with enthusiasm; and all those persons, whether Portuguese or British, who had blamed sir John Cradock's prudent caution, now anticipating a change of system, spake largely and confidently of the future operations: in truth, all classes were greatly excited, and an undefined yet powerful sentiment that something great would soon be achieved pervaded the public mind.

Appendix,
No. 16,

Sir Arthur's plans were, however, neither hastily adopted nor recklessly hurried forward; like Cradock, he felt the danger of removing far from Lisbon while Victor was on the Alemtejo frontier, and he anxiously weighed his own resources against those at the enemy's disposal. Not that he wavered between offensive and defensive movements; a general of his discernment could not fail to perceive that, if the French were acting upon any concerted plan, the false march of Lapisse to Merida had marred their combinations, by placing a whole nation, with all its fortresses and all its forces, whether insurgents, regular troops, or auxiliaries, between the armies of Victor and Soult; and that neither concert nor communication could longer exist between those marshals.

Soult's offensive strength, also, was evidently exhausted; he might establish himself firmly in the provinces beyond the Douro, but he could not, alone, force his way to Lisbon, a distance of two hundred miles, in a season when the waters were full, and through a country tangled with rivers, mountains, and defiles. He could not hope, with twenty-four thousand men, to beat a whole people in arms, assisted by an auxiliary army of as high reputation, and nearly as numerous as his own; and, moreover, there were discontents and conspiracy in his camp, and of this sir Arthur was aware.

Soult alone, then, was no longer formidable to the capital; but that which weakened him increased the offensive power of Victor, who was now at the head of thirty thousand men, and might march straight upon Lisbon, and through an open country, the only barrier being the Tagus, a river fordable in almost all seasons. Such a movement, or even the semblance of it, must perforce draw the British and native armies to that side, and then Soult, coming down to the Mondego, might, from thence, connect his operations with Victor's by the line of the Zezere, or advance at once on Lisbon as occasion offered.

Now, to meet the exigencies of the compaign, the military resources of the English general were,—

1°.—His central position.

2°.—The British and German troops, about twenty-six thousand in number; of which the present under arms, including sergeants, amounted to twenty-two thousand, with three thousand seven hundred horses and mules. In the British army corporals and privates only are understood in the present under arms, but in the French army that term includes all military persons. Officers, non-commissioned officers, soldiers and drummers, combatants and non-combatants, a distinction to be borne in mind when comparing the forces on each side.

3°.—The Portuguese troops of the line ; of which there might be organised and armed about sixteen thousand.

Nearly all these troops were already collected, or capable of being collected in a short time, between the Tagus and Mondego ; and beyond the latter river, Trant and Silveira commanded separate corps ; the one upon the Vouga, the other on the Tamega.

4°.—The militia and the *ordenanças*, which may be demominated the insurgent force.

5°.—The fortresses of Almeida, Ciudad Rodrigo, Elvas, Abrantes, Peniché, and Badajos.

6°.—The English fleet, the Portuguese craft, and the free use of the coast and river navigation for his supplies.

7°.—The assistance of Cuesta, who had six thousand cavalry and thirty thousand infantry of which twenty-five thousand were actually about the defiles of Monasterio in front of Victor's posts.

Sir Arthur Wellesley's moral resources were the high courage of his own troops ; his personal popularity ; the energy of an excited people ; a favourable moment ; the presentiment of victory, and a mind equal to the occasion.

In a strategic point of view, to fall upon Victor was best, because he was the most dangerous neighbour to Portugal ; because his defeat would prove most detrimental to the French, most advantageous to the Spaniards ; and because the greatest body of troops could be brought to bear against him. On the other hand, Soult held a rich province, from whence the chief supply of cattle for the army was derived; he was in possession of the second city in the kingdom, where he was forming a French party; the feelings of the regency and the people were greatly troubled by the loss of Oporto, and their desire to regain it was strongly expressed.

To attack Victor, it was indispensable to concert operations with Cuesta; but that general was ill disposed towards the British, and to insure his co-operation would have required time, which could be better employed in expelling Soult. For these reasons, sir Arthur Wellesley determined to attack the last-named marshal without delay; intending, if successful, to establish a good system of defence in the northern provinces, and then, in conjunction with Cuesta, to turn his arms against Victor, hoping thus to relieve Gallicia more effectually than by following the French into that province.

The security of Lisbon being the pivot of the operations against Soult, time was the principal object to be gained. If Victor came fiercely on, he could not be stopped, but his course might be impeded; his path could not be blocked, but it might be planted with thorns. To effect this, eight or ten thousand Portuguese troops were immediately directed upon Abrantes and Santarem, where two British battalions and two regiments of cavalry just disembarked, also marched and were there joined by three other battalions drafted from the army at Leiria.

A body of two thousand men, composed of a militia regiment, and the Lusitanian legion which remained near Castello Branco after Lapisse had crossed the Tagus, were placed under the command of colonel Mayne, and directed to take post at the bridge of Alcantara, having orders to defend the passage of the river, and, if necessary, to blow up the structure. At the same time, the flying bridges at Villa Velha and Abrantes were removed, the garrison of the latter place was reinforced, and general Mackenzie was appointed to command all the troops, whether Portuguese or British, thus distributed along the right bank of the Tagus. These precautions appeared sufficient, especially as there was a general disposition to believe the French weaker than they really were; Victor could not, by a mere demonstration, shake this line of defence; and if he forced the bridge of Alcantara, and penetrated by the sterile and difficult route formerly followed by Junot, it would bring him, without guns, upon Abrantes; but Abrantes was already capable of a short resistance, and Mackenzie would have had time to line the rugged banks of the Zezere.

If, however, Victor leaving Badajos and Elvas behind him, should pass through the Alemtejo, and cross the Tagus between Abrantes and Lisbon, he was to be feared; but Cuesta had promised to follow closely in the French general's rear, and it was reasonable to suppose that Mackenzie, although he might be unable to prevent the passage of the river, would not suffer himself to be cut off from the capital, where, having the assistance of the fleet, the aid of the citizens, and the chance of reinforcements from England, he might defend himself until the army could return from the Douro. Moreover, Victor was eighteen marches from Lisbon; it was only by accident that he and Soult could act in concert, and the allied army, having a sure and rapid mode of correspondence with Cuesta, was already within four marches of Oporto.

The main body of the allies was now directed upon Coimbra; four of the best Portuguese battalions were incorporated in the British brigades; Beresford retained, under his personal command, about six thousand native troops; Trant remained stedfast on the Vouga; Silveira on the Tamega; and sir Robert Wilson, quitting the command of the legion, was detached, with a small Portuguese force, to Viseu, where, hanging upon Franceschi's left flank, he also communicated with Silveira's corps by the way of Lamego.

The difficulty of bringing up forage and provisions, which had pressed so sorely on sir John Cradock, was now somewhat lessened. The land transport was indeed still scanty, and the admiral, dreading the long shore navigation for large vessels, was without the small craft necessary for victualling the troops by the coast; but the magazines at Caldas were partly filled, and twenty large country-boats loaded with provisions, the owners being induced by premiums to make the run, had got safely into Peniché and the Mondego. In short, the obstacles to a forward movement, although great, were not insurmountable.

Sir Arthur Wellesley reached Coimbra the 2d of May. His army was concentrated there on the 5th, in number about twenty-five thousand sabres and bayonets; nine thousand were Portuguese, three thousand Germans, the remainder British. The duke of Dalmatia was ignorant that the allies were thus assembled in force upon the Mondego; but many French officers knew it, and were silent, for they were engaged in a plot of a very extraordinary nature, which was probably a part of the conspiracy alluded to in the first volume of this work, as being conducted through the medium of the princess of Tour and Taxis.

The French soldiers were impatient of their toils, their attachment to Napoleon himself was unshaken, but human nature shrinks from perpetual contact with death, and they were tired of war. This feeling induced some officers of high rank, serving in Spain, to form a plan for changing the French government; generally speaking, these men were friendly to Napoleon personally, but they were republicans in their politics, and earnest to reduce the power of the emperor. Their project, founded upon the discontent of the troops in the Peninsula, was to make a truce with the English army, to elect a chief, and march into France with the resolution to abate the pride of Napoleon, or to pull him from his throne. These conspirators at first turned their eyes upon marshal Ney, but finally resolved to choose Gouvion St. Cyr for their leader; yet it was easier to resolve than to execute. Napoleon's ascendancy, supported by the love and admiration of millions, was not to be shaken by the conspiracy of a few discontented men: and, although the hopes of these last were not entirely relinquished until after Massena's retreat from Portugal in 1810, long before that period they discovered that the soldiers, tired as they were of war, were faithful to their great monarch, and would have slain any who openly stirred against him.

The foregoing facts are stated on the authority of a principal mover of the sedition; but many minor plots had cotemporary existence, for this was

the spring-time of folly.   In the second corps
conspirators were numerous, and by their discourses
and their slow sullen execution of orders, had continually thwarted the operations of marshal Soult, yet
without exciting his suspicions; as he penetrated
into Portugal, their counteractions increased, and,
by the time he arrived at Oporto, their design
was ripe for execution.

In the middle of April, John Viana, the son of an
Oporto merchant, had appeared at marshal Beresford's head-quarters, with proposals from the French
malcontents; who desired to have an English
officer sent to them, to arrange the execution of a
plan, which was to be commenced by seizing their
general, and giving him over to the British outposts: a detestable project, for it is not in the field,
and with a foreign enemy, that soldiers should
concert the overthrow of their country's institutions.   It would be idle and impertinent in a
foreigner to say how much and how long men shall
bear with what they deem an oppressive government, but there is a distinct and especial loyalty
due from a soldier to his general in the field; a
compact of honour, which it is singularly base to
violate, and so it has in all ages been considered.
When the Argyraspides, or silver-shields of the
Macedonians, delivered their general, Eumenes, in
bonds, to Antigonus, the latter, although he had
tempted them to the deed, and scrupled not to
slay the hero, reproached the treacherous soldiers
for their conduct, and with the approbation of all
men destroyed them: yet Antigonus was not a
foreign enemy, but of their own kin and blood.

An English lieutenant-colonel attached to the
Portuguese service reluctantly undertook the duty

of meeting these French conspirators, and penetrated, by night, but in uniform, behind the French outposts, by the lake of Aveiro or Ovar. He had previously arranged that one of the malcontents should meet him on the water, the boats unknowingly passed each other in the dark, and the Englishman returned to Aveiro, where he found John Viana, in company with the French adjutant-major, D'Argenton. The latter confirmed what Viana had declared at Thomar; he expressed great respect for Soult, yet dwelt upon the necessity of removing him before an appeal could be made to the soldiers; and he readily agreed to wait, in person, upon Beresford, saying he was himself too strongly supported in the French army to be afraid. Marshal Beresford was then at Lisbon, thither D'Argenton followed and having seen him and sir Arthur Wellesley, remained five days in that capital, and then returned to Oporto. While at Lisbon, he, in addition to his former reasons for this conspiracy, stated that Soult wished to make himself king of Portugal; an error into which he and many others naturally fell, from circumstances that I have already noticed.

When Sir Arthur Wellesley arrived at Coimbra, D'Argenton appeared again at the English head-quarters; this time, however, by the order of sir Arthur, he was conducted through bye-paths, and returned convinced, from what he had seen and heard, that although the allies were in force on the Mondego, many days must elapse before they could be in a condition to attack Oporto. During his absence, he had been denounced by general Lefebre, who was falsely imagined to be favourable to the conspiracy; being arrested, passports, signed by admiral Berkeley, which this unfortunate man, contrary to Sir A. Wellesley's urgent recommendation, had insisted upon having, completely proved his guilt, and Soult, until that moment, without suspicion, beheld with amazement the abyss that yawned beneath his feet: his firmness, however, did not desert him. He offered D'Argenton pardon, and even reward, if he would disclose the names of the other conspirators and relate truly what he had seen of the English and Portuguese armies; the prisoner, to save his life, readily told all that he knew of the British, but Sir A. Wellesley's foresight had rendered that tale useless, and with respect to his French accomplices D'Argenton was immoveable. Exaggerating the importance of the conspiracy, he even defied the marshal's power, and advised him, as the safest course, to adopt the conspirators' sentiments; nor was his boldness fatal to him at the moment, for Soult, anxious to ascertain the extent of the danger, delayed executing him, and he effected his escape during the subsequent operations.

He was not the only person who communicated secretly with the British general; colonel Donadieu and colonel Lafitte were engaged in the conspiracy. The latter is said to have had an interview with sir Arthur, between the outposts of the two armies, and from the first the malcontents were urgent that the movements of the allied forces should be so regulated as to favour their proceedings: sir Arthur Wellesley, however, having little dependence upon intrigue, sternly intimated that his operations could not be regulated by their plots, and hastened his military measures.

Under the impression that Silveira was successfully defending the line of the Tamega, the British general at first resolved to reinforce him by sending Beresford's and Wilson's corps across the Douro at Lamego, by which he hoped to cut Soult off from Tras os Montes; intending, when their junction was effected, to march with his own army direct upon Oporto, and to cross the Douro near that town, by the aid of Beresford's corps, which would then be on the right bank. This measure, if executed, would, including Trant's, Wilson's, and Silveira's people, have placed a mass of thirty thousand troops, regulars and irregulars, between the Tras os Montes and Soult, and the latter must have fought a battle under very unfavourable circumstances, or have fallen back on the Minho, which he could scarcely have passed at that season while pressed by the pursuing army. But the plan was necessarily abandoned when intelligence arrived that the bridge of Amarante was forced, and that Silveira, pursued by the enemy, was driven over the Douro. The news of this disaster only reached Coimbra the 4th of May, and, on the 6th, a part of the army was already in motion to execute a fresh project, adapted to the change of affairs. As this eagerness to fall on Soult may appear to justify those who censured sir J. Cradock's caution, it may here be well to shew how far the circumstances were changed.

When Cradock refused to advance, the Portuguese troops were insubordinate and disorganized; they were now obedient and improved in discipline.

Sir John Cradock had scarcely any cavalry; four regiments had since been added.

In the middle of April, Cuesta was only gathering the wrecks of his forces after Medellin; he was now at the head of thirty-five thousand men.

The intentions of the British government had been doubtful, they were no longer so. Sir John Cradock's influence had been restricted, the new general came out with enlarged powers, the full confidence of the ministers, and with Portuguese rank. His reputation, his popularity, and the disposition of mankind, always prone to magnify the future, whether for good or bad, combined to give an unusual impulse to public feeling, and enabled him to dictate at once to the regency, the diplomatists, the generals, and the people; to disregard all petty jealousies and intrigues, and to calculate upon resources from which his predecessor was debarred. Sir Arthur Wellesley, habituated to the command of armies, was moreover endowed by nature with a lofty genius, and a mind capacious of warlike affairs.

CHAPTER II.

CAMPAIGN ON THE DOURO.

AFTER the action of Amarante, Laborde's troops were recalled to Oporto, a brigade of cavalry and a regiment of infantry being left to keep up the communication with Loison. General Botilho, however, soon reappeared upon the Lima, Lorge's dragoons were detached to watch him, and meanwhile Mermet's division was pushed towards the Vouga. The French army was thus extended in detachments from that river to the Tamega, occupying two sides of a triangle, its flanks presented to the enemy, the wings separated by the Douro and without communication, except by the boat-bridge of Oporto. It required three days to unite on the centre, and five days to concentrate on either extremity.

The situation of the allies was very different;— sir Arthur Wellesley having assembled the bulk of his troops at Coimbra, had the choice of two lines of operation; the one, through Viseu and Lamego, by which, in four or five marches, he could turn the French left and cut them off from Tras os Montes; the other leading upon Oporto, whereby, in two marches, he could throw himself unexpectedly, and in very superior numbers, upon the enemy's right, with a prospect of crushing it between the Vouga and the Douro. On the first of these two lines, which were separated by the lofty

BOOK
VIII.
1809.
May.
ridges of the Sierra de Caramula, the march could
be covered by Wilson's corps, at Viseu, and by Silveira's, near Lamego. Along the second, the movement could be screened by Trant's corps on the Vouga.

The duke of Dalmatia's dispositions were made
in ignorance of sir Arthur Wellesley's position,
numbers, and intentions. He was not even aware
of the vicinity of such an antagonist, but sensible
that to advance directly upon Lisbon was beyond
his own strength, he meditated to cross the Tamega,
and then, covered by that river and the Douro, to
s.
Journal of
Operations
MSS.
follow the great route of Bragança, and so enter
the Salamanca country. It was in this view that
Loison had been directed to get possession of Mezamfrio and Pezo de Ragoa, Mermet's advance
towards the Vouga being only to support Franceschi's retreat, when the army should commence its
movement towards the Tamega.

The 9th of May, D'Argenton was arrested, the
film fell from Soult's eyes, and all the perils of his
position broke at once upon his view. Treason in
his camp which he could not probe; a powerful
enemy close in his front; the insurgents again active
in his rear; the French troops scattered from the
Vouga to the Tamega, from the Douro to the Lima,
and commanded by officers, whose fidelity was necessarily suspected, while the extent of the conspiracy was unknown. Appalling as this prospect was,
the duke of Dalmatia did not quail at the sight.
The general officers assured him of the fidelity of
the troops, he ordered Loison to keep Mezamfrio
and Ragoa, if he could, but, under any circumstances, to hold Amarante fast, and the greatest
part of the guns and stores at Oporto were directed
upon the Tamega; the ammunition that could

not be removed was destroyed, and Lorge was directed to withdraw the garrison of Viana and make for Amarante; D'Argenton was then closely, although vainly, pressed to discover his accomplices, and all the arrangements necessary for a movement upon the Tras os Montes were actively followed up. But the war was coming up with a full and swift tide; Loison, upon whose vigour the success of the operation depended, was giving way, Wellesley was already across the Vouga, and Franceschi was struggling in his grasp.

The English general had resolved to operate along both the routes before spoken of, but the greater facility of supplying the troops by the coast-line, and, above all, the exposed position of the French right wing, so near the allies and so distant from succour, induced him to make the principal attack by the high road leading to Oporto. He had one division of cavalry and three of infantry, exclusive of Beresford's corps. The first division, composed of two brigades of infantry and twelve guns, was commanded by lieutenant-general Paget. The second, of three brigades of infantry and six guns, by lieutenant-general Sherbrooke. The third, of two brigades of infantry and six guns, by major-general Hill. The cavalry by lieutenant-general Payne. The whole amounted to about fourteen thousand five hundred infantry, fifteen hundred cavalry, and twenty-four guns, of which six were only three-pounders.

The 6th of May, Beresford, with six thousand Portuguese, two British battalions, five companies of riflemen, and a squadron of heavy cavalry, marched upon Lamego by the road of Viseu.

The 7th, the light cavalry and Paget's division advanced towards the Vouga by the Oporto road, but halted, on the 8th, to give Beresford time to reach the Upper Douro, before the attack on the French right should commence. The 9th, they resumed their march for the bridge of Vouga ; Hill's division took the Aveiro road, and the whole reached the line of the Vouga river that evening ; but Paget's division was not brought up until after dark, and then with caution, to prevent the enemy's guard from seeing the columns, the intent being to surprise Franceschi the next morning.

That general, with all his cavalry, a regiment of Mermet's division, and six guns, occupied a village, eight miles beyond Vouga bridge, called Albergaria Nova ; the remainder of Mermet's infantry were at Grijon, one march in the rear, and on the main road to Oporto. Franceschi had that day informed Soult, that the allied forces were collecting on the Mondego and that Trant's posts had closed upon the Vouga ; he was, however, far from suspecting that the whole army was upon the last river, although, from the imprudent conversation of an English officer, bearing a flag of truce, he had reason to expect an attack of some kind.

Sir Arthur Wellesley's plan was partly arranged upon the suggestion of the field-officer who had met D'Argenton. He had observed, during his intercourse with the conspirators, that the lake of Ovar was unguarded by the French, although it extended twenty miles behind their outposts, and all the boats were at Aveiro, which was in possession of the allies. On this information it was decided to turn the enemy's right by the lake.

Accordingly, general Hill embarked on the evening of the 9th, with one brigade, the other being to follow him as quickly as possible. The fishermen looked on at first with surprise, but, soon comprehending the object, voluntarily rushed in crowds to the boats, and worked with such a will, that the whole flotilla arrived at Ovar precisely at sunrise on the 10th, when the troops immediately disembarked. That day, also, Beresford, having rallied Wilson's corps upon his own, reached Pezo de Ragoa, and he it was, that had repulsed Loison and pursued him to Amarante.

Both flanks of the French army were now turned, and at the same moment sir Arthur, with the main body, fell upon Franceschi, for while the flotilla was navigating the lake of Ovar, the attempt to surprise that general at Albergaria Nova, was in progress. Sherbrooke's division was not yet up; but general Cotton, with the light cavalry, crossing the Vouga, a little after midnight, endeavoured to turn the enemy's left, and get behind him while the head of Paget's division, marching a little later, passed through the defiles of Vouga, directly upon Albergaria. Trant's corps was to make way between Paget's division and the lake of Aveiro.

This enterprise, so well conceived, was baffled by petty events, such as always abound in war. Sir Arthur Wellesley did not perfectly know the ground beyond the Vouga, and late in the evening of the 9th, colonel Trant, having ascertained that an impracticable ravine, extending from the lake to Olivera de Azemiz, would prevent him from obeying his orders, passed the bridge of Vouga, and carried his own guns beyond the defiles; thinking thus to leave the bridge clear for the British artillery and

Richard Stewart's brigade, which had been charged to conduct the British cannon; this task was difficult; several carriages broke down, and Trant's corps took the lead of Paget's column, the march of which was impeded by the broken gun-carriages. Meanwhile the cavalry under Cotton were misled by the guides, and came, in broad daylight, upon Franceschi, who, with his flank resting upon a wood garnished with infantry, boldly offered a battle that Cotton dared not, under such circumstances, accept. Thus, an hour's delay, produced by a few trifling accidents, marred a combination that would have shorn Soult of a third of his infantry and all his light cavalry; for it is not to be supposed that, when Franceschi's horsemen were cut off, and general Hill at Ovar, Mermet's division could have escaped across the Douro.

When sir Arthur Wellesley came up to Albergaria with Paget's infantry, Franceschi was still in position, skirmishing with Trant's corps, and evidently ignorant of what a force was advancing against him; but being immediately attacked, and his foot dislodged from the wood, he retreated along the road to Oliveira de Azemis, briskly pursued by the allied infantry. Nevertheless, valiantly extricating himself from this perilous situation, he reached Oliveira without any serious loss, and continuing his march during the night by Feria, joined Mermet next morning at Grijon.

Franceschi, in the course of the 10th, could see the whole of the English army, including the troops with Hill, and it may create surprise that he should pass so near the latter general without being attacked; but Hill was strictly obedient to his orders, which forbade him to act on the enemy's rear; and those orders were wise and prudent, because the principle of operating with small bodies on the flanks and rear of an enemy is vicious. While the number of men on the left of the Douro was unknown, it would have been rash to interpose a single brigade between the advanced guard and the main body of the French; the object of Hill's being sent to Ovar was, 1°. that the line of march might be eased, and the enemy's attention distracted; 2°. that a division of fresh soldiers might be at hand to follow the pursuit, so as to arrive on the bridge of Oporto pell-mell with the flying enemy; and it was the soldierlike retreat of Franceschi that prevented the last object from being attained.

General Paget's division and the cavalry halted the night of the 10th at Oliveira; Sherbrooke's division passed the Vouga later in the day, and remained in Albergaria; the next morning the pursuit was renewed, and the men, marching strongly, came up with the enemy about eight o'clock in the morning.

COMBAT OF GRIJON.

The French were posted across the road on a range of steep hills, a wood, occupied with infantry, covered their right flank, and their front was protected by a village and broken ground, but their left was ill placed. The British troops came up briskly in one column, the head of which was instantly and sharply engaged. The 16th Portuguese regiment, then quitting the line of march, drove the enemy out of the wood covering his right, and at the same time the Germans, who were in the rear, bringing their left shoulders forward, with-

out any halt or check, turned the other flank of the
French : the latter immediately abandoned the
position, and, being pressed in the rear by two
squadrons of cavalry, lost a few killed and about a
hundred prisoners. The heights of Carvalho gave
them an opportunity to turn and check the pursuing
squadrons, yet, when the British infantry, with an
impetuous pace, again drew near, they fell back,
and thus fighting and retreating, a blow and a race,
wore the day away. During this combat, Hill
was to have marched by the coast-road towards
Oporto, to intercept the enemy's retreat, but by
some error in the transmission of orders, that general, taking the route of Feria, crossed Trant's
line of march, and the time thus lost could not be
regained.

The British halted at dark. The French passed
the Douro in the night, and destroyed the bridge, and
all the heavy artillery and baggage still in Oporto
were immediately sent off by this road to Amarante.
Mermet, without halting, followed the same route
as far as Vallonga and Baltar, having orders to
secure all the boats and vigilantly to patrole up the
right bank of the river, and Loison, his retreat from
Pezo de Ragoa being unknown, was again warned
to hold the Tamega as he valued the safety of
the army ; finally Soult having directed all the
craft in the Douro in his front to be secured, and
having placed guards at convenient points, resolved
to hold Oporto during the 12th, that Lorge's dragoon's and the different detachments might have
time to concentrate at Amarante.

The duke of Dalmatia's attention was now principally directed to the river in its course *below* the
city, for the reports of his cavalry led him to be-

lieve that Hill's division had been disembarked at Ovar from the ocean, and he expected that the empty vessels would come round to effect a passage at the mouth of the Douro. Nevertheless, thinking that Loison still held Mesamfrio and Pezo with six thousand men, and knowing that three brigades occupied intermediate posts between Amarante and Oporto, he was satisfied that his retreat was secured, and thought there was no rashness in maintaining his position for another day. But the conspirators were busy. His orders were neglected or only half obeyed, and false reports of their execution made to him.

In this state of affairs the heads of the British columns arrived at Villa Nova, and before eight o'clock in the morning of the 12th, the whole army was concentrated there, yet hidden from Soult by the height upon which the convent of Sarea stood. The Douro rolled between the hostile forces, and the French who had suffered nothing from the previous operations, could in two days take post behind the Tamega, from whence the retreat upon Bragança would be certain; and they might, in passing, defeat Beresford; for that general's force was feeble in numbers, in infancy as to organization, and the utmost sir Arthur expected from it was that, vexing the French line of march, and infesting the road of Villa Real, it would oblige Soult to take the less accessible route of Chaves and retire to Gallicia instead of Leon. This however could not happen unless the main body of the allies followed the French closely from Oporto, and as Soult at Salamanca would have been more formidable than ever, the ultimate object of the campaign and the immediate safety of Beresford's

corps, alike demanded, that the Douro should be
quickly passed.   But how force the passage of a
river, deep, swift, more than three hundred yards
wide, and with ten thousand veterans guarding the
opposite bank!   Alexander the Great might have
turned from it without shame!

The height of Sarea, round which the Douro
came with a sharp elbow, prevented any view of
the upper river from the town, and the duke of
Dalmatia, confident that all above the city was
secure, took his station in a house westward of
Oporto, whence he could discern the whole course
of the lower river to its mouth.   Meanwhile, from
the summit of Sarea, sir A. Wellesley, with an
eagle's glance, searched all the opposite bank and
the city and country beyond it.   He saw horses and
baggage moving on the road to Vallonga, and the
dust of columns in retreat, but no large body of
troops near the river; the enemy's guards were few
and distant from each other; his patroles neither
numerous nor vigilant, and an auspicious negligence seemed to pervade his camp.   Suddenly a
large unfinished building, called the Seminary,
caught the English general's eye.   This isolated
structure, having a short easy access from the river,
was surrounded by a high wall, which, extending
to the water on either side, enclosed an area sufficient for two battalions in order of battle; the only
egress was by an iron gate opening on the Vallonga
road, and the building itself commanded every
thing in its vicinity, except one mound, which was
within cannon-shot, but too pointed to hold a gun.
There were no French posts near, and the direct
line of passage from the height of Sarea, across
the river to the building, being to the right hand,

was hidden from the troops in the town. Here, then, with a marvellous hardihood, sir Arthur resolved, if he could find but one boat, to make his way, in the face of a veteran army and a renowned general.

PASSAGE OF THE DOURO.

A poor barber, evading the French patroles, had during the night come over the water in a small skiff. Colonel Waters, a staff officer, a quick daring man, discovered this, and aided by the barber, and by the prior of Amarante who gallantly offered his services, immediately passed the river, and in half an hour returned unperceived with three large barges. Meanwhile eighteen pieces of artillery were got up to the convent of Sarea, and major-general John Murray was directed, with the German brigade, some squadrons of the 14th dragoons, and two guns, upon the Barca de Avintas, three miles above. He had orders to seek for boats and effect a passage there also if possible, and when Waters returned, some of the English troops were pushed towards Murray in support, while others cautiously approached the brink of the river under Sarea.

It was now ten o'clock; the French were still tranquil and unsuspicious; the British wondering and expectant. Sir Arthur was informed that one boat was brought up to the point of passage. "*Well, let the men cross,*" was his reply, and at this simple order, an officer with twenty-five soldiers of the Buffs embarked, and in a quarter of an hour silently placed themselves in the midst of the enemy's army.

The Seminary was thus gained, all was quiet in

Oporto, and a second boat followed the first; no hostile movement was seen, no sound heard, and a third boat passed higher up the river, but scarcely had the men from this last set foot on shore, when a tumultuous noise arose in the city. The drums beat to arms, shouts arose from all parts, the people were seen vehemently gesticulating and making signals from the houses, confused masses of French troops, hurrying forth from the streets by the higher grounds, threw out swarms of skirmishers that came furiously down against the Seminary. The British army instantly crowded to the bank of the river; Paget's and Hill's divisions collected at the point of passage and Sherbrooke's division where the boat bridge had been cut away from Villa Nova. Paget himself had passed in the third boat, and having mounted the roof of the Seminary was already struck down with a dangerous wound. Hill took his place. The musketry was sharp, voluble, and encreasing as the numbers on both sides accumulated; but the French attack was eager and constant, their fire augmented faster than that of the English, and their artillery also began to play upon the building. The British guns from Sarea commanded indeed the whole enclosure round the Seminary, and swept the left of the wall in such a manner as to confine the French assault to the side of the iron gate; but Murray did not appear, and the struggle was so violent, and the moment so critical, that sir Arthur himself was only prevented from crossing by the earnest representations of those about him, and the just confidence he had in general Hill.

At this period some citizens pushed over to Villa Nova with several great boats, Sherbrooke's people

began to cross in large bodies, and at the same
moment, a loud shout in the town, and the waving
of handkerchiefs from all the windows, gave notice
that the enemy had abandoned the lower part of
the city: Murray's troops were now seen descending
the right bank from Avintas, three battalions were
in the Seminary, and Hill, advancing to the enclosure wall, opened a destructive fire upon the French
columns, as they passed, in haste and confusion,
by the Vallonga road. Five pieces of French
artillery came galloping out from the town on the
left, but appalled by the terrible line of musketry
to be passed, the drivers suddenly pulled up, and
while thus hesitating, a volley from behind stretched
most of the artillery-men on the ground; the rest
dispersing among the enclosures, left their guns on
the road. This volley was given by a part of
Sherbrooke's people, who, having forced their way
through the streets, thus came upon the rear: in
fine, the passage was won, and the allies were in
considerable force on the French side of the river.
To the left, general Sherbrooke, with the brigade
of guards, and the 29th regiment, was in the town,
and pressing the rear of the enemy, who were quitting it. In the centre, general Hill, holding the
Seminary and the wall of the enclosure, with the
Buffs, the 48th, the 66th, the 16th Portuguese,
and a battalion of detachments, sent a damaging
fire into the masses as they passed him, and his
line was prolonged on the right, although with a
considerable interval, by general Murray's Germans,
and two squadrons of the 14th dragoons. The remainder of the army kept passing the river at different points, and the artillery, from the height of

Sarea, still searched the enemy's columns as they hurried along the line of retreat.

If general Murray had then fallen boldly in upon the disordered crowds, their discomfiture would have been complete; but he suffered column after column to pass him, without even a cannon shot, and seemed fearful lest they should turn and push him into the river. General Charles Stewart and major Hervey, impatient of this timidity, charged with the two squadrons of dragoons, and riding over the enemy's rear-guard, as it was pushing through a narrow road to gain an open space beyond, unhorsed Laborde and wounded Foy; but on the English side Hervey lost an arm, and his gallant horsemen, receiving no support from Murray, had to fight their way back with loss. This finished the action, the French continued their retreat, and the British remained on the ground they had gained. The latter lost twenty killed, a general and ninety-five men wounded; the former had about five hundred men killed and wounded, and five pieces of artillery were taken in the fight; a considerable quantity of ammunition, and fifty guns (of which the carriages had been burnt) were afterwards found in the arsenal, and several hundred men were captured in the hospitals.

Napoleon's veterans were so experienced, so inured to warfare that no troops in the world could more readily recover from such a surprise, and before they reached Vallonga their columns were again in order, with a regular rear-guard covering the retreat; a small garrison at the mouth of the Douro which had been cut off, being guided by some friendly Portuguese, also rejoined the army in the

Plate 4. Vol. 2.

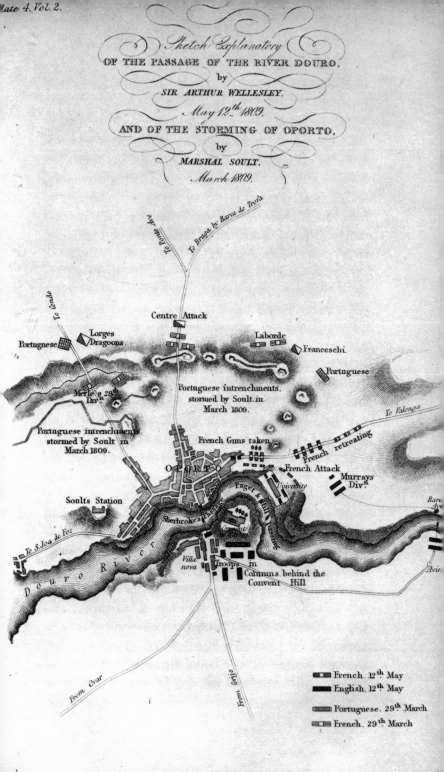

Sketch Explanatory

OF THE PASSAGE OF THE RIVER DOURO,

by

SIR ARTHUR WELLESLEY,

May 12th 1809.

AND OF THE STORMING OF OPORTO,

by

MARSHAL SOULT.

March 1809.

To Ponte Ave

To Braga by Barca de Trofa

To Conde

Centre Attack

Lorges Dragoons

Portuguese

Laborde

Franceschi

Portuguese

Merle's 28th Divn

Portuguese intrenchments stormed by Soult in March 1809.

To Valonga

Portuguese intrenchments stormed by Soult in March 1809.

French Guns taken

French retreating

OPORTO

French Attack

Murrays Divn

Soult's Station

Paget & Hill landing

University

Barca Ave

Sherbroke's landing

Convent

To S. Joa de Foz

Douro River

Villa nova

Troops in Columns behind the Convent Hill

Avin

From Ovar

From Grijo

☒☒ French. 12th May

▬▬ English. 12th May

▥▥ Portuguese. 29th March

☐☐ French. 29th March

London. Published by T. & W. BOONE.

night, and Soult, believing that Loison was at Amarante, thought he had happily escaped the danger.

Sir Arthur Wellesley employed the remainder of
the 12th, and the next day, in bringing over the
rear-guard of the army, the baggage, the stores,
and the artillery. Murray's Germans indeed pursued, on the morning of the 13th, but not further
than about two leagues on the road of Amarante, and
this delay has been blamed as an error in sir Arthur.
It is argued that an enemy once surprised should
never be allowed to recover, and that Soult should
have been followed up, even while a single regiment was left to pursue. The reasons for halting
were, first, that a part of the army was still on the
left bank of the Douro ;—secondly, that the troops
had outmarched provisions, baggage, and ammunition, and having passed over above eighty miles of
difficult country in four days, during three of which
they were constantly fighting, both men and animals required rest; thirdly, that nothing was known
of Beresford, whose contemporary operations it is
time to relate.

The moment of his arrival on the Douro was
marked by the repulse of Loison's division, which
immediately fell back, as I have already related, to
Mezamfrio, but followed by the Portuguese patroles
only, for Beresford halted on the left bank of the
river, because the British regiments were still in
the rear. This was on the 10th. Silveira, who
was at Villa Real, had orders to feel towards Mezamfrio for the enemy, and the marshal's force was
thus, with the assistance of the insurgents, in readiness to turn Soult from the route of Villa Real to
Bragança. The 11th Loison continued his retreat,

and Beresford finding him so timid, followed and skirmished with his rear-guard; at the same time Silveira advanced from Villa Real. On the 12th, the French outposts in front of Amarante were driven in, and the 13th Loison abandoned that town, and took the route of Guimaraens. These events were unknown to sir Arthur Wellesley on the evening of the 13th, but he heard that Soult, after destroying his artillery and ammunition, near Penafiel, had passed over the mountains towards Braga, and judging this to arise from Beresford's operations on the Tamega, he reinforced Murray with some cavalry, ordering him to proceed by Penafiel, and if Loison still lingered near Amarante, to open a communication with Beresford. The latter was at the same time directed to ascend the Tamega, and intercept the enemy at Chaves.

Meanwhile, the main body of the army marched in two columns upon the Minho, the one by the route of Barca de Troffa and Braga, the other by the Ponte d'Ave and Bacellos; but, on the evening of the 14th, the movements of the enemy about Braga gave certain proofs that not Valença and Tuy, but Chaves or Montalegre, would be the point of his retreat. Hereupon, the left column was drawn off from the Bacellos road and directed upon Braga, and Beresford was instructed to move by Monterey, upon Villa del Rey, if Soult should take the line of Montalegre. The 15th, sir Arthur reached Braga. Murray was at Guimaraens on his right, and Beresford, who had anticipated his orders, was near Chaves, having sent Silveira towards Salamonde, with instructions to occupy the passes of Ruivaens and Melgasso. At this time, however, Soult was

fifteen miles in advance of Braga, having, by a surprising effort, extricated himself from one of the
most dangerous situations that a general ever
escaped from ; but to understand this, it is necessary to describe the country through which his
retreat was effected.

I have already stated, that the Sierra de Ca-
breira and the Sierra de Catalina, line the right
bank of the Tamega ; but, in approaching the
Douro, the latter slants off towards Oporto, leaving
a rough but practicable slip of land, through which
the road leads from Oporto to Amarante : hence,
the French in retreating to the latter town had the
Douro on their right hand and the Sierra de Catalina on their left, both supposed impassable ; and
although between Amarante and Braga which is on
the other side of the Catalina, a route practicable
for artillery runs through Guimaraens, it was necessary to reach Amarante to fall into this road.
Soult, therefore, as he advanced along the narrow
pass between the mountains and the Douro, rested
his hopes of safety entirely upon Loison's holding
Amarante ; several days, however, had elapsed since
that general had communicated with the army, and
an aide-de-camp was sent, on the morning of the 12th,
to ascertain his exact position. Colonel Tholosé, the
officer employed, found Loison at Amarante, but
neither his remonstrances, nor the after-coming intelligence, that Oporto was evacuated and the army
in full retreat upon the Tamega, could induce that
general to remain there ; as we have seen, he
marched towards Guimaraens on the 13th, abandoning the bridge of Amarante, without a blow,
and leaving his commander and two-thirds of the

army to what must have appeared inevitable destruction.

The news of this unexpected calamity reached
Soult at one o'clock on the morning of the 13th,
just after he had passed the rugged banks of the
Souza river; the weather was boisterous, the men
were fatigued, voices were heard calling for a capitulation, and the whole army was stricken with
dismay; then it was that the duke of Dalmatia
justified, by his energy, that fortune which had
raised him to his high rank in the world. Being,
by a Spanish pedlar, informed of a path, that, mounting the right bank of the Souza, led over the Sierra
de Catalina to Guimaraens, he, on the instant,
silenced the murmurs of the treacherous or fearful
in the ranks, destroyed the artillery, abandoned the
military chest and baggage, loaded the animals with
sick men and musket ammunition, and repassing
the Souza, followed his Spanish guide with a hardy
resolution. The rain was falling in torrents, and
the path was such as might be expected in those
wild regions, yet the troops made good their passage over the mountains to Pombeira, and at Guimaraens, happily fell in with Loison. During the
night they were joined by Lorge's dragoons from
Braga, and thus, almost beyond hope, the whole
army was concentrated.

If Soult's energy in command was conspicuous
on this occasion, his sagacity and judgement were
not less remakably displayed in what followed.
Most generals would have moved by the direct
route upon Guimaraens to Braga; but he, with a
long reach of mind, calculated from the slackness
of pursuit after he passed Vallonga, that the bulk

of the English army must be on the road to Braga,
and would be there before him ; or that, at best, he
should be obliged to retreat fighting, and must
sacrifice the guns and baggage of Loison's and
Lorge's corps in the face of an enemy—a circumstance that might operate fatally on the spirit of his
soldiers, and would certainly give opportunities to
the malcontents; and already one of the generals
(apparently Loison) was recommending a convention
like Cintra. Wherefore, with a firmness worthy
of the highest admiration, Soult destroyed all the
guns and the greatest part of the baggage and ammunition of Loison's and Lorge's divisions ; then,
leaving the high road to Braga on his left, once
more took to the mountain paths, making for the
heights of Carvalho d'Este, where he arrived late
in the evening of the 14th, thus gaining a day's
march, in point of time. The morning of the 15th
he drew up his troops in the position he had occupied two months before, at the battle of Braga,
and by this spectacle, where twenty thousand men
were collected upon the theatre of a former victory,
and disposed so as to produce the greatest effect, he
aroused all the sinking pride of the French soldiers.
It was a happy reach of generalship, an inspiration
of real genius !

He now re-organised his army, taking the command of the rear-guard himself, and giving that of
the advanced guard to general Loison. Noble, the
French historian of this campaign, says, " *the
whole army was astonished ;*" as if it were not a stroke
of consummate policy, that the rear, which was
pursued by the British, should be under the general-
in-chief, and that the front, which was to fight its
way through the native forces, should have a com-

mander whose very name called up all the revenge-
ful passions of the Portuguese. *Maneta dared not
surrender !* and thus the duke of Dalmatia dex-
terously forced those to act with most zeal who were
least inclined to serve him; but in sooth, such was
his perilous situation, that all the resources of his
mind and all the energy of his character were
needed to save the army.

From Carvalho he retired to Salamonde, from
whence there were two lines of retreat; the one
through Ruivaens and Venda Nova, by which the
army had marched when coming from Chaves two
months before; the other, shorter, although more
impracticable, leading by the Ponte Nova and Ponte
Miserella into the road running from Ruivaens to
Montalegre. But the scouts brought intelligence
that the bridge of Ruivaens, on the little river of
that name, was broken, and defended by twelve
hundred Portuguese, with artillery, and that another
party had been, since the morning, destroying the
Ponte Nova on the Cavado river. The destruction
of the first bridge blocked the road to Chaves; the
second, if completed, and the passage well defended, would have cut the French off from Montalegre. The night was setting in, the soldiers
were harassed, barefooted, and starving; the ammunition was injured by the rain, which had never
ceased since the 13th, and which was now increasing in violence, accompanied with storms of
wind; the British army would certainly fall upon
the rear in the morning; and if the Ponte Nova,
where the guard was reported to be weak, could
not be secured, the hour of surrender was surely
arrived. In this extremity, Soult sent for major
Dulong, an officer justly reputed for one of the

most daring in the French ranks. Addressing himself to this brave man, he said, " I have chosen you from the whole army to seize the Ponte Nova, which has been cut by the enemy. Select a hundred grenadiers and twenty-five horsemen, endeavour to surprise the guards, and secure the passage of the bridge. If you succeed, say so, but send no other report; your silence will suffice." Thus exhorted and favoured by the storm Dulong reached the bridge unperceived of the Portuguese, killed the centinel before any alarm was given, and then, followed by twelve grenadiers, began crawling along a narrow slip of masonry, which was the only part undestroyed. The Cavado river was flooded and roaring in its deep channel, one of the grenadiers fell into the gulf, but the noise of the waters was louder than his cry, and Dulong with the eleven reaching the other side surprised the nearest post; the remainder of his men advanced at the same moment close to the bridge, and some crossing and others mounting the heights, shouting and firing, scared the poor peasantry, who imagined the whole army was upon them; thus the passage was gallantly won.

At four o'clock, the bridge was repaired and the advanced guards of the French commenced crossing; but the column of march was long, the road narrow and rugged, the troops filed over slowly, and beyond the Ponte Nova there was a second obstacle still more formidable. For the pass in which the troops were moving being cut in the side of a mountain, open on the left for several miles, at last came upon a torrent called the Misarella, which, breaking down a deep ravine, or rather gulph, was only to be crossed by a bridge constructed with a single

lofty arch, called *Saltador*, or the leaper, and so
narrow that only three persons could pass abreast.
Fortunately for the French, the Saltador was not
cut, but entrenched and defended by a few hundred
Portuguese peasants, who occupied the rocks on the
farther side, and here the good soldier Dulong again
saved the army; for, when a first and second
attempt had been repulsed, he carried the entrenchments by a third effort, and, at the same instant
fell deeply wounded. The head of the column
then poured over, and it was full time, for the
English guns were thundering in the rear, and the
Ponte Nova was choked with dead.

s.
Journal of
Operations
MS.

Sir Arthur Wellesley, quitting Braga on the
morning of the 16th, had come, about four o'clock,
upon Soult's rear-guard, which remained at Salamonde to cover the passage of the army over the
bridges. The right was strongly protected by a
ravine, the left occupied a steep hill, and a stout
battle might have been made; but men thus cir-
cumstanced, and momentarily expecting an order
to retreat, will seldom stand firmly; on this occasion, when some light troops turned the left, and
general Sherbrooke, with the guards, mounting
the steep hill, attacked the front, the French made
but one discharge, and fled in confusion to the
Ponte Nova. As this bridge was not on the direct line of retreat, they were for some time unperceived, and gaining ground of their pursuers,
formed a rear-guard; yet being at last descried,
some guns were brought to bear on them, and then
man and horse, crushed together, went over into
the gulph, and the bridge, and the rocks, and the
defile beyond were strewed with mangled bodies.
This was the last calamity inflicted by the sword

upon the French army in this retreat; a retreat attended by many horrid as well as glorious events; for the peasants in their fury, with an atrocious cruelty, tortured and mutilated every sick man and straggler that fell into their power, and on the other hand, the soldiers, who held together in their turn, shot the peasants, while the track of the columns might be discovered from afar by the smoke of the burning houses.

The French reached Montalegre on the 17th, being followed only by colonel Waters, with some cavalry, who picked up a few stragglers at Villella. Sir Arthur halted that day at Ruivaens, which seems to have been an error in principle, because there appears no adequate cause for the delay, but on the 18th he renewed the pursuit, and a part of his cavalry passed Montalegre, followed by the guards; the enemy was, however, drawn up behind the Salas in force, and no action took place. Silveira, indeed, had entered Montalegre, from the side of Chaves, before the British came up from Ruivaens; but instead of pursuing, he put his men into quarters; and a Portuguese officer of his division, who was despatched to marshal Beresford with orders to move from Villa Perdrices upon Villa del Rey, loitered on the road so long, that all chance of intercepting the French line of march was at an end; for though Beresford, on the 19th, sent colonel Talbot with the 14th dragoons as far as Ginjo, Franceschi turned in force, and obliged that officer to retire, and the pursuit terminated, with the capture of a few stragglers on the Salas.

Soult himself crossed the frontier by Allaritz on the 18th, and on the 19th entered Orense, without guns, stores, ammunition, or baggage; his men were exhausted with fatigue and misery, the greatest part without shoes, many without accoutrements, and in some instances even without muskets. He had quitted Orense seventy-six days before, with about twenty-two thousand men, and three thousand five hundred had afterwards joined him from Tuy. He returned with nineteen thousand five hundred, having lost by the sword and sickness, by assassination and capture, six thousand good soldiers; of which number above three thousand were taken in hospitals,* and about a thousand were killed by the Portuguese, or had died of sickness, previous to the retreat; the remainder were captured, or had perished within the last eight days. He had carried fifty-eight pieces of artillery into Portugal, and he returned without a gun; yet was his reputation as a stout and able soldier no wise diminished.

OBSERVATIONS.

The duke of Dalmatia's arrangements being continually thwarted by the conspirators, his military skill cannot be fairly judged of; nevertheless, the errors of the campaign may, without injustice, be pointed out, leaving to others the task of tracing them to their true sources.

1°.—The disposition of the army, on both sides of the Douro and upon such extended lines, when no certain advice of the movements and strength of the English force had been received, was rash. It was, doubtless, right, that to clear the front and to gather information, Franceschi should advance to the Vouga; but he remained too long in the same

---

* Viz.   1800 left in Viana and Braga.
          500 including the wounded taken in Oporto.
          1300 taken at Chaves, by Silveira.

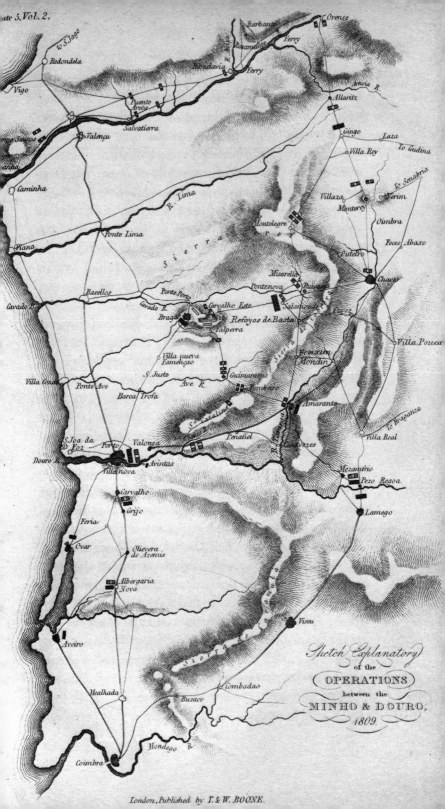

to S.Jago

Redondela

Vigo

R. Avia

Barbantes

Rosancotte

Orense

Ferry

Puente Arcos

Bradavia

Ferry

Allaritz

Gingo

Laza

To Gudina

Salvatierra

Villa Rey

Valença

Villazo

Monterey

Nerim

To Senabria

Oimbra

Caminha

R. Lima

Cudeiro

Feces Abaxo

Viana

Ponte Lima

Sierra

Chaves

Misarella

Pontenova

Ruivas

Bacellos

Porte Porto

Carvalho Este

Salamonde

Villa Pouca

Cavado R.

Braga

Refoyos de Basto

Cavado R.

Calperra

Sierra de Cabrara

Villa nueva Famelicao

Guimaraens

Frexim Mondin

S. Justo

Ave R.

Lombaro

Amaranto

Villa Conde

Ponte Ave

Barca Trofa

Santa Catalna

Peñafiel

Canavezes

Villa Real

To Braganza

S. Joa da Foz

Porto

Valonga

Avintas

Mezamfrio

Pezo Regoa

Douro R.

Villa nova

Carvalho

Lamego

Feria

Grijo

Ovar

Olievera de Azenis

Albergaria Nova

Viseu

Aveiro

Sierra de Alcoba

Mealhada

Busaco

Tombadao

Mondego R.

Coimbra

Sketch Explanatory
of the
OPERATIONS
between the
MINHO & DOURO,
1809.

London, Published by T. & W. BOONE.

position, and he should have felt Trant's force more positively. Had the latter officer (whose boldness in maintaining the line of the Vouga was extremely creditable) been beaten, as he easily might have been, the anarchy of the country would have increased; and as Beresford's troops at Thomar wanted but an excuse to disperse, the Portuguese and British preparations must have been greatly retarded.

2°.—That Soult, when he had secured, as he thought, all the boats on an unfordable river three hundred yards wide, should think himself safe from an attack for one day, is not wonderful. The improbability that such a barrier could be forced in half an hour might have rendered Fabius careless! yet there were some peculiar circumstances attending the surprise of the French army which indicate great negligence. The commanding officer of one regiment reported, as early as six o'clock, that the English were crossing the river; the report was certainly premature, because no man passed before ten o'clock, but it reached Soult, and he sent general Quesnel, the governor of Oporto, to verify the fact. Quesnel stated, on his return, and truly, that it was an error, and Soult took no further precaution; the patroles were not increased, no staff-officers appear to have been employed to watch the river, and no signals were established; yet it was but three days since D'Argenton's conspiracy had been discovered, and the extent of it was still unknown. This circumstance alone should have induced the duke of Dalmatia to augment the number of his guards and posts of observation, that the multiplicity of the reports might render it impossible for the malcontents to deceive him. The

Noble's
Campagne
de Galice.

surprise at Oporto must, therefore, be considered as a fault in the general, which could only be attoned for by the high resolution and commanding energy with which he saved his army in the subsequent retreat.

3°.—When general Loison suffered marshal Beresford to drive him from Pezo de Ragoa and Mezamfrio, he committed a grave military error, and when he abandoned Amarante, he relinquished all claim to military reputation, as a simple statement of facts will prove. The evening of the 12th he wrote to Soult that one regiment had easily repulsed the whole of the enemy's forces; yet he, although at the head of six thousand men, cavalry, infantry, and artillery, that night and without another shot being fired, abandoned the only passage by which, as far as he knew, the rest of the army could escape from its perilous situation with honour! It was not general Loison's fault if England did not triumph a second time for the capture of a French marshal.

MOVEMENTS OF THE BRITISH GENERAL.

1°.—If sir Arthur Wellesley's operation be looked at as a whole, it is impossible to deny his sagacity in planning, his decision and celerity in execution. When he landed at Lisbon, the nation was dismayed by previous defeats, distracted with anarchy, and menaced on two sides by powerful armies, one of which was already in possession of the second city in the kingdom. In twenty-eight days he had restored public confidence; provided a defence against one adversary; and having marched two hundred miles through a rugged country, and forced the passage of a great river—caused his other opponent to flee over the frontier, without artillery or baggage.

2°.—Such being the result, it is necessary to show that the success was due, not to the caprice of fortune, but to the talents of the general, that he was quick to see, and active to strike. And first, the secrecy and despatch with which the army was collected on the Vouga belongs entirely to the man; for, there were many obstacles to over-come, and D'Argenton, as the sequel proved, would, by his disclosures, have ruined sir Arthur's com-binations, if the latter had not providently given him a false view of affairs. The subsequent march from the Vouga to the Douro was, in itself, no mean effort; for it must be recollected, that this rapid advance against an eminent commander and a veteran army of above twenty thousand men, was made with a heterogeneous force, of which only sixteen thousand men were approved soldiers, the remainder being totally unformed by discipline, untried in battle, and, only three weeks before, in a state of open mutiny.

3°.—The passage of the Douro, at Oporto, would, at first sight, seem a rash undertaking; when examined closely, it proves to be an example of consummate generalship, both in the conception and the execution. The careless watch maintained by the French may, indeed, be called fortunate, because it permitted the English general to get a few men over unperceived; but it was not twenty-five, nor twenty-five hundred, soldiers that could have maintained themselves, if heedlessly cast on the other side. Sir Arthur, when he so coolly said—"*let them pass,*" was prepared to protect them when they had passed. He did not give that order until he knew that Murray had found boats at Avintas, to ferry over a considerable number of troops, and, consequently, that that general, descending the Douro, could cover the right flank of the Seminary, while the guns planted on the heights of Sarea could sweep the left flank, and search all the ground enclosed by the wall round the building. Had only general Murray's troops passed, they would have been compromised; if the whole army had made the attempt at Avintas, its march would have been discovered; but in the double passage all was secured; the men in the Seminary by the guns, by the strength of the building, and by Murray's troops; the latter by the surprise on the town, which drew the enemy's attention away from them. Hence, it was only necessary to throw a few brave men into the Seminary unperceived, and the success was almost certain; because, while that building was maintained, the troops in the act of passing could neither be prevented nor harmed by the enemy. To attain great objects by simple means is the highest effort of genius!

4°.—If general Murray had attacked vigorously, the ruin of the French army would have ensued. It was an opportunity that would have tempted a blind man to strike; the neglect of it argued want of military talent and of military hardihood; and how would it have appeared if Loison had not abandoned Amarante? If Soult, effecting his retreat in safety, and reaching Zamora or Salamanca in good order, had turned on Ciudad Rodrigo, he would have found full occupation for sir Arthur Wellesley in the north; and he would have opened a free communication with the duke of Belluno; the latter must then have marched either against Seville or Lisbon; and thus the boldness and excellent conduct of the English general, producing no adequate results, would have been overlooked, or, perhaps, have formed a subject for the abuse of some ignorant, declamatory writer.

5°.—Sir Arthur Wellesley's reasons for halting at Oporto the 13th, have been already noticed, but they require further remarks. Had he followed Soult headlong, there is no doubt that the latter would have been overtaken on the Souza river, and destroyed; but this chance, arising from Loison's wretched movements, was not to be foreseen. He knew nothing of Beresford's situation, but he naturally supposed that, following his instructions, he was about Villa Real; and that, consequently, the French would, from Amarante, either move by Villa Pouca to Chaves, or taking the road to Guimaraens and Braga, make for the Minho; hence, he remained where he could command the main roads to that river, in order to intercept Soult's retreat and force him to a battle; whereas, if he had once entered the defile formed by the Douro and the Sierra de Catalina, he could only have followed his enemy in one column by a difficult route, a process promising little advantage. Nevertheless, seeing that he detached general Murray by that route at last, it would appear that he should have ordered him to press the enemy closer than he did; but there a political difficulty occurred. The English cabinet, although improvident in its preparations, was very fearful of misfortune, and the general dared not risk the safety of a single brigade, except for a great object, lest a slight disaster should cause the army to be recalled. This circumstance often obliged him to curb his naturally enterprising dis-position; and to this burthen of ministerial inca-pacity, which he bore even to the battle of Sala-manca, may be traced that over-caution which has been so often censured as a fault, not only by mili-tary writers, but by Napoleon, who, judging from appearances, erroneously supposed it to be a cha-racteristic of the man, and often rebuked his generals for not taking advantage thereof.

6°.—The marches and encounters, from the 14th to the 17th, were excellent on both sides. Like the wheelings and buffeting of two vultures in the air, the generals contended, the one for safety, the other for triumph; but there was evidently a failure in the operations of marshal Beresford. Soult did not reach Salamonde until the evening of the 15th, and his rear-guard was still there on the evening of the 16th. Beresford was in person at Chaves on the 16th, and his troops reached that place early on the morning of the 17th. Soult passed Monta-legre on the 18th, but from Chaves to that place is only one march. Again, marshal Beresford was in possession of Amarante on the 13th, and as there was an excellent map of the province in existence, he must have known the importance of Salamonde, which was only thirty-two miles from Amarante, and that there was a road to it through Freixim and Refoyos de Basta, and another through Mondin and Cavez, both shorter than that by Guimaraens and Chaves. It is true that Silveira was directed to occupy Ruivaens and Melgasso; but he either dis-obeyed or executed his orders too slowly, and Misarella was totally neglected. Major Warre, an officer of the marshal's staff, endeavoured, indeed, to break down the bridges of Ponte Nova and

Ruivaens, and it was by his exertions that the peasants surprised at the former, had been collected; but he had only a single dragoon with him, and was without powder to execute this important task. The peasantry, also glad to be rid of the French, were reluctant to stop their retreat, and still more to destroy the bridge of Misarella, which was the key of all the communications, and all the great markets of the Entre Minho e Douro, and therefore sure to be built up again; in which case the people knew well that their labour and time would be called for without payment. It is however undoubted that Soult owed his safety, firstly, to the failure, whatever may have been the cause, in Beresford's general operations, and, secondly, to the particular failure in breaking down the bridges; and it is probable, from what he did do, that major Warre would have effectually destroyed them if he had been supplied with only the commonest means.

Silveira is accused of not moving either in the direction or with the celerity required of him by Beresford, but there seems to have been a misunderstanding between them, and some allowance must be made for the numerous mistakes necessarily arising in the transmission of orders by officers speaking different languages; and for the difficulty of moving troops not accustomed, and perhaps not perfectly willing to act together.

CHAPTER III.

BOOK
VIII.

1809.
May.

S.
Journal of
Operations
MS.

THE duke of Dalmatia halted at Orense the 20th,
and on the 21st put his troops in motion upon
Lugo, to succour general Fournier, of the 6th corps,
who, with three battalions of infantry and a regiment of dragoons, was besieged by twelve or fifteen thousand Spaniards, under the command of
general Mahi. But to explain this it is necessary
to resume the account of Romana's operations, after
his defeat at Monterey on the 6th of March.

Having reassembled the fugitives at Puebla de
Senabria, on the borders of Leon, he repaired his
losses by fresh levies, and was soon after joined by
three thousand men from Castile, and thus, unknown to Ney, he had, as it were, gained the rear
of the sixth corps. Villa Franca del Bierzo was, at
this time, only occupied by two weak French battalions, and as their nearest support was at Lugo,
Romana resolved to surprise them. Dividing his
forces, he sent Mendizabel with one division by
the valley of the Syl to take them in rear, and
marched himself by the route of Calcabellos; in
this manner he surrounded the French, who, after a
short skirmish, in which the Spaniards lost about
a hundred men, surrendered, and were sent into
the Asturias.

Romana then detached a part of his forces to
Orense and Ponte Vedra, to assist Morillo and the
insurrection in the western parts of Gallicia, where,
with the aid of the English ships of war, and notwithstanding the shameful neglect of the supreme

central junta, the patriots were proceeding vigorously. The moveable columns of the sixth corps daily lost a number of men, some in open battle, and a still greater number by assassinations; these last were however rigorously visited upon the districts where they took place, and thus, in Gallicia, as in every other part of Spain, the war hourly assumed a more horrid character. Referring to this period, colonel Barios afterwards told Mr. Frere that to repress the excesses of marshal Ney's troops, he, himself, had, in cold blood, caused seven hundred French pri- Parl. Papers, 1810. soners to be drowned in the Minho! an avowal recorded by Mr. Frere, without animadversion, but which, happily for the cause of humanity, there is good reason to believe was as false as it would, if true, have been detestable.

After the capture of Vigo, the Spanish force on the coast increased rapidly. Barios departed for Seville, Martin Carrera assumed the command of the troops near Orense, and the Conde Noroña of those near Vigo; general Maucune returned to St. Jago from Tuy, and Ney, apprized of the loss at Villa Franca, advanced to Lugo. Romana immediately abandoned Gallicia, and, entering the Asturias by the pass of Cienfuegos, marched along the line of the Gallician frontier, until he reached Navia de Suarna, where he left Mahi, with the army, to observe Ney, but repaired, himself, to Oviedo, to redress the crying wrongs of the Asturians.

It is unnecessary to recapitulate the evil doings of the Asturian junta, which was notoriously corrupt and incapable; Romana, after a short inquiry, dismissed the members in virtue of his supreme authority, and appointed new men; but this act of justice gave great offence to Jovellanos and others.

It appeared too close an approximation to Cuesta's manner, in Leon, the year before, and as the central government, always selfish and jealous, abhorred any indication of vigour or probity in a general, Romana was soon afterwards deprived of his command. Meanwhile he was resolutely reforming abuses, when his proceedings were suddenly arrested by an unexpected event.

As soon as Ney understood that the Spanish army was posted on the Gallician side of the Asturian frontier; and that Romana was likely to excite the energy of the Asturian people; he planned a combined movement, to surround and destroy, not only Romana and his army, but also the Asturian troops, which then amounted to about fifteen thousand men, including the *partida* of Porlier, commonly called the Marquisetto. This force, commanded by general Ballasteros and general Vorster, occupied Infiesta, on the eastern side of Oviedo, and Castropol on the coast. Ney, with the consent of Joseph, arranged that Kellerman, who was at Astorga, with six guns and eight thousand seven hundred men, composed of detachments, drawn together from the different corps, should penetrate the Asturias from the south east by the pass of Pajares; that Bonnet, who always remained at the town of St. Andero, should break in, from the north east, by the coast road; and that the sixth corps should make an irruption by the Concejo de Ibas, a short but difficult route leading directly from Lugo.

When the period for these combined movements was determined, Ney, appointing general Marchand to command in Gallicia during his own absence, left three battalions under Maucune at St. Jago, three others in garrison at Coruña under

general D'Armagnac, one at Ferrol, and three with
a regiment of cavalry under Fournier at Lugo.   He
then marched himself, with twelve battalions of infantry and three regiments of cavalry, against Mahi,
and the latter immediately abandoned his position
at Navia de Suarna, and drawing off by his left,
without giving notice to Romana, returned to
Gallicia and again entered the valley of the Syl.
Ney, either thinking that the greatest force was
near Oviedo, or that it was more important to
capture Romana than to disperse Mahi's troops, continued his route by the valley of the Nareca; and
with such diligence that he reached Cornellana and
Grado, one march from Oviedo, before Romana
knew of his approach.   The Spanish general, thus
surprised, made a feeble and fruitless endeavour
to check the French at the bridge of Peñaflor, after
which, sending the single regiment he had with
him to Infiesta, he embarked on board an English
vessel at Gihon, and so escaped.

The 18th, Ney entered Oviedo, where he was
joined by Kellerman, and the next day pursued
Romana to Gihon; Bonnet, likewise, executed his
part, but somewhat later, and thus Vorster, being
unmolested by Ney, had time to collect his corps
on the coast.   Meanwhile Ballasteros, finding that
Bonnet had passed between him and Vorster, boldly
marched upon St. Andero and retook it, making
the garrison and sick men (in all eleven hundred)
prisoners: the Amelia and Statira, British frigates,
arrived off the harbour at the same moment, and
captured three French corvettes and two luggers,
on board of which some staff-officers were endeavouring to escape.

Bonnet, however, followed hard upon Ballasteros, and, the 11th of June, routed him so completely that he, also, was forced to save himself on board an English vessel, and the French recovered all the prisoners, and, amongst them, the men taken at Villa Franca, by Romana. But, before this, Ney, uneasy for his posts in Gallicia, had returned to Coruña by the coast-road through Castropol, and Kellerman, after several trifling skirmishes with Vorster, had also retired to Valladolid. This expedition proved that Asturia was not calculated for defence, although, with the aid of English ships, it might become extremely troublesome to the French.

While Ney was in Asturia, Carrera, advancing from the side of Orense, appeared in front of St. Jago di Compostella at the moment that colonel D'Esmenard, a staff-officer sent by the marshal to give notice of his return to Coruña, arrived with an escort of dragoons in Maucune's camp. This escort was magnified by the Spaniards into a reinforcement of eight hundred men; but Carrera, who had been joined by Morillo, commanded eight thousand, and, on the 23d, having attacked Maucune, at a place called "*Campo de Estrella,*" totally defeated him, with a loss of six hundred men and several guns. The Spaniards did not pursue, and the French retreated in confusion to Coruña. Nor was this the only check suffered by the 6th corps, for Mahi, having united a great body of peasants to his army, drove back Fournier's outposts, and closely invested him in Lugo on the 19th.

Such was the state of affairs in Gallicia when Soult arrived at Orense; and as the inhabitants of that town, from whom he got intelligence of these events, rather exaggerated the success of their countrymen, the French marshal immediately sent

s.
Journal of
Operations
MSS.

forward an advanced guard of his stoutest men to
relieve Lugo, and followed himself, by the route of
Monforte, with as much speed as the exhausted
state of his troops would permit. The 22d, he
reached Gutin, and, the same day, his van being
descried on the mountains above Lugo, Mahi broke
up his camp, and fell back to Mondenedo.

The 23d, Soult entered Lugo, where he heard of
the emperor's first successes in Austria, and, with
renewed energy, prepared for fresh exertions himself. The 30th, he was joined by Ney, who, unformed of Mahi's position at Mondenedo, had
missed a favourable opportunity of revenging the
loss at St. Jago. Meanwhile Romana, disembarking
at Ribadeo, joined Mahi at Mondenedo, and immediately marched along the line of the Asturian
frontier, until he arrived at the sources of the
Neyra; then, crossing the royal road, a little above
Lugo, plunged, once more, into the valley of the
Syl; and, having gained Orense, the 6th of June,
opened a communication with Carrera at St. Jago,
and with the insurgents at Vigo. This movement
of Romana's was able, energetic, and worthy of
every praise.

In pursuance of an order from the emperor, Soult
now sent eleven - hundred men, composed of
dismounted dragoons and skeletons of cavalry
regiments, to France; and, having partially restored the artillery and equipments of the second
corps, from the arsenals of Coruña and Ferrol, he,
in concert with the duke of Elchingen, arranged
a fresh plan for the destruction of Romana; in
the execution it failed, as shall be hereafter
noticed, but at present, it is necessary to return to
the campaign south of the Tagus.

VICTOR'S OPERATIONS.

Semelé's
Journal of
Operations
MSS.

After the abortive effort to gain Badajos, the duke
of Belluno, in obedience to the king's orders, proceeded to recover Alcantara. His rear was still
within two marches of Merida when the head of
his columns, under Lapisse, driving back some cavalry
posts, entered the town of Alcantara, and the next
day attempted the passage of the bridge. The
Portuguese force consisted of two thousand infantry, fifty cavalry, and six guns, and some works
of defence were constructed on the right bank
of the river, but on the 14th of May, Lapisse,
lining the rocks on the left bank, skirmished so
sharply that the militia regiment of Idanha gave
way. Colonel Mayne then sprung a mine, yet the
explosion did little injury to the bridge, and the
French made good the passage; the Portuguese,
who had suffered considerably, retired to the Puente
de Segura, and Lapisse immediately sent patroles
towards Castello Branco, Salvatierra, and Idanha
Nova.

Intelligence of this attack having reached general Mackenzie, he directed preparations to be made
for destroying the boat-bridge at Abrantes, and
marched, in person, by Corticada to Sobreira Formosa; which movement, aided by a rumour that
Soult had retreated from Oporto, afforded an excuse
to Victor for again abandoning Alcantara, and resuming his former camp. During his absence,
Cuesta, true to the promise he had given, attacked
the fort of Merida, but, on the return of the French
advanced guard, recrossed the Guadiana, and fell
back to Zafra, having first ravaged all the flat

country, and obliged the inhabitants to withdraw
into the mountains.

Some time before this, king Joseph had received a despatch from the French minister of war, giving notice that reinforcements had sailed from England, and warning him to lose no time in marching against Lisbon, to create a useful diversion in favour of Soult. It might be supposed that the original plan of the emperor would then have been acted upon, and this was the first thought of Joseph himself; but other circumstances created doubt and hesitation in his councils, and, finally, induced him to abandon all thoughts of Portugal. It appears when Napoleon returned to Paris, he imagined that hostilities with Austria, although certain, would not break out so suddenly, but that he should have time to organise a sufficient army in Germany, without drawing his veteran troops from Spain; hence, he still left the imperial guards at Vittoria, and sending the prince of Neufchatel to command the troops on the Danube, he himself remained at Paris, to superintend the preparations for opening the campaign. The Austrians were, however, not inattentive observers of the perfidy which accompanied the invasion of Spain, and, aptly taking the hint, attacked the French outposts and published their own declaration of war at the same moment. Berthier, incapable of acting a principal part, was surprised, and made a succession of false movements that would have been fatal to the French army, if the emperor, journeying day and night, had not arrived at the very hour when his lieutenant was on the point of consummating the ruin of the army. Then, indeed, was seen the supernatural force of Napoleon's genius: in a few hours he

changed the aspect of affairs, and in a few days,
maugre their immense number, his enemies, baffled
and flying in all directions, proclaimed his mastery in
an art which, up to that moment, was imperfect;
for never, since troops first trod a field of battle,
was such a display of military skill made by man.
But previous to these successes, so threatening
had been the aspect of affairs in Germany, that the
imperial guards had been recalled from Vittoria,
and hurried to the Danube; the great reserve of
infantry was, as we have seen, struck off the rolls
of the army in Spain, and the skeletons of the
fourth squadrons of every cavalry regiment were
ordered to return to their depôts in France; even
the fifth corps, under Mortier, then on its way
to Valladolid from Zaragoza, was directed to halt,
and hold itself in readiness to march for Germany. Thus, while Victor was reluctant to move,
while Ney was demanding more troops to preserve
Gallicia, and while the fate of the second corps
was unknown, the whole army was actually diminished by forty thousand men, and fifteen thousand
more were paralysed with regard to offensive operations.

These things had rendered Joseph timid. Madrid, it was argued in his councils, was of more
consequence than Lisbon; Soult might be already
at the latter place; or, if not, he might extricate
himself from his difficulties, for the capital of
Spain must be covered. In pursuance of this
reasoning, Sebastiani was forbidden any forward
movement; and the duke of Belluno, whose army
was daily wasting with the Guadiana fever, took
a position at Torre-Mocha, a central point between
Truxillo, Merida, and Alcantara. His cavalry

posts watched all the passages over the Guadiana
and the Tagus; and his communications with Madrid, between the Tietar and the Tagus, were protected by twelve hundred men, detached for that
purpose by the king.

But one timid measure in war generally produces
another. The neighbourhood of the English force
at Castel Branco increased the energy of the Spanish
insurgents, who infested the valley of the Tagus,
and communicated secretly with those of the Sierra
de Guadalupe; hence, Victor, alarmed for his bridge
at Almaraz, sent a division there the 22d, and, as
from that period until the 10th of June, he remained
quiet, his campaign, which had opened so bril-
liantly, was annulled. He had neither assisted
Soult, nor crushed Cuesta, nor taken Badajos, nor
Seville; yet he had wasted and lost, by sickness, more
men than would have sufficed to reduce both Lisbon
and Seville; meanwhile the Spaniards were daily
recovering strength and confidence, and sir Arthur
Wellesley, after defeating Soult, had full leisure to
return to the Tagus, and to combine his future
operations with the Spanish armies in the south.

Information that Lapisse had forced the bridge
of Alcantara reached the English general on the
night of the 17th. That part of the army which
was still behind Salamonde received immediate
orders to retrace their steps to Oporto; and when
the retreat of Soult by Orense was ascertained,
the remainder of the troops, including three Portuguese brigades under Beresford, followed the
same route. Colonel Trant was appointed military
governor of Oporto, and it was thought sufficient
to leave Silveira with some regular battalions and

militia to defend the northern provinces, for Soult's army was considered a crippled force, which could not for a long time appear again in the field; a conclusion drawn, as we shall see, from false data, and without due allowance being made for the energy of that chief.

As the army proceeded southward, the narrow scope of Lapisse's movements was ascertained; Colonel Mayne was directed again to take post at Alcantara, and as a reinforcement of five thousand men had landed at Lisbon, the rapidity of the march slackened. Passing by easy journeys through Coimbra, Thomar, and Punhete, the troops reached Abrantes the 7th of June, and encamped on the left bank of the Tagus, but there was sickness and a great mortality in the ranks.

From the moment of his arrival in Portugal, sir Arthur Wellesley had looked to the defeat of Victor as the principal, and the operation against Soult as the secondary, object of the campaign; and the English government, acceding to his views, now gave him a discretionary power to enter the nearest province of Spain, if Portugal should not thereby be endangered. In his correspondence with the junta and with Cuesta, he had therefore strongly urged the necessity of avoiding any serious collision with the enemy until the British troops could act in concert with the Spanish armies, and this advice, approved of by the junta, was attended to by Cuesta, insomuch that he did not seek a battle; but he exposed his advanced posts, as if in derision of the counsel, and, disdainful of the English general's abilities, expressed his belief that the latter had no desire to act heartily; "because," said he, " the system of

Sir A. Wellesley's Correspondence, Parl. Papers, 1810.

the British appears to be never to expose their troops, owing to which, they never gain decisive actions by land."

Cuesta's knowledge of the enemy's strength and positions was always inaccurate, and his judgement false; hence he himself not only never gained any decisive action, but lost every army entrusted to his command. He was now discontented with the movement against Soult; asserting that the French hold of Gallicia would only be strengthened thereby, unless that favourite folly of all Spanish generals were adopted, namely, surrounding the enemy, without regarding whether the troops to be surrounded were more or less numerous than the surrounders. Sir Arthur Wellesley, however, affirmed that if Soult were first driven over the Minho, a combined attack afterwards made upon Victor would *permanently deliver Gallicia;* and this plan being followed, Gallicia was abandoned by the French, and they never returned to that province!

When the English army was again free to act, Cuesta was importunate that a joint offensive operation against Victor should be undertaken, yet, obstinately attached to his own opinions, he insisted upon tracing the whole plan of campaign. His views were however so opposed to all sound military principles, that sir Arthur, although anxious to conciliate his humour, could scarcely concede the smallest point, lest a vital catastrophe should follow. Valuable time was thus lost in idle discussions which might have been employed in useful action, seeing that the return of the British army from the Douro had falsified Victor's position at Torremocha. That marshal, as late as the 10th of June, had only one division guarding the bridge of Almaraz, and it

BOOK
VIII.
——
1809.
June.
was difficult for him to ascertain the movements of
sir Arthur Wellesley, covered, as they were, by
the Tagus, the insurgents, and Mackenzie's corps
of observation: hence, by rapid marches, it was
possible for the English general, while Victor was
still at Torremocha, to reach the valley of the
Tagus, and cutting the first corps off from Madrid,
Semelé's
Journal of
Operations
MS.
to place it between two fires. This did not escape
the penetration of either commander; but sir Arthur
was forced to renounce the attempt, partly because
of the sick and harassed condition of his troops, the
want of shoes and money, and the difficulty of
Appendix,
No. 16.
getting supplies; but chiefly that Cuesta's army
was scattered over the open country, between the
defiles of Monasterio and the Guadiana, and, as he
Parlia-
mentary
Papers,
1810.
refused to concentrate or retire, Victor might have
marched against and crushed him, and yet found
time to meet the British on the Tietar. Early in
June, however, three brigades were directed upon
Castello Branco, and the duke of Belluno, immediately taking the alarm, and being also assured,
by despatches from Madrid, of Soult's retreat,
resolved to recross the Tagus; but, previous to
commencing this movement, he resolved to secure
his flank, by causing the bridge of Alcantara to be
destroyed.

Colonel Mayne, as I have already observed, had
been again entrusted with that post, and unfortunately, his first orders to blow up the bridge, if
the enemy advanced, were not rescinded, although
the return of the army from the north rendered such
a proceeding unnecessary. Neither did Mayne keep
his instructions secret, and Victor hearing of them,
sent a detachment to the bridge with no other view
than to induce its destruction. He succeeded. That

noble monument of Trajan's genius was ruined! Yet such is the nature of war that, not long afterwards, both armies found its fall injurious to their interests, and, as a matter of taste and of military advantage, sighed alike over the broken arches of Alcantara.

Having completed this operation, Victor passed the Tagus, at Almaraz, on the 19th, without being molested by Cuesta, and, removing his boat-bridge, proceeded to take post at Plasencia. Meanwhile Beresford returned to the defence of the northern provinces of Portugal, which Soult was again menacing; for, during the forced inactivity of the British, at Abrantes, the cause of which I shall explain in another place, changes in the relative positions of the hostile armies were taking place; and it is important that these changes should be well understood, because on them the fate of the succeeding campaign hinged.

When Ney and Soult met at Lugo, they, although still on bad terms, agreed, after some discussion, that the first should march from Coruña, by the route of St. Jago and Vigo, against Carrera and the Conde de Noroña; and that the second, entering the valley of the Syl, should attack Romana, and drive him upon Orense, at which place, it was expected, that Ney, after taking or blocking Vigo, would be able to reach him, and thus the whole force of Gallicia be crushed at once. Soult was then to menace the Tras os Montes, by the side of Bragança, with the view of obliging sir Arthur Wellesley to remain in that province, while the second corps opened a direct communication with Madrid and with the first corps. This being arranged, Ney returned to Coruña; and, on the 1st of

June, two divisions of infantry and a brigade of dragoons, of the second corps, marched upon Monforte; they were followed, the next day, by two other divisions of infantry, and, at the same time, Franceschi, who was on the Fereira river, supported by La Houssaye's dragoons, was directed, after scouring the road to St. Jago, to fall down the right bank of the Tambuga, towards Orense.

From the 2d to the 9th, the main body halted at Monforte, to get up stores from Lugo, and to scour the country on the flanks, for Romana, in his passage, had again raised the peasantry of all the valleys. Loison was then sent with a division to the Val des Orres, having orders to feign a movement towards Villa Franca and Puente Ferrada, as if for the purpose of meeting a French column in that direction. The 10th, he passed the Syl, and took

post at the Puente de Bibey, and the 12th, Franceschi, reinforced with a division of infantry, arrived at Monte Furada also on the Syl, and, sent a detachment to Laronco, to connect his division with Loison's. The remainder of the infantry followed this movement, and detachments were sent up the course of the Syl, and towards Dancos, on the road from Villa Franca to Lugo. Loison then forced the passage of the Puente de Bibey, and drove the insurgents to Puebla de Tribes. The French army thus cleared all the valleys opening on the course of the Upper Minho, and Romana was confined to the lower part of that river.

The 13th, Franceschi, ascending the valley of the Bibey, took post at Bollo and the bridge of the Hermitage, and pushed his patroles to Gudina and Monterey on one side; and into the Sierra de Porto on the other, as far as the sources of the

Bibey, with a view to ascertain the exact direction which Romana would take to avoid Loison's column; and to prevent the Spanish general from passing the left of the French army, and gaining the Asturias by the route of Puebla de Senabria. These precautions occupied the duke of Dalmatia till the 19th, when, being assured that Romana had fallen back to Monterey, he judged that he would attempt the same march towards Puebla de Senabria, by which he had escaped after the action in the month of March; the French army was therefore directed up the valley of the Bibey, upon Viana, where there was a bridge, and where many of the mountain roads united. The same day Franceschi fell in with the head of Romana's army, and repulsed it; and the evening of the 20th the whole of the French troops were concentrated near Viana, intending to give battle to the Spaniards the next morning; but the latter retreated precipitately during the night, and many of the men dispersed.

Soult continued his movement by the left until he reached the great road running from Castile to Orense, and from thence, having sent Heudelet's division to Villa Vieja to threaten the Tras os Montes frontier, and Mermet's division and Lorge's dragoons towards La Canda to observe the road of Puebla de Senabria, he marched himself, with an advanced guard, to La Gudina, leaving Laborde and La Houssaye in reserve between Gudina and Villa Vieja. These divers movements, through the rugged passes of Gallicia, led to a variety of slight skirmishes, the most important of which took place at the Puente de Bibey, a place of such prodigious strength that it is scarcely conceivable how men, with arms, could be brought to abandon such a post.

Romana's situation was now nearly hopeless, but he was saved by a misunderstanding between the French marshals. It appears that Ney, having marched from Coruña, entered St. Jago with about ten thousand men, and Carrera fell back upon Ponte Vedra; the Conde de Noroña joined him there with some fresh troops, and assuming the command, continued the retreat to the Octavem river behind which he took post; placing his main body at the bridge of San Payo, and sending detachments to guard some secondary points. On the 7th of June, the French came up. The Spaniards had thirteen thousand men, two eighteen-pounders, and nine field pieces; of the troops only seven thousand were armed, but the whole of the artillery was in position to defend the passage at San Payo, and the bridge being cut, was overlooked by a battery of two eighteen-pounders. Three thousand men were in reserve at Redondela; and, at Vigo, about sixty stragglers, from sir John Moore's army were landed, and, in conjunction with a detachment of seamen and marines, occupied the forts. Some Spanish gun-boats, one of which was manned by English seamen, under captain Winter, also proceeded up the river to the bridge of San Payo.

During the 7th, a desultory and useless fire took place on both sides, and on the 8th, the French were repulsed in two feeble attempts to force a passage at San Payo and at Soto Mayor, the loss on either side being about a hundred men. These attacks were merely to keep the Spaniards employed until the reports of the officers, sent by Ney to ascertain the situation and projects of Soult's army, were received, but, in the evening of the 8th, those officers returned with information, obtained from the peasants, that the second corps was retreating upon Castile. I have been assured by persons, then on marshal Ney's staff, that he, amazed at these tidings, rashly concluded that Soult, swayed by personal feelings, wished to endanger the sixth corps; hence filled with indignation, he immediately retired to Coruña, while Soult, on the other hand, viewed this retreat as a breach of their engagements, and an underhand policy to oblige him to remain in Gallicia. Certain it is that by these ebullitions of temper, both Romana and Noroña were saved; for there was nothing to prevent Ney from sending a column against Orense, while he himself kept in check Noroña, on the Octavem; and, however spirited the conduct of the Spaniards was at San Payo, it would be ridiculous to imagine that ten thousand of the best soldiers of France, led by an officer so quick and resolute as Ney, could have been resisted by an equal number of raw troops and peasants, one-third of whom were without arms. But the history of the quarrel between these marshals is involved in mystery, the clearing of which must be left to those who shall write the memoirs of the men: for the purposes of this history it is sufficient to know that there was ill-blood, and that therein the Gallicians found safety.

Soult, informed of Ney's retreat and of sir Arthur Wellesley's arrival on the Tagus, ceased to pursue Romana, and marched to Zamora, where his sick had been before sent, and where his brother, general Soult, had conducted three or four thousand stragglers and convalescents. Here, also, he requested the king to send the artillery and stores necessary to re-equip the second corps; and here he proposed to give his harassed troops some rest, for they had now been for eight months incessantly marching and fighting, and men and officers were alike dispirited by the privations they had endured, and by the terrible nature of a war in which the most horrid scenes were daily enacted.

To put the king in possession of his views, Soult sent general Franceschi to Madrid; but this celebrated officer, refusing an escort, fell into the hands of the *Capuchino*. Being transferred to Seville, the central junta, with infamous cruelty, treated him as if he had been a criminal instead of a brave soldier, and confined him in a dungeon at Carthagena. The citizens there, ashamed of their government, endeavoured to effect his escape; but he perished in confinement, at the moment when his liberation was certain. When his young wife, a daughter of count Mathieu Dumas, heard of his fate, she refused all nourishment, and, in a few days, by her death, added one more to the thousand instances of the strength of woman's affections.

S.
Journal of
Operations
MSS.

The 25th of June, Soult reached Puebla de Senabria.

The 28th, he marched to Mombuey.

The 29th and 30th, he crossed the Esla, by the bridges of San Pelayo and Castro Gonzales.

The 2d of July, he entered Zamora, having previously rejected a proposition of Ney's, that the two corps should jointly maintain Gallicia, a rejection which induced the duke of Elchingen to evacuate that province.

To effect this, Ney formed a camp near Betanzos; and, on the 22d of July, withdrew his garrisons from Coruña and Ferrol, having previously destroyed all the stores and arsenals and disabled the land

Coruña

Betanzos

Mondoñedo

Castropol

M.ª Quadramen

Mondonedo

S. Jago
Compostella

Mellid

Lugo

M.te
Conceja

Ulla R.

Bia Sacra

Leyra R.

Neyra R.

Doncos

Villa

Unna R.

Monte Teystevro

R. Iarthua

Ponte Vedra

Vedra R.

Monforte

Pave Brigd

Ottaven R.

Parada

Valdes

Orres

Redondela

Oren

Tribez

Vigo

Sierra S.ᵗ Mahmed

Laronca

Ribadavia

Bollo

Hermitage

Minho R.

S.ª Seca

Viana

Porte

Tuy

Monterey

Gudiña

Cauda

Parada

a de Culebra

Mombuey

Villa Viega

R.º Benav

Braganza

P.ᵉ Pelag

Esla R.

Zamora

Sketch Explanatory of
NEY & SOULT'S
OPERATIONS IN GALLICIA,
in June 1809.

Salamanca

▦ Romana & Noroña's ⎫
▨ Ney and Soult's   ⎬ Positions

Douero R.

R. Tormes

Ciudad Rodrigo

defences. Nevertheless, his influence was still so powerful that captain Hotham, commanding the English squadron, off Coruña, seeing the hostile attitude maintained by the inhabitants, landed his seamen on the 24th, and spiked the guns on the sea-line; and, in like manner, compelled a Spanish garrison, left by Ney in the forts of Ferrol, to surrender on the 26th. The marshal, however, marched, unmolested, by the high road to Astorga, where he arrived on the 30th, having brought off all his own sick and those of the second corps also, who had been left in Lugo. Thus Gallicia was finally delivered.

This important event has been erroneously attributed to the exertions of the Spaniards. Those exertions were creditable to the Gallicians, although the most powerful motive of action was to protect their personal property; and when the French withdrew, this same motive led them to repair their losses by resisting the payment of tithes and rents, a compensation by no means relished by the proprietors or the church. But it is certain that their efforts were only secondary causes in themselves, and chiefly supported by the aid of England, whose ships, and arms, and stores were constantly on the coast. How can the operations of the Spaniards be said to have driven the sixth corps from Gallicia, when Ney retained every important post in that province to the last; when single divisions of his army, at two different periods, traversed the country, from Coruña to Tuy, without let or hindrance; and when the Spaniards could not prevent him from overrunning the Asturias without losing his hold of Gallicia? It is true, Soult, writing to Joseph, affirmed that the Gallicians would wear out the

BOOK
VIII.
────────
1809.
July.

Intercept-
ed De-
spatches,
Parl. Pap.
1810.

strongest army; that is, if a wrong system was
pursued by the French; but he pointed out the
right method of subduing them, namely, in pursuance of Napoleon's views, to fortify some principal
central points, from whence the moveable columns
could overrun the country; and this, he estimated,
would only require fifty thousand pounds and six
weeks' labour. It is plain the real causes of the
deliverance were—the quarrels between the marshals, which saved Romana and Noroña from destruction; and the movements of sir Arthur Wellesley on the Tagus; for, in an intercepted letter
from Soult to Joseph, that marshal expressly assigns
the danger hanging over Madrid and the first corps
as the reason of his refusing to remain in Gallicia.
Now, although Soult's views were undoubtedly
just, and his march provident, the latter necessarily
drew after it the evacuation of Gallicia; because,
it would have been absurd to keep the sixth corps
cooped up in that corner of the Peninsula, deprived
of communication, and estranged from the general
operations.

The movement of the second corps, after quitting
Monforte, being along the edge of the Portuguese
frontier, and constantly threatening the northern
provinces, drew marshal Beresford, as I have before
stated, from the south, and all the regular Portuguese forces capable of taking the field were immediately collected by him round Almeida. The
duke del Parque was at Ciudad Rodrigo; and as
that part of Romana's force, which had been cut
off by Soult's movement upon Gudina, fell back
upon Ciudad Rodrigo, not less than twenty-five
thousand men, Portuguese and Spaniards, were
assembled, or assembling, round those two fortresses.

The change of situation thus brought about in the armies on the great western line of invasion was rendered more important by the events which were simultaneously taking place in other parts, especially in Aragon, where general Blake, whose army had been augmented to more than twenty thousand men, inflated with his success at Alcanitz, had advanced to Ixar and Samper. Suchet, himself, remained close to Zaragoza, but kept a detachment, under general Faber, at Longares and Villa Muel, near the mountains on the side of Daroca. Blake, hoping to cut off this detachment, marched, in person, through Cariñena, and sent general Arisaga, with a column, to Bottorita, and the latter captured a convoy of provisions on the Huerba ; but Faber retired to Plasencia, on the Xalon.

The 14th of June, the advanced guards skirmished to Bottorita ; and Blake, endeavouring to surround the enemy, pushed a detachment to Maria, in the plain of Zaragoza.

The excitement produced in that city, and in Aragon generally, by this march, was so great, that Suchet doubted if he should not abandon Zaragoza, and return towards Navarre ; for the peasantry had assembled on many points in the mountains around, and it required great vigilance to keep down the spirit of insurrection in the city itself. The importance of that place, however, made him resolve to fight a battle, for which the near approach of Blake, who came on in the full confidence that the French general would retreat, furnished an opportunity which was not neglected.

BATTLE OF MARIA.

The 14th, after some skirmishing, the Spanish army was concentrated at Bottorita.

The 15th, Blake slowly and unskilfully formed his troops in order of battle, near the village of Maria, and perpendicular to the Huerba, of which he occupied both banks. Towards two o'clock in the day, he extended his left wing to outflank the right of the French; but Suchet, who had just then been rejoined by Faber, and by a brigade from Tudela, immediately stopped this evolution, by attacking the wing with some cavalry and light troops. The Spaniards then fell back to their line of battle, Blake drew men from his right to reinforce his centre and left, and was immediately engaged in a severe conflict; he repulsed the foremost of the enemy's columns, but so violent a storm arose at the moment, that neither army could see the other, although close together, and the action ceased for a time. Blake's position was so ill chosen, that he was surrounded by ravines, and had only one line of retreat, by the bridge of Maria, which was on the extremity of his right flank. Suchet, who had observed this error, when the storm cleared off a little, briskly engaged the centre and left of the Spaniards, and forming his cavalry and two regiments of infantry in column, by one vigorous effort broke quite through the Spanish horse, and seized the bridge of Maria. Notwithstanding this, Blake, who was at all times intrepid, collected the infantry of his centre and left wing in a mass, and stood for the victory, but the French troops overthrew his with a great slaughter. A general, twenty-five guns, and many stands of colours were taken, yet

Suchet's
Memoirs.

few prisoners, for the darkness enabled the dispersed Spaniards to escape by the ravines, and Blake rallied them the next day at Bottorita. The French lost nearly a thousand men, and general Harispé was wounded.

During the action, a French brigade held the position of Monte Torrero, without mixing in the fight, lest the citizens of Zaragoza, being released from their presence, should rise against the garrison; but after the victory, this brigade marched down the Ebro to cut off Blake's retreat; general Laval, who commanded it, did not, however, execute his orders, and the Spanish army retired on the night of the 16th.

The 17th, the rear guard suffered some loss at Torrecilla; and on the 18th, the two armies were again in presence at Belchite. Blake, reinforced by some detachments, was about fourteen thousand strong; but he had lost the greatest part of his artillery, and his men were dispirited. Suchet, on the contrary, having by the success at Maria awed the Aragonese, was able to bring twenty-two battalions and seven squadrons, or about fifteen thousand men, flushed with victory, into action.

BATTLE OF BELCHITE.

The Spaniards were drawn up on a range of hills half enclosing the town; their right, resting on a hermitage and some buildings, was inaccessible to cavalry; the left was also well covered; and behind the right, a hill with a building on it, overtopping all the position and occupied by a reserve, served as a rallying point, because there was an easy line of communication between it and the left wing. The centre, being on rough ground containing the

Suchet's Memoirs.

Blake's Despatch.

town of Belchite which had a wall and gates, was
also very strong, and the whole position was so
compact, that Blake, after completely filling his line,
had yet a considerable reserve in hand. His dispositions were made to fight by his centre and right,
his left being rather in the nature of an advanced
post.

A French battalion commenced the action, by
skirmishing with the Spanish centre, but, at the
same time, two columns of attack marched, the one
against the right, the other against the left. The
latter, which was the principal one, preceded by a
fire of artillery, soon closed upon the Spanish troops,
although Blake's guns opened heavily from his centre
and right. The rapid attack of the French, and
the accidental explosion of an ammunition-waggon,
created a panic, which, commencing on the left,
spread to all parts of the line. The Spanish general made a charge of cavalry to retrieve the day, it
was however easily repulsed, and the confusion
which followed is thus described by himself :—" One
giment fled without firing a shot, it was followed
by another, and a third, all flying without having
discharged a gun, and, in a few moments, the
whole position was abandoned."—" Thus we, the
generals and officers, were left alone, without being
able to rally a body which could make any opposition ; and I had the mortification to see our army
dispersed, abandoning all its baggage, and throwing
away its arms, and even its clothes, before a single
corps of the enemy; nor were we able to avail ourselves of the defence of any strong place, as it was
impossible to collect two hundred men to make head
against the enemy."

Blake, although a bad general, was a man of real

courage: stung to the quick by this disgrace, he reproached his troops with bitterness, demanded an inquiry into his own conduct, and, with a strong and sincere feeling of honour, restored to the junta the estate which had been conferred upon him for the success at Alcanitz.

This battle and the pursuit, in which Suchet took about four thousand prisoners, and all the artillery, ammunition, and baggage of the Spaniards, not only made him master of the operations in Aragon, but also rendered the fifth corps, under Mortier, who were now at Valladolid, completely disposable for offensive operations. Thus, on the 1st of July, there were, exclusive of Kellerman's and Bonnet's divisions, three complete *corps d'armée*, furnishing six thousand cavalry and fifty thousand infantry, collected between Astorga, Zamora, and Valladolid. The inroad on Portugal had failed, and the loss of Gallicia followed, but Napoleon's admirable system of invasion was unbroken; his troops, deprived of his presiding genius, had been stricken severely and shrunk from further aggression; they had been too widely spread for a secure grasp, but the reaction disclosed all the innate strength of his arrangements.

CHAPTER IV.

THE British army remained in the camp of Abrantes until the latter end of June. During this period, sir Arthur Wellesley, although burning to enter Spain, was kept back by a variety of difficulties. He had been reinforced with five thousand men immediately after his return from the Douro ; and, in the preceding operations, the killed and hurt in battle had not exceeded three hundred men, but the deaths by sickness was numerous. Four thousand in hospital, and fifteen hundred employed in escort and depôt duties, being deducted, the gross amount of the present under arms, as late even as the 25th of June, did not exceed twenty-two thousand men ; and these were, at any moment, liable to be seriously diminished, because the ministers, still intent upon Cadiz, had authorized Mr. Frere, whenever the junta should consent to the measure, to draw a garrison for that town from sir Arthur's force. As an army, therefore, it was weak in every thing but spirit ; the commissariat was without sufficient means of transport ; the soldiers nearly barefooted, and totally without pay ; the military chest empty, the hospitals full.

The cost, at a low estimation, was about two hundred thousand pounds a month ; with the most strenuous exertions, a hundred and sixty thousand pounds only had been procured in the two months of May and June, and of this, thirteen thousand had been obtained as a temporary loan in

CHAP.
IV.

1809.
June.

Parl. Pa-
pers, 1810.

Oporto. The rate of exchange in Lisbon was high, and, notwithstanding the increased value given to the government paper by the successes on the Douro, this rate was daily rising; the Spanish dollar was at five shillings, while Spanish gold sunk so much in value that the commissary-general sent all that he received from England, or could collect in Lisbon, to Cadiz, and other parts, to truck for dollars; but, in all places of commerce, the exchange was rising against England, a natural consequence of her enormous and increasing issues of paper. Those issues, the extravagant succours given to Spain, together with subsidies to Austria, made it impossible to supply the army in Portugal with specie, otherwise than by raising cash, in every quarter of the globe, on treasury-bills, and at a most enormous loss; an evil great in itself, opening a wide door to fraud and villany, and rendered the war between France and England not so much a glorious contest of arms as a struggle between pub lic credit and military force, in which even victory was sure to be fatal to the former.

The want of money, sickness, Cuesta's impracticable temper, and a variety of minor difficulties, too tedious to mention, kept the army in a state of inactivity until the end of June; but, at that period, the retreat of the first corps from Torremocha, and the consequent advance of Cuesta, removed one obstacle to offensive operations, and sir Arthur, having the certainty that eight thousand additional troops were off the rock of Lisbon, then commenced his march into Spain by the northern banks of the Tagus; meaning to unite with Cuesta on the Tietar, and to arrange, if possible, a plan of operations against Madrid.

But, before I embark on the full and broad stream
into which the surges and eddies of the complicated
warfare that succeeded Napoleon's departure from
the Peninsula settled, I must give a general view of
the state of affairs, that the reader, comprehending
exactly what strength each party brought to the
encounter, may judge more truly of the result.

FRENCH POWER.

	Men.	Horses.
The French, having received some reinforcements of conscripts, amounted, in the beginning of July, including the king's guards, to about	275,000	
In hospital ....61,000 ⎫		
Stragglers and prisoners borne on the states .... 7,000 ⎬	68,000	
Total under arms	207,000	36,000
The military governments, lines of correspondence, garrisons, and detachments, absorbed	32,000	3,000
Present under arms with the *corps d'armée*	175,000	33,000

The actual strength and situation of each *corps
d'armée* was as follows :—

Under the King, covering Madrid.

	Inf. & Art.	Cavalry.
First corps, in the valley of the Tagus	20,881	4,200
Fourth corps, La Mancha	17,490	3,200
Division of Dessolles, Madrid	6,864	
King's French guards, Madrid, about	4,000	1,500
Total 49,235		8,900

In Old Castile, under Marshal Soult.

	Inf. & Art.	Cavalry.
Second corps, Zamora, Tora, and Salamanca ..	17,707	2,883
Fifth corps, Valladolid	16,042	874
Sixth corps, Astorga, and its vicinity	14,913	1,446
Total	48,662	5,203

In Aragon, under General Suchet.

	Inf. & Art.	Cavalry.
Third corps, Zaragoza, Alcanitz, &c. ········	15,226	2,604

In Catalonia, under Marshal Augereau.

	Inf. & Art.	Cavalry.
Seventh corps, Vich, Gerona, and Barcelona ··	30,593	2,500

In addition to these corps there were twelve hundred men belonging to the battering train; four thousand infantry under Bonnet, at St. Andero; and two thousand two hundred cavalry under Kellerman, in the Valladolid country.

The fortresses and armed places in possession of the French army were—St. Sebastian, Pampeluna, Bilbao, Santona, St. Andero, Burgos, Leon, Astorga, on the northern line;

Jacca, Zaragoza, Guadalaxara, Toledo, Segovia, and Zamora, on the central line;

Figueras, Rosas, and Barcelona, on the southern line.

It needs but a glance at these dispositions and numbers to understand with what a power Napoleon had fastened upon the Peninsula, during his six weeks' campaign. Much had been lost since his departure, but his army still pressed the Spaniards down, and, like a stone cast upon a brood of snakes, was immoveable to their writhings. Nevertheless, the situation of Spain, at this epoch, was an ameliorated one compared to that which, four months before, the vehemence of Napoleon's personal warfare had reduced it to. The elements of resistance were again accumulated in masses, and the hope, or rather confidence, of success was again in full vigour; for, it was in the character of this people, while grovelling on the earth, to suppose themselves standing firm; and, when creeping in the gloom of defeat, to imagine they were soaring in the full blaze of victory.

The momentary cessation of offensive operations on the part of the French, instead of being traced to its true sources, the personal jealousies of the marshals, and the king's want of vigour, was, as usual, attributed, first—to fear and weakness, secondly—to the pressure of the Austrian war. It was not considered that the want of unity, checking the course of conquest, would cease when the French army was driven to the defensive; neither was the might of France duly weighed, while the strength of Austria was unduly exalted. The disasters at Ucles, at Almaraz, at Zaragoza, Rosas, Cardadeu, Valls, at Ciudad Real, Medellin, Braga, and Oporto, and in the Asturias, were all forgotten, the French had been repulsed from Portugal, and they had not taken Seville! This, to the Spaniards, was sufficient evidence of their weakness; and, when the French were supposed to be weak, the others, by a curious reasoning process, always came to the conclusion that they were themselves strong. Hence, the fore-boasting at this period was little inferior to what it had been after the battle of Baylen, and the statement of the relative numbers was almost as absurd. The utmost amount of the French force was not calculated higher than a hundred and fifteen, or a hundred and twenty, thousand men, of which about fifty thousand were supposed to be on the French side of the Ebro, and the whole only waiting for an excuse to abandon the Peninsula.

SPANISH POWER.

The Spanish armies, on paper, were, as usual,

numerous; and the real amount of the regular force was certainly considerable, although very inadequate to the exigencies or the resources of the country. Before the battle of Belchite had broken Blake's strength, there were, organized and under arms, twelve thousand cavalry, and about one hundred and twenty thousand infantry, exclusive of irregular bands and armed peasantry, who were available for particular defensive operations. After that defeat the number of regular forces, capable of taking the field in the south-eastern provinces, was not above twenty thousand men, of which about ten thousand, under Coupigny, were watching Barcelona, or, again, rallying under Blake; the remainder were in Valencia, where Caro, Romana's brother, had taken the command.

In the north-western provinces there were about twenty-five thousand men, of which fifteen thousand were in Gallicia; some thousands in the Asturias, under Vorster and Ballasteros, and the remainder, under the duke del Parque, who was directed to organize a new army in the neighbourhood of Ciudad Rodrigo.

In Andalusia, or covering it, there were about seventy thousand men. Of these twenty-three thousand infantry, and two thousand five hundred cavalry, were assembled in the Morena, near St. Elena and Carolina, under the command of general Venegas; and thirty-eight thousand, including seven thousand cavalry, were in Estremadura, under the orders of Cuesta, who was nominally commander-in-chief of both armies.

The troops, thus separated into three grand divisions, were called the armies of *the right, the centre, the left*. The fortresses were—Gerona, Hostalrich,

Lerida, Mequineza, Tarragona, Tortosa, Valencia,
Carthagena, and Alicant, for the army of the
right; Cadiz and Badajos for that of the centre;
Ciudad Rodrigo, Coruña, and Ferrol, for the army
of the left.

The Spanish troops were, however, far from
being serviceable in proportion to their numbers;
most of them were new levies, and the rest were
ill-trained. The generals had lost nothing of their
presumption, learnt nothing of war, and their
mutual jealousies were as strong as ever. Cuesta
still hating the junta, was feared and hated by that
body in return, and Venegas was placed at the
head of the Carolina army as a counterpoise to him.
Romana, also, was obnoxious to the junta, and in
return, with more reason, the junta was despised
and disliked by him. In Valencia and Murcia
generals and juntas appeared alike indifferent to
the public welfare, satisfied if the war was kept
from their own doors. In Catalonia there never
was any unanimity.

Blake, who had abandoned Romana in Gallicia,
and who was still at enmity with Cuesta, had been,
for these very reasons, invested with supreme
power in Valencia, Aragon, and Catalonia; and,
moreover, there were factions and bickerings among
the inferior officers in the armies of Venegas and
Cuesta. Albuquerque was ambitious of commanding in chief, and Mr. Frere warmly intrigued in his
cause, for that gentleman still laboured under the
delusion that he was appointed to direct the military instead of conducting the political service in
the Peninsula. In April, he had proposed to the
junta that a force of five thousand cavalry and some
infantry, taken from the armies of Cuesta and Ve-

negas, should, under the command of the duke of
Albuquerque, commence offensive operations in
La Mancha; this, he said, would, " *if the enemy
refused to take notice of it*," become " a very serious
and perhaps a decisive movement;" and he was so
earnest that, without communicating upon the
subject with sir Arthur Wellesley, without waiting
for the result of the operations against Soult, he
pretended to the junta that the co-operation of the
English army with Cuesta (that co-operation which
it was sir Arthur's most anxious wish to bring
about) could only be obtained, as the price of the
Spanish government's acceding to his own proposal. The plenipotentiary's greatest efforts were,
however, directed to procure the appointment of
Albuquerque to the commands of an army; but
that nobleman was under the orders of Cuesta, who
was not willing to part with him, and, moreover,
Frere wished to displace Venegas, not that any
fault was attributed to the latter, but merely to
make way for Albuquerque; a scheme so indeco-
rous that both the junta and Cuesta peremptorily
rejected it.

Mr. Frere did not hesitate to attribute this rejection to a mean jealousy of Albuquerque's high
birth and talents; yet the junta had sufficient
reason for their conduct, not only on this occasion,
but afterwards, when they refused to give him any
independent command. The duke, although a brave
and patriotic and even an able soldier, was the
dupe of a woman who corresponded with the
French; the junta, in the fear of offending him, for-
bore to punish her, at first, yet, finally, they were
obliged to shut her up, and they could not entrust
him with a command while her dangerous influence

Parlia-
mentary
Papers,
1810.

Appendix,
No. 8,

Parlia-
mentary
Papers,
1810.

lasted.   Hence, Mr. Frere's intrigue failed to serve
Albuquerque ; and his   military project for La
Mancha fell to the ground when sir Arthur Wellesley, unable to perceive its advantages, strongly
advised the junta, not to weaken but to reinforce
Cuesta's army ; not to meddle with the French
either in La Mancha or Estremadura, but to preserve a strict defensive in all quarters.

The *supreme junta* was itself in fear of the old
junta of Seville, and the folly and arrogance of the
first and its neglect of the public weal furnished
ample grounds of attack, as a slight sketch of its
administrative proceedings will suffice to prove.
The king, after the battles of Medellin and Ciudad
Real, had, through the medium of don Joachim
Sotelo, a Spanish minister in his service, made an
attempt to negotiate for the submission of the junta,
which was spurned at by the latter and in suitable
terms, for dignified sentiments and lofty expressions
were never wanting to the Spaniards ; yet, taken
with their deeds, they were but as a strong wind
and shrivelled leaves.

The junta did not fail to make the nation observe
their patriotism upon this occasion, and, indeed,
took every opportunity to praise their own proceedings ; nevertheless, men were not wanting in Spain
most anxious not only to check the actual abuses
of power, but to lay bare all the ancient oppressions
of the country, and recur to first principles, both
for present reform and future parmanent good government ; in short, to make public avowal of the
misrule which had led to their misfortunes, and, if
possible, to amend it.   Knowing that although
national independence may co-exist with tyranny,
it is necessarily attached to civil and religious free-

dom,—they desired to assemble the cortez; to give
the people an earnest that national independence
was worth having, and to convince them that their
sufferings and their exertions would lead to a sensible good, instead of a mere choice between an old
and a new despotism; this party was powerful
enough to have a manifesto, to their purpose, drawn
up by the junta, and it would have been published,
if the English ministers had not interposed; for, as
I have before said, their object was not Spain, but
Napoleon.

Mr. Frere vigorously opposed the promulgation
of this manifesto, and not ambiguously hinted that
the displeasure of England, and the wrath of the
partizans of despotism in Spain, would be vented
on the junta, if any such approach to real liberty
was made. In his despatches to his cabinet he
wrote that, from his knowledge of the members of
the junta, he felt assured they would " *shrink from
the idea of giving permanent effect to the measures
which they held out;*" and this expression he meant
in their praise! but still he thought it necessary to
check the tendency to freedom in the outset, and it
would be injustice not to give his sentiments in his
own words; sentiments which were at this time
perfectly agreeable to his immediate superior, Mr.
Canning, but offering a curious contrast to the political liberality which that politician afterwards
thought it his interest to affect.

Writing as a Spaniard, Mr. Frere thus addressed
don Martin Garay :—

" If we have indeed passed three centuries under
an arbitrary government, let us not forget that it is
a price which we pay for having conquered and
peopled the fairest portion of the globe; that the

integrity of this immense power rests solely on
these two words, religion and the king.   If the old
constitution has been lost by the conquest of America, our first object should be to recover it, but in
such a manner as not to lose what has cost us so
much in the acquisition.   From this consideration,
it appears to me that we ought to avoid, as *political
poison, any annunciation of general principles, the
application of which it would be impossible to limit or
qualify, even when the negroes and Indians should
quote them in favour of themselves.*   But let us
allow that we have made a *bad exchange in barter-
ing our ancient national liberty for the glory and ex-
tension of the Spanish name.*   Let us allow that the
nation has been deceived for three centuries, and
that this error should, at all hazards, be immediately done away.   Even though it were so, it does
not appear *very becoming the character of a well
educated person to pass censures upon the conduct of
his forefathers,* or to complain of what he has lost
by their negligence or prodigality ; and still less so,
if it is done in the face of all the world : and what
shall we say of a nation who would do this publicly,
and after mature deliberation ?"

The manifesto was suppressed, a new one more
consonant to Mr. Frere's notions was published, and
a promise to convoke the cortez given, but without
naming any specific time for that event.   The junta,
who, as Mr. Frere truly stated, were not at all
disposed to give any effect to free institutions, now
proceeded to prop up their own tottering power by
severity : they had, previous to the manifesto,
issued a menacing proclamation, in which they
endeavoured to confound their political opponents
with the spies and tools of the French ; and having

before established a tribunal of public security, they
caused it to publish an edict, in which all men, who
endeavoured to raise distrust of the junta, or who
tried to overturn the government, by popular commotions, or other means that had, by the junta,
been reprobated, were declared guilty of high
treason, undeserving the name of Spaniards and
sold to Napoleon : their punishment to be death,
and confiscation of property. Any person propagating rumours, tending to weaken or soften the
hatred of the people against the French, was instantly to be arrested and punished without re-
mission ; lastly, rewards were offered for secret information upon these heads.

This decree was not a dead letter. Many persons
were seized, imprisoned, and executed, without trial,
or knowing their accusers. But the deepest stain
upon the Spanish character, at this period, was the
treatment experienced by prisoners of war. Thousands, and amongst them part of Dupont's troops,
who were only prisoners by a breach of faith, were
sent to the Balearic Isles, without any order being
taken for their subsistence, and when remonstrated
with, the junta cast seven thousand ashore on the
little desert rock of Cabrera. At Majorca, numbers
had been massacred by the inhabitants, in the most
cowardly and brutal manner, but those left on
Cabrera suffered miseries that can scarcely be described. The supply of food, always scanty, was
often neglected altogether ; there was but one spring
on the rock, which dried up in summer ; clothes
were never given to them except by the English seamen, who, compassionating their sufferings, often
assisted them, in passing the island. Thus, afflicted
with hunger, thirst, and nakedness, they lived like

wild beasts while they could live, but perished in
such numbers, that less than two thousand remained
to tell the tale of this inhumanity; and surely, it
was no slight disgrace that the English government
failed to interfere on such an occasion.

But what were the efforts made for the defence
of the country by this barbarous junta, which, having been originally assembled to discuss the form of
establishing a central government, had, unlawfully,
retained their delegated power, and used it so
shamefully?   There was a Spanish fleet, and a sufficient number of sailors to man it, in Carthagena,
and there was another fleet, and abundance of seamen, in Cadiz.   Lord Collingwood, and others,
pressed the junta, constantly and earnestly, to fit
these vessels out, and to make use of them, or at
least to place them beyond the reach of the enemy,
yet his remonstrances were unheeded; the sailors
were rendered mutinous for want of pay, and even
of subsistence, and the government would neither

Appendix,
No. 9.

fit out ships themselves, nor suffer the English seamen to do it for them.   At the period when the
marquis of Romana and the insurgents in Gallicia
were praying for a few stands of arms and five

Lord Col-
lingwood's
Correspon-
dence.
General
Miller's
Memoirs.

thousand pounds, from sir John Cradock, the junta
possessed many millions of money, and their magazines, in Cadiz, were bursting with the continually
increasing quantity of stores and arms arriving from
England, but which were left to rot as they arrived,
while, from every quarter of the country not yet
subdued, the demand for these things was incessant.

The fleet in Cadiz harbour might have been at
sea in the beginning of February.   In a week it
might have been at Vigo, with money and succours

of all kinds for the insurgents in Gallicia; after
which, by skilful operations along the coast from
Vigo to St. Sebastian, it might have occupied an
enormous French force on that line of country;
instead of a fleet, the junta sent colonel Barios, an
obscure person, to steal through by-ways, and to
take the command of men who were not in want of
leaders. In the same manner, the fleet in Carthagena might have been employed on the Catalonian
and French coasts; but, far from using their means,
which were really enormous, with energy and judgement, the junta carried on the war by encouraging
virulent publications against the French, and confined their real exertions to the assembling of the
unfortunate peasants in masses, to starve for a while,
and then to be cut to pieces by their more experienced opponents.

The system of false reports, also, was persevered
in without any relaxation : " *The French were beaten
on all points; the marshals were slain or taken;
their soldiers were deserting, or flying in terror at
the sight of a Spaniard; Joseph had plundered and
abandoned Madrid; Zaragoza had not fallen.*"
Castro, the envoy to the Portuguese regency, so late
as April, anxiously endeavoured to persuade that
government and the English general, that Zaragoza
had never been subdued, and that the story of its
fall was a French falsehood. In June, official letters were written to marshal Beresford, from the
neighbourhood of Lugo and dated the very day
upon which Soult's army relieved that town, not to
give intelligence of the event, but to announce the
utter defeat of that marshal, and the capture of
Lugo itself; the amount of the killed and wounded,
and the prisoners taken, being very exactly stated,

and with such an appearance of truth, as to deceive Beresford, notwithstanding his previous experience of the people he had to deal with.

But the proofs of corruption and incapacity in the junta are innumerable, and not confined to the records of events kept by British officers. Romana, a few months later, upon the question of appointing a regency, thus describes their conduct: " *He himself,*" he said, " *had doubted if the central junta was a lawful government, and this doubt was general in the provinces through which he had passed; yet he had, to preserve the nation from anarchy, not only yielded obedience to it, but he had, likewise, forced the provinces of Gallicia, Leon, and Asturias to do the same; because he thought that an illegal government might be useful if it deserved the confidence of the people, and that they respected its authority. The central junta, however, was not thus situated: the people, judging of measures by their effects, complained that the armies were weak, the government without energy; that there were no supplies; that the promised accounts of the public expenditure were withheld; and yet, all the sums drawn from America, all the succours granted by England, the rents of the crown, and the voluntary contributions were expended. The public employments were not given to men of merit and true lovers of their country. Some of the members of the junta rendered their power subservient to their own advantage; others conferred lucrative appointments on their relations and dependents. Eeclesiastical offices had been filled up to enable individuals to seize those rents for themselves which ought to be appropriated for the public service. There was no unity to be found: many of the junta cared only for the interest*

*of their particular province, as if they were not
members of the Spanish monarchy; confirming the
appointments of the local juntas, without regard to
fitness; and even assigning recompenses to men
destitute of military knowledge, who had neither seen
service nor performed the duties assigned to them."*

" *The junta, divided into sections, undertook to
manage affairs in which they were unversed, and
which were altogether foreign to their professions.
Horses, taken from their owners under pretence of
supplying the armies, were left to die of hunger in
the sea-marshes: and, finally, many important
branches of administration were in the hands of
men, suspected, both from their own conduct and
from their having been creatures of that infamous
favourite who was the author of the general misery."*

It was at this period that the celebrated *Partidas*
first commenced the *guerilla,* or petty warfare, which
has been so lauded, as if that had been the cause
of Napoleon's discomfiture. Those bands were infinitely numerous, because, every robber, that feared
a jail, or that could break from one; every smug-
gler,* whose trade had been interrupted; every friar,
disliking the trammels of his convent; and every
idler, that wished to avoid the ranks of the regular
army, was to be found either as chief or associate in
the *partidas.* The French, although harassed by
the constant and cruel murders of isolated soldiers,
or followers of the army, and sometimes by the loss
of convoys, were never thwarted in any great object
by these bands; but the necessity of providing subsistence, and attaching his followers to his fortunes,
generally obliged the guerilla chief to rob his coun-

---

* The bands formed of smugglers were called Quadrillas.

trymen; and, indeed, one of the principal causes of the sudden growth of this system was the hope of intercepting the public and private plate, which, under a decree of Joseph, was bringing in from all parts to be coined in Madrid; for that monarch was obliged to have recourse to forced loans, and the property of the proscribed nobles and suppressed convents, to maintain even the appearance of a court.

This description will apply to the mass of the *partidas;* yet there were some actuated by nobler motives; by revenge; by a gallant enterprising spirit; or, by an honest ambition, thinking to serve their country better than by joining the regular forces. Among the principal chiefs may be placed, Renovales, and the two Minas, in Navarre and Arragon; Porlier named the *marquisetto*, and Longa, in the Asturias and Biscay; Juan Martin, or *El Empecinado*, who vexed the neighbourhood of Madrid; Julian Sanchez, in the Gata and Salamanca country; doctor Rovera, Perena, and some others, in Catalonia; Julian Palarea, or *El Medico*, between the Moreno and Toledo; the curate Merino, *El Principe*, and Saornil, in Castile; the friar Sapia, in Soria, and Juan Abril, near Segovia.

But these men were of very different merit. Renovales, a regular officer, raised the peasantry of the valleys between Pampeluna and Zaragoza, after the fall of the latter city, and was soon subdued. Juan Martin, Rovera, Julian Sanchez, and the student Mina, discovered military talent, and Sanchez was certainly a very bold and honest man; but Espoz y Mina, the uncle and successor of the student, far outstripped his contemporaries in fame. He shed the blood of his prisoners freely, yet rather

from false principle, and under peculiar circumstances, than from any real ferocity, his natural disposition being manly and generous; and, although
not possessed of any peculiar military genius, he
had a sound judgement, surprising energy, and a
constant spirit. By birth a peasant, he despised
the higher orders of his own country, and never
would suffer any *hidalgo*, or gentleman, to join his
band. From 1809, until the end of the war, he
maintained himself in the provinces bordering on
the Ebro; often defeated, and chased from place to
place, he yet gradually increased his forces, until,
in 1812, he yet was at the head of more than ten
thousand men, whom he paid regularly, and supplied from resources chiefly created by himself;
one of which was remarkable:—He established a
treaty with the French generals, by which articles,
not being warlike stores, coming from France, had
safe conduct from his *partida*, on paying a duty,
which Mina appropriated to the subsistence of his
followers.

That the guerilla system could never seriously
affect the progress of the French, is proved by the
fact, that the constant aim of the principal chiefs
was to introduce the customs of regular troops; and
their success against the enemy was proportionate
to their progress in discipline and organization.
There were not less than fifty thousand of these
irregular soldiers, at one time, in Spain; and so
severely did they press upon the country that it
may be assumed as a truth that if the English
army had abandoned the contest, one of the surest
means by which the French could have gained the
good will of the nation would have been the extir-
pating of the *partidas*. Nevertheless, a great and

unquestionable advantage was derived by the regular armies, and especially by the British, from
the existence of these bands; the French corps
could never communicate with each other, nor combine their movements, except by the slow method
of sending officers with strong escorts; whereas,
their adversaries could correspond by post, and
even by telegraph, an advantage equal to a reinforcement of thirty thousand men.

PORTUGUESE POWER.

The Portuguese military system has been already
explained. The ranks of the regular army, and of
the militia, were filling; the arms and equipments
were supplied by England; and means were taking
to give effect to the authority of the *Capitāos Mor*,
or chiefs of districts, under whom the *ordenanças*
were to be gathered for the defence of the country.
The people having been a second time relieved from
an invasion, by the intervention of a British army,
were disposed to submit implicitly to the guidance
of their deliverers; but the effect of former misgo-
vernment pervaded every branch of administration,
political and municipal, and impeded the efforts
made to draw forth the military resources of the
kingdom; and it is curious that, until the end of
the war, such was the reluctance of the people to
become soldiers, that, notwithstanding their undoubted hatred of the French, their natural docility,
and the visible superiority of the soldiers' condition
over that of the peasant or artizan, the recruiting
was always difficult; the odious spectacle was constantly exhibited, of men marched in chains, to
reinforce armies, which were fighting in what was
a popular, and ought to have been a sacred cause.

The actual number of regular troops, armed and organized, was about fifteen thousand, but notwithstanding the courage displayed by those employed in the late operations, marshal Beresford was still doubtful of their military qualities, and reluctant to act separately from the British troops. The most important fortresses in a condition for defence were Elvas, Albuquerque, and Almeida, in the first line; Abrantes and Peniché, in the second; the citadel, and forts of Lisbon, Palmela, and Setuval, in the third. But there were many other walled places, capable, if armed, of standing a siege, and presenting a variety of strong points for the irregular force of the country to assemble upon; and hence, Portugal offered, not only great resources in men, but a base of operations solid in itself; central with respect to the French armies, and enabling the English general to act, without reference to the Spanish government or Spanish commanders; an advantage more justly appreciated at the end of this campaign than at the commencement. Such were the relative situations of the contending hosts in the Peninsula; yet, to take an enlarged view of affairs, it is necessary to look beyond the actual field of battle; for the contest in Spain, no longer isolated, was become an integral part of the great European struggle against France.

Napoleon, after his first successes near Ratisbon, entered Vienna, and attempted to carry the war to the left bank of the Danube; but a severe check, received at the battle of Esling on the 21st of May, so shook his moral ascendancy in Europe, that he deemed it necessary to concentrate all the disposable strength of his empire for one gigantic effort, which should restore the terror of his name. The

appearance of inactivity assumed by him, while
thus mightily gathering his forces, deceived his
enemies; and, as their hopes rose, their boasts
became extravagant, more especially in England,
where, to express a doubt of his immediate overthrow was regarded as a heinous offence; and
where the government, buoyed up with foolish
expectations, thought less of supporting a noble
and effectual warfare in Portugal than of nourishing and aiding the secondary and rather degrading
hostility of conspirators, malcontents, and military
adventurers in Germany.

While sir Arthur Wellesley was waiting impatiently on the Tagus for the scanty reinforcements
afforded him, two other armies were simultaneously
preparing to act against the extremities of the
French empire; the one, consisting of about twelve
thousand men, drawn from Sicily, was destined to
invade Italy, the southern parts of which had been
denuded of troops to oppose the Austrians on the

Adjutant-
general's
Returns.
Tagliamento. The other was assembled on the
coast of England, where above forty thousand of
the finest troops the nation could boast of, and a
fleet of power to overthrow all the other navies of
the world combined, composed an armament, intended to destroy the great marine establishment
which the French emperor had so suddenly and
so portentously created at Antwerp. So vast an
expedition had never before left the British shores,
neither any one so meanly conceived, so impro-
vidently arranged, so calamitously conducted; for
the marine and land forces, combined, numbered
more than eighty thousand fighting men, and those
of the bravest, yet the object in view was compara-
tively insignificant, and even that was not obtained.

Delivered over to the leading of a man, whose
military incapacity has caused the glorious title of Chatham to be scorned, this ill-fated army, with spirit, and strength, and zeal to have spread the fame of England to the extremities of the earth, perished, without a blow, in the pestilent marshes of Walcheren! And so utterly had party spirit stifled the feeling of national honour that men were found in Parliament base enough to reprobate the convention of Cintra, to sneer at sir John Moore's operations, and yet to declare the Walcheren expedition wise, profitable, and even glorious!

The operation against Italy was less unfortunate rather than more ably conducted, and it was equally abortive. What with slow preparations, the voyage, and the taking of the petty islands of Ischia and Procida, thirteen weeks were wasted, although during that period, Murat, conscious of his inability to resist, was only restrained from abandoning Naples by the firmness of his queen, and the energy of Sallicetti, the minister of police. We have seen that it was the wish of the ministers to have the troops in Sicily employed in the south of Spain, but, yielding to the representations of sir John Stuart, they permitted him to make this display of military foolery: yet it is not with the bad or good success of these expeditions that this history has to deal, but with that direful ministerial incapacity which suffered two men, notoriously unfitted for war, to waste and dissipate the military strength of England on secondary objects, while a renowned commander, placed at the most important point, was left without an adequate force.

For the first time since the commencement of the peninsular war, sixty thousand Spanish troops, well

armed and clothed, were collected in a mass, and in
the right place, communicating with a British force;
for the first time since Napoleon swayed the destiny
of France, the principal army of that country had
met with an important check; the great conqueror's
fortune seemed to waver, and the moment had arrived when the British government was called to
display all its wisdom and energy. The duke of
York had performed his duty; he had placed above
ninety thousand superb soldiers, all disposable for
offensive operations, in the hands of the ministers;
but the latter knew not their value, and, instead of
concentrating them upon one, scattered them upon
many points. Sir Arthur Wellesley might have had
above eighty thousand British troops on the frontiers of Portugal, and he was a general capable of
wielding them. He was forced to commence a
campaign, upon which the fate of the Peninsula, a
quick triumph or a long-protracted agony of twelve
millions of people depended, with only twenty-two
thousand; while sixty thousand fighting men, and
ships numerous enough to darken all the coasts of
Spain, were waiting, in Sicily and England, for
orders which were to doom them, one part to scorn,
and the other to an inglorious and miserable fate.
Shall the deliverance of the Peninsula, then, be
attributed to the firmness and long-sighted policy
of ministers who gave these glaring proofs of im-
providence, or shall the glory of that great exploit
lighten round the head of him who so manfully
maintained the fierce struggle, under all the burden
of their folly?

CHAPTER V.

CAMPAIGN OF TALAVERA.

In the foregoing chapters the real state of affairs in the Peninsula has been described; but it appeared with a somewhat different aspect to the English general, because false informations, egregious boasts, and hollow promises, such as had been employed to mislead sir John Moore, were renewed at this period; and the allied nations were influenced by a riotous rather than a reasonable confidence of victory. The English newspapers teemed with letters, describing the enemy's misery and fears; nor was the camp free from these inflated feelings. Marshal Beresford was so credulous of French weakness as publicly to announce to the junta of Badajos that Soult's force, wandering and harassed by continual attacks, was reduced to eight or ten thousand distressed soldiers. Nay, sir Arthur Wellesley himself, swayed by the pertinacity of the tale-makers, the unhesitating assurances of the junta, perhaps, also, a little excited by a sense of his own great talents, was not free from the impression that the hour of complete triumph was come.

The Spanish government and the Spanish generals were importunate for offensive movements, and lavish in their promises of support; and the English general was as eager; for he was at the head of gallant troops, his foot was on the path of victory, and he felt that, if the duke of Belluno was not quickly disabled, the British army, threatened on both flanks, would, as in the case of sir

John Cradock, be obliged to remain in some defensive position, near Lisbon, until it became an object of suspicion and hatred to the Spanish and Portuguese people.

There were three lines of offensive operations open:—

1°. *To cross the Tagus, join Cuesta's army, and, making Elvas and Badajos the base of movements, attack Victor in front.* This line was circuitous. It permitted the enemy to cover himself by the Tagus, and the operations of the allies would have been cramped by the Sierra de Guadalupe on one side, and the mountains lying between Albuquerque and Alcantara on the other; strong detachments must also have been left to cover the roads to Lisbon, on the right bank of the Tagus. Finally, the communication between the duke of Belluno and Soult being free, Beresford's corps would have been endangered.

2°. *To adopt Almeida and Ciudad Rodrigo as the base of movements, and to operate in conjunction with Beresford, the duke del Parque, and Romana, by the line of Salamanca, while Cuesta and Venegas occupied the attention of the first andf ourth corps on the Tagus.* The objections to this line were, that it separated the British troops from the most efficient and most numerous, and obliged them to act with the weakest and most irregular of the Spanish armies; that it abandoned Cuesta to the ruin which his headstrong humour would certainly provoke; and as the loss of Seville or of Lisbon would inevitably follow, the instructions of the English ministers, (which enjoined the defence of the latter city as paramount to every object, save the military possession of Cadiz,) would have been neglected.

3°. *To march upon Plasencia and Almaraz, form a junction with Cuesta, and advance against Madrid, while Venegas operated in the same view, by the line of La Mancha.* The obstacles in the way of this plan were—1°. That it exposed Cuesta to be defeated by Victor before the junction; and after the junction, the combinations would still be dependent upon the accuracy of Venegas's movements. 2°. That sir Arthur Wellesley's march, with reference to Soult's corps, would be a flank march: an unsafe operation at all times, but, on this occasion, when the troops must move through the long and narrow valley of the Tagus, peculiarly dangerous. Nevertheless, this line was adopted, nor were the reasons in favour of it devoid of force. The number of French immediately protecting Madrid was estimated at fifty thousand; but confidential officers, sent to the head-quarters of Cuesta and Venegas, had ascertained that their strength was not overstated at thirty-eight thousand, for the first, and twenty-five thousand for the second; all well armed and equipped, and the last certainly the best and most efficient army that the Spaniards had yet brought into the field. Now the English force in Portugal amounted to thirty thousand men exclusive of the sick, twenty-two thousand being under arms on the frontier, and eight thousand at Lisbon: here, then, was a mass of ninety thousand regular troops that could be brought to bear on fifty thousand; besides which there were sir Robert Wilson's legion, about a thousand strong, and the Spanish *partidas* of the Guadalupe and the Sierra de Bejar.

The ridge of mountains which separate the valley of the Tagus from Castile and Leon being, as has been already related, impracticable for artillery, except at the passes of Baños and Perales, it was supposed that the twenty thousand men under Beresford and the duke del Parque would be sufficient to block those lines of march, and that Romana, moving by the Tras os Montes, might join the duke del Parque; thus thirty thousand men, supported by two fortresses, would be ready to protect the flank of the British army in its march from Plasencia towards Madrid. But this was a vain calculation, for Romana remained ostentatiously idle at Coruña, and sir Arthur Wellesley, never having seen the Spanish troops in action, thought too well of them ; having had no experience of Spanish promises he trusted them too far, and at the same time, made a false judgement of the force and position of his adversaries. The arrival of the sixth corps at Astorga and of the fifth at Valladolid were unknown to him ; the strength of the second corps, and, perhaps, the activity of its chief, were also underrated. Instead of fifteen or twenty thousand harassed French troops, without artillery, there were seventy thousand fighting-men behind the mountains !

The 27th of June, the English army, breaking up from the camp of Abrantes, and, being organized in the following manner, marched into Spain :—

Artillery.

Six brigades,　　　　30 guns,　　　comᵈ. by maj-gen. Howorth.

Cavalry.

Three brigades,　　　3047 sabres,　　comᵈ. by lt.-gen. Payne.

Infantry.

1st div. of 4 brigades,		6023 bayonets, comᵈ. by lt.-gen. Sherbrooke
2d　do.　2　do.	3947	do.	do.	maj.-gen. Hill.
3d　do.　2　do.	3736	do.	do.	m.-gen. Mackenzie.
4th do.　2　do.	2957	do.	do.	br.-gen. Campbell.

5　divs. 13 brigades. 19710 sabres and bayonets.

—　　　　—　　　　1287 Engineers, artillery, and waggon-train.

Grand total **••••** 20997 men, and 30 pieces of artillery.

Besides this force, the 40th regiment, so long detained at Seville by Mr. Frere, had arrived in Lisbon, and the troops on their march from that city, being somewhat less than eight thousand bayonets, were organized in three brigades, commanded by major-general Lightfoot and brigadier-generals Robert and Catlin Craufurd. But the leading brigade, under Robert Craufurd, only quitted Lisbon on the 28th of June.

The army moved by both banks of the Tagus; one column proceeding through Sobreira Formosa, the other by Villa Velha, where a boat-bridge was established. The 1st of July the head-quarters were at Castello Branco, and from thence the troops continued their route, in one column, by Moralejo and Coria; a flanking brigade, under general Donkin, being directed through Ceclaven and Torijoncillos, to explore the country between Zarza Mayor and the Tagus. The 8th, the head-quarters were established at Plasencia. The 10th, the army arrived at that place, and was, soon after, joined by a regiment of cavalry and two battalions of infantry from Lisbon.

At this period Cuesta was at Almaraz, and Victor, of whose intermediate movements it is time to take notice, was at Talavera de la Reyna. When that Marshal had retired from Torremocha, the valley of the Tagus was exhausted by the long sojourn of the fourth and fifth corps; but the valley of Plasencia was extremely fertile, and untouched, and the duke of Belluno, whose troops, weakened by the tertian sickness, required good nourishment, resolved to take post there, keeping a bridge at Bazagona, on the Tietar, by which he could, in two marches, fall upon Cuesta, if he ventured to

Semelé's Journal of Operations MSS.

pass the Tagus at Almaraz ; at Plasencia, also, he could open a communication with the second and fifth corps, and observe closely the movements of the English army on the frontier of Portugal. The bridge at Bazagona had been finished on the 21st of June, and the French light troops were scouring the country towards Plasencia, when the king, who had already withdrawn a division of infantry and a large part of the cavalry of the first corps to reinforce the fourth, ordered the duke of Belluno to retire instantly to Talavera, leaving rear guards on the Tietar and at Almaraz. This order, which arrived the 22d of June, was the result of that indecision which none but truly great men, or fools, are free from ; the first, because they can see their way clearly through the thousand difficulties that encumber and bewilder the mind in war ; the last, because they see nothing.

On the present occasion, general Sebastiani had reported that Venegas was reinforced, and ready to penetrate by La Mancha ; and the king, swayed by this false information, disturbed by the march of Cuesta, and still more by Blake's advance against Zaragoza (the result of which was then unknown), became so alarmed that he commanded St. Cyr to move into Aragon, repaired himself to Toledo, with his guards and reserve, withdrew the light cavalry and a division of infantry from Victor, obliged that marshal to fall back on Talavera ; a nd even commanded Mortier to bring up the fifth corps from Valladolid to Villa Castin, near Avila, although, following Napoleon's orders, it should have gone to Salamanca.

In the hope of meeting Venegas, Joseph had penetrated as far as the Jabalon river, in La Mancha ;

and as the Spaniard, fearful of the tempest approaching him, immediately took shelter in the Morena, the king, leaving some posts of the 4th corps at Toledo, restored the light cavalry to the first corps, and, with his guards and reserve, returned to Madrid. But, while he had been pursuing a shadow, Victor was exposed to great danger; for the Jabalon is six long marches from Madrid, and hence, for ten days, the duke of Belluno, with only two divisions of infantry and two thousand cavalry, in all about fourteen thousand men, had remained at Talavera without any support, although sixty thousand men were marching against him from different points.

Victor did not suffer as he might have done, but his numerical weakness was certainly the safety of Cuesta. For that general, having followed the retreat of the first corps from Torremocha, crossed the Tagus, at Almaraz, on the 23d of June, and pushed an advanced guard towards Oropesa. He had thirty-eight thousand men, yet he remained tranquil while (at a distance of only twelve miles) fourteen thousand French made a flank movement that lasted three days; and his careless method of acting, and his unskilful dispositions, were so evident, that the French cavalry, far from fearing, were preparing to punish him, when he suddenly took the alarm, and, withdrawing to Almaraz, occupied himself in finishing his bridges over the Tagus.

The 28th of June, Victor having removed his hospitals and depots from Arzobispo, had taken a position behind the Alberche, keeping, however, three battalions and the cavalry at Talavera, with advanced posts at Calera and Gamonal; a small detachment, also, watched the course of the Tagus

BOOK
VIII.
————
1809.
July.

Seméle's
Journal of
Operations
First Corps
MSS.

from the mouth of the Alberche to that of the Guadarama, and a moveable column was sent to Escalona, to observe the Vera de Plasencia, and the passes leading upon Avila. In executing this retrograde movement, Victor, having no means of transport, burnt ten out of the fifteen pontoons supporting his bridge over the Tietar, and, for the same reason, he threw a considerable quantity of powder and shot into the river. His troops had been for four days on quarter rations, and were suffering from sickness and hunger, and as the Tagus was fordable in several places, the danger of his position is evident; the British were, however, still at Abrantes, and Cuesta knew not how to profit by this opportunity before the king returned from La Mancha.

Such was the position of the different armies when the British general arrived at Plasencia. He had seen Soult's letters, found upon general Franceschi, and thus ascertained that the second corps was at Zamora, and from Franceschi himself, who passed as a prisoner, at the same time, he learned the arrival of the fifth corps at Valladolid; but the march of Ney's corps was not suspected, and the tenor of Soult's letters led to the notion that Gallicia was to be retained. A letter of Victor's to Joseph, dated the 23d of June, and written in the most desponding language, had been likewise intercepted; and, as Soult's correspondence also gave a strong picture of *his* difficulties, the general impression, that the French armies were not only weak but utterly dismayed, was rather augmented than lessened by this information. Sir Arthur Wellesley, however, could not but have some distrust, when he knew that *two corps* were beyond the mountains, on his left, and though far from suspecting the extent of his danger, he took additional precautions to protect that flank, and renewed his instructions to Beresford to watch the enemy's movements, and to look carefully to the defence of the *Puerto Perales*. But the pass of Baños was still to be guarded, and for this purpose sir Arthur applied to Cuesta.

CHAP.
V.

1809.
July.

Sir A.Wel-
lesley's
Correspon-
dence,
Parl. Pa-
pers, print-
ed in 1810.

The Spanish general was at first unwilling to detach any men to that quarter, yet finally agreed that two battalions from his army and two others from the town of Bejar, at the other side of the pass, should unite to defend Baños, and that the duke del Parque should also send a detachment to the pass of Perales. Although these measures appeared sufficient to obviate danger from Soult's corps, weakened as it was supposed to be, they were evidently futile to check the real force under that marshal; and they were rendered absolutely ridiculous by Cuesta, who sent two weak battalions, of three hundred men each, and with only twenty rounds of ammunition per man : and this was only a part of a system which already weighed heavily on the English general.

The 10th, sir Arthur Wellesley had proceeded to Cuesta's head-quarters, near the Col de Mirabete, to confer with him on their future operations. Ever since the affair of Valdez, in 1808, the junta had been sorely afraid of Cuesta, and, suspecting that he was meditating some signal vengeance, they endeavoured to raise up rivals to his power. In this view they had lavished honours and authority upon Blake, and when the defeat at Belchite crushed their hopes in that quarter, they turned their eyes upon Venegas, and increased his forces,

taking care to give him the best troops. Still
Cuesta's force was formidable, and to reduce it
was the object both of Mr. Frere and the junta :
the motive of the first being to elevate the duke
of Albuquerque ; the intention of the others being
merely to reduce the power of Cuesta.

But whatever might have been the latter's ultimate intention with respect to the junta, it is certain
that his natural obstinacy and violence were greatly
increased by a knowledge of these proceedings, and
that he was ill-disposed towards the English general,
as thinking him a party concerned in the intrigues.
When, therefore, sir Arthur, at the instigation of
Mr. Frere, proposed that a draft of ten thousand
Spanish troops should be detached towards Avila
and Segovia, Cuesta replied that it must be done
by the British, and absolutely refused to furnish
more than two battalions of infantry and a few
cavalry to strengthen sir Robert Wilson's partizan
corps, which was destined to act on the enemy's right.
This determination again baffled Mr. Frere's project of placing the duke of Albuquerque at the
head of an independent force, and obliged the
supreme junta to fall upon some other expedient for
reducing Cuesta's power ; however it was fortunate
that the old Spaniard resisted the proposal, because
the ten thousand men would have gone straight
into the midst of the fifth corps, which, in expectation of such a movement, was then at Villa
Castin, and, having been rejoined by the detachment of colonel Briche, from Catalonia, was eighteen thousand strong, and supported by Kellerman's
division of cavalry at Valladolid.

The discussion between the generals lasted two
days ; but, with the approbation of the supreme

Sir A.Wel-
lesley's
Correspon-
dence,
Parl. Pa-
pers, 1810.

junta, it was finally agreed that the British and
Spanish armies, under sir Arthur and Cuesta, should
march, on the 18th, against Victor, and that
Venegas, advancing, at the same time, through La
Mancha, should leave Toledo and Aranjues to his
left, and push for Fuente Duenas and Villa Mau-
rique on the Upper Tagus. If this movement should
draw Sebastiani, with the fourth corps, to that side,
Venegas was to keep him in play while the allied
forces defeated Victor. If Sebastiani disregarded
it, Venegas was to cross the Tagus and march upon
Madrid, from the south-east, while sir Robert
Wilson, reinforced by some Spanish battalions,
menaced that capital from the opposite quarter.

Previous to entering Spain, sir Arthur had ascertained that the valleys of the Alagon and the Arago
and those between Bejar and Ciudad Rodrigo were
fertile and capable of nourishing his army, and he
had sent commissaries to all these points to purchase
mules, and to arrange with the alcaldes of the different districts for the supply of the troops. He
had obtained the warmest assurances, from the supreme junta, that every needful article should be
forthcoming, and the latter had also sent the inten-
dant-general, don Lonzano de Torres, to the British
head-quarters, with full powers to forward all arrangements for the supply of the English soldiers.
Relying upon these preparations, sir Arthur had
crossed the frontier with few means of transport and
without magazines, for Portugal could not furnish
what was required, and, moreover, the Portuguese
peasants had an insuperable objection to quitting
their own country; a matter however apparently of
little consequence, because Mr. Frere, writing offi-

cially at the time, described the people of Estremadura as viewing " *the war in the light of a crusade,
and carrying it on with all the enthusiasm of such a
cause !*"

From Castello Branco to Plasencia is but seven
days' march, yet that short time was sufficient to
prove the bad faith of the junta, and the illusion
under which Mr. Frere laboured. Neither mules
for the transport of ammunition and provisions, nor
the promised help of the authorities, nor aid of
any kind could be procured; and don Lonzano de
Torres, although, to sir Arthur, he freely acknowledged the extent of the evil, the ill-will of the
inhabitants, and the shameful conduct of the supreme
junta, afterwards, without shame, asserted that the
British troops had always received and consumed
double rations, and were in want of nothing: an
assertion in which he was supported by don Martin
de Garay, the Spanish secretary of state; the whole
proceeding being a concerted plan, to afford the
junta a pretext for justifying their own and casting
a slur upon the English general's conduct, if any
disasters should happen.

Appendix,
No. 17.

Sir Arthur Wellesley, seriously alarmed for the
subsistence of his army, wrote, upon the 16th, to
Mr. Frere and to general O'Donoghue, the chief of
Cuesta's staff; representing to both the distress of
the troops, and intimating his resolution *not to proceed
beyond the Alberche*, unless his wants were immediately supplied; faithful, however, to his agreement with Cuesta, he prepared to put his force in
motion for that river. It was known at Plasencia,
on the 15th, that Ney had retreated from Coruña;
but it was believed, that his corps had been recalled

to France, and no change took place in the plan of campaign. It was not suspected that the sixth corps had then been sixteen days at Astorga!

The valley of the Tagus, into which the army was about to plunge, is intersected by several rivers, with rugged banks and deep channels; but their courses being very little out of the parallel of the Tagus, the Alberche is in a manner enclosed by the Tietar. Now, sir Robert Wilson, having a detachment of four thousand Portuguese and Spanish troops, had ascended the right bank of the latter river, and gained possession of the passes of Arenas, which lead upon Avila, and of the pass of San Pedro Bernardo, which leads upon Madrid; in this position he covered the Vera de Plasencia, and threatened Victor's communications with the capital. The French marshal was alarmed, and a movement of the whole army in the same direction would have obliged him to abandon the Lower Alberche; because, two marches effected beyond Arenas, in the direction of Escalona and Maqueda, would have placed sir Arthur Wellesley between the first corps and Madrid. But, on the other hand, the line of country was too rugged for rapid movements with a large body; and it was necessary first to secure a junction with Cuesta, because Victor, having recovered his third division on the 7th of July, was again at the head of twenty-five thousand men. With such a force he could not be trusted near the Spaniards, and the British general therefore resolved to cross the Tietar, at the Venta de Bazagona, and march by Miajadas upon Oropesa.

The 16th, two companies of the *staff corps*, with a working party of five hundred men, marched from Plasencia to Bazagona, to throw a bridge over the

Semelé's
Journal of
Operations
MSS.

BOOK
VIII.
───────
1809.
July.

Semelé's
Journal of
the First
Corps'
Operations
MSS.

Tietar. The duke of Belluno had wasted many days in dragging up fifteen pontoons from the Tagus, to form his bridge at that place, and when he retired upon Talavera, he destroyed the greatest part of the equipage; but the English officer employed on this occasion pulled down an old house in the neighbourhood, felled some pine-trees in a wood three miles distant, and, uniting intelligence with labour, contrived, without other aid than a few hatchets and saws, in one day, to throw a solid bridge over the Tietar.

The 18th, the army crossed that river, and taking the route of Miajadas, reached Talayuela.

The 19th, the main body halted at Centinello and Casa de Somas. The advanced posts at Venta de St. Juliens.

The 20th, the troops reached Oropesa; but as their marches had been long, and conducted through a difficult country, they halted the 21st; on which day, Cuesta, who had moved from Almaraz by Naval Moral and Arzobispo, passed Oropesa, and united his whole force at Velada, except a small detachment, which marched along the south bank of the Tagus, to threaten the French by the bridge of Talavera.

The duke of Belluno, aware of these movements, had supported his posts at Talavera with a division of infantry, which was disposed in successive detachments behind that town, but his situation appeared critical, because the allies, covered by the Alberche, might still gain a march and reach Escalona before him; and from thence either push for Madrid, by the pass of Brunete, or, taking post at Maqueda, cut him off from the capital. His sources of information were however sure, and he contented himself with sending a regiment of hussars to Cazar de Escalona, to watch the Upper Alberche, and to support the moveable column opposed to sir Robert Wilson.

The 21st, the allies being between Oropesa and Velada, Victor recalled all his foraging parties, altered his line of retreat from the Madrid to the Toledo road, removed his parc from St. Ollalla to Cevolla, and concentrated two divisions of infantry behind the Alberche.

The 22d, the allies moved in two columns, to drive the French posts from Talavera, and Cuesta, marching by the high road, came first up with the enemy's rear-guard, near the village of Gamonal; then commenced a display of ignorance, timidity, and absurdity, that has seldom been equalled in war; the past defeats of the Spanish army were rendered quite explicable; the little fruit derived from them by marshal Victor quite inexplicable. General Latour Maubourg, with two thousand dragoons, came boldly on to the table-land of Gamonal, and sustaining a cannonade, not only checked the head of the Spanish leading column, but actually obliged general Zayas, who commanded it, to display his whole line, consisting of fifteen thousand infantry and three thousand cavalry; nor did the French horsemen give back at all, until the appearance of the red uniforms on their right informed them that it was time to retire. Then, and not till then, Latour Maubourg, supported by some infantry, retreated behind the Alberche, and without loss, although many batteries, and at least six thousand Spanish horse, were close on his rear; the latter could never be induced to make even a partial charge, however favourable the opportunity, and by

two o'clock the whole French army was safely concentrated on its position. Ruffin's division on the
left touched the Tagus, and protected the bridge
over the Alberche, which was more immediately
defended by a regiment of infantry and fourteen
pieces of artillery. Villatte's and Lapisse's divisions,
drawn up in successive lines, on some high ground
that overlooked the surrounding country, formed
the right ; the heavy cavalry were in second line
near the bridge, and in this situation Victor rested
the 22d and 23d.

It was at all times difficult to obtain accurate information from the Spaniards by gentle means ;
hence, the French were usually better supplied with
intelligence than the British, while the native
generals never knew anything about the enemy,
until they felt the weight of his blows. Up to this
period, sir Arthur's best sources of information had
been the intercepted letters of the French ; and now,
although the latter had been in the same position,
and without any change of numbers since the 7th,
the inhabitants of Talavera could not, or would not,
give any information of their strength or situation ;
nor could any reasonable calculation be formed of
either, until some English officers crossed the Tagus,
and, from the mountains on the left bank of that
river, saw the French position in reverse. The
general outline of an attack was, however, agreed
upon for the next morning, but the details were
unsettled, and when the English commander came
to arrange these with Cuesta, the latter was gone
to bed ! The British troops were under arms at
three o'clock the next morning, Cuesta's staff were,
however, not aroused from slumber until seven
o'clock, and the old man finally objected to fight

that day, alleging, among other absurd reasons, that it was Sunday. There was something more than absurdity in these proceedings. Victor, who was not ignorant of the weak points of his own position, remained tranquil the 23d, being well assured that no attack would take place, for it is certain that he had a correspondence with some of the Spanish staff, and the secret discussions between sir Arthur Wellesley and Cuesta, at which only one staff officer of each party was present, became known to the enemy in twenty-four hours after; indeed, Cuesta was himself suspected of treachery by many, yet apparently without reason.

In the course of the 23d, the Spanish officer commanding the advanced posts, reported, that the French guns were withdrawn, and that it was evident they meant to retreat; Cuesta then became willing to attack, and proposed, in concert with sir Arthur Wellesley, to examine Victor's position, when, to the surprise of the English commander, the Spaniard arrived in a coach, drawn by six horses, to perform this duty, and as the inequalities of the ground obliged him to descend from his vehicle, he cast himself at the foot of a tree, and in a few moments went to sleep: yet he was always ready to censure and to thwart every proposal of his able coadjutor. This time, however, he consented to fall upon the enemy, and the troops were in motion early in the morning of the 24th; but the duke of Belluno was again duly informed of their intention, and having withdrawn his moveable column from Escalona, and relinquished the road to Madrid, retreated during the night to Torrijos. Thus, the first combination of the allies failed entirely, and each hour the troops of the enemy were accumu-

lating round them; for Venegas, who should have
been at Fuente Duenas, high up on the Tagus, had
not even passed Damyel; the king was collecting
his whole strength in front, between Toledo and
Talavera, and Soult was fast gathering his more
formidable power behind the mountains of Bejar.

The English general was indeed still ignorant
of the danger which threatened him from the Salamanca country, or he would, doubtless, have withdrawn at once to Plasencia, and secured his communications with Lisbon, and with Beresford's
troops; and other powerful reasons were not wanting to prevent his further advance. Before he quitted Plasencia he had completed contracts with the
alcaldes, in the Vera de Plasencia, for two hundred
and fifty thousand rations of forage and provisions;
this, together with what he had before collected,
would have furnished supplies for ten or twelve
days, a sufficient time to beat Victor, and carry the
army into a fresh country; but, distrustful, as he
had reason to be, of the Spaniards, he again gave
notice to Cuesta and the junta, that BEYOND THE
ALBERCHE he would not move, unless his wants
were immediately supplied; for, hitherto the rations contracted for had not been delivered, and his
representations to the junta and to Cuesta were,
by both, equally disregarded; there were no means
of transport provided; the troops were already on
less than half allowance; absolute famine approached, and when the general demanded food for
his soldiers, at the hands of those whose cause he
came to defend, he was answered with false excuses,
and insulted by false statements. Under any circumstances this would have forced him to halt, but
the advance having been made in the exercise of

his own discretion, and not the command of his
government, there could be no room for hesitation :
wherefore, remonstrating warmly, but manfully,
with the supreme junta, he announced his resolu- Sir A.Wel-
lesley's
Correspon-
dence,
Parl. Pa-
pers, 1810.
tion to go no farther, nay, even *to withdraw from
Spain altogether*.

It is evident that without these well-founded
reasons for pausing, Cuesta's conduct, and the state
of his army, offered no solid ground for expecting
success by continuing the forward movement ; yet
the faithless and perverse conduct of the supreme
junta, although hidden as yet from sir Arthur Wellesley, far exceeded the measure even of Cuesta's
obdurate folly. That body, after having agreed to
the plan upon which the armies were acting, concluded, in the fulness of their ignorance, that the
combined troops in the valley of the Tagus would
be sufficient to overthrow Joseph, and, therefore,
secretly ordered Venegas not to fulfil his part ;
arguing to themselves, with a cunning stupidity,
that it would be a master-stroke of policy to save
him from any chance of a defeat, and hoping thus
to preserve a powerful force, under one of their own
creatures, to maintain their own power. This was
the cause why the army of La Mancha had failed to
appear on the Tagus : and thus, the welfare of millions was made the sport of men, who yet were
never tired of praising themselves, and have not
failed to find admirers elsewhere.

As the Spaniards are perfect masters of the art of
saying every thing and doing nothing, sir Arthur's
remonstrances drew forth many official statements,
plausible replies, and pompous assertions, after their
manner, but produced no amelioration of the evils
complained of. Mr. Frere, also, thinking it neces-

sary to make some apology for himself, asserted
that the evil was deep rooted, and that he had had
neither time nor power to arrange any regular plan
for the subsistence of the English armies.   But all
the evils that blighted the Spanish cause were deep
seated, and Mr. Frere, who could not arrange a
plan for the subsistence of the troops, that indispensable preliminary to military operations, and which
was really within his province, thought himself
competent to direct all the operations themselves
which were in the province of the generals.   He
had found leisure to meddle in all the intrigues of
the day; to aim at making and unmaking Spanish
commanders; to insult sir John Moore; to pester
sir John Cradock with warlike advice; and to arrange the plan of campaign for sir Arthur Wellesley's
army, without that officer's concurrence.

CHAPTER VI.

THE English general's resolution to halt at Talavera made little impression upon Cuesta.   A French
corps had retreated before him, and Madrid, nay,
the Pyrennees themselves, instantly rose on the
view of the sanguine Spaniard : he was resolved to
be the first in the capital, and he pushed forward
in pursuit, reckless alike of military discipline and
of the friendly warnings of sir Arthur, who vainly
admonished him to open his communications as
quickly as possible with Venegas, and to beware
how he let the enemy know that the British and
Spanish armies were separated.   In the fulness of
his arrogant vanity, Cuesta crossed the Alberche on
the 24th, and being unable to ascertain the exact
route of the French, pursued them, by the road of
Toledo, as far as Cebolla, and, by the road of Madrid, as far as El Bravo.   On the 25th, still
inflated with pride, he caused the troops at Cebolla to move on to Torrijos, and marched himself
to St. Ollalla, as if chasing a deer, but the 26th
he discovered that he had been hunting a tiger.
Meanwhile sir Arthur Wellesley, foreseeing the
consequence of this imprudence, had sent general
Sherbrooke, with two divisions of British infantry
and all the cavalry, across the Alberche, to Cazalegas, where, being centrically situated with
respect to Talavera, St. Ollalla, and Escalona, he
could support the Spaniards, and, at the same time,
hold communication with sir Robert Wilson, who
had been at the latter town since the 23d.   But a

great and signal crisis was at hand, the full importance of which cannot be well understood without
an exact knowledge of the situation and proceedings of all the armies involved in this complicated
campaign.

The 30th of June, Soult, when at Zamora, had
received a despatch from the emperor, dated near
Ratisbon, conferring on him the supreme command
of the second, fifth, and sixth corps, with orders
to concentrate them, and act decisively against the
English. *" Wellesley,"* said Napoleon, *" will probably advance, by the Tagus, against Madrid: in
that case, pass the mountains, fall on his flank
and rear, and crush him;"* for, at that distance,
and without other information than what his own
sagacity supplied, this all-knowing soldier foresaw
the leading operations even as soon and as certainly
as those who projected them. The duke of Dalmatia immediately imparted these instructions to
the king, and, at the same time, made known his
own opinions and designs with respect to the probable projects of the allies. He was ignorant of
the precise object and exact position of sir Arthur
Wellesley, but, judging from the cessation of hostility in the north, that the English were in march
with the design of joining Cuesta, and acting by
the line of the Tagus, he proposed to concentrate
the third corps at Salamanca, besiege Ciudad Rodrigo, and menace Lisbon, which, he justly observed,
would bring the English army back to the northern
provinces of Portugal; and if, as some supposed,
the intention of sir Arthur was to unite, at Bragança, with Romana, and open the campaign to the
north of the Douro, the French army would still
be in a suitable position to oppose them.

In pursuance of this opinion, Soult ordered Mortier to approach Ciudad Rodrigo, with the double view of preparing for the siege and covering the quarters of refreshment so much needed by the second corps after its fatigues. Ney also was directed to march with the sixth corps, by the left bank of the Esla, to Zamora; but the spirit of discord was strong, and it was at this moment that the king, alarmed by Sebastiani's report, drew the fifth corps to Villa Castin, while marshal Ney, holding it imprudent to uncover Astorga and Leon, mortified, also, at being placed under the orders of another marshal, refused to move to Zamora. Soult, crossed by these untoward circumstances, sent the division of light cavalry, under his brother, and one of infantry, commanded by Heudelet, from Zamora and Toro to Salamanca, with orders to explore the course of the Tormes, to observe Alba and Ledesma, and especially to scour the roads leading upon Ciudad Rodrigo and Plasencia : these troops relieved a division of dragoons belonging to Kellerman, who was still charged with the general government of the province.

The 10th of July, the march of the British upon Plasencia became known, and it was manifest that sir Arthur had no design to act north of the Douro ; wherefore the duke of Dalmatia resolved to advance, with the remainder of the second corps, to Salamanca ; and, partly by authority, partly by address, he obliged Ney to put the sixth corps in movement for Zamora, leaving Fournier's dragoons to cover Astorga and Leon. Meanwhile, king Joseph, having returned from his fruitless excursion against Venegas, was at first incredulous of the advance of sir Arthur Wellesley and Cuesta, but he agreed to Soult's pro-

ject against Ciudad Rodrigo, and ordered Mortier
to return to Valladolid, where that marshal arrived,
with his first division, on the 16th of July: his
second division, under general Gazan, halted, however, at Medina del Campo and Nava del Rey, on
the route from Salamanca to Valladolid, and an
advanced guard was sent forward to Alba de Tormes.

The 13th of July, Soult, being assured that the
British army was on the eastern frontier of Portugal,
and that considerable reinforcements had been disembarked at Lisbon, became certain that sir Arthur
meant to operate by the line of the Tagus, and
therefore again addressed the king to move him to
an immediate siege of Ciudad Rodrigo, promising
to have the three corps under his own command in
full activity in fifteen days, provided his demands
were complied with, the most important being—
1°. The formation of a battering-train;—2°. The
concentration of an immense number of detachments, which weakened the active corps;—3°. A
reinforcement of fifteen or twenty thousand conscripts, drawn from France, to enable the old troops,
employed on the line of communication, to join the
corps d'armée. The first corps should, he said,
continue to watch the Spanish army of Estremadura, and be prepared either to prevent it from
uniting with the English to disturb the siege, or to
join the first, second, and sixth corps, and give
battle, if that should become necessary. The siege
might thus be pressed vigorously, Ciudad would
fall, Almeida be next invested, and the communications of the English army, with Lisbon, threatened.

S.
Journal of
Operations
MSS.

The 17th, the king replied, through marshal
Jourdan, that he approved of the plan, but had not
means to meet several of Soult's demands, and he

proposed that the latter should reinforce Kellerman and Bonnet, with ten thousand men, to enable them to seize the Asturias, and thus strengthen the communications with France. This drew from the duke of Dalmatia the following remonstrance :—" *Under present circumstances we cannot avoid some sacrifice of territory. Let us prepare, first, by concentrating, on a few points capable of defence and covering the hospitals and depôts which may be on the extremity of our general position. This will not be so distressing as it may appear, because the moment we have beaten and dispersed the enemy's masses we shall recover all our ground.*" Then reiterating his own advice, he concluded thus :—" *I conceive it impossible to finish this war by detachments. It is large masses only, the strongest that you can form, that will succeed.*" It is remarkable that sir Arthur Wellesley, writing at this time, says, " *I conceive that the French are dangerous only when in large masses.*"

Meanwhile, Heudelet's division, having pushed back the advanced guards of the duke del Parque upon Ciudad Rodrigo, ascertained that a great movement of troops was taking place near that city, and that sir Arthur Wellesley, advancing quicker than was expected, had already reached Plasencia ; wherefore, on the 18th, Soult directed Mortier to march upon Salamanca with the fifth corps, and, at the same time, reinforced Heudelet's division with Merle's ; the latter's place, at Zamora, being supplied by a division of the sixth corps, the remainder of which continued on the Esla, fronting the Tras os Montes. Thus, not less than fifty thousand men were at or close to Salamanca, with their cavalry-posts pointing to the passes of Baños, on the very day that sir Arthur Wellesley crossed the Tietar to effect his junction with Cuesta. Yet, neither through the duke del Parque, nor Beresford, nor the guerillas, nor the peasantry, did intelligence of this formidable fact reach him!

Having put the three corps in motion, Soult despatched general Foy to Madrid, with information of sir Arthur's march, and to arrange the future combinations of the two armies. " *It is probable,*" he said, " *that the concentration of my army at Salamanca will oblige the English general to change his plan; but, if he shall already have advanced on the road to Madrid, we should assemble all our forces, both on the Tagus and on this side, fall upon him altogether, and crush him. Thus, his campaign will be finished, and our operations may go on with advantage.*" Foy arrived, the 22d, at Madrid; and, a few hours afterwards, intelligence reached the king that the allies were at Talavera, in front of the first corps, and that sir Robert Wilson (whose strength was much exaggerated) was at Escalona. The die was now cast, Joseph directed Soult to march immediately upon Plasencia; then, leaving general Belliard, with only three thousand men, in the Retiro, set out himself, with his guards and reserve, by the road of Mostoles, to join Victor at Talavera. The 23d, being at Naval-Carneiro, he received notice that the first corps would retreat that night to Torrijos, and, in two days, would be behind the Guadarama river; whereupon, turning to the left, Joseph descended the Guadarama to Vargas, and effected his junction with the duke of Belluno on the 25th.

During this time, Sebastiani, who had been watching Venegas near Damyel, deceived that general, and, returning to Toledo by forced marches, left three thousand men there, with the design of obliging him to cross the Tagus, at Aranjues. With the remainder of the fourth corps Sebastiani joined the king, and thus nearly fifty thousand fighting men and ninety pieces of artillery were concentrated, on the morning of the 26th, behind the Guadarama, and within a few miles of Cuesta's advanced guard. But, on the side of the allies, the main body of the Spaniards was at St. Ollalla; Sherbrooke with two divisions and the cavalry, at Casalegas, and the rest of the English in Talavera. So that, while the French were concentrated and in full march to attack, the allies were separated in four nearly equal and unconnected parts, of which three were enclosed, as it were, in a net, between the Alberche and the Tagus! On such an occasion Napoleon would have been swift and deadly.

In retiring upon Toledo, instead of Madrid, the duke of Belluno showed himself an able commander. Toledo was the strategic pivot upon which every movement turned; it was the central point, by holding which the army of Venegas was separated from the allies on the Alberche. If the latter advanced, Soult's operations rendered every forward step a stride towards ruin; if, leaving Venegas to his fate, they retired, it must be rapidly, or there would be neither wisdom nor safety in the measure. The king knew that Foy would reach Soult the 24th, and as that marshal had already assembled his army about Salamanca, which was only four day's march from Plasencia, he might be in the valley of the Tagus by the 30th; hence, to insure complete success, the royal army needed only to keep the allies in check for four or five days.

BOOK VIII.

1809.
July.

This was the plan that Soult had recommended, that the king promised to follow, and that marshal Jourdan strenuously supported. The unskilful proceedings of Cuesta and Venegas, the separation of the allies, the distressed state of the English army, actually on the verge of famine, (a circumstance that could hardly be unknown to Victor,) greatly facilitated the execution of this project, which did not preclude the king from punishing the folly of the Spanish general, whose army, scattered and without order, discipline, or plan, so strongly invited an attack.

I have said that Cuesta was following a tiger: he had some faint perception of his danger on the 25th, and he gave orders to retreat on the 26th; but the French, suddenly passing the Guadarama, at two o'clock in the morning of that day, quickly drove the Spanish cavalry out of Torrijos, and pursued them to Alcabon; where general Zayas had drawn up four thousand infantry, two thousand horsemen, and eight guns, on a plain, and now offered battle.

COMBAT OF ALCABON.

The Spanish right rested on the road of Domingo Perez, and the left on a chapel of the same name. The French cavalry, under Latour Maubourg, advanced in a parallel line against the position and a cannonade commenced; but at that moment, the head of the French infantry appeared in sight, the Spaniards broke, and fled in disorder towards St. Ollalla, followed, at full gallop, by the horsemen, who pressed them so sorely that the panic would, doubtless, have spread through the whole army, but for the courage of Albuquerque, who, coming up with a division of three thousand fresh cavalry, held the enemy in play, while Cuesta retreated, in the greatest disorder, towards the Alberche.

After reaching St. Ollalla, the French slackened their efforts; the main body halted there, the advanced guards, save a few cavalry-posts, did not pass El Bravo, and no attempt was made to profit from the unconnected position of the allies—a gross and palpable error; for, either by the sword or dispersion, the Spaniards lost, on that day, not less than four thousand men, and such was their fear and haste that it required but a little more perseverance in the pursuit to cause a general rout. Albuquerque, alone, showed any front; but his efforts were unavailing, and the disorder continued to increase until general Sherbrooke, marching out of Cazalegas, placed his divisions between the scared troops and the enemy. Still the danger was imminent; there was no concert between the commanders, the ground on the left of the Alberche was unfavourable to a retiring party, and, as yet, no position upon which the combined forces could retire had been agreed upon! What, then, would have been the consequence if the whole French army had borne down, compact and strong, into the midst of the disordered masses?

Sir Arthur Wellesley, who, at the first alarm, had hastened to the front, seeing the confusion beyond the Alberche, knew that a battle was at hand, and, being persuaded that in a strong defensive position only could the Spaniards be brought to stand a shock, earnestly endeavoured to persuade Cuesta, while Sherbrooke's people could yet cover the movement, to withdraw to Talavera, where there was ground suited for defence; but

Cuesta's uncouth nature again broke forth; his people were beaten, dispirited, fatigued, bewildered, clustering on a narrow slip of low, flat land, between the Alberche, the Tagus, and. the heights of Salinas, and the first shot fired by the enemy must have been the signal of defeat; yet it was in vain that sir Arthur Wellesley pointed out those things, and entreated of him to avoid the fall of the rock that trembled over his head; he replied, that his troops would be disheartened by any further retreat, and that he would fight where he stood : in this mood he passed the night.

The 27th, at day-light, the British general renewed his solicitations, at first, fruitlessly, but when the enemy's cavalry came in sight, and Sherbrooke prepared to retire, Cuesta sullenly yielded, yet, turning to his staff with frantic pride, observed that " *He had first made the Englishman go down on his knees.*" Sir Arthur Wellesley, by virtue of his genius, now assumed the direction of both armies. General Mackenzie's division and a brigade of light cavalry were left on the Alberche, to cover the retrograde movement, and the rest of the allied troops was soon in full march for the position, which was about six miles in the rear. Sir Robert Wilson, who had reached Naval Carneiro on the 25th, and opened a communication with Madrid, and who would certainly have entered that capital but for the approaching battle, was also recalled. He returned, on the 28th, to Escalona, and hung on the enemy's rear, but did not attempt to join the army.

Between the Alberche and the town of Talavera, the country was flat, and covered with olives and cork-trees; but nearly parallel to the Tagus, and at a distance of about two or three miles, a chain of round steep hills bounded the woody plain. Beyond these hills, and separated from them by a deep and rugged valley, something less than half a mile wide, was the mountain-ridge which divides the bed of the Alberche from that of the Tietar. Hence, a line drawn perpendicularly from the Tagus would cross the first chain of hills at the distance of two miles, and at two miles and a half would fall on the mountains.

Sir Arthur Wellesley, taking the town of Talavera, which was built close to the river, as his fixed point, placed the right of the Spaniards there, drawing their army up in two lines, with the left resting upon a mound, where a large field-redoubt was constructed, and behind which a brigade of British light cavalry was posted; all this front was covered by a convent, by ditches, mud walls, breast-works, and felled trees. The cavalry was posted behind the infantry; and the rear was supported by a large house in the wood, well placed, in case of defeat, to cover a retreat on to the main roads leading from Talavera to Arzobispo and Oropesa. In this position they could not be attacked seriously, nor their disposition be even seen, and thus, one-half of the line necessary to be occupied by the allies was rendered nearly impregnable, and yet held by the worst troops.

The front of battle was prolonged by the British infantry. Campbell's division, formed in two lines, touched the Spanish left, and Sherbrooke's division stood next to Campbell's, but arranged on one line only, because Mackenzie's division, destined to form the second line, was then near the Alberche. It was intended that Hill's division should close the left of the British, by taking post on the highest hill, in the chain before mentioned, as bounding the flat and woody country; but, from some cause unknown, the summit of this height was not immediately occupied.

The whole line thus displayed was two miles in length, the left resting on the valley between the round hills and the mountain, and the front covered by a water-course, which, commencing about the centre of the line, opened deeply as it passed the left and became a wide chasm in the valley. Part of the British cavalry was with general Mackenzie, part in the plain beyond the left, and part behind the great redoubt, at the junction of the allied troops. The British and Germans under arms that day were somewhat above nineteen thousand sabres and bayonets, with thirty guns. The Spaniards, after their previous defeat, could only produce from thirty-three to thirty-four thousand men, but they had seventy guns. The combined army, therefore, offered battle with forty-four thousand infantry, nearly ten thousand cavalry, and a hundred pieces of artillery; the French came on with eighty guns, and, including the king's guards, nearly fifty thousand men, of which seven thousand were cavalry. But what a difference in the quality of the troops! The French were all hardy veterans, while the genuine soldiers of the allied army did not exceed nineteen thousand.

The king passed the night of the 26th at St. Ollalla, but put his troops in motion before daylight, on the 27th. Latour Maubourg, with the cavalry, preceded the column, and the first and fourth corps, the royal guards, and reserve, followed in succession. The appearance of the leading

squadrons, near Cazalegas, hastened, as we have
seen, Cuesta's decision, and, about one o'clock in
the afternoon, the first corps reached the heights
of Salinas, from whence the dust of the allies, as
they took up their position, could be perceived;
but neither their situation nor disposition could
be made out, on account of the forest, which,
clothing the country from the Tagus nearly to the
foot of the first range of hills, masked all their
evolutions. The duke of Belluno, however, being
well acquainted with the ground, instantly guessed
their true position, and, in pursuance of his advice, the king directed the fourth corps against the
left of the allies, the cavalry against the centre,
and Victor himself, with the first corps, against the
right: the guards and the reserve supported the
fourth corps.

Semelé's
Journal of
Operations
MSS.

Two good routes, suitable to artillery, led from the
Alberche to the position. The one, being the royal
road to Talavera, was taken by the fourth corps
and the reserve; the other, passing through a place
called the *Casa des Salinas*, led directly upon sir
Arthur Wellesley's extreme left, and was taken
by the first corps: but to reach this Casa, which
was situated near the plain in front of the British
left wing, it was necessary to ford the Alberche,
and to march for a mile or two through the woods.
A dust, which was observed to rise near the Casa
itself indicated the presence of troops at that
place, and, in fact, general Mackenzie's division,
and a brigade of light cavalry, were there posted,
the infantry in the forest, the cavalry on the plain:
yet no patroles had been sent to the front, and this
negligence gave rise to the

COMBAT OF SALINAS.

About three o'clock, Lapisse and Ruffin's division having crossed the Alberche, marched in two columns towards the *Casa de Salinas*, and their light infantry came so suddenly on the British outposts that the latter were surprised, and sir Arthur Wellesley, who was in the *Casa*, nearly fell into the enemy's hands. The French columns followed briskly, and charged so hotly, that the English brigades were separated, and being composed principally of young battalions, got into confusion, one part fired upon another, and the whole were driven into the plain. But, in the midst of this disorder, the forty-fifth, a stubborn old regiment, and some companies of the fifth battalion of the sixtieth, were seen in perfect array, and when sir Arthur rode up to the spot, the fight was restored, and maintained so steadily, that the enemy was checked. The infantry, supported by two brigades of cavalry, then crossed the plain, and regained the left and centre of the position, having lost about four hundred men. General Mackenzie, with one brigade, immediately took post in second line behind the guards; the other was commanded by colonel Donkin, who finding the hill on the left unoccupied, drew up there without orders, and so accidentally completed the position. The cavalry was formed in column behind the left of the line.

Victor, animated by the success of this first operation, brought up Villatte's division, together with all the artillery and light cavalry, to the Casa de Salinas, and then, issuing from the forest, rapidly crossed the plain, advancing, with a fine military display, close up to the left of the position, where he seized an isolated hill, directly in front of colonel Donkin's ground, and immediately opened a heavy cannonade upon that officer's brigade. Meanwhile, the fourth corps and the reserve, approaching the right more slowly, and being unable to discover the true situation of Cuesta's troops, sent their light cavalry forward to make that general shew his lines. As the French horsemen rode boldly up to the front, and commenced skirmishing with their pistols, the Spaniards made a general discharge of small arms, and then, as if deprived of all sense, ten thousand infantry, and all the artillery, breaking their ranks, fled to the rear: the artillery-men carried off their horses, the infantry threw away their arms, the adjutant-general O'Donoghue was amongst the foremost of the fugitives, and even Cuesta himself was in movement towards the rear. The panic spread, and the French would fain have charged home, but sir Arthur Wellesley, who was at hand, immediately flanked the main road with some English squadrons, and the ditches on the other side rendered the country impracticable; the fire of musketry was then renewed by those Spaniards who remained, the enemy lost some men, and finally retreated in disorder.

The greatest part of Cuesta's runaways fled as far as Oropesa, giving out, that the allies were totally defeated and the French army in hot pursuit; thus, the rear became a scene of incredible disorder; the commissaries went off with their animals, the paymasters carried away their money chests, the baggage was scattered, and the alarm spread far and wide; nor is it to be concealed, that some English officers disgraced their uniform on this oc-

BOOK
VIII.
───────
1809.
July.

casion.   Cuesta, however, having recovered from
his first alarm, sent many of his cavalry regiments to
head the fugitives, and drive them back and a part
of the artillery, and some thousands of the infantry
were thus recovered during the night ; but, in the
next day's fight, the Spanish army was less by six
thousand men than it should have been, and the
great redoubt in the centre was silent for want of
guns.

COMBAT ON THE EVENING OF THE 27TH.

The hill on the left of the British army was the
key of the whole position. It was steep and rugged
on the side towards the French, and it was rendered
more inaccessible by the ravine at the bottom, but
towards the English side it was of a smoother ascent.

Semelé's
Journal
of Opera-
tions,
MSS.

Victor, however, observing that the extreme summit
was unoccupied and that Donkin's brigade was
feeble, conceived the design of seizing it by a sudden
assault.   The sun was sinking, and the twilight
and the confusion among the Spaniards on the
right, appeared so favourable to his project, that,
without communicating with the king, he immediately directed Ruffin's division to attack, Villatte to
follow in support, and Lapisse to fall on the
German legion, so as to create a diversion for
Ruffin, but without engaging seriously himself.
Although the assault was quick and vigorous, colonel Donkin beat back the enemy in his front, but his
force was too weak to defend every part, and
many the French turning his left, mounted to the
summit behind him.   At this moment, general Hill
was ordered to reinforce him, and it was not yet
dark, when that officer, while giving orders to
the colonel of the 48th regiment, was shot at by

PENINSULAR WAR.

389

CHAP.
VI.

1809.
July.

some troops from the highest point; thinking they were stragglers from his own ranks, firing at the enemy, he rode up to them, followed by his brigade-major, Fordyce, and in a moment found himself in the midst of the French. Fordyce was killed, and Hill's horse was wounded by a grenadier, who immediately seized the bridle; but the general, spurring the animal hard, broke the man's hold, and galloping down the descent met the 29th regiment, and, without an instant's delay, led them up with such a fierce charge, that the enemy could not sustain the shock.

The summit being thus recovered, the 48th regiment and the first battalion of detachments were immediately brought forward, and, in conjunction with the 29th and colonel Donkin's brigade, presented a formidable front of defence, and in good time; for the troops thus beaten back were only that part of the 9th French regiment, which formed the advance of Ruffin's division; the two other regiments of that division had lost their way in the ravine and hence the attack had not ceased, but only subsided for a time. Lapisse also was in motion, and soon after opened his fire against the German legion, and all the battalions of the 9th, being re-formed in one mass, again advanced up the face of the hill with redoubled vigour. The fighting then became vehement, and, in the darkness, the opposing flashes of the musketry shewed with what a resolute spirit the struggle was maintained; the combatants were scarcely twenty yards asunder, and for a time the event seemed doubtful; but soon the well known shout of the British soldier was heard, rising above the din of arms, and the enemy's broken troops were driven once more into the ravine below: Lapisse, who had made some impression on the German legion, immediately abandoned his false attack, and the fighting of the 27th ceased. The British lost about eight hundred men, and the French about a thousand on that day.

The bivouac fires now blazed up on both sides, and the French and British soldiers were quiet; but, about twelve o'clock, the Spaniards on the right being alarmed at some horse in their front, opened a prodigious peal of musketry and artillery, which continued for twenty minutes without any object; and during the remainder of the night, the whole line was frequently disturbed by desultory firing from the allied troops, by which several men and officers were unfortunately slain. The duke of Belluno, who had learned, from the prisoners, the exact position of the Spaniards, until then unknown to the French generals, now reported his own failure to the king, and proposed that a second attempt should be made in the morning, at daylight; marshal Jourdan opposed this, as being a partial enterprize, which could not lead to any great result; yet Victor was so earnest for a trial, and, resting his representation on his intimate knowledge of the ground, pressed the matter so home, that he won Joseph's assent, and immediately made dispositions for the attack.

The guns of the first corps, being formed in one mass, on the height corresponding to that on which the English left was posted, were enabled to command the great valley on their own right, to range the summit of the hill in their front, and obliquely to search the whole of the British line to the left, as far as the great redoubt between the allied armies.

Ruffin's division was placed in advance, and Villatte's in rear, of the artillery; but the former kept one regiment close to the ravine.

Lapisse occupied some low table-land, opposite to Sherbrooke's division.

Latour Maubourg's cavalry formed a reserve to Lapisse; and general Beaumont's cavalry formed a reserve to Ruffin.

On the English side, general Hill's division was concentrated; the cavalry was massed behind the left; the parc of artillery and hospitals established under cover of the hill, between the cavalry and Hill's division.

COMBAT ON THE MORNING OF THE 28TH.

About daybreak, Ruffin's troops were drawn up, two regiments abreast, supported by a third, in columns of battalions, and, in this order, went forth against the left of the British; a part moving directly against the front, and a part by the valley on the right, thus embracing two sides of the hill. Their march was rapid and steady, they were followed by Villatte's division, and their assault was preceded by a burst of artillery, that rattled round the height, and swept away the English ranks by whole sections. The sharp chattering of the musketry succeeded, the French guns were then pointed towards the British centre and right, the grenadiers instantly closed upon general Hill's division, and the height sparkled with fire. The inequalities of the ground broke the compact formation of the troops on both sides, and small bodies were seen here and there struggling for the mastery with all the virulence of a single combat; in some places the French grenadiers were overthrown at once, in others they would not be denied, and reached the summit, but the reserves were always ready to vindicate their ground, and no permanent footing was obtained. Still the conflict was maintained with singular obstinacy; Hill himself was wounded, and his men were falling fast, yet the enemy suffered more, and gave back, step by step at first, and slowly, to cover the retreat of their wounded, but, finally, unable to sustain the increasing fury of the English, and having lost above fifteen hundred men in the space of forty minutes, the whole mass broke away in disorder, and returned to their own position, covered by the renewed play of their powerful artillery.

To this destructive fire no adequate answer could be made, for the English guns were few, and of small calibre, and when sir Arthur Wellesley desired a reinforcement from Cuesta, the latter sent him only two pieces; yet even those were serviceable and the Spanish gunners fought them gallantly. The principal line of the enemy's retreat was by the great valley, and a favourable opportunity for a charge of horse occurred, but unfortunately the English cavalry, having retired, during the night, for water and forage, were yet too distant to be of service. However, these repeated efforts of the French against the hill, and the appearance of some of their light troops on the mountain, beyond the left, taught the English general that he had committed a fault in not prolonging his flank across the valley, and he hastened to rectify it. For this purpose, he brought up the principal mass of his cavalry behind his left, with the leading squadrons looking into the valley, and having obtained, from Cuesta, general Bassecour's division of infantry, posted it on the mountain itself, in observation of the French light troops. Meanwhile, the duke of Albuquerque, discontented with Cuesta's arrangements, came, with his division, to sir Arthur Wellesley, who placed him behind the British, thus displaying a formidable array of horsemen, six lines in depth.

Immediately after the failure of Ruffin's attack, king Joseph, having in person examined the whole position of the allies, from left to right, demanded of Jourdan and Victor if he should deliver a general battle. The former replied that the great valley and the mountain being unoccupied, on the 27th, sir Arthur Wellesley's attention should have been drawn to the right by a feint on the Spaniards; that, during the night, the whole army should have been silently placed in column, at the entrance of the great valley, ready, at daybreak, to form a line of battle, to the left, on a new front, and so have attacked the hill from whence Victor had been twice repulsed. Such a movement, he said, would have obliged the allies to change their front also, and, during this operation, they might have been assailed with hopes of success. But this project could not now be executed ; the English, aware of their mistake, had secured their left flank, by occupying the valley, and the mountain and their front were alike inattackable. " *Hence, the only prudent line was to take up a position on the Alberche, and await the effect of Soult's operations on the English rear.*"

Marshal Victor opposed this counsel; he engaged to carry the hill on the English left, notwithstanding his former failures, provided the fourth corps

Letter from Marshal Jourdan, MSS.

would attack the right and centre at the same moment; and he finished his argument by declaring that, if such a combination failed, " *It was time to renounce making war.*"

The king was embarrassed. His own opinion coincided with Jourdan's; but he feared that Victor would cause the emperor to believe a great opportunity had been lost ; and, while thus wavering, a despatch arrived from Soult, by which it appeared that his force could only reach Plasencia between the 2d and 5th of August. Now, a detachment from the army of Venegas had already appeared near Toledo, that general's advanced guard was approaching Aranjuez; and the king was much troubled by the danger thus threatening Madrid, because all the stores, the reserve artillery, and the general hospitals of the whole army in Spain were deposited there ; and, moreover, the tolls received at the gates of that town formed almost the only pecuniary resource of his court; so narrowly did Napoleon reduce the expenditure of the war. These considerations overpowered his judgement ; adopting the worse and rejecting the better counsel, he resolved to succour the capital, but, before separating the army, determined to try the chance of a battle. Indecision is a cancer in war : Joseph should have adhered to the plan arranged with Soult ; the advantages were obvious, the ultimate success sure, and the loss of Madrid was nothing in the scale, because it could only be temporary ; but, if the king thought otherwise, he should have decided to fight for it before ; that is, he should have drawn the fifth corps to him, prepared his plan, and fallen, with the utmost rapidity, upon Cuesta, the 26th ; his advanced guard should have been on

the Alberche that evening, and, before twelve
o'clock on the 27th, the English army would have
been without the aid of a single Spanish soldier.
But, after neglecting the most favourable opportunity when his army was full of ardour, he now,
with singular inconsistency, resolved to give battle,
when his enemies were completely prepared,
strongly posted, and in the pride of success, and
when the confidence of his own troops was shaken
by the partial action of the morning.

While the French generals were engaged in
council, the men on both sides took some rest,
and the English wounded were carried to the rear ;
but the soldiers were suffering from hunger ; the
regular service of provisions had ceased for several
days, and a few ounces of wheat, in the grain,
formed the whole subsistence of men who had
fought, and who were yet to fight, so hardly. The
Spanish camp was full of confusion and distrust.
Cuesta inspired terror, but no confidence, and Albuquerque, whether from conviction or instigated
by momentary anger, just as the French were
coming on to the final attack, sent one of his staff
to inform the English commander that Cuesta was
betraying him. The aide-de-camp, charged with
this message, delivered it to colonel Donkin, and
that officer carried it to sir Arthur Wellesley. The
latter, seated on the summit of the hill which had
been so gallantly contested, was intently watching
the movements of the advancing enemy ; he listened
to this somewhat startling message without so much
as turning his head, and then drily answering—
" *Very well, you may return to your brigade*," continued his survey of the French. Donkin retired,
filled with admiration of the imperturbable resolu-

tion and quick penetration of the man; and, indeed,
sir Arthur's conduct was, throughout that day,
such as became a general upon whose vigilance
and intrepidity the fate of fifty thousand men depended.

BATTLE OF TALAVERA.

The dispositions of the French were soon completed. Ruffin's division, on the extreme right,
was destined to cross the valley, and, moving
by the foot of the mountain, to turn the British
left.

Villatte's orders were to menace the contested
height with one brigade, and to guard the valley
with another, which, being strengthened by a battalion of grenadiers, connected Ruffin's movement
with the main attack.

Lapisse, supported by Latour Maubourg's dragoons, and by the king's reserve, was instructed to
pass the ravine in front of the English centre, and
to fall, with half his infantry, upon Sherbrooke's
division, while the other half, connecting its attack
with Villatte's brigade, mounted the hill, and made
a third effort to master that important point.

Milhaud's dragoons were left on the main road,
opposite Talavera, to keep the Spaniards in check;
but the rest of the heavy cavalry was brought into
the centre, behind general Sebastiani, who, with
the fourth corps, was to assail the right of the
British army. A part of the French light cavalry
supported Villatte's brigade in the valley, and a part
remained in reserve.

A number of guns were distributed among the
divisions, but the principal mass remained on the
hill, with the reserve of light cavalry; where, also,

the duke of Belluno stationed himself, to direct the movements of the first corps.

From nine o'clock in the morning until mid-day the field of battle offered no appearance of hostility; the weather was intensely hot, and the troops, on both sides, descended and mingled, without fear or suspicion, to quench their thirst at the little brook which divided the positions; but, at one o'clock in the afternoon, the French soldiers were seen to gather round their eagles, and the rolling of drums was heard along the whole line. Half an hour later, the king's guards, the reserve, and the fourth corps were descried, near the centre of the king's position, marching to join the first corps; and, at two o'clock, the table-land and the height on the French right, even to the valley, were covered with the dark and lowering masses. At this moment some hundreds of English soldiers, employed to carry the wounded to the rear, returned in one body, and were, by the French, supposed to be sir Robert Wilson's corps joining the army; nevertheless, the duke of Belluno, whose arrangements were now completed, gave the signal for battle, and eighty pieces of artillery immediately sent a tempest of bullets before the light troops, who, coming on with the swiftness and violence of a hailstorm, were closely followed by the broad, black columns, in all the majesty of war.

Sir Arthur Wellesley, from the summit of the hill, had a clear view of the whole field of battle; and first he saw the fourth corps rushing forwards, with the usual impetuosity of French soldiers, clearing the intersected ground in their front, and falling upon Campbell's division with infinite fury; but that general, assisted by Mackenzie's brigade,

and by two Spanish battalions, withstood their
utmost efforts. The English regiments, putting the
French skirmishers aside, met the advancing columns with loud shouts, and, breaking in on their
front, and lapping their flanks with fire, and giving
no respite, pushed them back with a terrible carnage.
Ten guns were taken, but as Campbell prudently
resolved not to break his line by a pursuit, the
French instantly rallied on their supports, and made
head for another attack; then the British artillery
and musketry played vehemently upon their masses,
a Spanish cavalry regiment charged their flank, and
they retired in disorder: thus the victory was secured in that quarter.

But, while this was passing on the right, Villatte's
division, preceded by the grenadiers, and supported
by two regiments of light cavalry, was seen advancing up the great valley against the left, and,
beyond Villatte, Ruffin was discovered marching
towards the mountain. Sir Arthur Wellesley immediately ordered Anson's brigade of cavalry,
composed of the twenty-third light dragoons and
the first German hussars, to charge the head of
these columns; these regiments, coming on at a
canter, and increasing their speed as they advanced,
rode headlong against the enemy, but, in a few
moments, came upon the brink of a hollow cleft,
which was not perceptible at a distance. The
French, throwing themselves into squares, opened
their fire; and colonel Arentschild, commanding
the hussars, an officer whom forty years' experience
had made a master in his art, promptly reined up
at the brink, exclaiming, in his broken phrase,
" *I will not kill my young mens!* " But in front of
the twenty-third, the chasm was more practicable,

the English blood hot, and the regiment plunged down without a check; men and horses rolling over each other in dreadful confusion; the survivors still untamed, mounted the opposite bank by two's and three's, and Colonel Seymour being severely wounded, major Frederick Ponsonby, a hardy soldier, rallied all who came up, and passing through the midst of Villatte's columns, which poured in a fire from each side, fell with inexpressible violence upon a brigade of French *chasseurs* in the rear. The combat was fierce but short; Victor had perceived the first advance of the English, and detached his Polish lancers, and Westphalian light-horse, to the support of Villatte; and these fresh troops coming up when the twenty-third, already overmatched, could scarcely hold up against the chasseurs, entirely broke them. Those who were not killed or taken, made for Bassecour's Spanish division, and so escaped, leaving behind two hundred and seven men and officers, or about half the number that went into action.

During this time the hill, the key of the position, was again attacked, and Lapisse, crossing the ravine, pressed hard upon the English centre; his own artillery, aided by the great battery on his right, opened large gaps in Sherbrooke's ranks, and the French columns came close up to the British line in the resolution to win; but they were received with a general discharge 'of all arms, and so vigorously encountered, that they gave back in disorder. Under the excitement of the moment, the brigade of English guards, quitting the line, followed up their success with inconsiderate ardour, when the enemy's supporting columns, and their dragoons advanced, the men who had been repulsed turned again, and the heavy French batteries pounded the flank and front of the guards.

Thus maltreated, the latter drew back, and, at the same time, the German legion, being sorely pressed, got into confusion. At this moment, although Hill's and Campbell's divisions, on the extremities of the line, held fast, the centre of the British was absolutely broken, and the fortune of the day seemed to incline in favour of the French, when, suddenly, colonel Donellan, with the forty-eighth regiment, was seen advancing through the midst of the disordered masses. At first, it seemed as if this regiment must be carried away by the retiring crowds, but, wheeling back by companies, it let them pass through the intervals, and then, resuming its proud and beautiful line, marched against the right of the pursuing columns, and plied them with such a destructive musketry, and closed upon them with such a firm and regular pace, that the forward movement of the French was checked. The guards and the Germans immediately rallied, a brigade of light cavalry came up from the second line at a trot, the artillery battered the enemy's flanks without intermission, the French wavered, lost their advantage, and the battle was restored.

In all actions there is one critical and decisive moment which will give the victory to the general who knows how to seize it. When the guards first made their rash charge, sir Arthur Wellesley, foreseeing the issue of it, had ordered the forty-eighth down from the hill, although a rough battle was going on there, and, at the same time, he directed Cotton's light cavalry to advance. These dispositions gained the day. The French relaxed their efforts by degrees, the fire of the English grew hotter, and their loud and confident shouts—sure augury of success—were heard along the whole line.

In the hands of a great general, Joseph's guards and the reserve, which were yet entire, might have restored the combat, but all combination was at an end on the French side; the fourth corps, beaten back on the left with the loss of ten guns, was in confusion; the troops in the great valley on the right, amazed at the furious charge of the twenty-third, and awed by the sight of four distinct lines of cavalry, still in reserve, remained stationary; no impression had been made on the hill; Lapisse was mortally wounded, his division gave way, and the whole army finally retired to the position from whence it had descended to the attack. This retrograde movement was covered by skirmishers and an increasing fire of artillery, and the British, exhausted by toil and want of food, and reduced to less than fourteen thousand sabres and bayonets, could not pursue. The Spanish army was incapable of any evolution, and about six o'clock all hostility ceased, each army holding the position of the morning. But the battle was scarcely over when, the dry grass and shrubs taking fire, a volume of flames passed with inconceivable rapidity across a part of the field, scorching, in its course, both the dead and the wounded.

On the British side, two generals (Mackenzie and Langworth), thirty-one officers of inferior rank, and seven hundred and sixty-seven serjeants and soldiers were killed upon the spot; three generals, a hundred and ninety-two officers, three thousand seven hundred and eighteen serjeants and privates wounded. Nine officers, six hundred and forty-

BOOK
VIII.
————
1809.
July.

three serjeants and soldiers were missing; thus making a total loss of six thousand two hundred and sixty-eight, in the two days' fighting, of which five thousand four hundred and twenty-two fell on the 28th.

The French suffered more severely; nine hundred and forty-four, including two generals, were Marshal
Jourdan
MSS. killed! six thousand two hundred and ninety-four wounded, one hundred and fifty-six prisoners, furnished a total of seven thousand three hundred and Semelé's
Journal of
Operations
of the First
Corps,
MSS. eighty-nine men and officers, of which four thousand were of Victor's corps, ten guns were taken by general Campbell's division, and seven were left in the woods by the French.

The Spaniards returned above twelve hundred men, killed and wounded, but the correctness of the report was very much doubted at the time.

The 29th, at day-break, the French army quitted its position, and, before six o'clock, was in order of battle on the heights of Salinas, behind the Alberche. That day, also, general Robert Craufurd reached the English camp, with the forty-third, fifty-second, and ninety-fifth regiment, and immediately took charge of the outposts. These troops, after a march of twenty miles, were in *bivouac* near Malpartida de Plasencia, when the alarm caused by the Spanish fugitives spread to that part. Craufurd, fearing that the army was pressed, allowed the men to rest for a few hours, and then, withdrawing about fifty of the weakest from the ranks, commenced his march with the resolution not to halt until he reached the field of battle. As the brigade advanced, crowds of the runaways were met with, and although not all Spaniards, all propagating the vilest falsehoods: " *the army was de-*

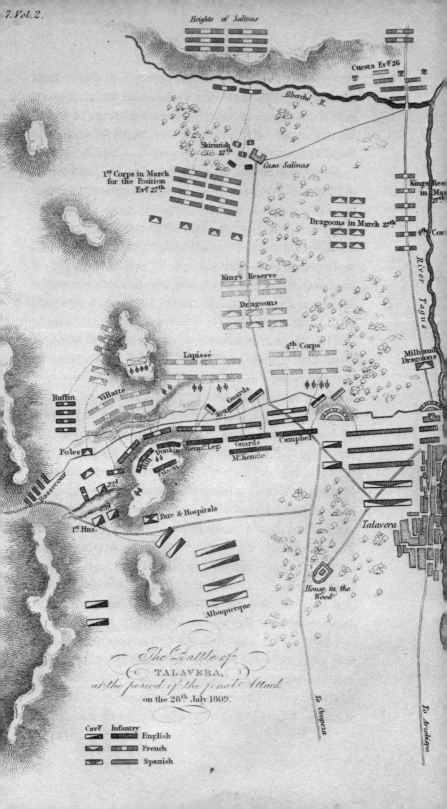

7. Vol. 2.

Heights of Salinas

Cuesta Ev.^g 26

Alberché R.

Skirmish 27th

Casa Salinas

1st Corps in March
for the Position
Ev^g 27th

King's Res.
in Ma
27th

4th Cor

Dragoons in March 27th

River Tagus

King's Reserve

Dragoons

Lapisse

4th Corps

Milhand
Dragoons

Ruffin

Villatte

Guards
48th

Poles

Hill Donkin Germ.ⁿ Leg.
Tilson

Guards
M.Kenzie

Campbel

Bassecour

2nd

2nd

Talavera

1st Hns.

Parc & Hospitals

Albuquerque

House in the
Wood

To Oropesa

To Arzobispo

The Battle of
TALAVERA,
at the period of the final Attack
on the 28th July 1809.

Cav^y Infantry
           English
           French
           Spanish

feated,"—" Sir Arthur Wellesley was killed,"—" the French were only a few miles distant;" nay, some, blinded by their fears, affected even to point out the enemy's advanced posts on the nearest hills. Indignant at this shameful scene the troops hastened, rather than slackened, the impetuosity of their pace, and leaving only seventeen stragglers behind, in twenty-six hours crossed the field of battle in a close and compact body ; having, in that time, passed over sixty-two English miles, and in the hottest season of the year, each man carrying from fifty to sixty pounds weight upon his shoulders. Had the historian Gibbon known of such a march, he would have spared his sneer about the " delicacy of modern soldiers !"

OBSERVATIONS.

1°. The moral courage evinced by sir Arthur Wellesley, when, with such a coadjutor as Cuesta, he accepted battle, was not less remarkable than the judicious disposition which, finally, rendered him master of the field. Yet it is doubtful if he could have maintained his position had the French been well managed, and their strength reserved for the proper moment, instead of being wasted on isolated attacks during the night of the 27th, and the morning of the 28th.

A pitched battle is a great affair. A good general must bring all the moral, as well as the physical, force of his army into play at the same time if he means to win, and all may be too little. Marshal Jourdan's project was conceived in this spirit, and worthy of his reputation ; and it is possible, that he might have placed his army, unperceived, on the flank of the English, and then by a sudden and general attack have carried the key of his position, thus commencing his battle well : but sir Arthur Wellesley's resources would not then have been exhausted. He had foreseen such an occurrence, and was prepared, by a change of front, to keep the enemy in check with his left wing and cavalry; while the right, marching upon the position abandoned by the French, should cut the latter off from the Alberche. In this movement the allies would have been reinforced by Wilson's corps, which was near Cazalegas, and the contending armies would then have exchanged lines of operation. The French could, however, have gained nothing, unless they won a complete victory, while the allies would, even though defeated, have ensured their junction with Venegas. Madrid and Toledo would thus have fallen to them, and before Soult could unite with Joseph, a new line of operations, through the fertile country of La Mancha, might have been obtained. But these matters are only speculative.

2°. The distribution of the French troops for the great attack cannot be praised. The attempt to turn the English left with a single division was puerile. The allied cavalry was plainly to be seen in the valley; how, then, could a single division hope to develope its attack upon the hill, when five thousand horsemen were hanging upon its flank? and, in fact, the whole of Ruffin's, and the half of Villatte's division, were paralyzed by the charge of a single regiment. To have rendered this movement formidable, the principal part of the French cavalry should have preceded the march of the infantry; but the great error was fighting at all before Soult reached Plasencia.

3°. It has been said, that to complete the victory

sir Arthur Wellesley should have caused the Spaniards to advance; this would, more probably, have led to a defeat. Neither Cuesta, nor his troops, were capable of an orderly movement. The infantry of the first and the fourth corps were still above twenty thousand strong, and, although a repulsed, by no means a discomfited force; the cavalry, the king's guards, and Dessolle's division, had not been engaged at all, and were alone sufficient to beat the Spaniards; a second panic, such as that of the 27th, would have led to the most deplorable consequences, as those, who know with what facility French soldiers recover from a repulse, will readily acknowledge.

The battle of Talavera was one of hard honest fighting, and the exceeding gallantry of the troops honoured the nations to which they belonged. The English owed much to the general's dispositions and something to fortune. The French owed nothing to their commander; but when it is considered that only the reserve of their infantry were withheld from the great attack on the 28th, and that, consequently, above thirty thousand men were closely and unsuccessfully engaged for three hours with sixteen thousand British, it must be confessed that the latter proved themselves to be truly formidable soldiers; yet the greatest part were raw men, so lately drafted from the militia regiments that many of them still bore the number of their former regiments on their accoutrements.

CHAPTER VII.

BOOK
VIII.
———
1809.
July.

THE French rested the 29th at Salinas; but, in the night, the king marched with the 4th corps and the reserve to St. Ollalla, from whence he sent a division to relieve Toledo. The 31st, he halted. The 1st of August he marched to Illescas, a central position, from whence he could interpose between Venegas and the capital. The duke of Belluno, with the first corps, remained on the Alberche, having orders to fall upon the rear-guard of the allies, when the latter should be forced to retire, in consequence of Soult's operations. Meantime, sir Robert Wilson, who during the action was near Cazalegas, returned to Escalona, and Victor, displaying an unaccountable dread of this small body, which he supposed to be the precursor of the allied army, immediately retired, first to Maqueda, and then to Santa Cruz del Retamar; he was even proceeding to Mostoles, when a retrograde movement of the allies recalled him to the Alberche.

The British army was so weak, and had suffered so much, that the 29th and 30th were passed, by sir Arthur, in establishing his hospitals at Talavera, and in fruitless endeavours to procure provisions, and the necessary assistance to prevent the wounded men from perishing. Both Cuesta and the inhabitants of Talavera possessed the means, but would not render the slightest aid, nor would they even assist to bury the dead; the corn secreted in Talavera was sufficient to support the army for a month, yet the starving troops were kept in ignorance of it, although

the inhabitants, who had fled across the Tagus with
their portable effects at the beginning of the battle,
had now returned. It is not surprising that, in
such circumstances, men should endeavour to save
their property, especially provisions; but the
apathy with which they beheld, the wounded men
dying for want of aid, and those who were sound,
sinking from hunger, did in no wise answer
Mr. Frere's description of them, as men who
" *looked upon the war in the light of a crusade,
and carried it on with all the enthusiasm of such
a cause.*"

This conduct left an indelible impression on the
minds of the English soldiers. From that period to
the end of the war their contempt and dislike of
the Spaniards were never effaced, and long afterwards, Badajos and St. Sebastian suffered for the
churlish behaviour of the people of Talavera. The
principal motive of action with the Spaniards was
always personal rancour: hence, those troops who
had behaved so ill in action, and the inhabitants,
who withheld alike their sympathy and their aid
from the English soldiers to whose bravery they owed
the existence of their town, were busily engaged
after the battle, in beating out the brains of the
wounded French as they lay upon the field; and
they were only checked by the English soldiers,
who, in some instances, fired upon the perpetrators
of this horrible iniquity. Cuesta also gave proofs
of his ferocious character; he, who had shown himself alike devoid of talent and real patriotism, he
whose indolence and ignorance of his profession had
banished all order and discipline from his army,
and whose stupid pride had all but caused its
destruction, now assumed the Roman general, and

proceeded to decimate the regiments that had fled in the panic on the 27th. Above fifty men he slew in this manner; and if his cruelty, so contrary to reason and the morals of the age, had not been mitigated by the earnest intercession of sir Arthur Wellesley, more men would have been destroyed in cold blood, by this savage old man, than had fallen in the battle.

Sir A.
Welles-
ley's
Correspon-
dence,
Parl.
Papers,
1810.

Hitherto the allied generals had thought little of the duke of Dalmatia's movements, and their eyes were still fixed on Madrid; but, the 30th, information was received at Talavera, that twelve thousand rations had been ordered, for the 28th, at Fuente Dueña by that marshal, and twenty-four thousand at Los Santos, a town situated between Alba de Tormes and the pass of Baños. Cuesta, conscious of the defenceless state of the latter post, suggested that sir Robert Wilson should be sent there; but sir Arthur Wellesley wished Wilson to remain at Escalona, to renew his intercourse with Madrid, and proposed that a Spanish corps should go: indeed, he still slighted the idea of danger from that quarter, and hoped that the result of the battle would suffice to check Soult's march. Cuesta rejected this proposal at the moment, and again, on the 31st, when sir Arthur renewed his application; but, on the 1st of August, it was known that Soult had entered Bejar; and, on the 2d, general Bassecour was detached by Cuesta to defend the Puerto de Baños, from which he was absent four long marches, while the enemy had been, on the 31st, within one march.

The day that Bassecour marched, intelligence arrived that Soult had entered Plasencia. Baños had been abandoned to the enemy without a shot;

for the battalions from Bejar had dispersed, and those sent by Cuesta had been withdrawn to Almaraz by their general the marquis de la Reyna, who also proclaimed that he would destroy the boat-bridge at that place. This news roused Cuesta; he proposed that half the allied army should march to the rear, and attack Soult; sir Arthur Wellesley however refused to divide the English army, yet offered to go or stay with the whole; and, when the other desired him to choose, he answered that he would go, and Cuesta appeared satisfied.

On the night of the 2d August, letters were received from Wilson, announcing the appearance of the French near Nombella, whither he, unconscious of the effect produced by his presence at Escalona, had retreated with his infantry, sending his artillery to St. Roman, near Talavera. As sir Arthur Wellesley could not suppose that sir Robert Wilson's corps alone would cause the first corps to retire, he naturally concluded that Victor's design was to cross the Alberche at Escalona, crush Wilson, and operate a communication with Soult by the valley of the Tietar. As such a movement, if persisted in, would necessarily dislodge Cuesta from Talavera, sir Arthur, before he commenced his march, obtained the Spanish general's promise that he would collect cars, for the purpose of transporting as many of the English wounded as were in a condition to be moved, from Talavera, to some more suitable place. This promise, like all the others, was shamefully violated, but the British general had not yet learned the full extent of Cuesta's bad faith, and thinking that a few days would suffice to drive back Soult, marched, on the 3d of August, with seventeen thousand men, to

BOOK
VIII.
───────
1809.
August.
S.
Journal of
Operations
2d corps,
MS.

Oropesa, intending to unite with Bassecour's division, and to fight Soult, whose force he estimated at fifteen thousand.

Meanwhile, Soult being, by the return of general Foy, on the 24th of July, assured of the king's concurrence in the combined movements to be executed, ordered Laborde, Merle, and La Houssaye to march from Zamora and Toro upon Salamanca and Ledesma, and to scour the banks of the Tormes. The sixth corps was also directed upon the same place, and, the 25th, Soult repaired to Salamanca in person, intending to unite the three corps there. Hearing, however, of Victor's retrograde movement from the Alberche to the Guadarama, he desired marshal Mortier to march, on the 28th, to Plasencia, by Fuente Roble and Bejar, and he placed La Houssaye's and Lorge's dragoons under his command; the remainder of the second corps and the light cavalry were to follow when the sixth corps should be in motion. This done, Soult wrote to the king, saying, " *My urgent desire is that your majesty may not fight a general battle before you are certain of the concentration of all my forces near Plasencia. The most important results will be obtained if your majesty will abstain from attacking until the moment when a knowledge of my march causes the enemy to retrace his steps, which he must do, or he is lost.*"

The 29th, the fifth corps was at Fuente Roble; but information being received that Beresford, with an army, had reached Almeida on the 27th, the march was covered by strong detachments on the side of Ciudad Rodrigo. The long-expected convoy of artillery and ammunition for the second corps had, however, arrived in Salamanca the 29th; and Ney wrote, from Toro, that he also would be there the 31st.

The 30th, the fifth corps drove the marquis de la Reyna from the pass of Baños, and took post at Aldea Neuva del Camina and Herbas; and the second corps, quitting Salamanca, arrived, the same day, at Siete Carrera.

The 31st, the fifth corps entered Plasencia; the second corps reached Fuente la Casa, Fuente Roble, San Estevan, and Los Santos.

Plasencia was full of convalescents, detachments, and non-combatants, and when the French arrived, about two thousand men, including five hundred of the Lusitanian legion, evacuated the town, taking the road to Moraleja and Zarza Mayor; yet four hundred sick men, following the enemy's accounts, were captured, together with a few stores. During these rapid marches, the French were daily harassed by the Spanish peasantry, the villages were deserted, the cavalry wandered far and near to procure subsistence, and several slight skirmishes and some pillage took place.

The 1st of August, the second corps passed the Col de Baños, and the head of the column entered Plasencia, which was, like other places, deserted by the greatest part of the inhabitants. Vague reports that a battle had been fought between the 26th and 29th was the only intelligence that could be procured of the situation of the allies, and on the 2d, the advanced guard of the army marched to the Venta de Bazagona, while scouting parties were, at the same time, directed towards Coria, to acquire news of marshal Beresford, who was now said to be moving along the Portuguese frontier.

The 3d of August, the fifth corps and the dra-

goons, passing the Tietar, reached Toril, the outposts were pushed to Cazatejada and Sierra de
Requemeda, but the second corps remained at Plasencia, awaiting the arrival of the sixth corps, the
head of which was now at Baños. Hence, on the
3d of August, the king and Sebastiani being at Illescas and Valdemoro, Victor at Maqueda, Cuesta
at Talavera, sir Arthur Wellesley at Oropesa, and
Soult on the Tietar, the narrow valley of the Tagus
was crowded in its whole length by the contending
troops.

The allies held the centre, being only one day's
march asunder, but their force, when concentrated,
was not more than forty-seven thousand men.
The French could not unite under three days, but
their combined forces exceeded ninety thousand
men, of which fifty-three thousand were under

Soult. This singular situation was rendered more
remarkable by the ignorance in which all parties
were as to the strength and movements of their
adversaries. Victor and the king, frightened by
Wilson's partizan corps of four thousand men, were
preparing to unite at Mostoles, while Cuesta,
equally alarmed at Victor, was retiring from Tala
vera. Sir Arthur Wellesley was supposed, by
Joseph, to be at the head of twenty-five thousand
British ; and the former, calculating on Soult's
weakness, was marching, with twenty-three thousand Spanish and English, to engage fifty-three
thousand French ; while Soult, unable to ascertain
the exact situation of either friends or enemies, little
suspected that the prey was rushing into his jaws.
At this moment the fate of the Peninsula hung by
a thread, which could not bear the weight for

c. 8. Vol. 2.

Sierra Coopeceno

Guadalaxara
Fuente Dueñas
Ocaña   Tembleque
Xarama R.   To Dayma
Aranjuez   Consuegra
Valdemoro   P.Largo   Yepes
MADRID
Mostoles   Illescas   Almonacid
Escurial   Guazalete R.
Navalcarnero   Vargas
Segovia   Guadarama R.   Toledo
                    Toledo Mts.
Sierra de Guadarama   Torijos
Villa Castin   Brunete   Maqueda
                    Escalona   S.Malla
Valladolid   Alberche R.
          Avila   Nombella   Sierra Guadalupe
                    Gaza.vegas
          Gredos   Pedro Bernardo   Talacon
                    Velada   Aldea Nueva
          Puerto   Mombeltran   Calera
          Arenas   Centinello
          Vianda   Arzobispo
Tormes R.   Sierra Gredos   Oropeza
                    Gordo   Puebla Nauida
          Sierra Gata   Julien   Mirabete
          Fuente Roble   Vera de Plasencia   Navalmoral
Los Santos   Miajadas
Salamanca   Siete Careras   Toril
          S.Estevan   Lumareus   Almaras
          Beja   Banos   Bazagona   Jaraic
          Huerbas   Tietar R.
                    Placencia

          Ponte Cardenal

Ciudad
Rodrigo   River Tagus
                    Coria
Perales   Alagon R.
          Moraleja
Almeida   Zarza mayor
          Elga R.   Salvatierra   Alcantara

Operations of the
BRITISH, FRENCH & SPANISH ARMIES,
in July & August 1809.

twenty-four hours, yet fortune so ordained that no irreparable disaster ensued.

At five o'clock in the evening of the 3d, it was known at the English head-quarters that the French were near Naval Moral, and, consequently, between the allies and the bridge of Almaraz.

At six o'clock, letters from Cuesta advised sir Arthur, that the king was again advancing, and that, from intercepted despatches addressed to Soult, it appeared that the latter must be stronger than was supposed ; wherefore Cuesta said, that wishing to aid the English, he would quit Talavera that evening : in other words, abandon the British hospitals !

To this unexpected communication sir Arthur replied that the king was still some marches off, and that Venegas should be directed to occupy him on the Upper Tagus ; that Soult's strength was exceedingly overrated, and Victor's movements not decided enough to oblige the Spanish army to quit Talavera ; wherefore he required that Cuesta should at least wait until the next morning, to cover the evacuation of the English hospitals. But, before this communication reached Cuesta, he was in full march, and, at day-break on the 4th, the Spanish army was descried moving, in several columns, down the valley towards Oropesa ; Bassecour's division soon after joined it from Centinello, and, at the same time, the cavalry patroles found the French near Naval Moral.

Sir Arthur Wellesley having, by this time, seen the intercepted letters himself, became convinced that Soult's force was not overrated at thirty thousand ; and the duke of Dalmatia, who had also intercepted some English letters, learned that, on

the first of August, the allies were still at Talavera,
and ill-informed of his march. Thus, the one general perceived his danger and the other his advantage at the same moment.

Mortier was immediately ordered, by the duke
of Dalmatia, to take a position with the fifth corps
at Cazatejada, to seize the boat-bridge at Almaraz,
if it was not destroyed, and to patrole towards Arzobispo; the second corps was, likewise, directed
upon the same place, and the head of the sixth
entered Plasencia. The further progress of the
allies was thus barred in front; the Tagus was on
their left; impassable mountains on their right; and
it was certain that Cuesta's retreat would immediately bring the king and Victor down upon their
rear. The peril of this situation was apparent to
every soldier in the British ranks, and produced a
general inquietude. No man felt the slightest confidence in the Spaniards, and the recollection of
the stern conflict at Talavera, aided by a sense of
exhaustion from long abstinence, depressed the
spirits of men and officers. The army was, indeed,
ready to fight, but all persons felt that it must be
for safety, not for glory.

In this trying moment, sir Arthur Wellesley
abated nothing of his usual calmness and fortitude.
He knew not indeed the full extent of the danger;
but, assuming the enemy in his front to be thirty
thousand men, and Victor to have twenty-five
thousand others in his rear, he judged that to continue the offensive would be rash, because he must
fight and beat those two marshals separately within
three days, which, with starving and tired troops,
inferior in number, was scarcely to be accomplished.
To remain where he was, on the defensive, was

equally unpromising; because the road from Talavera to Arzobispo led through Calera, in the rear of
Oropesa, and thus Victor could intercept the only
line of retreat; a battle must then be fought,
in an unfavourable position, against the united
forces of the enemy, estimated, as we have seen, to
be above fifty thousand men. One resource remained : to pass the bridge of Arzobispo immediately, and take up a line of defence behind that
river, before the French could seize the Col de Mirabete, and so cut off the road to Truxillo and
Merida—a hard alternative; but the long cherished
error relative to Soult's weakness had dried up the
springs of success, and left the campaign, like a
withered stem, without fruit or foliage.

Cuesta doggedly opposed this project, asserting
that Oropesa was a position suitable for a battle,
and that he would fight there. Further concession
to his humours would have been folly, and sir
Arthur sternly declared that he would move forth-
with, leaving the Spanish general to do that which
should seem meet to him; and, assuredly, this decided conduct saved the Peninsula, for not fifty,
but ninety thousand enemies were at hand.

It was now six o'clock in the morning, the baggage and ammunition were already in motion for
the bridge of Arzobispo, but the army, which had
been reinforced by a troop of horse-artillery, and
some convalescents that escaped from Plasencia,
remained in position for several hours, to cover
the passage of stores and wounded men from
Talavera, who had just arrived at Calera in the
most pitiable condition. About noon, the road
being clear, the columns marched to the bridge,
and, at two o'clock, the whole army was in position

at the other side, the immediate danger was averted, and the combinations of the enemy were baffled. During the passage, several herds of swine, which, following the custom of the country, had been feeding in the woods, under charge of the swineherds, were fallen in with, and the soldiers, instigated by hunger, broke their ranks, and ran in upon the animals as in a charge, shooting, stabbing, and, like men possessed, cutting off the flesh while the beasts were yet alive ; nor can this conduct be much censured under the circumstances of the moment, although it was a severe misfortune to the poor peasants, whose property was thus destroyed.

From Arzobispo, the army moved towards Deleytoza, and general Craufurd's brigade, having six pieces of artillery attached, was directed to gain the bridge of Almaraz by a forced march, lest the enemy, discovering the ford below that place, should cross the river, and seize the Puerto de Mirabete. The roads were exceedingly rugged, and the guns could only be dragged up the Meza d'Ibor by the force of men ; nevertheless, Craufurd reached his destination on the evening of the 5th, and the head-quarters were established at Deleytoza, on the 7th, the artillery being at Campillo, the rear-guard occupying the Meza d'Ibor. The sick and wounded were then forwarded to Merida, but the paucity of transport was such, that sir Arthur Wellesley was obliged to unload both ammunition and treasure carts for the conveyance of these unfortunate men. Meanwhile Soult, little thinking that his object was already frustrated, continued his march on the 5th, and Mortier took post at Naval Moral ; the advanced guard entered Puebla de Naciada, and the patroles,

scouring the roads to Oropesa and the bridge of
Arzobispo, fell in with and were chased by the
Spanish cavalry from Arzobispo; for Cuesta would
not retire on the 4th, and was in the act of passing
the bridge when the French came in view. The
movements were now hurried on both sides. Before
dark, the Spanish army was across the Tagus, with
the exception of a rear-guard, which remained on
the right bank that evening, but it was driven
across the river, on the morning of the 6th, by the
fifth corps, which afterwards took post at Valdeveja
and Puebla de Naciada. Ney also reached Naval
Moral, and the second corps entered Gordo.

The 7th Mortier examined the Spanish position,
and reported that Cuesta, having thrown up entrenchments, and placed twenty guns in battery, to
rake the bridge, which was also barricadoed, had
left two divisions of infantry and one of cavalry to
hold the post, and withdrawn the rest of his army
towards Meza d'Ibor. Hereupon, Soult detached
his light cavalry towards Talavera, to communicate
with the king, and brought up the second corps to
Arzobispo. Meanwhile, the duke of Belluno having, on the 5th, ascertained the retreat of the
allies from Talavera, retraced his steps, and entered that town on the 6th; thus the English
wounded, left there, fell into his hands, and their
treatment was such as might be expected from a
gallant and courteous nation; between the British
soldiers and the French, there was no rancour, and
the generous usages of a civilized and honourable
warfare were cherished.

The 7th, Victor crossed the Tagus, at the bridge
of Talavera, and pushed his advanced guard to
Aldea Nueva de Balbaroya, on the left bank, within

a few leagues of the Spanish position, which Soult was preparing to attack in front ; for he had observed that, at a certain point, the Spanish horses, when brought to drink, came far into the stream ; and, the place being sounded in the night of the 7th, a deep but practicable ford was discovered, about half a mile above the bridge.

The fifth and second corps and a division of the sixth were concentrated, to force this passage, early on the morning of the 8th ; but Soult being just then informed of Victor's movement, and perceiving that Albuquerque had withdrawn the Spanish cavalry, leaving only a rear guard in the works, judged that the allies were retreating; wherefore, without relinquishing the attack at Arzobispo, he immediately sent the division of the sixth corps back to Naval Moral, and, at the same time, transmitted a plan of the ford below Almaraz, directed Ney to cross the Tagus there, seize the Puerto de Mirabete, and be in readiness to fall upon the allies, as they came out from the defiles between Deleytoza and Truxillo. Meanwhile the heat of the day had induced Albuquerque to seek shelter for his horsemen in a wood, near Azutan, a village about five miles from the bridge; and the Spanish infantry, keeping a bad guard, were sleeping or loitering about without care or thought, when Mortier, who was charged with the direction of the attack, taking advantage of their want of vigilance, commenced the passage of the river.

COMBAT OF ARZOBISPO.

The French cavalry, about six thousand in number, were secretly assembled near the ford, and, about two o'clock in the day, general Caulaincourt's

brigade suddenly entered the stream. The Spaniards, running to their arms, manned the batteries,
and opened upon the leading squadrons, but Mortier, with a powerful concentric fire of artillery,
immediately overwhelmed the Spanish gunners;
and Caulaincourt, having reached the other side of
the river, turned to his right, and, taking the batteries in reverse, cut down the artillerymen, and
dispersed the infantry who attempted to form. The
duke of Albuquerque, who had mounted at the
first alarm, now came down with all his horsemen
in one mass, but without order, upon Caulaincourt,
and the latter was in imminent danger, when
the rest of the French cavalry, passing rapidly,
joined in the combat; one brigade of infantry followed at the ford, another burst the barriers on the
bridge itself, and, by this time, the Spanish foot
were flying to the mountains. Albuquerque's effort
was thus frustrated, a general route ensued, and
five guns and about four hundred prisoners were
taken.

Soult's intention being to follow up this success,
he directed that the first corps should move, in two
columns, upon Guadalupe and Deleytoza, intending
to support it with the second and fifth, while the
sixth corps crossed at Almaraz, and seized the pass
of Mirabete. This would undoubtedly have completed the ruin of the Spanish army, and forced sir
Arthur to make a rapid and disastrous retreat; for
so complete was the surprise and so sudden the
overthrow that some of the English foragers also
fell into the hands of the enemy; and that Cuesta's
army was in no condition to have made any resistance, if the pursuit had been continued with vigour,
is clear, from the following facts :—

1°. When he withdrew his main body from the bridge of Arzobispo to Peralada de Garbin, on the 7th, he left fifteen pieces of artillery by the road-side, without a guard. The defeat of Albuquerque placed these guns at the mercy of the enemy, who were, however, ignorant of their situation, until a trumpeter attending an English flag of truce, either treacherously or foolishly, mentioned it in the French camp, from whence a detachment of cavalry was sent to fetch them off. 2°. The British military agent, placed at the Spanish head-quarters, was kept in ignorance of the action; and it was only by the arrival of the duke of Albuquerque, at Deleytoza, on the evening of the 9th, that sir Arthur Wellesley knew the bridge was lost. He had before advised Cuesta to withdraw behind the Ibor river, and even now contemplated a partial attack to keep the enemy in check; but when he repaired in person to that general's quarter, on the 10th, he found the country covered with fugitives and stragglers, and Cuesta as helpless and yet as haughty as ever. All his ammunition and guns (forty pieces) were at the right bank of the Ibor, and, of course, at the foot of the Meza, and within sight and cannon-shot of the enemy, on the right bank of the Tagus; they would have been taken by the first French patroles that approached, but that sir Arthur Wellesley persuaded the Spanish staff-officers to have them dragged up the hill, in the course of the 10th, without Cuesta's knowledge.

In this state of affairs, the impending fate of the Peninsula was again averted by the king, who recalled the first corps to the support of the fourth, then opposed to Venegas. Marshal Ney, also, was unable to discover the ford below the bridge of

Almaraz, and, by the 11th, the allies had re-established their line of defence. The head-quarters of the British were at Jaraicejo, and those of the Spaniards at Deleytoza; the former, guarding the ford of Almaraz, formed the left; the latter, occupying the Meza d'Ibor and Campillo, were on the right. The 12th, Cuesta resigned. General Eguia succeeded to the command, and at first gave hopes of a better co-operation, but the evil was in the character of the people. The position of the allies was, however, compact and central; the reserves could easily support the advanced posts; the communication to the rear was open, and if defended with courage, the Meza d'Ibor was impregnable; and to pass the Tagus at Almaraz, in itself a difficult operation, would, while the Mirabete and Meza d'Ibor were occupied, have been dangerous for the French, as they would be enclosed in the narrow space between those ridges and the river.

The duke of Dalmatia, thus thwarted, conceived that sir Arthur Wellesley would endeavour to repass the Tagus by Alcantara, and so rejoin Beresford and the five thousand British troops under Catlin Craufurd and Lightburn, which were, by this time, near the frontier of Portugal. To prevent this he resolved to march at once upon Coria, with the second, fifth, and sixth corps, threaten both Beresford's and sir Arthur's communication with Lisbon, and, at the same time, prepare for the siege of Ciudad Rodrigo; but Marshal Ney absolutely refused to concur in this operation. He observed that sir Arthur Wellesley was not yet in march for Alcantara; that it was exceedingly dangerous to invade Portugal in a hasty manner; and

that the army could not be fed between Coria,
Plasencia, and the Tagus; finally, that Salamanca,
being again in possession of the Spaniards, it was
more fitting that the sixth corps should retake that
town, and occupy the line of the Tormes to cover
Castile. This reasoning was approved by Joseph,
who dreaded the further fatigue and privations
that would attend a continuance of the operations
during the excessive heats, and in a wasted country;
and he was strengthened in his opinion by the
receipt of a despatch from the emperor, dated
Schoenbrun, the 29th of July, in which any further
offensive operations were forbad, until the reinforcements which the recent victory of Wagram
enabled him to send should arrive in Spain. The
second corps was, consequently, directed to take
post at Plasencia; the fifth corps relieved the first
at Talavera; and the English wounded being, by
Victor, given over to marshal Mortier, the latter,
with a chivalrous sense of honour, would not permit
his own soldiers, although suffering severe privations themselves, to receive rations until the hospitals were first supplied; the sixth corps was
directed upon Valladolid, for Joseph was alarmed
lest a fresh insurrection, excited and supported by
the duke del Parque, should spread over the whole
of Leon and Castile.

Ney marched on the 11th; but, to his surprise,
found that sir Robert Wilson, with about four
thousand men, part Spaniards, part Portuguese,
was in possession of the pass of Baños. To explain this, it must be observed, that when the
British army marched from Talavera, on the 3d,
Wilson, being at Nombella, was put in communication with Cuesta. He had sent his artillery to

the army on the 3d, and on the 4th, finding that the
Spaniards had abandoned Talavera, he fell back
with his infantry to Vellada, a few miles north
of Talavera. He was then twenty-four miles from
Arzobispo, and, as Cuesta did not quit Oropesa
until the 5th, a junction with sir Arthur Wellesley
might have been effected; but it was impossible to
know this at the time, and Wilson, very prudently,
crossing the Tietar, made for the mountains, trusting
to his activity and local knowledge to escape the
enemy. Villatte's division pursued him, on the 5th,
to Nombella; a detachment from the garrison of
Avila was watching for him in the passes of Arenas
and Monbeltran; and general Foy waited for him
in the Vera de Plasencia. Nevertheless, baffling his
opponents, he broke through their circle at Viandar,
passed the Gredos at a ridge called the Sierra de
Lanes, and, getting into the valley of the Tormes,
reached Bejar: from thence, thinking to recover
his communications with the army, he marched
towards Plasencia, by the pass of Baños, and thus,
on the morning of the 12th, met with Ney, returning
to the Salamanca country.

The dust of the French column being seen from
afar, and a retreat to Ciudad Rodrigo open, it is not
easy to comprehend why sir Robert Wilson should
have given battle to the sixth corps. His position,
although difficult of approach, and strengthened by
the piling of large stones in the narrowest parts,
was not one in which he could hope to stop a
whole army; and, accordingly, when the French,
overcoming the local obstacles, got close upon his
left, the fight was at an end; the first charge broke
both the legion and the Spanish auxiliaries, and
the whole dispersed. Ney continued his march,

and, having recovered the line of the Tormes, resigned the command of the sixth corps to general
Marchand, and returned to France. But, while
these things happened in Estremadura, La Mancha
was the theatre of more important operations.

CHAPTER VIII.

WHEN the duke of Belluno retired from Salinas to Maqueda, the king, fearing that the allies were moving up the right bank of the Alberche, carried his reserve, in the night of the 3d, to Mostoles; but the fourth corps remained at Illescas, and sent strong patroles to Valdemoro. Wilson, however, retired, as we have seen, from Nombella, on the 4th; and the king, no longer expecting the allies in that quarter, marched in the night to Valdemoro, where he was joined by the fourth corps from Illescas.

The 5th, the duke of Belluno returned to St. Ollalla; and the king marched against general Venegas, who, in pursuance of the secret orders of the junta, before mentioned, had loitered about Daymiel and Tembleque until the 27th of July. It was the 29th before Venegas reached Ocaña, his advanced posts being at Aranjuez, his rear-guard at Yepes, and one division, under Lacy, in front of Toledo; the same day, one of the *partidas,* attending the army, surprised a small French post on the other side of the Tagus, and Lacy's division skirmished with the garrison of Toledo.

The 30th, Venegas heard of the battle of Talavera, and at the same time Lacy reported that the head of the enemy's columns were to be seen on the road beyond Toledo. Hereupon, the Spanish commander reinforced Lacy, and gave him Mora as a point of retreat; but, on the 2d of August, being falsely informed by Cuesta that the allied troops would immediately march upon Madrid, Venegas recalled his divisions from Toledo, pretending to concentrate his army at Aranjuez, in order to march also upon the capital; yet he had no intention of doing so, for the junta did not desire to see Cuesta, at the head of sixty thousand men, in that city, and, previous to the battle of Talavera, had not only forbidden him to enter Madrid, but appointed another man governor. This prohibition would, no doubt, have been disregarded by Cuesta, but Venegas was obedient to their secret instructions, and under pretence of danger to his flanks, if he marched on the capital, remained at Aranjuez, where his flank being equally exposed to an enemy coming from Toledo, he yet performed no service to the general cause.

The 3d, he pushed an advanced guard to Puente Largo, and leaving six hundred infantry, and some cavalry, near Toledo, concentrated his army between Aranjuez and Ocaña. In this position he remained until the 5th, when his advanced guard was driven from the Puente Largo, and across the Tagus; his line of posts on that river was then attacked by the French skirmishers, and, under cover of a heavy cannonade, his position was examined by the enemy's generals: but when the latter found that all the bridges above and below Aranjuez were broken down, they resolved to pass the Tagus at Toledo. With this intent, the French army recrossed the Xarama river, and marched in the direction of that city; but Venegas still keeping his posts at Aranjuez, foolishly dispersed his other divisions at Tembleque, Ocaña, and Guardia. He himself was desirous of defending La Mancha; the central junta, with more prudence, wished him to retreat into the

Sierra Morena; but Mr. Frere proposed that his army should be divided, one part to enter the Morena, and the other to march by Cuença, upon Aragon, and so to menace the communications with France! The admirable absurdity of this proposal would probably have caused it to be adopted, if Sebastiani's movements had not put an end to the discussion. That general, crossing the Tagus at Toledo, and at a ford higher up, drove the Spanish left, back upon the Guazalate, on the 9th of August; on the 10th, Venegas concentrated his whole army at Almonacid, and, holding a council of war, resolved to attack the French on the 12th; the time was miscalculated, Sebastiani advanced on the 11th, and commenced

THE BATTLE OF ALMONACID.

The army of Venegas, including two thousand five hundred cavalry, was somewhat more than twenty-five thousand strong, with forty pieces of artillery. It was the most efficient Spanish force that had yet taken the field ; it was composed of the best regiments in Spain, well armed and clothed, and the generals of divisions were neither incapacitated by age, nor destitute of experience, most of them having been employed in the previous campaign. The village of Almonacid was in the centre of the Spanish position, and, together with some table-land in front of it, was occupied by two divisions of infantry under general Castejon. The left wing, under general Lacy, rested on a hill which covered the main road to Consuegra. The right wing, commanded by general Vigodet, was drawn up on some rising ground covering the road to Tembleque. A reserve, under general Giron, and the greatest part of the artillery, were posted behind the centre, on a rugged hill, crowned by an old castle. The cavalry were placed at the extremity of each wing.

General Dessolles, with the French reserve, was still some hours' march behind, but Sebastiani, after observing the dispositions made by Venegas, resolved to attack him with the fourth corps only. The Polish division immediately marched against the front, Laval's Germans turned the flank of the hill, on which the Spanish left was posted, and two French brigades were directed upon the centre. After a sharp fight, the Spanish left was put to flight; Venegas, however, outflanked the victorious troops with his cavalry, and charging threw them into disorder; but at this moment, the head of Dessolles's column arrived, and enabled Sebastiani's reserves to restore the combat. The Spanish cavalry, shattered by musketry, and by the fire of four pieces of artillery, was, in turn, charged by a French regiment of horse, and broken. Venegas rallied his troops again on the castle-hill, behind the village; but the king came up with the remainder of the reserve, and the attack was renewed. The Poles and Germans continued their march against the left flank of the Spaniards, nine fresh battalions fell upon their centre, and a column of six battalions forced the right; the height and the castle were thus carried at the first effort. Venegas attempted to cover his retreat, by making a stand in the plain behind; but two divisions of dragoons charged his troops before they could re-form, and the disorder became irremediable; the Spaniards, throwing away their arms, dispersed in every direction, and were pursued and slaughtered by the horsemen for several hours.

Following the French account, three thousand of the vanquished were slain, and four thousand taken prisoners; and all the guns, baggage, ammunition, and carriages fell into the hands of the victors, whose loss did not exceed fifteen hundred men. The remnants of the defeated army took shelter in the Sierra Morena; the head-quarters of the fourth corps were then established at Aranjuez, those of the first at Toledo, and the king returned in triumph to the capital.

The Anglo-Spanish army, however, still held its positions at Deleytosa and Jaraicejo, and sir Arthur Wellesley was not, at the first, without hopes to maintain himself there, or even to resume offensive operations; for he knew that Ney had returned to Salamanca, and he erroneously believed that Mortier commanded only a part of the first corps, and that the remainder were at Toledo. On the other hand, his own strength was about seventeen thousand men; Beresford had reached Moraleja, with from twelve to fourteen thousand Portuguese; and between the frontier of Portugal and Lisbon there were at least five thousand British troops, composing the brigades of Catlin Craufurd and Lightburn. If Soult invaded Portugal, the intention of the English general was to have followed him. If the French remained in their present position, he meant to recross the Tagus, and, in conjunction with Beresford's troops, to fall upon their right at Plasencia. For his own front he had no fear; and he was taking measures to restore the broken arch of the Cardinal's bridge over the Tagus, with a view to his operation against Plasencia, when the misconduct of the Spanish government and its generals

Parl. Papers 1810.

again obliged him to look solely to the preservation
of his own army.

From the 23d of July, when the bad faith of the
junta, the apathy of the people in Estremadura,
and the wayward folly of Cuesta, had checked the
forward movements of the British, the privations of
the latter, which had commenced at Plasencia, daily
increased. It was in vain that sir Arthur, remonstrating with Cuesta and the junta, had warned
them of the consequences; it was in vain that he
refused to pass the Alberche until the necessary
supplies were secured; his reasonings, his representations, and even the fact of his having halted
at Talavera, were alike disregarded by men who,
judging from their own habits, concluded that his
actions would also be at variance with his professions. If he demanded food for his troops, he
was answered by false statements of what had been,
and falser promises of what would be done; the
glorious services rendered at Talavera, far from
exciting the gratitude or calling forth the activity
of the Spanish authorities, seemed only to render
them the more perverse. The soldiers in the
ranks were weakened by hunger, the sick were
dying for want of necessary succours, the commissaries were without the means of transport; and
when sir Arthur Wellesley applied for only ninety
artillery horses to supply the place of those killed
in the action, Cuesta, on the very field of battle,
and with the steam of the English blood still reeking in his nostrils, refused this request; two days after,
he abandoned the wounded men to an enemy that he
and his countrymen were hourly describing as the
most ferocious and dishonourable of mankind.

The retreat of the allies across the Tagus increased the sufferings of the troops, and the warmth of their general's remonstrances rose in proportion to the ill-treatment they experienced ; but the replies, nothing abating in falseness as to fact, now became insulting both to the general and his army: " *The British were not only well but over supplied :"—* " *they robbed the peasantry, pillaged the villages, intercepted the Spanish convoys, and openly sold the provisions thus shamefully acquired :"—*" *the retreat of the army across the Tagus was unnecessary ; Soult ought to have been destroyed ; and the English general must have secret motives for his conduct, which he dare not avouch :"*—and other calumnies of the like nature.

Now, from the 20th of July to the 20th of August, although the Spaniards were generally well fed, the English soldiers had not received ten full rations. Half a pound of wheat in the grain, and, twice a week, a few ounces of flour, with a quarter of a pound of goat's flesh, formed the sole subsistence of men and officers; and this scanty supply was procured with much labour, for the goats were to be caught and killed by the troops ; it was, perhaps, upon this additional hardship that the accusation of selling provisions was founded, for, in such cases, it is in all armies the custom that the offal belongs to the men who slaughter the animals;. but the famine in the camp was plainly proved by this very fact; for a goat's offal sold, at this time, for even three or four dollars, or about double the usual price of the whole animal, and men and officers strove to outbid each other for the wretched food.

It has been said that the British soldiers are less

BOOK
VIII.

1809.
August.
intelligent in providing for themselves, and less
able to sustain privations of food than the soldiers
of any other nation. This is one of many vulgar
errors which have been promulgated respecting them.
That they should be constantly victorious, and yet
inferior to all other nations in military qualification,
does not, at first sight, appear a very logical conclusion; but the truth is, that, with the exception
of the Spanish and Portuguese, who are, undoubtedly, more sober, the English soldiers possess all the
most valuable military qualities in as high, and many
in a much higher degree than any other nation. They
are as rapid and as intelligent as the French, as
obedient as the German, as enduring as the Russian,
and more robust than any; and, with respect to
food, this is sure, that no man, of any nation, with
less than two pounds of solid food, of some kind,
daily, can do his work well for any length of time.
A general charge of pillaging is easily made and
hard to be disproved, yet it is certain that the
Spanish troops themselves did not only pillage, but
wantonly devastate the country, and that without
any excuse, for, with the exception of the three
days succeeding the defeat of Arzobispo, their rations were regular and sufficient. With respect
to the interruption of their convoys, by the British
soldiers, the reverse was the fact. *The Spanish
cavalry intercepted the provisions and forage destined
for the English army, and fired upon the foragers,
as if they had been enemies.*

Appendix,
No. 18.

Parlia-
mentary
Papers,
1810.
Before the middle of August there were, in the
six regiments of English cavalry, a thousand men
dismounted, and the horses of seven hundred others
were unserviceable; the baggage animals died in
greater numbers; the artillery cattle were scarcely

able to drag the guns, and one third of the reserve ammunition was given over to the Spaniards, because the ammunition carts were required for the conveyance of sick men, of which the number daily increased. Marshal Beresford experienced the same difficulties in the neighbourhood of Ciudad Rodrigo. The numerous desertions that took place in the Portuguese army, when it became known that the troops were to enter Spain, prevented him from taking the field so soon as he had expected ; but, in the last days of July, being prepared to act, he crossed the Portuguese frontier, and, from that moment, the usual vexatious system of the Spaniards commenced. Romana still continued at Coruña ; the duke del Parque was full of mighty projects, and indignant that Beresford would not blindly adopt his recommendations. Both generals were ignorant of the real strength of the French ; but the Spaniard was confident, and insisted upon offensive movements, while Beresford, a general by no means of an enterprising disposition when in the sole command of an army, contented himself with taking up a defensive line behind the Agueda. In this he was justified ; first, by his instructions, which obliged him to look to the pass of Perales and the defence of the frontier line ; secondly, by the state of his army, which was not half organized, and without horsemen or artillery ; thirdly, by the conduct of the Spanish authorities.

The Portuguese troops were not only refused provisions, but those which had been collected by sir Arthur Wellesley, and put into the magazines at Ciudad Rodrigo, with a view to operate in that quarter, were seized by the cabildo, as security for a debt pretended to be due for the supply of sir

John Moore's army. The claim itself was of doubt-ful character, for Cradock had before offered to pay it if the cabildo would produce the voucher for its being due, a preliminary which had not been complied with. There was also an English com-missary at Ciudad Rodrigo, empowered to liquidate that and any other just claim upon the British military chest; but the cabildo, like all Spaniards, mistaking violence for energy, preferred this display of petty power to the interests of the common cause. Meanwhile, Soult having passed the Sierra de Gredos, by the Baños, Beresford, moving in a parallel direction, crossed the Sierra de Gata, at Perales; reached Moraleja about the 12th of August, and having rallied the troops and con-valescents cut off from Talavera, marched to Salva-tierra, where he arrived the 17th, and took post behind the Elga, covering the road to Abrantes.

Such was the state of affairs when the supreme junta offered sir Arthur Wellesley the rank of captain-general, and sent him a present of horses; and when he, accepting the rank, refused the pay as he had before refused that of the Por-tuguese government, they pressed him to renew offensive operations; but, acting as if they thought the honours conferred upon the general would amply compensate for the sufferings of the troops, the junta made no change in their system. Sir Arthur Wellesley was, however, now convinced that Spain was no longer the place for a British army. He relinquished the notion of further operations in that country, sent his cavalry to the neighbourhood of Caceres, broke down another arch of the Cardinal's bridge, to prevent the enemy from troubling him, and, through the British ambassador, informed the junta that he would immediately retire into Portugal.

This information created the wildest consternation; for, in their swollen self-sufficiency, the members of the government had hitherto disregarded all warnings upon this subject, and now acting as, in the like case, they had acted, the year before, with sir John Moore, they endeavoured to avert the consequences of their own evil doings by vehement remonstrances and the most absurd statements:— " *The French were weak and the moment most propitious for driving them beyond the Pyrenees :*" " *the uncalled-for retreat of the English would ruin the cause :*" and so forth. But they had to deal with a general as firm as sir John Moore ; and, in the British ambassador, they no longer found an instrument suited to their purposes. Lord Wellesley, a man with two many weaknesses to be called great, but of an expanded capacity, and a genius at once subtle and imperious, had come out on a special mission,—and Mr. Frere, whose last communication with the junta had been to recommend another military project, was happily displaced ; yet, even in his private capacity, he made an effort to have some of the generals superseded ; and the junta, with a refined irony, truly Spanish, created him *marquis of* UNION.

At Cadiz, the honours paid to lord Wellesley were extravagant and unbecoming, and his journey from thence to Seville was a scene of triumph, but these outward demonstrations of feeling did not impose upon him beyond the moment, his brother's correspondence and his own penetration soon enabled him to make a just estimate of the junta's protestations. Disdaining their intrigues, and fully appreciating a general's right to direct the operations of his own army, he seconded sir Arthur's remonstrances with firmness, and wisely taking the latter's statements as a guide and basis for his own views, urged them upon the Spanish government with becoming dignity.

The junta, on their part, always protesting that the welfare of the British army was the principal object of their care, did not fail to prove, very clearly upon paper, that the troops, ever since their entry into Spain, had been amply supplied; and that no measures might be wanting to satisfy the English general, they invested don Lorenzo Calvo, a member of their body, with full powers to draw forth and apply all the resources of the country to the nourishment of both armies. This gentleman's promises and assurances, relative to the supply, were more full and formal than M. de Garay's, and equally false. He declared that provisions and forage, in vast quantities, were actually being delivered into the magazines at Truxillo, when, in fact, there was not even an effort making to collect any. He promised that the British should be served, although the Spanish troops should thereby suffer, and, at the very time of making this promise, he obliged the alcaldes of a distant town to send, into the Spanish camp, provisions which had been already purchased by an English commissary. In fine, lord Wellesley had arrived too late; all the mischief that petulance, folly, bad faith, violence, and ignorance united, could inflict, was already accomplished, and, while he was vainly urging a vile, if not a treacherous government, to provide sustenance for the soldiers, sir Arthur withdrew the latter from a post where the vultures, in their pre-science of death, were already congregating.

The 20th, the main body of the British army quitted Jaraicejo, and marched by Truxillo upon Merida. The light brigade, under Craufurd, being relieved at Almaraz by the Spaniards, took the road of Caceras to Valencia de Alcantara; but the pass of Mirabete bore ample testimony to the previous sufferings of the troops. Craufurd's brigade, which, only three weeks before, had traversed sixty miles in a single march, were now with difficulty, and after many halts, able to reach the summit of the Mirabete, although, only four miles from their camp; and the side of that mountain was covered with baggage, and the carcases of many hundred animals that died in the ascent.

When the retreat commenced, the junta, with the malevolence of anger engendered by fear, ca-lumniated the man to whom, only ten days before, they had addressed the most fulsome compliments, and to whose courage and skill they owed their own existence. " *It was not the want of provisions*," they said, " *but some other motive that caused the English general to retreat.*" This was openly and insultingly stated by Garay, by Eguia, and by Calvo, in their correspondence with lord Wellesley and sir Arthur; and at the same time the junta industriously spread a report that the true reason was their own firm resistance to the ungenerous demands of the English ministers, who had re-quired the cession of Cadiz and the island of Cuba, as the price of further assistance. But the only firmness they had shewn was in resistance to the

just demands of their ally.   At Talavera, sir Arthur
Wellesley had been forced to give over to the Spaniards the artillery taken from the enemy; at Meza
d'Ibor, he had sacrificed a part of his ammunition,
to obtain conveyance for the wounded men ; and to
effect the present movement from Jaraicejo, without
leaving his sick behind, he was obliged to abandon
all his parc of ammunition and stores ; then, however, the Spanish generals, who had refused the
slightest aid to convey the sick and wounded men,
immediately found ample means to carry off all
these stores to their own magazines.   In this manner, almost bereft of baggage and ammunition,
those soldiers, who had withstood the fiercest efforts
of the enemy, were driven, as it were, ignomini-
ously from the country they had protected to their
own loss.

The 24th, the head-quarters being at Merida, a
despatch from lord Wellesley was received. He
painted in strong colours the terror of the junta,
the distraction of the people, the universal confusion; and with a natural anxiety to mitigate their
distress, he proposed that the British army should,
notwithstanding the past, endeavour to cover
Andalusia, by taking, in conjunction with the Spanish army, a defensive post behind the Guadiana,
in such manner that the left should rest on the
frontier of Portugal : to facilitate this he had, he
said, presented a plan to the junta for the future
supply of provisions, and the vicinity of the frontier and of Seville would, he hoped, obviate any
difficulty on that point.   But he rested his project
entirely upon political grounds, and it is worthy
of observation, that he, who for many years had,

with despotic power, controlled the movements of immense armies in India, carefully avoided any appearance of meddling with the general's province.

" I am," said he, " fully sensible not only of the *indelicacy*, but of the inutility of attempting to offer to you any opinion of mine in a situation where your own judgement must be your best guide."— " Viewing, however, so nearly, the painful consequences of your immediate retreat into Portugal, I have deemed it to be my duty to submit it to your consideration the possibility of adopting an intermediate plan." Let this proceeding be compared with Mr. Frere's conduct to sir John Moore on a similar occasion.

On the receipt of this despatch, sir Arthur Wellesley halted at Merida for some days, he was able in that country to obtain provisions, and he wished, if possible, to allay the excitement occasioned by his retreat; but he refused to co-operate again with the Spaniards. " Want," he said, " had driven him to separate from them, but their shameful flight at Arzobispo would alone have justified him for doing so. To take up a defensive position behind the Guadiana would be useless, because that river was fordable, and the ground behind it weak. The line of the Tagus, occupied at the moment by Eguia, was so strong, that if the Spaniards could defend any thing they might defend that. His advice then was that they should send the pontoon-bridge to Badajos, and remain on the defensive at Deleytoza and Almaraz. But, it might be asked, he said, was there no chance of renewing the offensive? To what purpose? The French were as numerous, if not more so, than the allies; and, with respect to the Spaniards at least, superior in discipline and every military quality. To advance again was only to play the same losing game as before. Baños and Perales must be guarded, or the bands in Castile would again pour through upon the rear of the allied army; but who was to guard these passes? The British were too few to detach, and the Spaniards could not be trusted; and if they could, Avila and the Guadarama passes remained, by which the enemy could reinforce the army in front,—for there were no Spanish troops in the north of Spain capable of making a diversion."

" But there was a more serious consideration, namely, the constant and shameful misbehaviour of the Spanish troops before the enemy. We, in England," said sir Arthur, " never hear of their defeats and flights, but I have heard Spanish officers telling of nineteen or twenty actions of the description of that at the bridge of Arzobispo, accounts of which, I believe, have never been published." " In the battle of Talavera," he continued, " in which the Spanish army, with very trifling exception, was not engaged—whole corps threw away their arms, and ran off, when they were neither attacked nor threatened with an attack. When these dastardly soldiers run away they plunder every thing they meet. In their flight from Talavera they plundered the baggage of the British army, which was, at that moment, bravely engaged in their cause."

For these reasons he would not, he said, again co-operate with the Spaniards; yet, by taking post on the Portuguese frontier, he would hang upon the enemy's flank, and thus, unless the latter came with very great forces, prevent him from crossing the Guadiana. This reasoning was conclusive, but ere it reached lord Wellesley, the latter found that so far from his plans, relative to the supply, having been adopted, he could not even get an answer from the junta; that miserable body, at one moment shrinking with fear, at the next bursting with folly, now talked of the enemy's being about to retire to the Pyrenees, or even to the interior of France! and assuming the right to dispose of the Portuguese army as well as of their own, importunately pressed for an immediate, combined, offensive operation, by the troops of the three nations, to harass the enemy in his retreat! but, at the same time, they ordered Eguia to withdraw from Deleytoza, behind the Guadiana.

The 31st, Eguia reached La Serena, and Venegas having rallied his fugitives in the Morena, and being reinforced from the depôts in Andalusia, the two armies amounted to about fifty thousand men, of which eight or ten thousand were horse, for, as I have before observed, the Spanish cavalry seldom suffered much. But the tide of popular discontent was now setting full against the central government. The members of the ancient junta of Seville worked incessantly for their overthrow. Romana, Castaños, Cuesta, Albuquerque, all, and they were many, who had suffered dishonour at their hands, were against them; and the local junta of Estremadura insisted that Albuquerque should command in that province. Thus pressed, the supreme junta, considering Venegas as a man devoted to their wishes, resolved to increase his forces. For this purpose they gave Albuquerque the command in Estremadura, yet furnished him with only twelve thousand men, and sent the remainder of Eguia's army to Venegas; at the same time, they made a last effort to engage the British general in their proceedings, offering to place Albuquerque under his orders, provided he would undertake an offensive movement.   By these means, they maintained their tottering power, but their plans, being founded upon vile political intrigues, could in no wise alter sir Arthur Wellesley's determination, which was the result of enlarged military views.   He refused Appendix, No: 17. their offers; and, the 4th of September, his headquarters were established at Badajos.   Meanwhile, Romana delivering over his army to the duke del Parque, repaired to Seville; and Venegas again advanced into La Mancha, but at the approach of a very inferior force of the enemy, retired, with all the haste and confusion of a rout, to the Morena. The English troops were then distributed in Badajos, Elvas, Campo Mayor, and other places, on both banks of the Guadiana; the brigades already in Portugal were brought up to the army, and the lost ammunition and equipments were replaced from the magazines at Lisbon, Abrantes, and Santarem; Beresford, leaving some light troops and militia on the frontier, retired to Thomar, and this eventful campaign, of two months, terminated.

The loss of the army was considerable; above three thousand five hundred men had been killed, or had died of sickness, or fallen into the enemy's hands.   Fifteen hundred horses had perished from want of food, exclusive of those lost in battle; the spirits of the soldiers were depressed, and a heartburning hatred of the Spaniards was engendered by the treatment all had endured.   To fill the cup,

the pestilent fever of the Guadiana, assailing bodies
which fatigue and bad nourishment had already
predisposed to disease, made frightful ravages;
dysentery, that scourge of armies, raged, and, in a
short time, above five thousand men died in the
hospitals.

CHAPTER IX.

OBSERVATIONS.

DURING this short, but important campaign, the armies on both sides acted in violation of the maxim which condemns " *double external lines of operation*," but the results vindicated the soundness of the rule. Nothing permanent or great, nothing proportionate to the number of the troops, the vastness of the combinations, or the reputation of the commanders, was achieved; yet, neither sir Arthur Wellesley, nor the duke of Dalmatia, nor marshal Jourdan can be justly censured, seeing that the two last were controlled by the king, and the first by circumstances of a peculiar nature. The French marshals were thwarted by superior authority; and the English general, commanding an auxiliary force, was obliged to regulate his movements, not by his own military views, but by the actual state of the Spaniards' operations, and with reference to the politics and temper of that people.

La Mancha was the true line by which to act against Madrid; but the British army was on the frontier of Portugal, the junta refused Cadiz as a place of arms, and without Cadiz, or some other fortified sea-port, neither prudence, nor his instructions, would permit sir Arthur to hazard a great operation on that side : hence he adopted, not what was most fitting, in a military sense, but what was least objectionable among the few plans that could be concerted at all with the Spanish generals and government. Now, the latter being resolved to act

with strong armies, both in Estremadura and La
Mancha, the English general had but to remain on
a miserable defensive system in Portugal, or to unite
with Cuesta in the valley of the Tagus.   His terri-
torial line of operations was therefore a matter of
necessity, and any fair criticism must be founded on
the management of his masses after it was chosen.
That he did not greatly err in his conception of the
campaign, is to be inferred from the fact, that Napoleon, Soult, Victor, and Jourdan, simultaneously
expected him upon the very line he followed.   He
was thwarted by Cuesta at every step, Venegas
failed to aid him, and the fatal error relative to
Soult's forces, under which he laboured throughout,
vitiated all his operations; yet he shook the intrusive monarch roughly, in the midst of fifty thousand
men.

Let the project be judged, not by what did happen,
but by what would have happened, if Cuesta had
been active, and if Venegas had performed his part
loyally.   The junction of the British and Spanish
forces was made at Naval Moral, on the 22d of
July.   The duke of Belluno, with twenty-one thousand men, was then in position behind the Alberche,
the fourth corps near Madrilejos in La Mancha,
and Joseph at Madrid, where general Foy had just
arrived, to concert Soult's movement upon Plasencia.
It is evident that the king and Sebastiani could
not reach the scene of action before the 25th or 26th
of July, nor could Soult influence the operations
before the 1st or 2d of August.   If then, the allied
army, being sixty thousand strong, with a hundred
pieces of artillery, had attacked Victor on the morning of the 23d, it is to be presumed that the latter
would have been beaten, and obliged to retreat,

either upon Madrid or Toledo ; but the country immediately in his rear was open, and ten thousand
horsemen could have been launched in the pursuit. Sir Robert Wilson, also, would have been
on Victor's flank, if, neglecting a junction with the
fourth corps, that marshal had taken the road to
Madrid ; and if that of Toledo, the first and fourth
corps would have been separated from the king, who
did not reach Vargas until the evening of the 25th,
but who would not, in this case, have been able to
advance at all beyond Naval Carneiro.

Now, admitting that, by superior discipline and
experience, the French troops had effected their
retreat on either line without any serious calamity,
what would have followed ?

1°. If Victor joined the king, the latter could
only have retired, by Guadalaxara, upon the third
corps, or have gone by the Guadarama towards
Soult.

2°. If Victor joined Sebastiani, the two corps
must have retreated to Guadalaxara, and the king
would have joined them there, or, as before said,
have pushed for the Guadarama to join Soult.

No doubt, that marshal, having so powerful an
army, would, in either case, have restored Joseph
to his capital, and have cut off sir Arthur's communication with Portugal by the valley of the Tagus.
Nevertheless, a great moral impression would have
been produced by the temporary loss of Madrid,
which was, moreover, the general depôt of all the
French armies ; and, meanwhile, Venegas, Cuesta,
and sir Arthur Wellesley would have been united,
and on one line of operations (that of La Mancha),
which, under such circumstances, would have forced
the junta to consent to the occupation of Cadiz. In

this view it must be admitted that the plan was conceived with genius.

Victor's position on the Alberche was, however, strong; he commanded twenty-five thousand veterans; and, as the Spaniards were very incapable in the field, it may be argued that a general movement of the whole army to Escalona, and from thence to Maqueda, would have been preferable to a direct attack at Salinas; because the allies, if thus suddenly placed in the midst of the French corps, might have beaten them in detail, and would certainly have cut the king off from the Guadarama, and forced him back upon the Guadalaxara. But, with Cuesta for a colleague, how could a general undertake an operation requiring celerity and the nicest calculation?

The false dealing of the junta no prudence could guard against; but experience proves that, without extraordinary good fortune, some accident will always happen to mar the combinations of armies acting upon " *double external lines.*" And so it was with respect to Venegas; for that general, with a force of twenty-six thousand men, suffered himself to be held in check for five days by three thousand French, and at the battle of Almonacid shewed, that he knew neither when to advance nor when to retreat.

The patience with which sir Arthur Wellesley bore the foolish insults of Cuesta, and the undaunted firmness with which he sought to protect the Spanish army, require no illustration. When the latter fell back from St. Ollalla on the 26th, it was impossible for the British to retreat with honour; and there is nothing more memorable in the history of this war, nothing more creditable to the personal character of the English chief, than

the battle of Talavera, considered as an isolated
event. Nevertheless, that contest proved that the
allies were unable to attain their object; for, notwithstanding Victor's ill-judged partial attacks on
the night of the 27th and morning of the 28th,
and notwithstanding the final repulse of the French,
all the advantages of the movements, as a whole,
were with the latter. They were, on the 31st of
July, including the garrison of Toledo, still above
forty thousand men, and they maintained their
central position, although it was not until the 1st of
August that Soult's approach caused any change in
the views of the allied generals ; and this brings us
to the fundamental error of sir Arthur Wellesley's
operations.

That so able a commander should engage himself
in the narrow valley of the Tagus with twenty
thousand British and forty thousand Spanish troops,
when fifty thousand French were waiting for him
at the further end, and above fifty thousand more
were hanging on his flank and rear, shews that the
greatest masters of the art may err : but he who
wars, walks in a mist through which the keenest eyes
cannot always discern the right path. " *Speak to
me of a general who has made no mistakes in war,*"
said Turenne, " *and you speak of one who has seldom
made war.*"

Sir Arthur Wellesley thus excused his error :—
" When I entered Spain I had reason to believe
that I should be joined by a Spanish army in such
a respectable state of discipline and efficiency, as
that it had kept in check, during nearly three
months after a defeat, a French army, at one time
superior, and at no time much inferior."

" I had likewise reason to believe that the French

corps, in the north of Spain, were fully employed;
and although I had heard of the arrival of marshal ———
Soult at Zamora, on the 29th of June, with a view
to equip the remains of his corps, I did not think
it possible that three French corps, consisting of
thirty-four thousand men, under three marshals,
could have been assembled at Salamanca without
the knowledge of the governor of Ciudad Rodrigo,
or of the junta of Castile; that these corps could
have been moved from their stations in Gallicia,
the Asturias, and Biscay, without setting free, for
general operations, any Spanish troops which had
been opposed to them, or without any other inconvenience to the enemy than that of protracting, to
a later period, the settlement of his government in
those provinces; — and that they could have
penetrated into Estremadura, without a shot being
fired at them by the troops deemed sufficient to
defend the passes by the Spanish generals."

Thus it was, that like the figures in a phantas-
magoria, the military preparations of Spain, however
menacing in appearance, were invariably found to
be vain and illusory. That sir Arthur Wellesley's
error was not fatal is to be attributed to three
causes :—

1°. The reluctance of marshal Ney to quit Astorga;—2°. The march of the fifth corps upon
Villa Castin instead of Salamanca;—3°. The vehemence with which Victor urged the battle of Talavera: in short, jealousy among the marshals, and
the undecided temper of the king.

If Soult had not been thwarted, he would have
concentrated the three corps near Salamanca before
the 20th, and he would have reached Plasencia
before the 28th of July. The allies must then

have forced their way into La Mancha, or been
crushed; but could they have done the former
without another battle? without the loss of all
the wounded men? could they have done it at all?
The British, including Robert Craufurd's brigade,
were seventeen thousand fighting men on the 29th,
yet wasted with fatigue and hunger. The Spaniards
were above thirty thousand; but in them no trust
could be placed for an effort requiring fine discipline
and courage of the highest order. The intrusive
king was at the head of forty thousand good troops.
Venegas, at once ignorant and hampered by the
intrigues of the junta, was as nought in the operations, while Soult's step, stealthy when the situation
of affairs was obscure, would have been impetuous
when a light broke on the field of battle; it is
scarcely possible to conceive that the allies could
have forced their way in front before that marshal
would have fallen on their rear.

FRENCH OPERATIONS.

Joseph was finally successful; yet it may be
safely affirmed that, with the exception of uniting
his three corps behind the Guadarama, on the evening of the 25th, his proceedings were an almost un-
interrupted series of errors. He would not suffer
Soult to besiege Ciudad Rodrigo with seventy thousand men, in the end of July. To protect Madrid
from the army of Venegas overbalanced, in his mind,
the advantages of this bold and grand project,
which would inevitably have drawn sir Arthur
Wellesley from the Tagus, and which, interrupting
all military communication between the northern
and southern provinces, and ensuring possession of
Castile and Leon, would, by its success, have

opened a broad way to Lisbon. Cuesta and Venegas,
meanwhile, would have marched against Madrid ! ——— Cuesta and Venegas, acting on external lines, and whose united force did not exceed sixty-five thousand men! The king, holding a central position, with fifty thousand French veterans, was alarmed at this prospect, and, rejecting Soult's plan, drew Mortier, with the fifth corps, to Villa Castin. Truly, this was to avoid the fruit-tree from fear of a nettle at its stem !

Sir Arthur Wellesley's advance to Talavera was the result of this great error, but he having thus incautiously afforded Soult an opportunity of striking a fatal blow, a fresh combination was concerted. The king, with equal judgment and activity, then united all his own forces near Toledo, separated Venegas from Cuesta, pushed back the latter upon the English army, and obliged both to stand on the defensive, with eyes attentively directed to their front, when the real point of danger was in the rear. This indeed was skilful; but the battle of Talavera which followed was a palpable, an enormous, fault. The allies could neither move forward nor backward, without being infinitely worse situated for success than in that strong position, which seemed marked out by fortune herself for their security. Until the 31st, the operations of Venegas were not even felt, hence, till the 31st, the French position on the Alberche might have been maintained without danger ; and, on the first of August, the head of Soult's column was at Plasencia.

Let us suppose that the French had merely made demonstrations on the 28th, and had retired behind the Alberche the 29th, would the allies have dared to attack them in that position ? The conduct of the Spaniards, on the evening of the 27th, answers the question; and, moreover, Joseph, with an army compact, active, and experienced, could, with ease, have baffled any efforts of the combined forces to bring him to action; he might have covered himself by the Guadarama river and by the Tagus in succession, and the farther he led his opponents from Talavera, without uncovering the line of La Mancha, the more certain the effect of Soult's operation: but here we have another proof that double external lines are essentially vicious.

The combined movement of the French was desirable, from the greatness of the object to be gained, and safe, from the powerful force on each point; and the occasion was so favourable that, notwithstanding the imprudent heat of Victor, the reluctance of Ney, and the unsteady temper of the king, the fate of the allies was, up to the evening of the 3d, heavy in the scale. Nevertheless, as the central position held by the allies, cut the line of correspondence between Joseph and Soult, the king's despatches were intercepted, and the whole operation, even at the last hour, was thus baffled. The first element of success in war is, that every thing should emanate from a single head; and it would have been preferable that the king, drawing the second and fifth corps to him by the pass of the Guadarama, or by that of Avila, should, with the eighty thousand men thus united, have fallen upon the allies in front. Such a combination, although of less brilliant promise than the one adopted, would have been more sure; and the less a general trusts to fortune the better:—she is capricious!

When one Spanish army was surprised at Arzobispo, another completely beaten at Almonacid, and when Wilson's Portuguese corps was dispersed at Baños, the junta had just completed the measure of their folly by quarrelling with the British which was the only force left that could protect them. The French were, in truth, therefore, the masters of the Peninsula, but they terminated their operations at the very moment when they should have pursued them with redoubled activity, because the general aspect of affairs and the particular circumstances of the campaign were alike favourable. For Napoleon was victorious in Germany; and of the British expeditions against Italy and Holland, the former had scarcely struggled into life,—the latter was already corrupting in death. Hence, Joseph might have been assured that he would receive reinforcements, but that none, of any consequence, could reach his adversaries; and, in the Peninsula, there was nothing to oppose him. Navarre, Biscay, Aragon, and the Castiles were subdued; Gerona closely beleaguered, and the rest of Catalonia, if not quiescent, totally unable to succour that noble city. Valencia was inert; the Asturias still trembling; in Gallicia there was nothing but confusion. Romana, commanding fifteen thousand infantry, but neither cavalry nor artillery, was then at Coruña, and dared not quit the mountains. The duke del Parque held Ciudad Rodrigo, but was in no condition to make head against more than a French division. The battle of Almonacid had cleared La Mancha of troops. Estremadura and Andalusia were, as we have seen, weak, distracted, and incapable of solid resistance. There remained only the English and Portuguese armies, the one being at Jaraceijo, the other at Moraleja.

The line of resistance may, therefore, be said to

have extended from the Sierra Morena to Coruña—
weak from its length; weaker, that the allied corps,
being separated by mountains, by rivers, and by
vast tracts of country, and having different bases of
operation, such as Lisbon, Seville, and Ciudad
Rodrigo, could not act in concert, except offensively; and with how little effect in that way the
campaign of Talavera had proved. But the French
were concentrated in a narrow space, and, having
only Madrid to cover, were advantageously situated
for offensive or defensive movements. The allied
forces were, for the most part, imperfectly organised,
and would not, altogether, have amounted to ninety
thousand fighting men. The French were above
one hundred thousand, dangerous from their discipline and experience, more dangerous that they
held a central position, and that their numbers
were unknown to their opponents; and, moreover,
having, in four days, gained one general and two
minor battles, their courage was high and eager.

See Calvo
Garay and
Lord Wel-
lesley's
Correspon-
dence,
Parl. Pa-
pers, 1810.
At this period, by the acknowlegement of the
Spaniards themselves, the fate of the country depended entirely upon the British troops, and, doubtless, the latter were soldiers of no ordinary stamp;
yet there is a limit to human power, in war as well
as in other matters. Sir Arthur Wellesley was at
the head of some seventeen thousand men, of all
arms, and about five thousand were between Lisbon
and Alcantara: but the whole French army could,
in two days, have been concentrated in the valley
of the Tagus. Soult, alone, of all the associated
generals, appears to have viewed this crisis with
the eye of a great commander. Had he been permitted to follow up the attack at Arzobispo, on the
8th of August, what could the seventeen thousand

starving British troops, encumbered with the terror-
stricken Spaniards, have effected against the seventy
thousand French that would have stormed their
positions on three sides at once? The hardy, enduring English infantry might, indeed, have held
their ground in one battle, but could they have
fought a second? Would not a movement of the
first corps by Guadalupe, would not famine alone,
have forced the ten or twelve thousand men remaining (if, indeed, so many were left) to abandon the
banks of the Tagus, to abandon, also, their parcs
of ammunition and their wounded men, and to
retreat towards Portugal? and to retreat, also, with
little hope, harassed, as they would have been,
by six thousand horsemen, for Soult had eighteen
regiments of cavalry.

Let it be supposed, however, that the strength of
the Meza d'Ibor and the Mirabete had baffled all
the enemy's efforts, and that, seeing the allies fixed
in those positions, the sixth corps, in pursuance of
Soult's second proposal, had crossed the frontier of
Portugal: sir Arthur Wellesley, contemplating Parl. Papers, 1810.
such an event, affirmed that he meant to follow
them in any movement they might make against
Lisbon. There were, however, two ways of following,
the one by the south and the other by the north
bank of the Tagus. Now, if he designed to cross
the Tagus at the Cardinal's bridge, and so, connecting his right with Beresford, to hang on the enemy's
rear, it could only have been while he was ignorant of Venegas' defeat, and when he imagined
the French to have but thirty thousand men in the
valley of the Tagus; but they had above seventy
thousand; and, without endangering Madrid, they
could have invaded Portugal with, at least, fifty

thousand men under arms.   If, on the other hand,
he designed to move by the south side of the Tagus,
the French line of march upon Abrantes and Lisbon
was shorter than his; and Beresford, who only
reached Moraleja on the 12th, would have been
cut off, and thrown back upon Almeida.   It is true
that marshal Ney alleged the difficulty of feeding
the troops in the country about Plasencia and Coria,
and the prudence of Soult's project might, in that
respect, have been somewhat questionable.   But
the duke of Elchingen was averse to *any* invasion
of Portugal, and, to an unwilling mind, difficulties
enlarge beyond their due proportion; moreover,
his talents were more remarkable in a battle than
in the dispositions for a campaign, and Soult's
opinion must, on this occasion, be allowed greater
weight; because the Vera de Plasencia and the
valleys of the Bejar and the Gata mountains were
exceedingly fertile, and had been little injured,
and the object was, not to fix a base of operations, but to obtain a momentary subsistence until
a richer country could be opened.

Admitting, however, that a march on Lisbon
was not feasible at that moment, there could have
been no well-founded objection to the siege of
Ciudad Rodrigo, which Soult again proposed.   The
emperor's instructions were indeed pleaded, but
those were general, and founded on the past errors
of the campaign, which made him doubtful of the
future; they were not applicable to the peculiar
circumstances of the moment, and would have been
disregarded by a general with a tithe of his own
genius.   Fortunately for Spain, the intrusive king
was not a great commander; when he might
have entered the temple of victory with ban-

ners flying, he stretched himself at the threshold and slept.

The departure of the English army was a remarkable epoch in the Peninsular war. The policy of combining operations with the Spanish armies, and of striking directly at the great masses of the French, had been fairly acted upon, and had failed ; and the long-cherished delusion, relative to Spanish enthusiasm and Spanish efficiency, was at last dissipated. The transactions of the campaign of 1809 form a series of practical comments upon the campaign of 1808. All the objections which had been made to sir John Moore's conduct, being put to the test of experience, proved illusory, while the soundness of that general's views were confirmed in every particular. The leading events of the two campaigns bear a striking resemblance to each other.

Both sir Arthur Wellesley and sir John Moore advanced from Portugal to *aid the Spanish armies.* The first general commanded about twenty thousand, the last about twenty-three thousand men ; but there was this difference : that, in 1808, Portugal was so disorganised as to require a British force to keep down anarchy ; whereas, in 1809, Portugal formed a good base of operations, and a Portuguese army was acting in co-operation with the British.

Sir John Moore was joined by six thousand men, under Romana, and there was no other Spanish army in existence to aid him.

Sir Arthur Wellesley was joined by thirty-eight thousand Spaniards, under Cuesta, and he calculated upon twenty-six thousand, under Venegas ; while from twenty to twenty-five thousand others were acting in Gallicia and Leon.

Sir John Moore was urgent to throw himself into the heart of Spain, to aid a people represented as abounding in courage and every other military virtue. Judging of what he could not see by that which was within his view, he doubted the truth of these representations, and thinking that a powerful army, commanded by a man of the greatest military genius, was likely to prove formidable, he was unwilling to commit his own small force in an unequal contest. Nevertheless, feeling that some practicable demonstration of the difficulties to be encountered was required by the temper of the times, he made a movement, too delicate and dangerous to be adopted, unless for a great political as well as military purpose. To relieve the southern provinces, and to convince the English government and the English public that they had taken a false view of affairs, were the objects of his advance to the Carrion river; but, although he carried his army forward with a boldness that marked the consciousness of superior talents, he never lost sight of the danger he was incurring by exposing his flank to the French emperor. To obviate this danger as much as possible, he established a second line of retreat upon Gallicia, and he kept a watchful eye upon the cloud gathering at Madrid. Arrived in front of Soult's corps, and being upon the point of attacking him, the expected storm burst, but, by a rapid march to Benevente, Moore saved himself from being taken in flank and rear and destroyed. Benevente was, however, untenable against the forces brought up by Napoleon, and the retreat being continued to Coruña, the army, after a battle, embarked.

It was objected—1°. That Moore should have gone to Madrid;—2°. That he should have fought

at Astorga, at Villa Franca, and at Lugo, instead
of at Coruña ;—3°. That he overrated the strength of the enemy, and undervalued the strength and enthusiasm of the Spaniards ; and that, being of a desponding temper, he lost the opportunity of driving the French beyond the Ebro, for, that a battle gained (and it was assumed that a battle must have been gained had he attacked) would have assuredly broken the enemy's power, and called forth all the energies of Spain.

Sir John Moore reasoned that the Spanish enthusiasm was not great, that it evaporated in boasting and promises, which could not be relied upon ; that the British army was sent as an auxiliary, not as a principal force, and that the native armies being all dispersed before he could come to their assistance, the enemy was far too strong to contend with single-handed ; wherefore, it was prudent to re-embark, and to choose some other base of operations, to be conducted upon sounder views of the actual state of affairs, or to give up the contest altogether ; for that little or no hope of final success could be entertained, unless the councils and dispositions of the Spaniards changed for the better. He died ; and the English ministers, adopting the reasoning of his detractors, once more sent an auxiliary army to Spain, although the system still existed which he had denounced as incompatible with success.

Sir Arthur Wellesley, a general of their own choice, and assuredly a better could not have been made, was placed at the head of this army ; and, after giving Soult a heavy blow on the Douro, he also advanced to deliver Spain. Like sir John Moore, he was cramped for want of money, and,

like sir John Moore, he was pestered with false
representations, and a variety of plans, founded
upon short-sighted views, and displaying great
ignorance of the art of war; but, finally, he adopted,
and, as far as the inveterate nature of the people he
had to deal with would permit, executed a project,
which, like sir John Moore's, had for its object to
overpower the French in his front, and, by forcing
them to concentrate, relieve the distant provinces; and give full play to the enthusiasm of the
Spaniards.

When sir John Moore advanced, there were no
Spanish armies to assist him; the French were
above three hundred and twenty thousand strong,
and of these two hundred and fifty thousand were
disposable to move against any point; moreover,
they were commanded in person by Napoleon, of
whom it has been said by the duke of Wellington,
that his presence, alone, was equal to forty thousand good troops.

When sir Arthur Wellesley advanced, the French
forces in the Peninsula did not exceed two hundred
and sixty thousand men, of which only one hundred thousand could be brought to bear on his
operations; and he was assisted by sixty thousand
Spaniards, well armed, and tolerably disciplined.
His plans were certainly laid with great ability upon
the data furnished to him, but he trusted to Spanish
promises and to Spanish energy, and he did not
fail to repent his credulity. He delivered and
gained that battle which sir John Moore had been
reproached for not essaying; but it was found that
a veteran French army, even of inferior numbers,
was not to be destroyed, or even much dispirited,
by one defeat; and while this battle was fighting,

Soult, with fifty thousand men, came down upon the flank and rear of the English, a movement precisely similar to that which Napoleon had made from Madrid upon the flank and rear of sir John Moore. This last general saved himself by crossing the Esla, in the presence of the French patroles; and in like manner, sir Arthur evaded destruction by crossing the Tagus, within view of the enemy's scouts; so closely timed was the escape of both.

When sir John Moore retreated, the Spanish government, reproaching him, asserted that the French were on the point of ruin, and Romana, even at Astorga, continued to urge offensive operations.

When sir Arthur Wellesley retired from Jaraceijo, the junta in the same manner asserted that the French were upon the point of retiring from Spain, and general Eguia proposed offensive operations.

In explaining his motives, and discussing the treatment he had met with, sir John Moore wrote thus to his own government: " *The British were sent to aid the Spanish armies, but they are not equal to encounter the French, who have at least eighty thousand men,* and we have nothing to expect from the Spaniards, who are not to be trusted; they are apathetic, lethargic, quick to promise, backward to act, improvident, insensible to the shame of flying before the enemy, they refuse all assistance, and I am obliged to leave ammunition, stores and money, behind. The Spanish armies have shewn no resolution, the people no enthusiasm nor daring spirit, and that which has not been shown hitherto, I know not why it should be expected to be displayed hereafter." Such were his expressions.

When sir Arthur Wellesley had proved the Spaniards, he, also, writing to his government, says :—
" We are here worse off than in a hostile country ;
never was an army so ill used ;—the Spaniards have
made all sorts of promises ;—we had absolutely no
assistance from the Spanish army ; on the contrary,
we were obliged to lay down our ammunition, to
unload the treasure, and to employ the cars in the
removal of our sick and wounded. The common
dictates of humanity have been disregarded by
them, and I have been obliged to leave ammunition,
stores, and money behind. *Whatever is to be done
must be done by the British army, but that is certainly not capable, singly, to resist a French army
of at least seventy thousand men.*"

The last advice given to the government, by sir
John Moore, was against sending an auxiliary force
to Spain. Sir Arthur Wellesley, in the same spirit,
withdrew his troops ; and, from that moment, to the
end of the struggle, he warred, indeed, for Spain,
and in Spain, but never with Spain. " I have
fished in many troubled waters, but Spanish
troubled waters I will never try again," was his
expression, when speaking of this campaign; and
he kept his word. That country became, indeed,
a field, on which the French and English armies
contended for the destiny of Europe; but the defeats or victories, the promises or the performances
of the Spaniards scarcely influenced the movements.
Spain, being left to her own devices, was beaten
in every encounter, foiled in every project, yet
made no change in her policy ; and while Portugal
endeavoured to raise her energy on a level with
that of her ally, Spain sought to drag down England to the depth of folly and weakness, in which

she herself was plunged. The one would not sacrifice an atom of false pride to obtain the greatest
benefits; the other submitted, not with abject dependence, but with a magnanimous humility, to
every mortification, rather than be conquered; and
the effects of their different modes were such as
might be expected. Portugal, although assaulted
by an infinitely greater number of enemies, in proportion to her strength, overthrew the oppressors
the moment they set foot upon her soil; while in
Spain, town after town was taken, army after army
dispersed, every battle a defeat, and every defeat
sensibly diminished the heat of resistance.

Napoleon once declared that a nation resolved to
be free could not be conquered, and the Spaniards re-
echoed the sentiment in their manifestos, as if to say
it was all that was necessary. But Napoleon contemplated a nation, like the Portuguese, making use of
every means of defence, whether derived from themselves or their alliances; not a people puffed with
conceit, and lavish of sounding phrases, such as "perishing under the ruins of the last wall," yet beaten
with a facility that rendered them the derision of the
world; a people unable to guide themselves, yet ar-
rogantly refusing all advice. Such a nation is ripe
for destruction, and such a nation was Spain.

The campaign of 1809 finished the third epoch
of the war, and it was prolific of instruction. The
jealousy of the French marshals, the evils of disunion, the folly of the Spanish government, and the
absurdity of the Spanish character, with respect to
public affairs, were placed in the strongest light;
while the vast combinations, the sanguinary battles,
the singular changes of fortune, the result so little
suitable to the greatness of the efforts, amply de-

monstrated the difficulty and the uncertainty of
military affairs.   It was a campaign replete with
interest; a great lesson from which a great commander profited :   sir Arthur Wellesley had now
experienced the weakness of his friends and the
strength of his enemies, and he felt all the emptiness
of public boasting.   Foreseeing that if the contest
was to be carried on, it must be in Portugal, and
that unless he himself could support the cause of
the Peninsula, it must fall, his manner of making
war changed; his caution increased tenfold, yet,
abating nothing of his boldness, he met and baffled
the best of the French legions in the fulness of their
strength.   He was alike unmoved by the intrigues
of the Portuguese regency, and by the undisguised
hatred of the Spanish Government; and when some
of his own generals, and two of them on his personal staff, denouncing his rashness and predicting
the ruin of the army, caused the puny energy of
the English ministers to quail as the crisis approached, he, with gigantic vigour, pushed aside
these impediments, and, steadily holding on his own
course, proved himself a sufficient man, whether to
uphold or to conquer kingdoms.

APPENDIX.

APPENDIX.

No. I.

SECTION I.—GENERAL STATE OF THE FRENCH
ARMY IN SPAIN, EXTRACTED FROM THE IMPE-
RIAL MUSTER-ROLLS, SIGNED BY THE PRINCE
OF NEUFCHATEL.

Commanded by the Emperor Napoleon, in person, 15th Jan. 1809.

Present under arms.		Detached.		Hospital.	Prisoners.	Total.	
Men.	Horses.	Men.	Horses.	Men.	Men.	Men.	Horses.
241,010	48,821	24,549	3,521	58,026	826	324,411	52,342

King Joseph, commanding—15th Feb. 1809.

Present under arms.		Detached.		Hospital.	Prisoners.	Total Effective.	
Men.	Horses.	Men.	Horses.	Men.	Men.	Men.	Horses.
193,446	3,339	36,326	9,523	56,404	1,843	288,219	43,704

Note.—The imperial guards, the reserve of infantry, and several thousand non-commissioned officers and old soldiers, wanted for the war in
Austria, in all above 40,000 men, were struck off the rolls since the last
returns.

1st. July 1809.

Present under arms.		Detached.		Hospital.	Prisoners and Stragglers.	Total Effective.	
Men.	Horses.	Men.	Horses.	Men.	Men.	Men.	Horses.
24,082	31,537	19,596	4,513	60,785	7,301	288,766	36,050
Deduct detached men comprised in governments						19,596	4,513
Real total						269,170	31,537

15th July, 1809.

196,144	31,131	19,122	4,608	58,230	8,089	281,585	35,739
Deduct detached in governments						19,122	4,608
Real total						262,463	31,131

15th August, 1809.

187,560	30,319	12,697	3,930	58,588	7,403	266,248	34,880
Deduct for governments						12,697	3,930
Real total...........						253,551	30,950

SECTION II.—RETURN OF THE FRENCH ARMY BY
CORPS.

Troops immediately under the king—1st June, 1809.

The king's guards, about 5000 men, of all arms, are never borne on the rolls.

First corps, marshal Victor commanding.

Head-quarters, Torremocha.

		Present under arms. Men.	Total. Men.
4 divisions of infantry	41 battalions	21,268	32,819
2 ditto cavalry	27 squadrons	5,232	7,344
Artillery and equipage	40 companies	2,984	3,610
Number of guns, 48			
Total present under arms		29,484	Grand total 43,773

First Corps—21st June, 1809.

Head-quarters, Almaraz.

		Present under arms. Men.	Total. Men.
3 divisions of infantry	33 battalions	18,367	25,633
2 ditto cavalry	20 squadrons	4,259	5,762
Artillery and equipage	,,	2,535	2,860
Total present under arms		25,161	Grand total 34,255

First Corps—15th July, 1809.

Head-quarters, Cazalegas.

3 divisions of infantry	33 battalions	18,890	26,373
2 ditto cavalry	18 squadrons	3,781	5,080
Artillery and equipage	,,	2,586	3,005
Total present under arms		25,257	Grand total 34,458

First Corps—1st August, 1809.

Head-quarters, Maqueda.

3 divisions of infantry	33 battalions	15,066	25,068
2 ditto cavalry	18 squadrons	4,987	4,983
Artillery and equipage	,,	2,362	2,873
Total present under arms		22,415	Grand total 32,924

Fourth Corps, General Sebastiani—10th July, 1809.

Head-quarters, Alcala.

		Present under arms. Men.	Total. Men.
3 divisions of infantry	27 battalions	17,100	25,960
2 ditto cavalry	25 squadrons	3,670	5,859
Number of artillerymen omitted in the returns		,,	,,
30 guns			
Total present under arms		20,770	Grand total 31,819

15th August, 1809.

3 divisions of infantry	27 battalions	14,259	25,801
2 ditto cavalry	25 squadrons	3,420	5,801
Total present under arms		17,679	Grand total 31,602

Division of Reserve, General Dessolles—15th July, 1809.
Head-quarters, Madrid.

		Present under arms. Men.	Total. Men.
1 division of infantry	10 battalions	7,681	10,254

Number of guns unknown.

Kellerman's division—21st April, 1809.
Head-quarters, Astorga.

	Men.	Horses.	Guns.
Total, composed of detachments	8,753	805	8

10th June, 1809.
Head-quarters, Oviedo.

	Under arms.		Total.	
	Men.	Horses.	Men.	Horses.
Total, composed of detachments	7,423	2,549	7,681	2,690

15th July, 1809.
Head-quarters, Valladolid.

8 squadrons	2,291	2,360	2,469	2393
6 guns				

SECTION III.

1st February, 1809.
Under arms.
Men.

Division Lapisse	infantry	12 battalions	7,692
Brigade Maupetit	cavalry	6 squadrons	910

Total under general Lapisse at Salamanca   8,602 sabres and bayonets.
Number of guns and artillerymen unknown.

SECTION IV.— RETURN OF TROOPS UNDER THE IMMEDIATE COMMAND OF MARSHAL SOULT.

Second Corps, Soult—15th July, 1809.
Head-quarters, Toro.

		Present under arms. Men.	Total. Men.
4 divisions of infantry	47 battalions	16,626	35,188
3 ditto cavalry	19 squadrons	2,883	4,540
Artillery	,,	1,081	1,620
40 guns			
Total present under arms		20,590 Grand total 41,348	

Fifth Corps, Mortier.
Head-quarters, Valladolid.

2 divisions of infantry	24 battalions	15,036	19,541
1 brigade of cavalry	6 squadrons	896	1,491
Artillery	,,	618	803
30 guns			
Total present under arms		16,580 Grand total 21,835	

Sixth Corps, Ney.
Head-quarters, Benevente.

		Present under arms. Men.	Total. Men.
2 divisions of infantry	24 battalions	13,700	17,587
1 ditto cavalry	10 squadrons	1,446	2,092
Artillery	,,	1,113	1,293
37 guns			

Total present under arms ....16,259 Grand total 20,972

General total under Soult, 15th July, 1809.

	Under arms. Men.	Total. Men.
95 battalions—35 squadrons	53,529	84,155
107 guns		

SECTION V.—TROOPS EMPLOYED IN THE SIEGE OF ZARAGOZA, UNDER MARSHAL LASNES.

15th January, 1809.

	Present under arms. Men.	Detached. Men.	Hospital. Men.	Total effective. Men.
Third corps	17,406	5,789	13,668	36,863
Fifth-corps	18,284	,,	4,189	22,473
Total	35,690	5,789	17,857	59,336

15th February, 1809.

Third corps	16,035	5,891	13,259	35,269
Fifth corps	17,933	1,735	3,859	23,626
Total....	33,968	7,526	17,118	58,895

SECTION VI.—RETURN OF THE SEVENTH CORPS, GENERAL ST. CYR.

15th January, 1809.

Present under arms. Men.	Detached. Men.	Hospital. Men.	Prisoners. Men.	Total. Men.	Horses.
41,386	,,	6,589	543	48,518	5,403

15th May, 1809.

42,246	2,341	10,243	435	55,265	5,537

15th June, 1809.

42,146	1,699	10,222	406	54,473	5,365

No. II.

SECTION I.—STATE OF SPAIN.

Colonel Kemmis to sir J. Cradock, December 17, 1808.

" In consequence of the unfavourable news from Spain, yesterday, the populace, in Badajos, murdered a Spanish colonel, and one or two more of note."

Lieutenant Ellis (an officer employed to gain intelligence) to colonel Kemmis, Loboa, December 27.

" The French entered Truxillo, yesterday, at eleven o'clock; and, from the circumstance of their having reconnoitred the intermediate villages, might be expected to arrive at Merida in two hours after we left it."

Colonel Kemmis to sir John Cradock, Elvas, December 28.

" Badajos cannot make resistance in any degree, either to check or to stop the progress of the enemy. From the statement made to me, last night, by the governor, they want *arms, ammunition,* and *provisions.*"—" The enemy marched into Truxillo, on the 26th, at half-past twelve o'clock in the day; but, at two, on the following morning, a French officer arrived there, and they fell back four leagues."

Lieutenant Ellis to colonel Kemmis, December 28.

" I proceeded cautiously to Truxillo. The main body of the enemy, six thousand in number, had retired across the bridge of Almaraz, and had not taken the road to Madrid, but had proceeded to Plasencia, leaving behind more than half the requisition for money which had been imposed on the town of Truxillo."

Mr. Stuart to sir John Moore, Seville, January 2, 1809.

" The corps of four thousand infantry and two thousand cavalry, which had marched from Talavera, and had actually passed the bridge of Almaraz, has fallen back, and is already near Plasencia, on its way northward."—" The extreme attention of Buonaparte being at this moment directed to the English army, every thing which can be collected is opposed to you alone."

SECTION II.

Mr. Stuart to sir J. Moore, December 27, 1808.

" You will receive, together with this, several letters from Doyle, which describe events in Catalonia *no way differing from what we have witnessed in other parts of Spain!*"—" The junta have established themselves here, and, whatever may have been the expectation which their alarm on the road may have induced Mr. Frere to form of their future proceedings, *a culpable relapse into their former apathy* seems susceptible of no other remedies but such as will be much stronger than any Spaniard is likely to adopt."—" Although Caro promised to write every particular of his conversation with you to the junta, I have hitherto been unable to see his letter. I therefore thought it expedient to put the whole to writing, and, *at the same time, to express my conviction both of the justice and propriety of your whole conduct during the late events, when it was impossible, under any circumstances, to have adopted other determination consistently with the safety of the army committed to your charge.* Though I doubt if this will stop the clamour which has been raised on the subject; and, though events have probably since taken place, which may materially change the state of affairs, it may be satisfactory to tell you that Mr. Frere *appears* to enter into the reasons alleged by you, and to feel, in their full force, the motives which induced you to act so cautiously, and to ground no operation on the hope of any effectual support from the Spaniards."

Mr. Stuart to sir J. Moore, Seville, January 2.

" The president, Florida Blanca, died two days since, and I was in hopes that the junta would have availed themselves of this event to make some change in their government."—" I see, however, little but good disposition, and *am still to look for that* energy in rewarding service and punishing treachery which can alone mend matters."

Mr. Stuart to sir J. Moore, Seville, January 10.

" Reding is at *Tarragona*, expecting to be attacked, and possessing a force composed chiefly of peasantry, but of which he certainly cannot command above ten thousand men in a situation to face his opponents at any given point."—" Whittingham arrived here yesterday, last from the duke of Infantado's head-quarters. He assures me the duke had already twenty thousand men when he *left Cuença*."—" *On the side of Estremadura,* matters are not going on well : Galluzzo, who allowed the enemy to pass the bridges, is here prisoner, and his corps is placed under the command of Cuesta. I cannot say, however, that I see much activity since the change ; parties of the enemy cover the country between Madrid and Almaraz, while the corps of six thousand men, which had been pushed forward from Madrid, have, I under-stand, already passed Plasencia, and probably are on the other side of the Puerto, for the purpose of falling on the Salamanca country, and, if possible, cutting off your communication with Ciudad Rodrigo."

SECTION III.

Mr. Frere to Mr. Canning, Seville, May 8.

" Besides the advantages which may be looked for from placing so extensive a command under a person of such tried abilities as general Blake, it is to be hoped that it will put an end to the distractions arising from the contracted views of those who directed the provincial junta, particularly that of Valencia, which have been so embarrassing to his predecessors."

Mr. Frere to Mr. Canning, Seville, July 10, 1809.

" As the devastations which have been committed have, in many instances, deprived the peasants of the means of paying what is due to the proprietors and to the church, a general spirit of resistance to all claims of this kind has begun to show itself."

Sir John Cradock to lord Castlereagh, December 24, 1808.

" I much fear that alarm and despondency has gained ground about Badajos and that part of Spain, and that there is so little co-operation in the acts of their several juntas, and such a want of subordination and common consent among the armed bodies, to which the defence of the country is entrusted, against such an united force as that of the French, that extreme confusion prevails everywhere."

Colonel Kemmis to sir John Cradock, Elvas, December 30.

" He (lieutenant Ellis) has been living with general Cuesta for
the last two days,"—" who has assured him that the Spanish
troops, in Madrid, forced their way through the French army;
and he expressed great sorrow in adding that, though a Spanish
force is often collected, the smallest check disperses them; that
in few instances depôts were provided, and those ill supplied,"
&c.—" that, such was the dispersion and flight of the Spanish
armies, between Badajos and Madrid, there did not remain a
single man."

*Colonel Kemmis to lieut.-colonel Reynel, military secretary
to sir John Cradock, Seville, February* 7, 1809.

" In passing through the Sierra Morena mountains, where
Nature has done much for the defence of this province, it was
painful to observe the pitiful works they were about to throw up.
In this whole direction there is but one body that has anything
like the appearance of a soldier, viz. dismounted cavalry."

General Mackenzie to sir John Cradock, Cadiz, February 9,
1809.

" The Spaniards here seem lulled in the most fatal security.
They are ignorant of the events in the north of Spain, or will not
give credit when they do hear them. Vague reports of the emperor of Austria's having declared war, and Buonaparte's return
to France gains unlimited credit."—" The equipment of the fleet
goes on very slowly, though there is no want of exertion now on
the part of admiral Purvis or Mr. Stuart; offers of every assistance are daily made, but they will neither work themselves nor
permit our people to work for them. The preparations of the ships
for carrying off the French prisoners goes on equally ill."

Duc de Albuquerque to Mr. Frere, Talavera, July 31, 1809.

" During our marches we stop to repose, like flocks of sheep,
without taking up any position, so that, if the enemy knew the
condition we were in, they would defeat us wherever they attacked
us. If, in the evening of the 26th, I had not gone out directly
with my division, and succeeded in checking the enemy, the
whole army would have dispersed, and all the artillery and
baggage, which were in the streets of St. Ollalla, would have been

lost; and as a proof of what would have happened, had not the
enemy, who was within musket-shot, been checked, for many
had already thrown away their arms, &c. the commissaries abandoning more than fifteen hundred rations of bread, the carts
occupying and blocking up the streets of the town; and to this,
I repeat, we are daily exposed, as we march, as if it were on a
pilgrimage, without any regard to distance, order, or method, and
with the whole parc of artillery, which ought always to remain at
the distance of two, three, or more leagues."

*Sir Arthur Wellesley to lord Wellesley, Merida, September 1,
1809.*

" I am much afraid, from what I have seen of the proceedings
of the central junta, that, in the distribution of their forces, they
do not consider military defence and military operations so much
as they do political intrigue and the attainment of trifling political
objects."

Lord Wellesley to Mr. Canning, Seville, September 2, 1809.

" While the intelligence received from sir Arthur Wellesley, to
the date of the 24th instant, continued to furnish irresistible proofs
of the failure of every promise or effort made by this government
for the immediate relief of our troops, no satisfaction was afforded
to me respecting any permanent plan for their future supply."—
" The troops of Portugal, which entered Spain, under general
Beresford, suffered similar distress, and experienced similar ill-
treatment; although the efforts of Portugal, in the cause of Spain,
have been as gratuitous as those of Great Britain; and although
Spain possesses no claim, of any description, to the aid of a
Portuguese army."—" In this calamity, the people of Spain cannot fail to acknowledge the natural consequences of their own
weakness, nor to discover the urgent necessity of enforcing a more
steady, pure, and vigorous system, both of council and action.   A
relaxed state of domestic government and an indolent reliance on
the activity of foreign assistance have endangered all the high
and virtuous objects for which Spain has armed and bled.   It
must now be evident that no alliance can protect her from the
inevitable result of internal disorder and national infirmity.   She
must amend and strengthen her government; she must improve
the administration of her resources, and the structure and discipline of her armies, before she can become capable of deriving

benefit from foreign aid.   Spain has proved untrue to our alliance,
because she is not true to herself."—" Until some great change
shall be effected in the conduct of the military resources of Spain,
and in the state of her armies, no British army can safely attempt
to co-operate with the Spanish troops in the territory of Spain."

No. III.

JUSTIFICATORY EXTRACTS FROM SIR J. CRADOCK'S CORRESPONDENCE, MSS.

SECTION I.— STATE OF PORTUGAL.

Sir J. Cradock to sir R. Wilson, Oporto, December 8, 1808.

" I press this measure" (to move the legion from Oporto to
Villa Real) " upon your adoption, for many reasons, &c. &c.;
but the more especially that it will give an impulse to military
preparation in general, and tend to eradicate *the notion that,
since the evacuation of Portugal by the French, the prospect
of a future war is at an end.*"

Sir J. Cradock to sir John Moore, December 9, 1808.

" I have pressed the adoption of such measures as appeared
most likely *to revive some notion of danger*, and the necessity
of activity and energy."

Sir J. Cradock to lord Castlereagh, December 14, 1808, *Lisbon.*

" The inaction of the regency was apparent at Oporto to a
lamentable degree; and, though I saw general Bernadim Friere,
I could not gain from him any information as to the state or
numbers of the Portuguese troops, where they were stationed,
or who commanded them.   I apprehend, from his conversation,
that the general officers are all of equal authority; and that even
seniority had not its usual effect.   He concluded his observations
to me with the strong expression, ' *That, from the evacuation
of Portugal by the French, the nation had thought all war
at an end.*'"

Sir J. Cradock to sir J. Moore, December 28, 1808.

" Mr. Villiers and myself have both concurred upon the

*absolute necessity to arouse and animate the Portuguese to
some sense of their situation."*

Colonel Kemmis to sir J. Cradock, Elvas, December 30, 1808.

" *The apathy of the Portuguese is not to be expressed.*
Their general, Leite, is a most excellent character: a theorist,
and, like his countrymen, *supine.*"

*Extract from the Report of lieutenant Brotherton, (an
officer employed to obtain intelligence in the north of
Portugal,) February* 11, 1809. *Head-quarters of Romana's
army.*

" From the totally defenceless state in which the two northern
provinces are left, it will require at least eight days (I speak from
authority) to prepare any thing like adequate means of defence."

SECTION II.—LUSITANIAN LEGION.

Lord Castlereagh to sir J. Cradock, November 27, 1808.

" Its formation was proposed by the chevalier de Souza."—
" The pay, allowances, and clothing were settled by the chevalier
de Souza. The former regulated, as I understood, upon the
scale *of increased pay, which the provisional government of
Oporto had adopted for all the troops they were in progress
of levying.*"

Sir J. Cradock to lord Castlereagh, December 24, 1808.

" I have considerable doubt if ever they" (the legion) " can
be incorporated, with effect and conciliation, with the body of the
Portuguese army."—" They are viewed with *extreme jealousy
by the regency;* and the *commanding officers of the Portuguese
battalion resisted, universally, the allowing of volunteers
from their regiments to enter into the legion.*"

Sir J. Cradock to lord Castlereagh, January 19, 1809.

" The Lusitanian legion continues to give considerable uneasiness, from its peculiar state, under present circumstances."

*Captain Morgan (Lusitanian legion) to sir J. Cradock,
January* 19, 1809.

" Should a retreat be adopted, sir Robert would not retire to

Oporto. *It is the government of a mob, of which he has had too much experience.*"

Sir J. Cradock to sir J. Moore, December 9, 1808.

" I am sorry to state that I find, as far as my limited observation reaches, the Portuguese army, and every other military concern, *in the worst possible state.*"

Sir J. Cradock to Mr. Villiers, December 18, 1809.

" I am sure that the state of the Portuguese army is quite misunderstood in England; *and that a reliance is placed upon it for the defence of the country that is entirely without foundation.* Their" (Portuguese) " ministers will avow this to you after ten minutes' conversation."—" Even of the reduced numbers of their men enrolled, (not amounting to twenty thousand, at the very highest computation,) to make any thing out of them, it is necessary to recur to first principles, and give them *officers, arms, clothing, accoutrements, horses,* &c.; and I need not say that money is wanting to effect this: and the ministers positively declare that they have none; and that no collection of their forces can take place, much less a movement to the frontier, without a supply."—" M. Forjas, secretary to the government, in answer to a strong question from me, stated that *their army have not in possession ten thousand firelocks fit for use.*"

Sir J. Cradock to lord Castlereagh, December 24, 1808.

" I am exerting myself to bring to account ' the *supposed* Portuguese army.'"—" Your lordship will perceive that *I talk of the regulars as if it were a regular force*; but I should be guilty of a deceit, that might lead to bad consequences, if I did not fairly state that *I conceive them to be of no moment at this time.*"

Sir J. Cradock to Mr. Villiers, January 8, 1809.

" I am ready to go to the utmost verge of prudence; but *Mr. Frere, when he talks of Portuguese troops and arrangements, really* (as I believe you will allow) *fait bâtir les chateux.*"

Major-general Cotton to sir J. Cradock, April 7, 1809.

" I yesterday inspected the Portuguese cavalry."—" This cavalry is unformed, and totally unfit for any sort of service."

Sir J. Cradock to lord Castlereagh, February 12.

" It appears that a report has reached your lordship that a conscription for horses in this country had been attended with great effect, and that above three thousand had been collected. It is, indeed, a matter of serious concern that such *serious misrepresentations* should be transmitted ; for it is a well-known fact that many of the Portuguese regiments of cavalry *are without horses;* and, if I am to pursue the subject, their *battalions of infantry are one-half without arms or clothing !* But the total want of all means of regulations for subsistence form so deplorable a view, in the event of co-operation, that the result, in my opinion, cannot be attended with success. *It is, however, but justice to say, that the disposition of the Portuguese seems well-inclined and faithful to the common cause ; and that a very efficient soldiery may be formed under more favourable circumstances.*"

Sir J. Cradock to Mr. Frere, February 27, 1809.

" I fear that your excellency is led to entertain a more favourable notion of the efficacy of the Portuguese army than, in any shape, it is entitled to. In short, my opinion is that they want every thing that constitutes a respectable force, except about ten thousand English arms. I believe they have no others. Many of their *cavalry regiments are without horses, without swords, pistols, &c. Their battalions are not clothed ; and, as to subsistence, they live at free quarters upon the villages where they are stationed.* To take the field with effect, or an assurance of food, seems to me out of the question. Since the first moment of my arrival, I wished to procure the advance of a small Portuguese force to Alcantara ; but it has been impossible. It is a matter of serious lamentation that such misrepresentations of the Portuguese force should go home, or reach your excellency."

Sir J. Cradock to lord Castlereagh, April 3.

" No reliance whatever can be placed upon the Portuguese troops in their present state. *If I said that the whole were ready to mutiny or revolt, I believe I speak general Beresford's sentiments. They will not be commanded by their own officers, and they do just as they please."*

SECTION IV.—CONDUCT OF THE REGENCY—TREATMENT OF
FRENCH PRISONERS.

Sir J. Cradock to Mr. Villiers, January 26, 1809.

" I have hitherto directed that these prisoners should be subsisted at our charge, but I have no authority in this measure; they are *in a most deplorable state,* and really are a *disgrace to all concerned."*

Sir J. Cradock to Mr. Villiers, February 5, 1809.

" It is absolutely necessary that the regency should give in an answer about the French prisoners. The whole is an unauthorised heavy charge, for which I give my warrant; and I see no end to the case : and, added to this, *their situation is a reflection upon humanity."*

SECTION V.—NEGLECT, DUPLICITY, AND TIMIDITY.

Colonel Kemmis to sir J. Cradock, Elvas, December 17.

" Lalyppe, on which the very existence of Elvas depends, has not been supplied with provisions as I have been taught to expect."

Colonel Kemmis to sir J. Cradock, Elvas, December 25.

" The great importance of this fort" (Lalyppe) " is well known to the Portuguese; and, therefore, they are jealous, notwithstanding the miserable condition of their troops, and total incapacity to defend the fort, if attacked."

Sir J. Cradock to Mr. Villiers, December 26, 1808.

" *The promises and apparently satisfactory language of the Portuguese government* are, in my opinion, by no means sufficient to meet the case. *I want to see* some steps actually taken before my mind is decided that the nation will defend itself."—" Indeed, I am told, on good authority, that *the go-*

vernment are afraid to allow the people to arm."—" The moment I see any materials to work upon, it will be my most anxious duty to give every effect, &c."—" But, under the present *inactivity and indifference,* it is, &c."

Reports of colonel Donkin (quarter-master-general) to sir J. Cradock, March 21.

" I cannot, however, order officers of my department to check this irregularity" (forcing quarters) " *when it originates solely in the neglect of the Portuguese civil magistrates;* for troops will not obey orders, which expose them wantonly to great privations."

Sir J. Cradock to Mr. Villiers, March 25.

" I have repeatedly urged this subject" (quarters of troops) " to the regency, in the strongest manner, but, as you perceive, without effect."

Sir J. Cradock to lord Castlereagh, March 17.

" Whatever suits the momentary purpose, upon the most superficial view, seems to be the guide in the Portuguese councils. Ultimate objects, which, in the course of things, must arrive, are never brought into the calculation."

Cradock to Berkely, January 17.

" The regency seems to decline giving any specific directions relative to the guns in fort St. Julian and the river batteries, and, *above all, not to write any thing;* but they are very willing to acquiesce in any thing we shall do, only anxious that, on a future day, it *shall appear to be our act, not theirs.*"

Admiral Berkely to sir J. Cradock, February 19, 1809.

" I imagine Mr. Villiers has transmitted a copy of the extraordinary note sent him by the regency; in which they complain of the conduct of the artillery-officer who dismantled the Bugio fort, and intimate their intention of sending for all the guns and powder from fort St. Julian; and add many particulars, as novel as they are suspicious."—" Whether the language of this note arises from duplicity, or any other cause, it is equally to be resisted; and, therefore, stated some facts which may be retorted upon them, and which will not place their conduct in the *most favourable point of view towards either their own sovereign or Great Britain.*"

Extract from an official note, drawn up by sir John Cradock, Lisbon, February 20, 1809.

" It was told me two or three times, by Mr. Villiers, that M. Forjas, or some other member of the regency, had expressed extreme solicitude about the forts on the Tagus, &c."—" I always urged Mr. Villiers to get from M. Forjas, or any other member, a declaration of what they wished, that we might exactly conform to it; for they seemed to be anxious to go beyond what we should venture to propose. Mr. Villiers, after some time, told me that the Portuguese government were *unwilling to put down any thing upon paper*, or give any specific instruction; but they would willingly leave all the arrangement to us."—" After the above statement, which I declare, upon my honour, to be the accurate description of what has passed, I must express my surprise, and even indignation, at the protest now made by the regency: and when it is considered that the Bugio fort is often inaccessible for a week together, this part of their complaint is shameful to the highest degree. *Their general object is, however, to be distinguished.*"

SECTION VI.—ANARCHY IN PORTUGAL.

Sir J. Cradock to lord Castlereagh, February 20, 1809.

" *Northern parts.*—It may be difficult to manage any money-transactions in Oporto, for the populace in that town have been suffered to become the masters; and it was only by an exchange of public and private property that the commissariat money has been lately secured."

Sir J. Cradock to Mr. Villiers, February, 1809.

" To gratify a mob, the other day, at Oporto, a guard of the sixtieth regiment was given up, and disarmed by baron Eben."

Captain Brotherton to sir J. Cradock, March 17, 1809, *Lamego.*

" Considering the tumults, and the state of effervescence of the public mind, and the blind fury of the populace—it will neither be so useful nor safe to remain amongst them."

Sir J. Cradock to lord Castlereagh, March 26, 1809.

" The disposition is good, but the proceedings are those of an ungovernable mob, *exposed to the evil effects of designing persons*."—" I confine myself to the north of Portugal and Oporto, for the same excesses have not taken place at this side the Douro; but the principles of insubordination, I should fear, would prevail."—" If the confusion and anarchy that prevail at Oporto will permit a defence, some exertion may be expected."—" Ammunition has been abundantly supplied, *but no quantity would meet the consumption expended in the manner it has been in the Tras os Montes;* an attempt to save which was, I believe, the occasion of Bernadim Friere's death."

Sir J. Cradock to Lord Castlereagh, March, 30, 1809.

" The anarchy that prevails at Oporto must, I fear, render every exertion unavailable for defence; and such is the ungovernable spirit of the populace, *that it is very difficult to say what part they might take if the proceedings of the British did not suit their views*."

Sir J. Cradock to Mr. Frere, March 29.

" Oporto and all its concerns, with the bishop, nominally, at its head, is in the hands of a wild ungovernable populace, *that has already committed the most cruel excesses.* I fear the same spirit exists in what is called the Portuguese army."

Sir J. Cradock to Mr. Frere, January 29, *Lisbon.*

" Without a British force in Lisbon, the authority of the regency would pass away, and the scenes of Oporto would take place here."

Report of Captain Lawson, January 30, *Lisbon.*

" Last night, my servant returning from the post-office was attacked by a party of Portuguese pike-men, headed by one of their own officers, who severely wounded the horse in two places, and slightly in several places, and obliged him, the servant, to put himself under the protection of the guard at the town-major's office, to save his own life : the outrage was committed without the slightest provocation."

General Langwerth to sir J. Cradock, February 1, Lisbon.

" The orderly with the general orders, on his way to St. Julian's, was stopped by a Portuguese serjeant and twenty men with pikes; the serjeant forced the orderly to deliver the letter containing the orders, broke it open, read the contents, and returned the enclosed receipt; the same guard stopped captain Clives, Royal Grenadiers, and lieutenants Beurman and Liners; these officers were in full uniform."

General Sontag's Official Report, February 3.

" Mr. Usher, deputy purveyor, and Mr. M'Carty, interpreter, both British subjects, arrived this day from Oporto, went to Moore's Hotel, where they were arrested and brought to the minister of police. Mr. Usher was in his British uniform."

Sir J. Cradock to Lord Castlereagh, January 30.

" Some unpleasant incidents have lately occurred on the part of the Portuguese armed inhabitants of Lisbon towards British individuals, but I cannot persuade myself that they have proceeded from any fixed evil disposition."—" The British army has not, in any instance, departed from the most regular discipline, and continues to manifest the greatest temper and moderation."— " The excesses on the part of the Portuguese commence by an *uncontrolled pursuit, without any authority from the police, after all persons whom they please to call Frenchmen,* and, in their indiscriminate career, they *often attack every foreigner, and will not even abstain from* those in our service. Those *persons seek refuge in our guard-room,* and though the guards and patroles have positive orders not to interfere under any pretext with the police, yet it is very difficult to smother the feelings of humanity when the wretched persons are flying from a furious and unauthorised rabble. *Mr. Villiers has exerted himself much with the Regency to check this disorder, and prevent the assembly of armed persons in the streets at night, who beat drums and discharge their pieces at all hours; but as yet his remonstrances have not had the desired effect.*"

Mr. Villiers to sir J. Cradock, January 30.

" Finding the people beat to arms, and paraded about the streets after dark, *on the very evening after the regency had settled that these irregularities should be restrained,* I addressed the ministers of the home department upon the subject; and as other excesses came to my knowledge, I followed up my complaint."

Sir J. Cradock to Mr. Villiers, January 30.

" I have, this morning, been taking such steps as appear necessary to secure our general situation from insult; and, at the same time, if practicable, not to manifest a distrust in the Portuguese nation, which, if sanctioned from head-quarters, would destroy any reason for our being here. I can assure you, every officer and soldier has received impressions that it is most difficult to act against, but I am determined to persevere in keeping the army from aggression to the last moment."

Sir J. Cradock to Mr. Villiers, February.

" When I reflect upon the frequent declarations of individual members of the regency, that they cannot control the populace; that there are at least seventy thousand armed inhabitants in Lisbon; that the regency dare not let them parade (their exercise has been at an end for some time, and the regency, at this moment, say they cannot look upon themselves as responsible,) it appears impossible that I should depart from the reasoning of my own mind, to meet a sensation of *I do not know whom,* and lessen the proper military appearance of our only guard. We are now beyond the power of surprise or insult, and I cannot, as my own individual act, alter the state of things. However, I never am devoted to my own way of thinking, and if you recommend the measure (the political reasoning, when the enemy is at a distance, may always be weighed against military regulation), or see any good consequences, I will immediately *order back the guns* to their former station in the artillery barracks."

Marshal Beresford to sir J. Cradock, April 7, *Santarem.*

" I, this morning, met no less than *three expresses,* communicating to me the *horrible state of mutiny, for I can call it no less, in which the troops every where are, and the in-*

habitants are in equal insubordination, and they encourage each other. I find two or three regiments have marched away (to what they call to oppose the enemy) where they pleased, in despite of their officers and generals, who are entirely commanded by them. This you will say is a pleasing state to be in; however, we must face it, and I hope for the best result, and I am sanguine enough to look for such. Colonel Trant will shortly have a pretty strong corps, if the regiments continue thus to volunteer for him."

Mr. Villiers to sir J. Cradock, February 15.

" I should almost doubt whether the British subjects *could be left in safety in Lisbon.*"

SECTION VII.—FALSE INTELLIGENCE.

Sir J. Cradock to colonel Donkin.

" I believe it is certain that we cannot depend upon the activity of the Portuguese government upon this head," (intelligence,) " either as to promptitude or security."

Colonel Donkin to sir J. Cradock, January 1, *Lisbon.*

" Experience has *shewn how utterly impossible it is to get correct intelligence here ;* an enemy may be within four or five days march of this city before it is known, unless he attacks on the very line our troops occupy."

Sir J. Cradock to Mr. Frere, March 29.

" It is singular how imperfectly all intelligence, though of such important events, reaches this, and we have not had, for two days, any account from Oporto."

Sir J. Cradock to lord Castlereagh, March 26.

" Yesterday the chevalier de Castro stated, from authority, a movement on the part of the French, quite different from a *direct report* from the junta of Badajos."

No. IV.

SECTION I.—EXTRACTS FROM SIR JOHN CRADOCK'S
INSTRUCTIONS.

Lord Castlereagh to sir J. Cradock, December 24, 1808.

" Upon the actual approach of the enemy towards Lisbon in such strength as may render further resistance ineffectual, you will take care that measures may be taken in due time, for withdrawing both the British army and *such Portuguese as may be desirous of accompanying it.*"—" The British admiral will be directed to take effectual measures, with your assistance, for depriving the enemy of all the resources, more especially those of a naval description, which the Tagus contains. Every thing of a naval and military description, that cannot be brought away, must, in the last extremity, be destroyed."

Lord Castlereagh to sir J. Cradock, November 25, 1808.

" I am to signify his majesty's pleasure that, in the event of any application being made to you from the regency of Portugal, on the subject of the occupation of the fortresses with his majesty's troops, you do *refer the subject to Mr. Villiers,* who has received instruction, &c. and you will not make any alteration as to the mode prescribed for garrisoning the fortresses *without directions from Mr. Villiers.*"

Lord Castlereagh to general Sherbrooke, January 12, 1809.

" Sir J. Cradock will be directed to comply with any requisition you may make *for horses for your guns,* or any other species of supply the service may require."

Extracts from certain queries put to lord Castlereagh by sir J. Cradock, with the answers thereto.

QUERY.	ANSWER.
" What may be the situation of my command ?"	" The relations with the government of Portugal will be arranged when Mr. Villiers arrives."
" In what light is the force under my command to be considered ?" &c. &c.	" Ditto."
" May any Portuguese bat-	" The taking Portuguese bat-

talions be levied for English pay?"

" If any want of provisions should appear in Portugal, may I be allowed to adopt measures, in conjunction with the regency, for obtaining a supply?

" If any Portuguese corps can be got into such forwardness as to be fit to enter Spain, and they should be willing to join sir J. Moore, are they to be put on British pay?"

talions into English pay will, if adopted, be managed *through Mr. Villiers.*"

" The general measures of supplying Portugal with provisions will be *referred to Mr. Villiers.*"

" *Mr. Villiers will be authorised* to enter upon the discussion of this subject with the regency, availing himself of your assistance," &c.

No. V.

JUSTIFICATORY EXTRACTS FROM SIR J. CRADOCK'S PAPERS.

WANT OF SUPPLIES.

Commissary Rawlings, deputy-commissary-general, to Cradock, December 22.

" Your excellency is aware of the exhausted state of this country. The difficulties encountered by sir J. Moore were of the most serious nature, even before the sources of supply were so much drained as they now are."

WANT OF TRANSPORT AND SUPPLIES.

Sir J. Cradock to lord Castlereagh, March 17.

" I have been obliged to send officers of the artillery and commissariat department to Gibraltar to attempt the supply of horses from the Barbary coast; and such is our actual want, that the proper movement of even the force we have is nearly impracticable."

Sir J. Cradock to lord Castlereagh, March 26.

" The means of transport are so confined that I must not expose any thing to loss; and the artillery must be preserved with the greatest care, for I cannot equip more than two brigades of six-pounders, and one light brigade of three-pounders, the latter being of a very inferior description."

Commissary Rawlings to sir John Cradock, March.
" The precarious tenure of this country by British troops has hitherto precluded the possibility of establishing such an advantageous contract for the public as, in more permanent cases, might necessarily be expected : we have literally been supplied from hand to mouth."

Colonel Robe to sir J. Cradock, March 20.
" It is necessary for me to add that every exertion has been made to supply the artillery with horses and mules by the deputy-commissary-general, from the exhausted state of the country, and the demands upon it for the Portuguese army, no more than two brigades have been furnished with those animals, and these are much too slight for the general service of the artillery."

Sir J. Cradock to Mr. Villiers, March 20.
" From the first moment of my arrival in this country, unceasing exertion has been employed to purchase and procure them" (horses and mules) " at any price or by any means, but the adequate supply for even the former small number of the British army could not be obtained. I have also made repeated representations to England."

Sir J. Cradock to Mr. Frere, March 29.
" I want eight hundred horses and mules for the common conveyance of provision and the equipment of the artillery."

Commissary Rawlings to sir J. Cradock, April 9.
" Some of the persons employed to provide cattle for the troops have returned without effecting their mission. This disappointment must be attributed to the movements of the enemy in the north, from whence our supply has hitherto been obtained."

Sir J. Cradock to marshal Beresford, Caldas, April 18.
" You can form no adequate idea of the difficulty to procure supplies. The subject of forage for the cavalry keeps me in alarm without intermission, and there is no certainty for a single day. The country appears to be without the ability to furnish straw."—
" In short, the supply is just for the day and barely sufficient."
—" I have begged of Mr. Villiers to desire the regency would

send a person, in special authority, to this district to furnish supplies, if they are to be found. I shall act like the French, and make requisition, with this difference, that we are ready to pay for every thing to the utmost."

Cradock to Berkely, Caldas, April 17.

" Such is the dearth of supply in this part of the country, and even in advance as far as we could go, that, unless victuallers are sent (or some other arrangement to the same effect) to Peniché and St. Martinho Bay, we cannot maintain our position. We cannot advance, for all our means of transport are gone back to Lisbon; and even in a retreat the cavalry could not be fed."— " If there is insurmountable risk in sending the victuallers to Peniché, I request your declaration to this effect; for I must, in that case, retire the army to a station close to Lisbon, to be fed from thence."

Cradock to Villiers, April 17.

" This letter is plainly to state that, unless some victuallers are sent, even at a risk, to Peniché and St. Martinho Bay, we cannot maintain our position, and must retreat."—" If the articles are in the country we must have them, and all ceremony must be dispensed with. The enemy would have them without paying for them : we must equally exact and pay."

Cradock to Beresford, April 20.

" All the recommendations you point out upon the assistance to be derived from the coast have been long since acted upon to the utmost of my exertion; but the difficulties started by the admiral and the commissary were so great, that I cannot say I have much dependence upon immediate aid."

General Cotton to Cradock, April 21.

" I wish I could once see the cavalry together; but I much fear that before that happens they will be very much out of condition. The fourteenth have already fallen off very much, owing to the frequent want of straw and their being supplied with Indian corn, which they will not eat : added to these circumstances, the commissary obliges the cavalry to carry (on the horses) three days' forage."

G. Harrison to Mr. Rawlins, Treasury-chambers,
February 25.

" It having been represented to the lords commissioners of his majesty's treasury that the troops at Lisbon are experiencing the greatest hardships from the want of shoes, I have received their lordships' commands," &c. &c.

Sir J. Cradock to colonel Willoughby Gordon, military
secretary, February 11.

" I trust that the importance of the subject will plead my excuse for thus repeating my representations of the wretched state of the clothing and the great coats in particular of his majesty's troops serving in this country."

Lord Castlereagh to general Sherbrooke, January 12.

" Sir John Cradock will be directed to comply with any requisition you make for horses for your guns, or any other species of supply the service may, from time to time, require.

No. VI.

SECTION I.—MISCELLANEOUS.

Captain Morgan, Lusitanian Legion, to sir J. Cradock,
Lisbon, January 19, 1809.

" I left sir R. Wilson very critically situated, occupying a pass on the Agueda. Sir Robert is wholly unsupported; he has been advised by colonel Guard to fall back; and, from his information, he imagines that sir John Moore is withdrawing his troops through Gallicia. On the other hand, he has received *positive orders from you** to defend the frontiers,* and pressing letters to that effect from the bishop of Oporto."

Sir John Cradock to Lord Castlereagh, 30th January.

" The regency and the bishop of Oporto are not pleased at his" (sir R. Wilson) " quitting the bounds of Portugal."

---

* Note by sir J. Cradock. This is not a correct statement, but quite the contrary; it must have been the bishop.

Ditto to Ditto, 6th March.

" I had a letter from sir R. Wilson, from Ciudad Rodrigo (24th February,) wherein he says, that many French prisoners state their expectations that the French army will retire behind the Ebro. Sir Robert's own persuasion is *that the French will retire altogether from Spain.*

SECTION II.

General Cameron to sir J. Cradock, Lamego, January 16.

" I have collected several detachments of recovered men belonging to sir J. Moore's army, whom I found scattered in all directions, without necessaries, and some of them committing every possible excess that could render the name of a British soldier odious to the nation."

Sir J. Cradock to admiral Berkely, March 16.

" There are about one hundred and twenty persons confined on board the *Rosina,* whose conduct has rendered them a disgrace to the army."

SECTION III.

Captain Brotherton to sir J. Cradock, Oimbra, Head-Quarters of Romana, February 21.

" The marquis of Romana seems to think that the serious *intention of the enemy is to retreat from Gallicia altogether;* and even that he will find much difficulty *in extricating himself.* I must confess that *I am not so sanguine;* and I judge that the present retrograde movement from the Minho is more with an intent to advance from Orense on Montalegre, and in this direction."

Captain Brotherton to sir J. Cradock, March.

" I still believe Romana had intention to fall back on Chaves, and join himself to the Portuguese army. *His troops had been much vexed by the unfriendly conduct of the Portuguese,* and a cordial co-operation was not to be expected ; but that he should separate altogether is what I neither could expect nor conceive.

He suddenly informed me of his resolution to retreat to Bragança. He had just received a letter from Silveira, which he also answered to that effect, and which created no small surprise, as a plan of operations had already been settled between them."

Major Victor Arentschild to sir J. Cradock, Oporto, March 16.

" General Silveira has only one regiment with him; and his conduct has been such, that the people have lost all confidence in him, and consider him a traitor. I merely mention this to your excellency as the opinion of the public.••••••The marquis of Romana's army is retreating to Orres, in Gallicia, and is, I fear, in a wretched condition. The opinion entertained of him is far from good."

Mr. commissary Boys to Mr. commissary Rawlings, Almeida, January 13.

" Sir John Moore, with his army, was retreating, and ten thousand men had deserted from the marquis of Romana, and were pillaging the country."

Mr. Canning to Mr. Frere, January 23.

" No effort appears to have been made by the Spaniards, either to second the British operations, or even to defend Ferrol, or save the naval means (whatever they may be) in that harbour."

Lord Castlereagh to marshal Beresford, February 15.

" The Portuguese government having solicited that a British general officer should be appointed to command and organize their army, his majesty has been graciously pleased to select you for this important trust."

No. VII.

EXTRACTS FROM MR. FRERE'S CORRESPONDENCE.

(N.B. The Italics are not in the original.)

Mr. Frere to Sir John Cradock, Seville, March 14.

" Our hope of offensive operations in Aragon is so much diminished by the defeat of general Reding, that I should much doubt whether any reinforcement, such as we could now send there, would enable us to attempt them with the prospect of a degree of success, such as might compensate for the inconvenience liable to arise from the derangement of calculations which may have been formed at home."—" On the other hand, there seems reason to *apprehend*, that general Soult may at last, in consequence of the resistance he has experienced, *desist from his unaccountable project, of entering Portugal and occupying Gallicia*. His return would, of course, add largely to the disposable and moveable force of the enemy, while it would not increase ours by any force of that description."—" In this view of the subject there are two points for the employment of a British force; one, *by making a push to drive the enemy from Salamanca, and the neighbouring towns*, while the Asturians should make an effort on their side to occupy Leon and Astorga, thus re-establishing the communication between the northern and southern province. The other, by moving from the bridge of Alcantara along the northern bank of the Tagus, in concert with general Cuesta, to attack and *drive the enemy from Toledo, and consequently from Madrid*. In the latter alternative, the British could have the advantage of acting in concert with a disciplined army. They would, likewise, have immediately the start of any reinforcement from the army of general Soult, supposing him to abandon Gallicia for the sake of moving southward ; and these movements would not tend in the same degree to draw him from his present position, in which, for so many reasons, *it is desirable he should continue*. It would, I should imagine, at the same time, cover Andalusia, and the points of the greatest interest and importance in this province, more effectually than the same force employed in any other manner."

Mr. Frere to Sir John Cradock, March 22.

" The fortieth remains here : under the present circumstances I could not think of their removal, unless to meet a British force from Elvas."

Mr. Frere to sir A. Wellesley, Seville, May 4.

Extracted from Parliamentary Papers, 1810.

" As it was my object to obtain *a diversion in La Mancha as the price of co-operation* on your part, and the impression which they (the junta) received from colonel Alava's report was that your intention was, after defeating or driving Soult into Gallicia, to come down upon Estremadura to attack general Victor, I was under some disadvantage, inasmuch as they imagined that the point which I wanted to make a condition was already conceded."

No. VIII.

EXTRACTS RELATIVE TO CADIZ.

Sir J. Cradock to Mr. Villiers, January 16.

" The troops from England for Cadiz may or may not arrive, at least we may expect delay; but I think the subject of sending a force from this requires immediate deliberation and settlement. I am prepared to appropriate for this service any number that may be deemed proper under existing circumstances. It is only upon the political part of the subject I can have any hesitation, and whether the Spaniards will receive the force as they ought. The orders from England are to send it if the supreme junta shall make the requisition. The question is, whether we shall anticipate the demand or not?"

Sir J. Cradock to Mr. Frere, January 29.

" This measure (sending troops to Cadiz) is certainly one of considerable responsibility to those concerned; but upon its adoption, Mr. Villiers, Admiral Berkely, and myself, could not well hesitate, after the despatches that were communicated to us, as addressed to you, as well as those directed to ourselves, which placed Cadiz in so prominent a point of view, upon the unfavourable termination of the campaign in the north of Spain."—" The force in Portugal is weakened to a degree, especially in British regiments, that reduces it to almost nothing; but I may look to the arrival of the force of five thousand men, announced to be on their way; and if it is intended to maintain Portugal, it will be but fair to replace the present detachment from them."

Sir J. Cradock to general Mackenzie, March 9.

" I yesterday received orders from his majesty's government to press, in the most expeditious manner, the immediate return of the forces under your command to the Tagus."

Sir John Cradock to lord Castlereagh, March 9.

" Your lordship will find, by the present communication, that major-general Mackenzie, at the express desire and advice of Mr. Frere, has actually left Cadiz with his whole force, (the fortieth regiment, from Seville, will be united,) and proceeded to Tarragona, unless your lordship's orders may have overtaken major-general Sherbrooke, who passed this port four days ago (without any communication). It may be presumed that he will follow the same course, upon the same motives that influenced general Mackenzie ; and at present a new scene of operations is entered upon in that part of Spain."

No. IX.

NARRATIVE OF THE PROCEEDINGS OF MAJOR-GENERAL MACKENZIE'S DETACHMENT FROM LISBON TO CADIZ.

" The detachment sailed from Lisbon on the 2d February, 1809, and arrived in Cadiz harbour on the 5th, at night. I immediately waited on rear-admiral Purvis, and from him I learnt there are some difficulties started by the marquis Villel (the commissioner from the central junta, as well as a member of it) to our landing and occupying Cadiz. I then waited on sir George Smith, on shore, where this intelligence was, in some degree, confirmed ; but sir George still expressed an expectation that the objections would be got over. These objections had been, it seems, but lately started. Next morning I saw Mr. Charles Stewart, who was acting under a diplomatic authority from Mr. Frere, and had a conference with him and sir G. Smith, when I explained the nature of my orders, and it was determined to wait on the marquis Villel. Mr. Stuart explained to the marquis that the object of my coming was to offer our assistance in the occupation and defence of Cadiz, and in making the necessary preparations for such an event ; that we were only the advance of a larger corps coming from England, to act from this side against the common enemy. The marquis hesitated, and, after some speeches of compliment, said his authority did not extend so far ; that he must wait for instructions from the central government; and, in the mean time, said he could permit our landing at Port St. Mary's. This I declined, as an unnecessary loss of time, and contrary to my orders; and it was then agreed to wait for the decision of the central junta from Seville. I thereupon wrote to Mr. Frere, and sent him a copy of my instructions from sir J. Cradock.

The decision of the junta was received on the 8th: and I received a letter from Mr. Frere, which put an end, for the moment, to our hope of occupying Cadiz. The reason assigned by the junta was of the most flimsy nature, viz. " That they had ordered two of their own battalions to occupy Cadiz;" a measure which was evidently the thought of the moment, and a mere pretext.

Although I cannot presume to judge of the evil political consequences which might arise from such a measure, as alluded to in Mr. Frere's, yet I had every reason to believe, as well from the opinion of sir G. Smith, as of all others conversant in the sentiments of the people of Cadiz, that our landing and occupying the place would be a very popular measure. Mr. Frere's letter expressed a great desire that we should not appear to have made an offer that was refused; and was desirous that we should not immediately depart, but that we should land and occupy the cantonments offered to us. On consulting with sir G. Smith and Mr. Stuart, this appeared to be contrary to the grounds on which we had set out; but as we were equally desirous not to appear at variance with the Spanish government, we agreed to submit to Mr. Frere, whether it would not be better for the troops to remain for the present in their transports, as we had already stated that we were in expectation of being immediately joined by a force from England, the scene of whose operations was uncertain; and our remaining in the harbour under this idea would answer every purpose Mr. Frere proposed by a landing.

I had, besides, some military objections to a landing; for, without reckoning the uncertainty of an embarkation from Port St. Mary's, I knew how dilatory all proceedings are in Spain. That if we were once placed in the scattered cantonments proposed, and we had a sudden call for embarkation, above a week would have been lost in effecting it; and from former experience, the effects of a certain disorder would, probably, have thrown a large number of our men into the hospitals. It is further evident that the detachment could not have been re-embarked without some stain on the national honour. It must have very soon marched into the interior of Spain, and thus have involved our country in its support, without having obtained the object for which it was detached,—the possession of Cadiz. On all these considerations I thought it right to defer landing, until we should hear further from Mr. Frere, to whom both Mr. Stuart and myself wrote, and I presume he was satisfied with the reasons given. In all these proceedings I had the cordial approbation of sir G. Smith, who, notwithstanding unfavourable appearances, seemed sanguine to the last that the point would be carried. I therefore wrote to sir J. Cradock, by the Hope brig, on the 9th, stating what had been done, and that we should remain in Cadiz harbour (with Mr. Frere's approbation) until we received orders from him or from England. And I wrote, by the same conveyance, to the same purport, to Lord Castlereagh.

On the 15th, we had the misfortune to lose sir G. Smith, who died that morning; and on the 18th, I received a letter from Mr. Frere, in which he seemed to have altered his opinion as to the propriety of our occupying Cadiz, and stating that the only mode which appeared to him likely to succeed in obtaining the possession was my leaving a small part of my detachment there, and proceeding with the rest to join Cuesta's army; that, as a force was expected from England for the same purpose for which my detachment came, what I left behind might follow me on their arrival.

I confess I was much disappointed at this proposal, the whole of my detachment not appearing more than equal to the charge of the place; but as it had not been laid before the junta, I considered it my duty to state the objections to it, as they arose out of my instructions. Such a measure would have completely committed our country, in a particular point, in the interior, with a very small detachment, a thing which I was instructed his majesty's ministers wished to avoid; whilst the admittance of a handful of men could not be considered as any possession of the place, where there were about four thousand volunteers well drilled. I therefore submitted to Mr. Frere, to defer the proposition of this measure until the arrival of troops from England, which might be looked for, according to his statement, every hour. We should be, then, in a condition to take possession of Cadiz effectually, and advance, in some point, respectably, towards the enemy. If, however, Mr. Frere should determine to bring forward the measure immediately, I further informed him, that I was ready to move on, as soon as we could obtain the necessary equipments.

Mr. Stuart embarked on the 21st, on board the Ambuscade, on a secret mission. On the 22d, and before I received any further communication from Mr. Frere, a popular commotion broke out suddenly at Cadiz, in consequence of the measure which the junta had adopted, of marching some of their own troops into the town, as the reason (or rather pretext) for declining to receive us. The regiment now on its march in, was composed of Poles, Swiss, and other foreigners, deserters from the French army, whose entrance the people were determined to resist. The utmost care was taken to prevent our officers or soldiers from taking any part whatever on this occasion; and, except in some cases where I was applied to by the governor, for the interference of some British officers as mediators, we steered perfectly clear. It was now evident that the people were favourable to our landing and occupying the town, for it was frequently called for during the tumult.

As soon as I could safely send an account of this commotion to Mr. Frere, I despatched an officer (captain Kelly, assistant quarter-master-general) with a detail. The Fisguard sailed on the 24th, for Lisbon and England, by which ship I informed sir J. Cradock, as well as lord Castlereagh, of all that had passed since my last; and just at that time colonel Roche arrived from Seville. He was sent down, by Mr. Frere, to Cadiz, in consequence of Mr. Stuart's mission. I had till now expected Mr. Frere's decision, on the subject of the proposition in his letter of the 18th; but as so much time had elapsed, I conjectured he might have dropped it for the present; and conceiving that something favourable to the object of my mission might be drawn from the present state of things, I had a full conversation with colonel Roche on the subject. He told me the junta were dissatisfied with our not having accepted the cantonments offered to us; but he did not seem to think our views unattainable, particularly at the present moment. I asked his opinion as to the practicability of general Stuart's being admitted, with two of my three battalions, into Cadiz, if I advanced with the third to Seville to join the fortieth regiment, thus making an equal division of my force. Colonel Roche was of opinion that this would be acceded to; and I, therefore, despatched him, as soon as possible, with a proposal to this effect to Mr. Frere. Though two battalions could not be considered a sufficient garrison, yet, from the evident popularity of our troops, and the speedy expectation of a reinforcement from England, I thought it would be extremely proper to make the trial.   It also appeared to me that by advancing to Seville I should not run much risk of involving those two battalions in any operations before the arrival of general Sherbrooke, which could embarrass him in the execution of the orders he might bring from home.

This proposition certainly exceeded any thing authorised by my instructions, but, I trust, the circumstances will be found to warrant it.

After colonel Roche's departure for Seville, Captain Kelly returned from thence, on the 26th, with a verbal confidential message from Mr. Frere, stating that marshal Soult was marching from Gallicia into Portugal, in three columns, and that Mr. Frere would write to me by express, or by next post.   On the 27th, I received this promised letter, enclosing the copy of an intercepted letter from Soult to Joseph Buonaparte ; and Mr. Frere expresses his opinion that my detachment may now be more useful in Portugal than at Cadiz.

Knowing, as I did before I left Lisbon, that every proper step was taking for evacuating Portugal, in case of necessity, and that nothing else than succours from home could enable sir John Cradock to hold his ground there, it became more than ever necessary to ascertain whether his army will be received into Cadiz, in case of the evacuation of Portugal.   In case the present negotiation succeeded, I had arranged with admiral Purvis to send a frigate with the intelligence to Lisbon immediately,   If it failed, every thing was in readiness to sail with the detachment thither ; for, although the assistance I should bring might not be sufficient of itself to make any alteration in the resolutions already taken, yet, if reinforcements arrived from England, we should be a welcome addition.

On the morning of the 2d of March I received a letter from colonel Roche, dated February 28, stating that my proposition had not yet been decided on, but that it would be taken into consideration that day.   He expressed much apprehension of a party in the French interest.

The morning of the 3d having passed without any letter from Mr. Frere or colonel Roche, as I had been assured by the latter I should receive, at furthest by the post of that morning, I despatched another courier, dreading some accident.   In the afternoon, however, I received a long and important letter from Mr.

Frere, from which I concluded the negotiation had failed (although he did not say so in terms); and a letter I received shortly after-wards from colonel Roche confirmed this failure. Mr. Frere's letter entered very minutely into the state of the Spanish and French armies; mentioned the failure of Soult's attempt to penetrate into Portugal by the Minho, and the improbability of his persisting in it, from the position of the Spanish army, assisted by the Portuguese. He then points out, in strong terms, the essential use my detachment could be of at Tarragona, in giving spirit and vigour to the cause in that country, where it is most in need of support.

As the return of my detachment to Portugal, except in the case of resisting the enemy, would not have a favourable appearance; and the proceeding to Tarragona would so evidently shew our determination to support the general cause, and leave the Spanish government without an excuse afterwards for refusing to admit our troops into Cadiz, it was my intention to have complied with Mr. Frere's solicitations, as the employment of my detachment on the sea-coast would easily admit of its being afterwards withdrawn, without committing any other British force for its support; and the motives urged by Mr. Frere were so strong, that I scarcely thought myself vindicable in hesitating to comply.

I accordingly wrote on the night of the 3d March to this effect to Mr. Frere, sir J. Cradock, and lord Castlereagh. But on the 4th, in the evening, captain Cooke, of the Coldstream guards, arrived from England with despatches from general Sherbrooke, who had not yet arrived. Captain Cooke came in the Eclair brig of war, and had stopped at Lisbon, which he again left on the evening of the 2d, and brought me a message to the following purport from sir J. Cradock, viz. " That he was determined to defend Portugal to the utmost of his power; that in this situation he considered my detachment as the choice part of his little army; that the enemy were actually on the borders, though there was not yet any intelligence of their having entered Portugal; and that unless some extraordinary circumstance, of which he could form no idea, prevented it, he should look for my immediate return to Lisbon."

This order, of course, put an end to all further deliberation The idea of proceeding to Tarragona was abandoned. I wrote to this effect to Mr. Frere, and embarked at midnight on the 4th. Contrary winds detained in Cadiz harbour the whole of the 5th.

but on the 6th the fleet sailed, and arrived in the Tagus on the 12th.

I trust, in the whole of these proceedings, in a very intricate and delicate situation, an honest and anxious desire has been evinced on my part, to accomplish the object of my mission ; the failure of which, I am persuaded, will be found to arise from the apprehensions and disunion of the central junta, and not from the inclinations of the people at Cadiz.

(Signed)

J. R. MACKENZIE,
Major-general.

Lisbon, March 13, 1809.

No. X.

COMMUNICATIONS WITH MINISTERS—NEGLECT OF PORTUGAL.

SECTION I.

Mr. Canning to Mr. Villiers, January 24, 1809.

" You are aware, by my despatch, No. 4, of the 24th of December, enclosing copies, &c. &c. *that, in the event of the evacuation of Portugal, by the force under sir J. Cradock's command, an event rendered the more probable by the transactions in Gallicia."*

Lord Castlereagh to sir J. Cradock, February 6.
" *Should you be compelled to evacuate Portugal,"* &c.

Admiral Berkely to sir J. Cradock, February 6.
" The period of the British army's stay in this place *appearing to draw near to its conclusion."*

SECTION II.

Sir J. Cradock to colonel Guard, January 3.

" The garrisons of Elvas and Almeida have engaged my most serious thoughts."—" But, as they were occupied by the command of his majesty's ministers, and *we remain without any fresh instructions under the present critical circumstances.*"

Sir J. Cradock to general Richard Stewart, January 10.

" I feel what a risk I run in thus leaving Lisbon defenceless, but *I obey the original orders of government.*"

Sir J. Cradock to general Richard Stewart, January 12.

" *We are still without any instructions whatever from England.*"

Sir J. Cradock to captain Halket, January 13.

" Though we cannot say *when* it may take place, and it shall be deferred to the last moment, *in hopes of hearing from England*, yet I believe it to be our duty to prepare every thing for the event of an embarkation."

Sir J. Cradock to admiral Berkely, January 17.

" I lament to say that there appears nothing before us but the resolution *to remain in Portugal to the last proper moment, awaiting orders from England.*"

Sir J. Cradock to Mr. Frere, January 19.

" With our force inferior and ill-composed, as it is, *we are determined to remain to the last proper moment, in the hopes of receiving orders from England.*"

Sir J. Cradock to admiral Berkely, February 9.

" The orders we daily expect may be either for *immediate embarkation, or to maintain Portugal.*"—" I am persuaded we have but this one wish, which is to act for the credit of our country, and endeavour, under the *want of all information, to discover what may be the object of the government we serve.*"

Sir J. Cradock to general Mackenzie, February 26.

" Since the 14th of January *we are without instructions from England.*"

SECTION III.

Sir J. Cradock to Mr. Villiers, January 15.

" What appears to be my duty is to keep the fixed idea that the
army in Portugal should remain to the last moment."

Sir J. Cradock to Mr. Villiers, February 15.

" I am just favoured with your communication about the dangerous effects likely to be produced by the measure of withdrawing
the troops from Lisbon to occupy the military position of Oyeras,
Passo d'Arcos, &c. I fear (though the contrary was intended to
be expressly stated) that you are led into the idea that the position
in question was solely intended for embarkation. My avowed
design was to await (in a military post suited to our force) orders
from England, or to defend ourselves with reasonable prospect of
success against any attempt from the enemy, or even from thence
to make a forward movement, should future events lead to such a
proceeding."—" What I must object to is to take up a false
position, say Alcantara, or other heights about the town, which
would only defend a certain position and leave the remainder to
the power of the enemy, one which we must leave upon his approach and seek another bearing the appearance of flight and yet
not securing our retreat. The whole having announced the
intention to defend Lisbon, but giving up that idea upon the
appearance of the enemy : for positions liable to be turned on
every side cannot be persevered in by an inferior force."—" My
political reasoning upon this subject was contained in the letter I
wrote the admiral, and, I must repeat, it continues unweakened,"
&c.—" After your strong representations of this morning, I shall
certainly not persevere ; and, as there is no instant necessity for
the measure, will await the progress of events."

No. XI.

STATE AND DISTRIBUTION OF THE FORCE UNDER SIR J. CRADOCK, JANUARY 6, 1809, EXTRACTED FROM THE HEAD-QUARTER STATES.

Disposable for the Field.

Garrisons.	Artillery. Men.	Cavalry. Men.	Infantry. Men.	
Santarem	68	199	2,492	General Richard Stewart
Saccavem	97	169	1,450	General M'Kenzie.
Lisbon	..	519	....	General Cotton.
	..	..	236	attached to different battalion
	165	879	4,178	

Total   5,222

Garrisons.	Artillery. Men.	Cavalry. Men.	Infantry. Men.
Almeida	38	..	1,440
Elvas	33	..	679
Oporto	..	..	379
Lisbon and Forts	315	..	2,682
Total	486	..	5,170

General total   10,392

Note.   Every man capable of bearing arms is included in this state.

ORDER OF BATTLE, APRIL 6, 1809, CALDAS.

Sir J. Cradock, commander-in-chief.

Major-general Sherbrooke, second in command.

Artillery.—Major-general Howarth.   Cavalry.—Major-general Cotton.

Under arms.

	Men.
First line, five brigades	10,418
Second line, three brigades	3,810
Reserve, one brigade	1,858
Cavalry	800
Total	16,886

STATE OF THE ARMY UNDER SIR A. WELLESLEY, APRIL 22.

Head-quarters, Leyria.

	Under arms. Men.	Sick. Men.	Command. Men.	Effective. Men.
Artillery	441	88	408	937
Cavalry	1,439	13	418	1,870
Infantry	16,539	1,937	314	18,790
Total	18,419	2,038	1,140	21,597

	6lb.	3lb.	Howitzers.
Number of guns	20	6	4

Total   30

STATE OF SIR A. WELLESLEY'S ARMY, MAY 1, 1809.

Head-quarters, Coimbra.

Artillery. Men.	Cavalry. Men.	Infantry. Men.	Waggon train. Men.	Total rank and file. Men.
1,413	3,074	19,510	230	24,227

Deduct { Hospital 2,357 / Absent 1,217

Total present under arms 20,653

STATE OF SIR A. WELLESLEY'S ARMY, JUNE 25, 1809.

Head-quarters, Abrantes.

Artillery. Men.	Cavalry. Men.	Infantry. Men.	Waggon train. Men.	Total rank and file. Men.
1,586	3,736	21,267	406	26,995

Deduct { Hospital 3,246 / Commands 1,396

30 Pieces of artillery.

Total present under arms 22,353

STATE OF SIR A. WELLESLEY'S ARMY, JULY 25, 1809.

Head-quarters, Talavera.

Artillery. Men.	Cavalry. Men.	Infantry. Men.	Waggon train. Men.	Total rank and file. Men.
1,584	3,734	29,694	398	35,410

Deduct { Hospital 4,827 / Commands 1,596

Total present under arms   28,987
Deduct regiments on march   9,141

30 Pieces of artillery.

Real present under arms   19,846

STATE OF SIR A. WELLESLEY'S ARMY, SEPTEMBER 25, 1809.

Head-quarters, Badajos.

Artillery. Men.	Cavalry. Men.	Infantry. Men.	Waggon train. Men.	Total rank and file. Men.
1,947	4,273	28,409	389	35,018

In Hospital   8,827 }   Total absent   11,353

Command and missing 2,526 }

Total present under arms   23,765

No. XII.

SECTION I.

MARSHAL BERESFORD TO SIR J. CRADOCK.

March 29, 1809.

SIR,

I HAVE the honour to annex your excellency a copy of requisitions, from their excellencies the government of this kingdom, for the speedy succouring of Oporto, which your excellency is informed is so immediately in danger, from the approach of the French army, whose advance posts are now within four leagues of that town.

I annex, for the information of your excellency, the instructions which, under the existing circumstances, I had issued to the general commanding beyond the Douro; but the object of which has been frustrated by events, at once unfortunate and melancholy.

The corps of brigadier-general Victoria, consisting of two battalions of the line, which, on the appearance of the urgent danger in the north, I had directed to cross the Douro, are now in Oporto, as is the second battalion of the Lusitanian legion, part of the regiment of Valença, and some regiments of militia; but I cannot get any return of the troops there, though, I understand, the number is considerable; and to this must be added a considerable number of ordenanza from without, and the armed population, which will, I understand, amount to eight or ten thousand men, and of the arms come from England, three thousand stand that were sent to the army north of the Douro, are probably now in Oporto, with a proportion of ammunition. I have thought it right to give this statement of the actual state of things at Oporto, as far as I can get information of, that your excellency may be aware of it; and it is with regret that I farther add that there prevails, in the town, the greatest anarchy and insubordination,— and that, in short, by the latest accounts, the populace entirely govern the law, civil and military.

Upon the subject of marching a British force to Oporto under the actual circumstances, and under the consideration of the various points from which the enemy at present threaten us, we had yesterday a full discussion, and which renders it unnecessary for me now to recapitulate the several reasons which induced me to submit to your excellency's consideration the propriety of advancing the British force to Leyria, to be then pushed on to Oporto, or otherwise, as the information from different parts may render expedient. But my principal reason was that, as there appeared an intention of co-operation (of which, however, there is no certainty) between the marshals Victor and Soult, it would be most desirable, by either driving back or overcoming one, before the other could give his co-operating aid to defeat their plan, and if we should, or not, be able, to do this, would be merely a matter of calculation of time, as, supposing, on our arrival at Leyria, Oporto offered a prospect of holding out till we could reach it, and that Victor continued his southern pursuit of Cuesta, he would get so distant from us, as to permit the army, pushing from Leyria to Oporto, without apprehension from the army of Victor, who, by the time he could possibly hear of our movement, would be in the Sierra Morena, which would clearly show that his principal object, and from which he did not seem willing to be diverted, was either the destruction of Cuesta's army, to enter more securely into Portugal, or to push to Seville; but, at all events, he would be too distant to give us apprehensions of any surprise upon this capital, as we have daily information of his movements, and which would enable us, wherever we were in Portugal, even to reach it before him. If, however, the final co-operation of these two armies is intended for the conquest of this kingdom, and that Soult does not think that of his army from Gallicia and that from Salamanca sufficient, then he will satisfy himself, until Victor is ready to act with him, in the possession of the country beyond the Douro, where he will refresh and rest his troops, re-equip them, and otherwise provide them, to be ready for the projected co-operation,—whilst the army from Salamanca will, probably, satisfy itself with the capture of Ciudad Rodrigo and Almeida, and act and wait in conjunction with Soult, both waiting till Victor has settled his present objects, and then all co-operating.

It is for your excellency to judge, under the actual circumstances, of the propriety of this movement towards Oporto, not only for the British troops, but, also, of those of the allies, as, by my instructions, I must consider you as commanding the allied armies; and the time is now certainly arrived, for what efforts they can make being combined: undoubtedly, their being employed in separate projects will cause each falling separately, and without advantage to the common cause.

I would, however, certainly, under present circumstances, be unwilling to send the few troops I could spare from the army, between the Tagus and the Mondego, to Oporto, as, unsupported by British, I fear it would be losing so many men, that on a future occasion, with such support, may weigh in the scale; and indeed, the very insubordinate state of the troops, of which I have just received a second report and complaint, from general Miranda, would render it highly unwise to send them to a town in the state that Oporto now is, where the best disposed troops, except a great body went there, if they were not debauched to insubordination, would be borne down by the multitude; and it is to be feared that whatever Portuguese troops enter the town will fall with it, as the temper of the people prevents the possibility of even any preparations for retreat, in case of misfortune, to the outward and very extended lines of defence. Having stated so much, I must leave the question to your excellency, &c.

I have the honour, &c.

W. C. BERESFORD.

SIR J. CRADOCK TO MARSHAL BERESFORD.

Lisbon, March 29, 1809.

DEAR SIR,

I HAVE the honour to acknowledge, at the earliest moment, your excellency's letter of this evening, conveying a copy of the request from the regency, &c. that I should move the British troops to the succour of Oporto, at this moment menaced, &c.

Upon a subject of such importance, I experience considerable relief, that the general view of approaching circumstances has been, for a length of time, within my reflection, and that all my reasoning (whatever it may be) has been transmitted to the government in England, and the part I am now called upon to act is simply but the execution of those measures I have long thought it prudent to pursue, and which the present critical and involved state of affairs seems to confirm and give no reason to alter in any part.

It has always appeared, to my judgement, that the enemy has but two objects to attain in this kingdom; the possession of Lisbon and Oporto. I believe it to be universally admitted, and I need not point out to your discrimination the infinitely superior value of the former above the latter. There are such positive local disadvantages attached to Oporto, independent of its remote position, that no military disposition, in which a small English army is to bear part, can apply. It pains me, therefore, to decline obedience to an application from so high an authority as the governors of the kingdom. It may be their duty to make the request, though I much doubt if their judgement goes along with it; but it appears to be mine not to transfer the small British force, under my command, (totally inadequate to separate objects,) from the defence of this part of the kingdom to the very doubtful succour of a place two hundred miles distant, and by a movement to the north with this professed view, feel myself engaged in a war that leaves Lisbon and the Tagus defenceless and unprotected from the inroads of other bodies of the enemy that may be prepared to combine in a general invasion.

I shall hasten, therefore, from all general observation, to the exact case before us, and state, in a concise manner, our actual situation, leaving to your judgement, how far it may be necessary to communicate some particulars that relate to the British army, and lay before the governors and your excellency the best ideas I can form for the employment of the British auxiliary force, in conjunction with the Portuguese, for the ultimate protection of Portugal under the pressure of all existing circumstances.

It may be granted that the enemy, with a force from seventeen to twenty thousand, a considerable portion of which (it is said five thousand) is cavalry, is directly menacing Oporto, there is reason to believe that the division at Salamanca, estimated from nine to twelve thousand, with a powerful force of artillery, is

moving to Ciudad Rodrigo, either for the investment of that
place, or to act in conjunction with general Soult, by an advance
into the Upper Beira. In the present view it is necessary to
state, with the weight it so well deserves, that the united forces
of generals Victor and Sebastiani are, apparently, pursuing
general Cuesta, just retiring before them; but it appears that a
part of the enemies had diverged to Merida, and had spread alarm
and dismay, even to the town of Badajos, on the frontiers of
Portugal, from whence, to the heights of Almeida, or the opposite
of Lisbon, through the whole of the Alemtejo: except the weak
garrison of Elvas, there is nothing to interrupt the immediate
passage.

Against such an attempt from the enemy I derive no security
from the contiguity of general Cuesta's army; for, besides the
general disinclination he has so strongly marked to the British
character, he has other objects to pursue, and his principal wish
is to gain time for the organization of his own force. To a person
so well acquainted with Portugal, and the circumstances of the
present hour, as your excellency is, it is quite superfluous to enter
upon further details, &c. It is only required to lay before you, in
confidence, the exact amount of the British forces, as the real point
upon which the whole subject depends: I may state it at twelve
thousand effective men, to take the field, if the necessary garrison
to maintain Lisbon in some tranquillity, and retain possession of the
maritime forts, is left. It may be increased to fourteen thousand,
if these points are risked; but even to gain the advantage of numbers to so limited a force, I cannot recommend the measure, for
the anarchy that prevails at Oporto, and would be, perhaps, worse
at Lisbon, is more to be dreaded than the presence of an enemy,
and may render all exertion useless. The necessary means of
transport for our army, notwithstanding every effort, from the
earliest moment, are quite inadequate, and not more than two and
a half brigades of artillery (fifteen guns) can be equipped. To adventure upon an advance to Oporto, two hundred miles from
Lisbon, when the very object is, perhaps, at this moment lost,
seems to be a point only to gratify the good feelings of every
soldier, but quite opposed to the sober dictates of the understanding, and the ultimate view of things. If the British army
sets out with the declared object to succour Oporto, or expel the
enemy, the impression on the public mind is the same; nothing
but the accomplishment will suit the English character; and I

confess that the best reasoning of my judgement, upon every public and private principle, for the credit of the British army, and the hope of any effectual assistance from the Portuguese nation, is, that the British troops should never make one retrograde step: from that moment I will date the extinction of all Portuguese aid, military as well as civil. The British army, from its description, may disregard this common occurrence in war, but I am persuaded, in the present state of the Portuguese army, and with the sentiments of suspicion now alive, all explanation would be vain, and that it would be left to the small body of English, alone, to sustain the whole future conflict.

I have now only to state what my inferior judgement points out; and as the arduous situation of command is allotted to me, I must try to execute to the best of my power. I shall remain faithful to my first principles, and persevere in the defence of Lisbon and the Tagus. I invite the co-operation of the Portuguese force, and, under your guidance and auspicious control, I look to a very powerful accession of strength. I am convinced nothing will be done by them in detached parties or in any isolated situation. They will acquire confidence by number, and emulation will arise, a rapid discipline will ensue from their connection with us, and the whole, animated by your presence, will give the best promise of success. Until we have consulted again I shall not say whether our general position should be at Lumiar, extending the whole right to Saccavem, or any other station more in advance. At this moment I have only to express the indispensable circumstance of some fixed basis, upon which the allied army will act, and by our united strength try to counteract the peculiar disadvantages that attend the defence of Portugal from positions that cannot be properly embraced, and always leave some part exposed.

Allow me to conclude, with the solemn expression of my own conviction, that nothing will give so much chance of a prosperous result to the arduous scene in which we are engaged (either as to reality or view) as the knowledge to the enemy, that, before he conquers Portugal, he must defeat an army of some magnitude, determined to fight him, and awaiting his approach, unbroken and not exposed to the danger of a false movement. Such a conquest cannot be an easy one, and must prove, if he pursue it, a powerful diversion in favour of Spain.

It will give me the sincerest pleasure, &c.

                                        JOHN CRADOCK.

No. XIII.

JUSTIFICATORY EXTRACTS RELATING TO THE
CONDUCT OF MARSHAL SOULT.

Captain Brotherton to colonel Donkin, (quarter-master-general,) Lamego, March 17, 1809.

" The enemy has, however, on this occasion, practised those arts which Frenchmen are so expert in — circulating proclamations and insidiously abandoning, for a moment, their usual system of terror, plunder, and desolation, *treating the inhabitants with feigned moderation and kindness.*"

Sir J. Cradock to lord Castlereagh, April 20, 1809, Caldas.

" It also appears to be the object of the enemy to ingratiate himself with the populace of Oporto, *by even feeding them* and granting other indulgences."—" It is also said that a Portuguese legion, to consist of *six thousand* men, has been instituted."

Extract from Soult's Official Report of the expedition to Portugal.

" Dans, quinze jours. Les villes de *Braga, Oporto, Bacellos, Viana, Villa de Conde, Povoa de Barcim, Feira*, et *Ovar*, eurent exprimé leurs vœux, des nombreuses deputations se rendirent à Oporto pour les remettre au marechal Soult et le prier de le faire parvenir à l'empereur. Des adresses qui renfermaient l'expression de ce vœu étaient couverts de plus de trente mille signatures du clergé, de la noblesse, des négocians, et du peuple."—" Pendant son séjour à Oporto. Le M. Soult fit des proclamations et rendit divers arrêtés sur l'administration et la police de la province *Entre Minho e Douro.* Il nomma au nom de l'empereur aux emplois qui étaient vacans, et après avoir reçu la manifestation politique des habitants, il organiza le garde national ainsi qu'une légion de cinq battallions."—" *Aucune contribution ne fût frappée;* les fonds trouvés dans les caisses royales suffirent pour fournir aux besoins des troupes, *et même pour donner de secours aux Portugais.*"

Intercepted letter of the duke of Dalmatia's to general La Martiniere, Orense, March 2, 1809.

" J'ai reçu vôtre lettre du 27 Jan. J'éprouve toutes les dispositions que vous avez faites. Je vous ai déjà dit que vous pouviez disposer pour le service des fonds qui sont dans la caisse royale de Tuy. Faites entrer en ville le plus de subsistance que vous pourriez. Si de valence on vous tier de coups de canon envoyez leurs des bomber. Bientôt vous pourrez mettre les chevaux au vert, mais faites les garder. Dans les equipages qui sont à Tuy, il y a douze cent pair de souliers, de cuir pour en égal nombre, et un peu de drap, vous pouvez en disposer pour vôtre troupe. Ralliez au depôt général tout ce qui appartient au corps d'armée et qui étoit resté en arrière, ainsi vous auriez bientôt une petite armée qui se soutiendra d'elle-même et faire la police dans le province dont vous devez tirerde quoi vivre, soignez bien les hôpitaux et n'envoiez personne sur Ribidavia. J'espère que sous peu je vous aurai ouvert une autre communication, le province d'Orence est en très grande partie pacifié, je marche sur les débris du corps de Romana pour en finir avec eux, ils sont du côté de Monterey. Si après cette expédition il y avoit encore en Gallice des troubles, je reviendrai avec tout mon armée pour les appaiser, et alors malheur à ceux qui les auroient occasionné : *je veux la paix et la tranquillité, que les habitans se livrent aux travaux de la campagne, qu'ils soient protegés et que la troupe se conduise bien. Les mutins et les malintentionés François et Espagnols, doivent étre sévèrement punis.* Il faut de tems en tems des examples. Je crois que vous pourriez correspondre avec moi par des gens du pays. Mais il faut bien leur payer ou leur promettre, qu'en arrivant près de moi ils le seront généreusement et prendre de gages pour reponde de leur fidelité, donnez de vos nouvelles au général Marchand. Pour le même moyen dite au colonel l'Abbeville de bien mettre en étât son artillerie.

" MARECHAL DUC DE DALMATIE."

No. XIV.

SIR ARTHUR WELLESLEY TO SIR J. CRADOCK.

Lisbon, April 23.

Mr. Villiers will have informed you of my arrival here yesterday, and of the concurrence of my opinion with that which you appear to entertain in respect to the further movements to the northward. I conclude that you will have determined to halt the army at Leyria. I think that, before any further steps are taken in respect to Soult, it would be desirable to consider the situation of Victor; how far he is enabled to make an attack upon Portugal, and the means of defence of the east of Portugal while the British will be to the northward, and, eventually, the means of defence of Lisbon and the Tagus, in case this attack should be made upon the country.

All these subjects must have been considered by you; and, I fear, in no very satisfactory light, as you appear to have moved to the northward unwillingly: and I should be glad to talk them over with you.

In order to consider of some of them, and to make various arrangements, which can be made only here, I have requested marshal Beresford to come here, if he should not deem his absence from the Portuguese troops, in the present state, likely to be disadvantageous to the public service; and I have directed him to let you know whether he will come or not.

It might, probably, also be more agreeable and convenient to you to see me here than with the army; and if this should be the case, it would be a most convenient arrangement to me to meet you here. I beg, however, that you will consider this proposition only in a view to your own convenience and wishes. If you should, however, choose to come, I shall be very much obliged to you if you will bring with you the adjutant-general and quarter-master-general, the chief engineer and the commanding officer of the artillery, and the commissary.

Ever yours, &c.

ARTHUR WELLESLEY.

N.B. Some paragraphs of a private nature are omitted.

No. XV.

*Extracts of a Letter from sir Arthur Wellesley to lord
Castlereagh, Lisbon, April* 24, 1809.

" I arrived here on Saturday, and found that sir John Cradock
and general Beresford had moved up the country, to the northward, with the troops under their command respectively; the
former to Leyria, and the latter to Thomar. Sir John Cradock,
however, does not appear to have entertained any decided intention of moving forward; on the contrary, indeed, he appears, by
his letters to Mr. Villiers, to have intended to go no further till
he should hear that Victor's movements were decided, and, therefore, I consider affairs in this country to be exactly in the state
in which, if I found them, it was the intention of the king's
minister that I should assume the command; and, accordingly, I
propose to assume it as soon as I shall communicate with sir John
Cradock. I have written to him, and to general Beresford, to
apprize him that I conceive advantage will result from our meeting
here, and I expect them both here as soon as possible. In respect
to the enemy, Soult is still at Oporto, and he has not pushed his
posts to the southward further than the river Vouga. He has
nothing in Tras os Montes since the loss of Chaves, of which
you have been most probably apprized; but he has some posts on
the river Tamega, which divides that province from Minho, and
it is supposed that he wishes to reserve for himself the option of
retreating through Tras os Montes into Spain, if he should find
it necessary. General Silveira, with a Portuguese corps, is in
Tras os Montes, but I am not acquainted with its strength or
its composition. General Lapisse, who commands the French
corps which, it was supposed, when I left England, was marching
from Salamanca into Portugal, has turned off to his left, and has
marched along the Portuguese frontier to Alcantara, where he
crossed the Tagus, and thence he went to Merida, on the Guadiana, where he is in communication with, indeed I may say, part
of the army of Victor; he has an advanced post at Montejo,
nearer to the Portuguese frontier than Merida. Victor has continued at Medellin since the action with Cuesta; he is either fortifying that post, or making an entrenched camp there. Cuesta

is at Llerena, collecting a force again, which, it is said, will soon
be twenty-five thousand infantry and six thousand cavalry, a
part of them good troops; I know nothing of the marquis de la
Romana, or of anything to the northward of Portugal.   I intend
to move upon Soult, as soon as I can make some arrangements
upon which I can depend for the defence of the Tagus, either to
impede or delay Victor's progress, in case he should come in while
I am absent.   I should prefer an attack upon Victor, in concert
with Cuesta, if Soult was not in possession of a fertile province
of this kingdom and of the favourite town of Oporto, of which
it is most desirable to deprive him; and if any operation upon
Victor, connected with Cuesta's movements, did not require time
to concert it, which may as well be employed in dislodging Soult
from the north of Portugal.   If Soult should go, I think it most
advisable, for many reasons, in which I need not enter at present,
to act upon the defensive in the north of Portugal, and to bring
the British army to the eastern frontier.   If the light brigade
should not have left England, when you receive this letter, I trust
that you will send them off without loss of time; and I request
you to desire the officer commanding them to endeavour to get
intelligence, as he will go along the coast, particularly at Aveiro
and the mouth of the Mondego; and I wish that he should stop
at the latter place for orders, if he should find that the British
army is engaged in operations to the northward, and if he should
not already have received orders at Aveiro.   The twenty-third
dragoons might also receive directions to a similar purport.   The
hussars, I conclude, have sailed before this time.   We are much
in want of craft here; now that we are going to carry on an
operation to the northward constant convoys will be necessary,
and the admiral does not appear to have the means in his power
of supplying all that is required of him.   The twenty-fourth
regiment arrived this day, &c. &c.

(Signed)   " ARTHUR WELLESLEY."

No. XVI.

LETTER FROM SIR ARTHUR WELLESLEY TO LORD
CASTLEREAGH.

Abrantes, June 22, 1809.

MY LORD,

When I wrote to you last I was in hopes that I should have
marched before this time, but the money is not yet arrived.
Things are in their progress as they were when I wrote on the
17th. The French are continuing their retreat. Sebastiani has
also fallen back towards Toledo, and Venegas has advanced, and
Cuesta had his head-quarters at Truxillo, on the 19th. I am
apprehensive that you will think I have delayed my march unne-
cessarily since my arrival upon the Tagus. But it was, and is,
quite impossible to move without money. Not only were the
officers and soldiers in the greatest distress, and the want of
money the cause of many of the disorders of which I have had
occasion to complain; but we can no longer obtain the supplies of
the country, or command its resources for the transport of our
own supplies either by land or by water. Besides this, the army
required rest, after their expedition to the frontiers of Gallicia,
and shoes, and to be furbished up in different ways; and I was
well aware that, if necessity had not obliged me to halt at the
present moment, I should have been compelled to make a longer
halt some time hence. To all this add, that, for some time after
I came here, I believed that the French were retiring, (as appears
by my letters to your lordship,) and that I should have no opportunity of striking a blow against them, even if I could have
marched. I hope that you will attend to my requisitions for
money; not only am I in want, but the Portuguese government,
to whom Mr. Villiers says that we owe £125,000. I repeat, that
we must have £200,000 a month, from England, till I write you
that I can do without it; in which sum I include £40,000 a
month for the Portuguese government, to pay for twenty thousand
men. If the Portuguese government are to receive a larger sum
from Great Britain, the sum to be sent to Portugal must be
proportionably increased. Besides this, money must be sent to
pay the Portuguese debt and our debts in Portugal. There are,

besides, debts of sir John Moore's army still due in Spain, which I am called upon to pay. In short, we must have £125,000, and £200,000 a month, reckoning from the beginning of May, &c. &c.

(Signed) " ARTHUR WELLESLEY."

NO. XVII.

LETTER FROM LORD WELLINGTON TO THE MARQUIS WELLESLEY.

Badajos, October 30, 1809.

MY LORD,

I have had the honour of receiving your excellency's despatch, (marked I.) of the 17th instant, containing a copy of your note to M. de Garay, of the 8th of September, and a copy of his note, in answer to your excellency, of the 3d of October.

I am not surprised that M. de Garay should endeavour to attribute to the irregularities of the English commissariat the deficiencies of supplies and means of transport experienced by the British army in its late service in Spain; I am not disposed to justify the English commissariat where they deserve blame ; but I must think it but justice to them to declare that the British army is indebted to their exertions for the scanty supplies it received.

From some of the statements contained in M. de Garay's note it would appear that the British army had suffered no distress during the late service ; others have a tendency to prove that great distress was suffered, at a very early period, by both armies ; particularly the quotation of a letter from general Cuesta, of the 1st of August, in answer to a complaint which I am supposed to have made, that the Spanish troops and *their prisoners* were better supplied than the British army. The answer to all these statements is a reference to the fact that the army suffered great distress for want of provisions, forage, and means of equipment; and, although that distress might have been aggravated, it could not have been occasioned by the inexperience or irregularity of the English commissariat.

I know nothing of the orders which M. de Garay states were sent by the government to the different provincial juntas, to provide provisions and means of transport for the British army on its passage through the different towns in the provinces. If such orders were sent, it was obvious that the central junta, as a government, have no power or influence over the provincial juntas and magistrates, to whom their orders were addressed, as they produced no effect; and the supplies, such as they were, were procured only by the requisitions and exertions of the English commissaries. But it is obvious, from M. de Garay's account of these orders, that the central junta had taken a very erroneous view of the operations to be carried on by the army, and of the provision to be made for the troops while engaged in those operations. The government provided, by their orders, for the troops only while on their passage through the towns; relying upon their immediate success, and making no provision for the collection of one body, of not less than fifty thousand men, even for one day. At the same time that they were guilty of this unpardonable omission, which paralyzed all our efforts, they rendered that success doubtful, by countermanding the orders given to general Venegas by general Cuesta, and thus exposing the combined armies to a general action with the enemy's concentrated force. The effect of their orders will appear more fully in the following detail:—

As soon as the line of my operations in Spain was decided, I sent a commissary to Ciudad Rodrigo, to endeavour to procure mules to attend the army, in concert with don Lozano des Torres, that city and its neighbourhood being the places in which the army commanded by the late sir John Moore had been most largely supplied. M. de Garay expresses the astonishment of the government that the British army should have entered Spain unprovided with the means of transport, notwithstanding that a few paragraphs preceding this expression of astonishment, he informs your excellency, in the name of the government, that they had given orders to the provincial juntas of Badajos and Castile (at Ciudad Rodrigo) and the magistrates, to provide and supply us with the means which, of course, they must have been aware that we should require. No army can carry on its operations if unprovided with means of transport; and the British army was, from circumstances, particularly in want at that moment.

The means of transport, commonly used in Portugal, are carts, drawn by bullocks, which are unable, without great distress, to move more than twelve miles in a day, a distance much shorter than that which the state of the country in which the army was to carry on operations in Spain, and the nature of the country, would oblige the army to march. The number of carts which we had been able to bring from Portugal was not sufficient to draw our ammunition, and there were none to carry provisions.

Having failed in procuring, at Ciudad Rodrigo and in the neighbourhood, the means of transport which I required, I wrote to general O'Donaghue, on the 16th of July, a letter, in which after stating our wants and the failure of the country in supplying them, I gave notice that if they were not supplied I should discontinue my co-operation with general Cuesta, after I should have performed my part in the first operation which we had concerted, viz. the removal of the enemy from the Alberche; and, if not supplied as I required, I should eventually withdraw from Spain altogether. From this letter of the 16th July, it will appear that I called for the supplies, and gave notice that I should withdraw from Spain if they were not furnished, not only long previous to the retreat across the Tagus of the 4th of August, but even previous to the commencement of the operations of the campaign.

Notwithstanding that this letter of the 16th of July was communicated to the central junta, both by Mr. Frere and general Cuesta, the British army has, to this day, received no assistance of this description from Spain, excepting twenty carts, which joined at Merida, ten on the 30th of August, and ten on the 2d of September; and about three hundred mules of about five hundred which were hired at Bejar, and joined at a subsequent period. None of the mules stated to have been hired and despatched to the army from Seville, or by Igea or Cevallos, or the two brigades of forty each, or the horses, have ever joined the British army; and I conclude that they are with the Spanish army of Estremadura, as are the remainder of the (one hundred) ten brigades of carts which were intended and are marked for the British army. But none of these mules or carts, supposing them to have been sent from Seville for our use, reached Estremadura till after the 21st of August, the day on which, after five weeks' notice, I was obliged to separate from the Spanish army.

It is not true, therefore, that my resolution to withdraw from Spain, as then carried into execution, was " sudden," or ought to have surprised the government : nor does it appear to have been perilous from what has since appeared in this part of Spain.

I ought, probably, on the 16th of July, to have determined to suspend all operations till the army should be supplied with the means required ; but having, on the 11th of July, settled with general Cuesta a plan of operations to be carried into execution by the armies under the command of general Venegas, general Cuesta, and myself, respectively, I did not think it proper to disappoint general Cuesta. I believed that general Venegas would have carried into execution that part of the plan of operations allotted to his army, although I was afterwards disappointed in that expectation ; and I preferred that the British army should suffer inconvenience than that general Venegas's corps should be exposed alone to the attack of the enemy ; and, above all, I was induced to hope that I should be supplied.

Accordingly, I marched, on the 18th of July, from Plasencia, the soldiers carrying on their backs their provisions to the 21st, on which day a junction was formed with general Cuesta's army ; and, from that day to the 24th of August, the troops or their horses did not receive one regular ration. The irregularity and deficiency, both in quality and quantity, were so great that I considered it a matter of justice to the troops to remit to them, during that period, half of the sum usually stopped from their pay for rations.

The forage for the horses was picked up for them by their riders wherever they could find it, and was generally wheat or rye, which are considered unwholesome food ; and the consequence was that, exclusive of the loss by engaging with the enemy, the army lost, in the short period of five weeks, not less than one thousand five hundred horses.

I have no knowledge of what passed between general Cuesta and don Lozano des Torres and the intendant of provisions of the Spanish army. I never saw the latter gentleman excepting twice ; the first time on the 22d of July, when he waited upon me to claim, for the Spanish army, sixteen thousand rations of bread which had been brought into Talavera, and had been sent to my quarters, and which were delivered over to him, notwithstanding that the British troops were in want ; and the second time, on the 25th of July, when he waited upon me, also at Talavera, to desire that the ovens of that town might be delivered over for the use of the Spanish army, they having moved to St. Ollalla, and the British army being still at Talavera. This request, which was not complied with, is an example of the preference which was given to the British troops while they were in Spain.

The orders stated to have been given by the central to the provincial juntas and magistrates, were not more effectual in procuring provisions than in procuring means of transport. In the interval between the 15th and 21st of July, the British commissaries had made contracts with the magistrates in the different villages of the Vera de Plasencia, a country abounding in resources of every description, for the delivery at Talavera, on different days before the 24th of July, of two hundred and fifty thousand rations of provisions. These contracts were not performed; the British army was consequently unable to move in pursuit of the enemy when he retired on that day; and, I conclude, that the French army have since subsisted on these resources.

The British army never received any salt meat, nor any of the rice or other articles stated to have been sent from Seville for their use, excepting to make up the miserable ration by which the men were only prevented from starving during the period to which I have adverted; nor was it attended by the troop of biscuit bakers, nor did it enjoy any of the advantages of their labours, nor was the supposed magazine of four hundred thousand pounds of biscuit ever performed. These are notorious facts, which cannot be disputed, of the truth of which every officer and soldier in the army can bear testimony. I assure your excellency, that not only have the supplies furnished to the army under my command been paid for whenever the bills for them could be got in, but the old debts due to the inhabitants for supplies furnished to the army, under the command of the late sir John Moore, have been discharged; and I have repeatedly desired the Spanish agents, and others acting with the army, and the different juntas with which I have communicated, to let the people know that all demands upon the British government, which could be substantiated, would be discharged.

I beg to refer your excellency to my despatches of the 21st of August, No. 12, for an account of the state of the magazine at Truxillo, on the 20th of August. Of the state of supplies and provisions at that period, lieutenant-colonel Waters had, by my desire, made an arrangement with the Spanish commissariat for the division of the magazine at Truxillo between the two armies; and he as well as I was satisfied with the principle and detail of that arrangement. But if the British army received only one-third of a ration on the 18th of August, and only one-half of a ration on the 19th, not of bread, but of flour; if the horses of the army received nothing; and if the state of the magazine at Truxillo was such, at that time, as to hold out no hope, not of improvement, (for it was too late to wait for improvement,) but of a full and regular supply of provisions and forage of all descriptions, I was justified in withdrawing from Spain. In point of fact, the magazine at Truxillo, which, under the arrangement made by lieutenant-colonel Waters was to be the sole source of the supply to both armies, did not contain, on the 20th of August, a sufficiency to supply one day's demand upon it.

But it is said that M. de Calvo promised and engaged to supply the British army; upon which I have only to observe that I had trusted too long to the promises of the Spanish agents, and that I had particular reason for want of confidence in M. de Calvo; as, at the moment he was assuring me that the British army should have all the provisions the country could afford, in preference to, and to the exclusion of the Spanish army, I had in my possession an order from him, (of which your excellency has a copy,) addressed to the magistrates of Guadalupe, directing him to send to the head-quarters of the Spanish army provisions which a British commissary had ordered to be prepared and sent to the magazines at Truxillo, to be divided between both armies, in conformity to the agreement entered into with the Spanish commissaries by lieutenant-colonel Waters.

As the state of the magazine at Truxillo was the immediate cause (as far as the want of provisions went) of my withdrawing from Spain, I beg to observe to your excellency that I was not mistaken in my opinion of its insufficiency; as, if I am not misinformed, general Eguia's army suffered the greatest distress in the neighbourhood of Truxillo, even after that part of the country and the magazines had been relieved from the burthen of supporting the British army.

In respect to the conduct of the operations in Spain by the Spanish general officers, many things were done of which I did not approve; some contrary to my expectations, and some contrary to positive agreements.

M. de Garay has stated that the orders of the marquis de

Romana were framed in conformity with suggestions from marshal Beresford; and thence he infers that the operations of that corps were approved of by me.

The marquis de Romana was still at Coruña on the 5th, and I believe as late as the 9th of August; and the armies of Estremadura retired across the Tagus on the 4th of August. This reference to dates shews that there was, and could have been no connexion in the operations of those different armies. In fact, I knew nothing of the marquis of Romana's operations; and till I heard, on the 3d of August, that marshal Ney's corps had passed through the mountains of Estremadura at Baños, and was at Naval Moral, I did not believe that that part of the enemy's army had quitted Astorga, or that the marquis was at liberty, or had it in his power to quit Gallicia.

Marshal Beresford's corps was collected upon the frontiers of Portugal in the end of July, principally for the purpose of forming the troops; and it was hoped he would keep in check the enemy's corps under Soult, which was at Zamora, and threatened Portugal; that he would act as a corps of observation in that quarter, and on the left of the British army; and I particularly requested marshal Beresford to attend to the Puerto de Perales. But I never intended, and never held out any hope to the Spanish officers that the corps under marshal Beresford could effect any operation at that period of the campaign, and never was a party to any arrangement of an operation in which that corps was to be concerned.

In the cases in which measures were carried on in a manner of which I did not approve, or which I did not expect, or contrary to the positive agreement, those who acted contrary to my opinion may have been right; but still they acted in a manner of which they were aware I did not approve: and the assertion in the note, that the operations were carried on with my concurrence, is unfounded.

I expected, from the communications I had with general Cuesta, through sir Robert Wilson and colonel Roche, that the Puerto de Baños would have been effectually occupied and secured; and, at all events, that the troops appointed to guard that point, upon which I was aware that all the operations, nay, the security, of the army depended, would not have retired without firing a shot.

It was agreed, between general Cuesta and me, on the 11th of July, that general Venegas, who was under his command, should march by Tembleque, Ocaña, Puerte Dueños, to Arganda, near Madrid; where he was to be on the 22d and 23d of July, when the combined armies should be at Talavera and Escola. This agreement was not performed, and the consequence of its non-performance (which had been foreseen) occurred; viz. that the combined armies were engaged with the enemy's concentrated force. I have heard that the cause of the non-performance of this agreement was that the central junta had countermanded the orders which general Venegas had received from general Cuesta; of which countermand they gave us no notice. I shall make no observation upon this proceeding, except that the plan of operations, as agreed upon with me, was not carried into execution, by general Venegas, in this instance.

It was agreed, by general Cuesta, on the 2d of August, that when I marched against Soult on the 3d, he would remain at Talavera. That agreement was broken when he withdrew from Talavera, in my opinion without sufficient cause. And it is also my opinion that he ought not to have withdrawn, particularly considering that he had the charge of my hospital, without my consent. I do not conceive that if general Cuesta had remained at Talavera, it would have made any difference in the result of the campaign. When Soult added thirty-four thousand to the numbers already opposed to the combined armies in Estremadura, the enemy was too strong for us; and it was necessary that we should retire across the Tagus. But if general Cuesta had held the post of Talavera, according to agreement, I should have been able to remove my hospital, or, at least, to know the exact situation of every individual left there; and I think that other disadvantages might have been avoided in the retreat.

When adverting to this part of the subject, I cannot avoid to observe upon the ambiguity of language used in the note respecting the assistance afforded by general Cuesta to remove the hospital from Talavera. That assistance amounted to four carts on the 4th of August, at Oropesa. In the subsequent removal of the wounded, and of the men subsequently taken sick, we had absolutely no assistance from the Spanish army or the country. We were obliged to lay down our ammunition, which was delivered over to the Spanish army, and to unload the treasure, and employ the carts in the removal of the wounded and sick. At Truxillo, in particular, assistance which could have been afforded was withheld, on the 22d and 23d of August, M. de Calvo and don Lozano de Torres being in the town.

In respect to the refusal to make movements recommended by me, I am of opinion that if general Bassecourt had been detached towards Plasencia on the 30th of July, when I recommended that movement, and if the troops had done their duty, Soult would have been stopped at the Tietar, at least for a sufficient length of time to enable me to secure the passage of the Tagus at Almaraz; and here again the hospital would have been saved.

He was not detached, however, till the 2d; and then I understood, from M. de Garay's note, that it was general Cuesta's opinion that the movement was useless.

It could not have been considered as useless by general Cuesta on the 30th, because the proposition for making a detachment from the combined armies originated with himself on that day; and it could not have been considered as useless even on the morning of the 2d, as, till the evening of that day, we did not receive intelligence of the arrival of Soult at Plasencia. A reference to the date of the period at which the general considered this detachment as useless would have been desirable.

I cannot account for the surprise stated to have been felt by general Cuesta upon finding the British army at Oropesa on the morning of the 4th of August. The army had left Talavera on the morning of the 3d, and had marched to Oropesa, six leagues, or twenty-four miles, on that day; which I conceive a sufficient distance for a body of men which had been starving for many days before. The accounts received, on the evening of the 3d, of the enemy's position at Naval Moral, and of his strength, and of general Cuesta's intended march on that evening, leaving my hospital to its fate, were sufficient to induce me to pause and consider our situation, and, at least, not to move before daylight on the 4th; shortly after which time, general Cuesta arrived at Oropesa.

Upon considering our situation at that time, it was evident to me that the combined armies must retire across the Tagus, and that every moment's delay must expose them to the risk of being cut off from their only remaining point of retreat. A battle, even if it had been successful, could not have improved our situation; two battles, or probably three, must have been fought and gained

before our difficulties, resulting from the increased strength of the
enemy in Estremadura, could be removed.   I did not consider the
British army, at least, equal to such an exertion at that moment.
It is unnecessary to make any observation upon the Spanish
army ; but the occurrences at Arzobispo, a few days afterwards,
shewed that they were not equal to any great contest.

M. de Garay complains of the alteration in the line of our
operations, and of the sudden changes in the direction of our
marches, to which he attributes the deficiency of our supplies,
which, in this part of the note, he is disposed to admit that the
British army experienced.   I know of but one alteration in the
plan of operations and in the direction of the march, which was
occasioned by the circumstances to which I have just referred.

When intelligence was first received of the arrival of the enemy
at Plasencia, and of the retreat, without resistance, of the corps
appointed to guard the Puerto de Baños, my intention was to
move towards Plasencia, to attack the enemy's corps which had
passed through the Puerto.   That intention was altered only
when I heard of the numbers of which that corps consisted ; and
when I found that, by general Cuesta's movement from Talavera,
the rear of the army was not secure, that the only retreat was
liable to be cut off, and that the enemy had it in their power, and
at their option, to join or to attack us in separate bodies.

It could not be attributed to me, that this large reinforcement
was allowed to enter Estremadura, or that we had not earlier
intelligence of their approach.

The Puerto de Baños was abandoned, without firing a shot, by
the Spanish troops sent there to guard it; and the junta of Castile,
if they knew of the collection of the enemy's troops at Salamanca,
sent no notice of it ; and no notice was in fact received, till the
accounts arrived that the enemy had ordered rations at Fuente
Noble and Los Santos; and they arrived on the following day.
But when the enemy arrived at Naval Moral, in Estremadura, in
such strength, and the post of Talavera was abandoned, the central junta will find it difficult to convince this country and the
world that it was not expedient to alter the plan of our operations
and the direction of our march.

But this alteration, instead of aggravating the deficiency of our
supplies, ought to have alleviated our distresses, if any measures
had been adopted at Seville to supply the British army, in consequence of my letter of the 16th July.   The alteration was from

the offensive to the defensive; the march was retrograde; and if any supplies had been prepared and sent, the army must have met them on the road, and must have received them sooner. Accordingly, we did meet supplies on the road, but they were for the Spanish army; and although our troops were starving at the time, they were forwarded, untouched, to their destination.

I have sent to marshal Beresford a copy of that part of M. de Garay's note which refers to the supplies for the Portuguese army under his command, upon which he will make his observations, which I propose to forward to your excellency. I shall here, therefore, only repeat that the want of magazines, and the apathy and disinclination of the magistrates and people in Spain to furnish supplies for the armies, even for payment, were the causes that the Portuguese army, as well as the British army, suffered great distress from want, while within the Spanish frontier.

Till the evils, of which I think I have reason to complain, are remedied, till I shall see magazines established for the supply of the armies, and a regular system adopted for keeping them filled, and an army, upon whose exertions I can depend, commanded by officers capable and willing to carry into execution the operations which may have been planned by mutual agreement, I cannot enter upon any system of co-operation with the Spanish armies. I do not think it necessary now to enter into any calculations to shew the fallacy of M. de Garay's calculations of the relative numerical strength of the allies, and of the enemy, in the Peninsula; if the fallacy was not so great, as I am certain it is, I should be of the same opinion, respecting the expediency of co-operating with the Spanish troops. But if the British and the Portuguese armies should not actively co-operate with them, they will at least do them no injury; and if M. de Garay is not mistaken, as I believe he is, in his calculations of numbers; and if the Spanish armies are in a state of efficiency in which they are represented to be, and which they ought to be, to invite our co-operation, the deficiency of thirty-six thousand men, which the British and Portuguese armies might add to their numbers, can be no objection to their undertaking, immediately, the operations which M. de Garay is of opinion would give to his countrymen the early possession of those blessings for which they are contending.

I have the honour to be, &c.

(Signed)   WELLINGTON.

No. XVIII.

COPY OF A LETTER FROM GENERAL HILL TO
SIR ARTHUR WELLESLEY.

Camp, August 17, 1809.

SIR,

I beg leave to report to you that the parties sent out by the officers of my division, yesterday, to procure forage, were, in more instances than one, opposed by the Spaniards. The following circumstances have been made known to me, and I take the liberty of repeating them for your excellency's information.

My servants were sent about three leagues on the Truxillo road, in order to get forage for me; and after gathering three mule loads, a party of Spanish soldiers, consisting of five or six, came up to them with their swords drawn, and obliged them to leave the corn they had collected. My servants told me, that the same party fired two shots towards other British men employed in getting forage. The assistant-commissary of my division likewise states to me, that the men he sent out for forage were fired at by the Spaniards.

I have the honour to be, &c.

(Signed)   R. HILL, major-general.

COPY OF A LETTER FROM COLONEL STOPFORD TO
LIEUTENANT-GENERAL SHERBROOKE.

Jaraceijo, August 16, 1809.

SIR,

I beg leave to inform you that I have just received intimations of some Spaniards having fired at some of the guards, for taking some forage. As there is no forage given us by the commissary, I wish to know what I am to do, in order to get some for the horses.

(Signed)   E. STOPFORD, second brigade of guards.

END OF VOL. II.